SGT FROG™

KERORO GUNSO

VOL #16 BY
MINE YOSHIZAKI

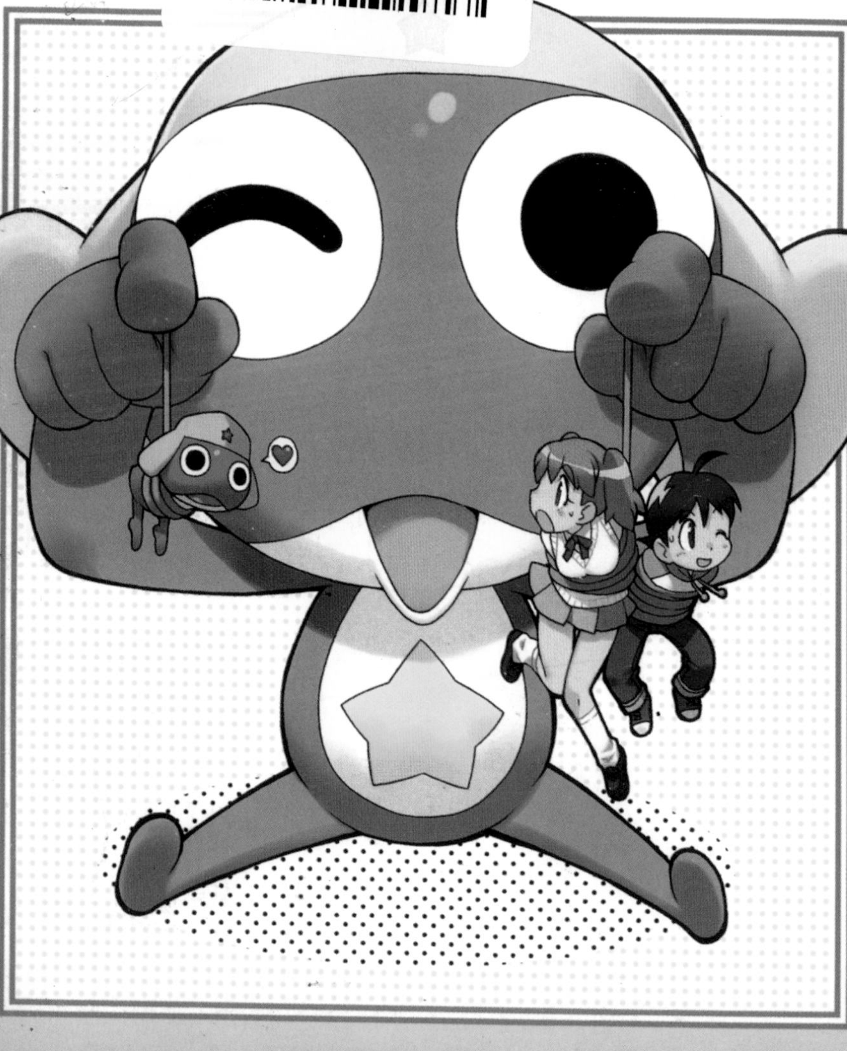

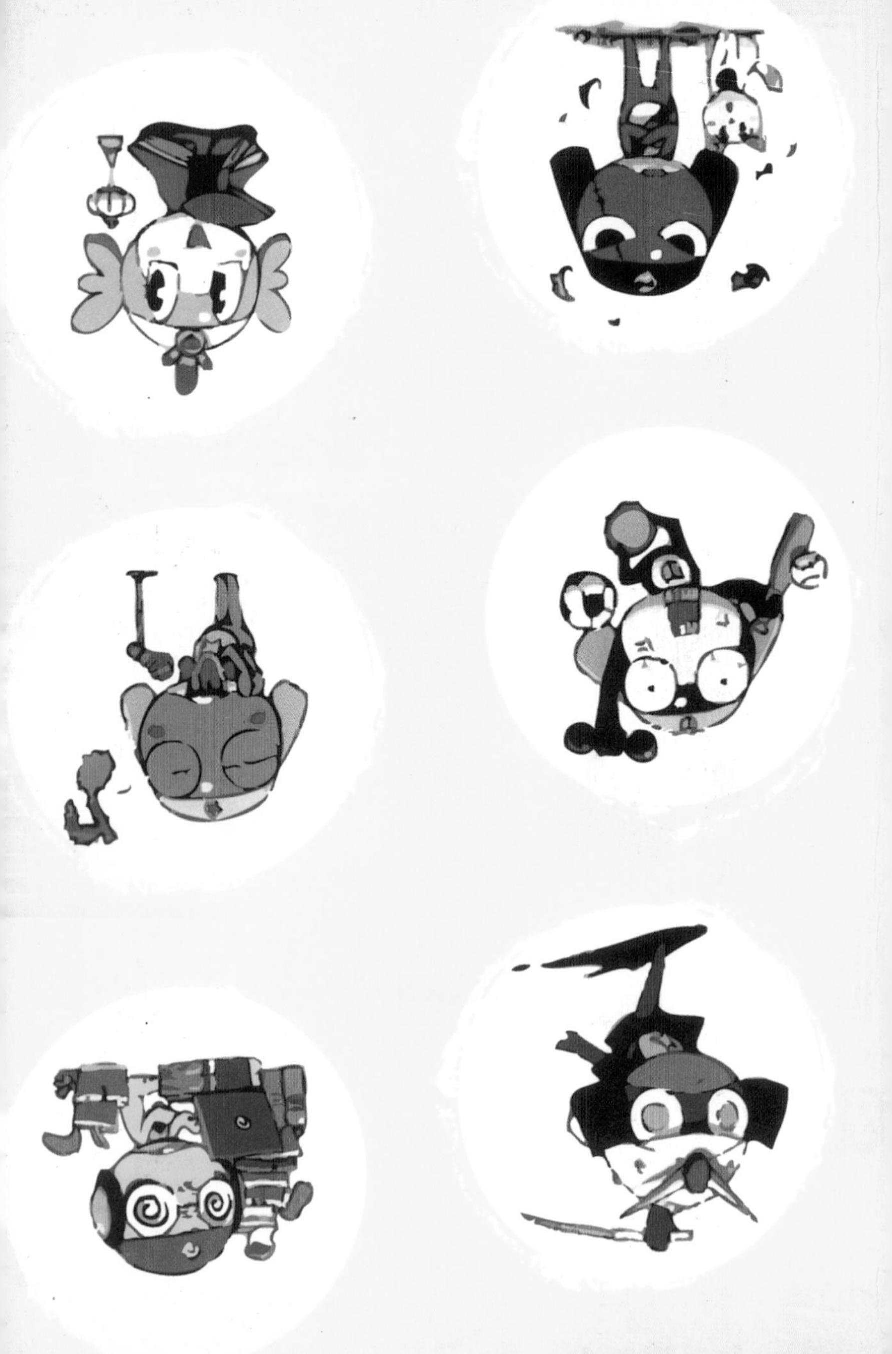

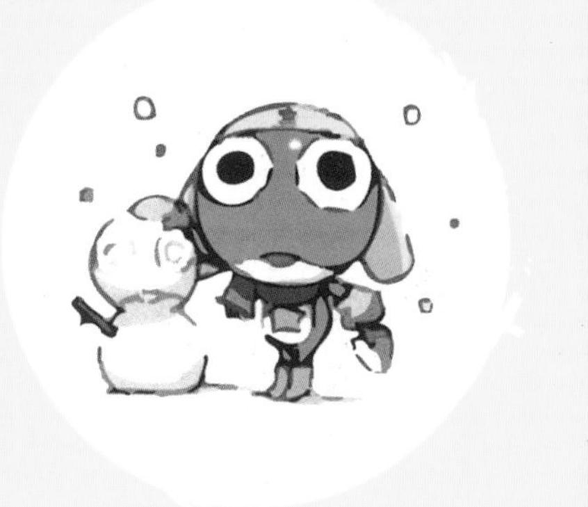

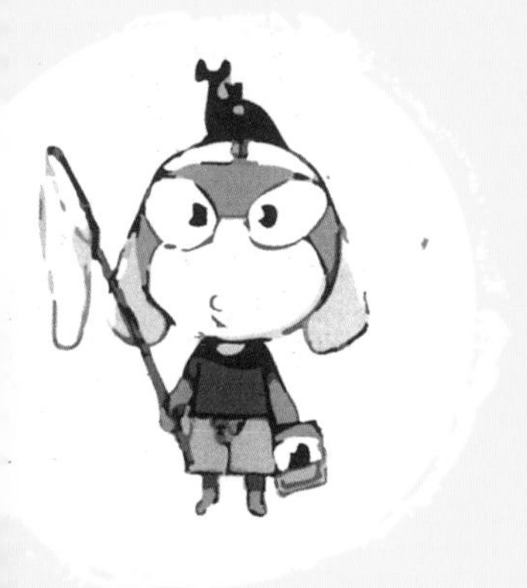

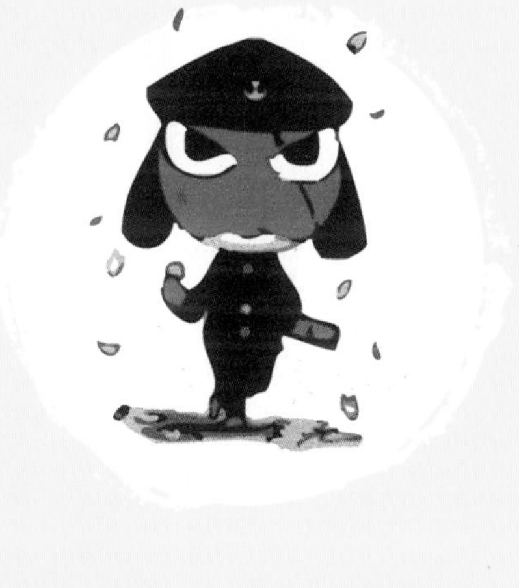

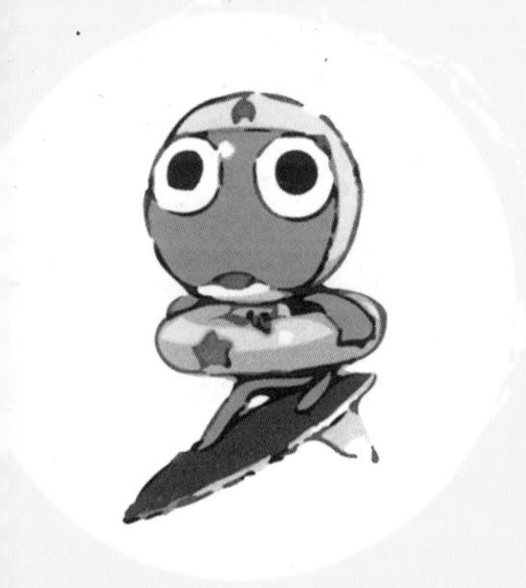

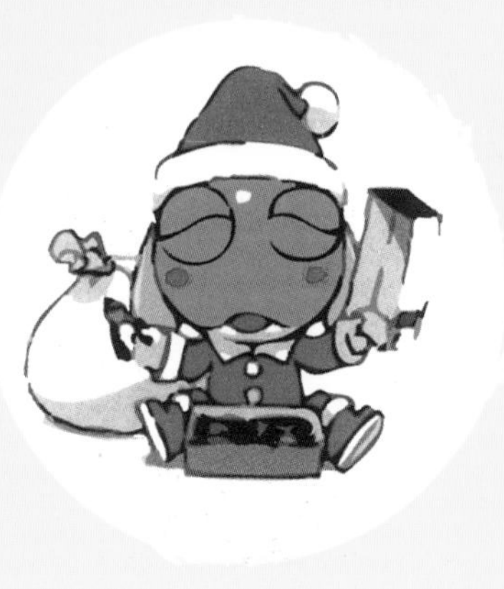

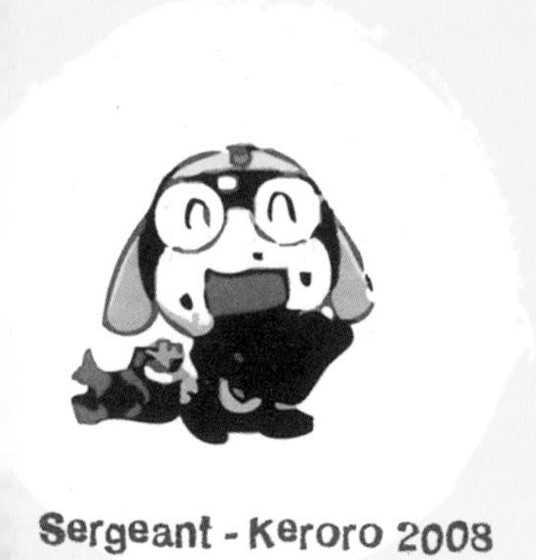

SGT. FROG 16. TABLE OF CONTENTS

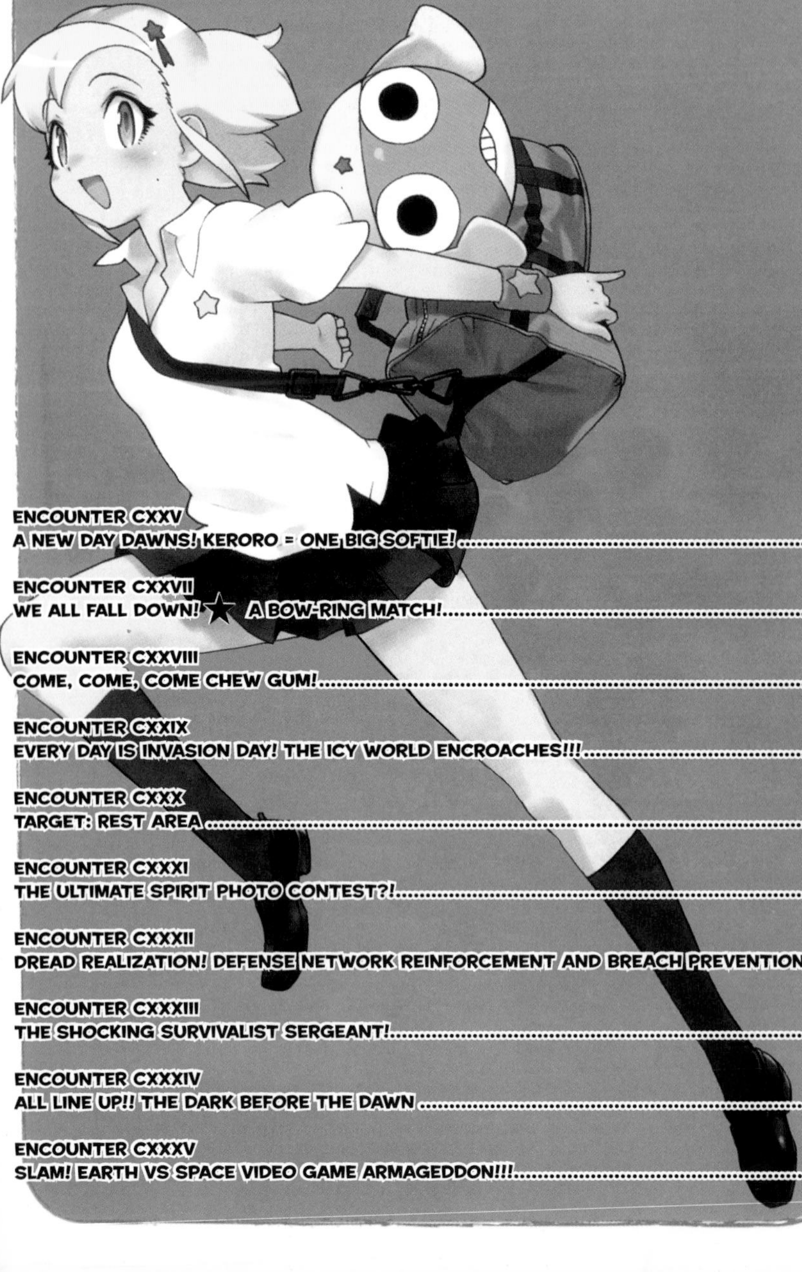

SGT FROG
KERORO GUNSOU

VOLUME #16

BY
MINE YOSHIZAKI

Sgt. Frog Volume 16
Created by Mine Yoshizaki

Translation - Yuko Fukami
English Adaptation - Ysabet Reinhardt MacFarlane
Retouch and Lettering - Star Print Brokers
Production Artist - Vicente Rivera, Jr.
Graphic Designer - Jose Macasocol, Jr.

Editor - Alexis Kirsch
Pre-Production Supervisor - Vicente Rivera, Jr.
Pre-Production Specialist - Lucas Rivera
Managing Editor - Vy Nguyen
Senior Designer - Louis Csontos
Senior Designer - James Lee
Senior Editor - Bryce P. Coleman
Senior Editor - Jenna Winterberg
Associate Publisher - Marco F. Pavia
President and C.O.O. - John Parker
C.E.O. and Chief Creative Officer - Stu Levy

A **TOKYOPOP** Manga

TOKYOPOP Inc.
5900 Wilshire Blvd. Suite 2000
Los Angeles, CA 90036

E-mail: info@TOKYOPOP.com
Come visit us online at www.TOKYOPOP.com

KERORO GUNSO Volume 16 © Mine YOSHIZAKI 2008
First published in Japan in 2008 by KADOKAWA SHOTEN
PUBLISHING CO., LTD., Tokyo. English translation rights
arranged with KADOKAWA SHOTEN PUBLISHING CO., LTD.,
Tokyo through TUTTLE–MORI AGENCY, INC., Tokyo.
English text copyright © 2008 TOKYOPOP Inc.

ISBN: 978-1-4278-1462-3

First TOKYOPOP printing: December 2008
10 9 8 7 6 5 4 3 2 1
Printed in the USA

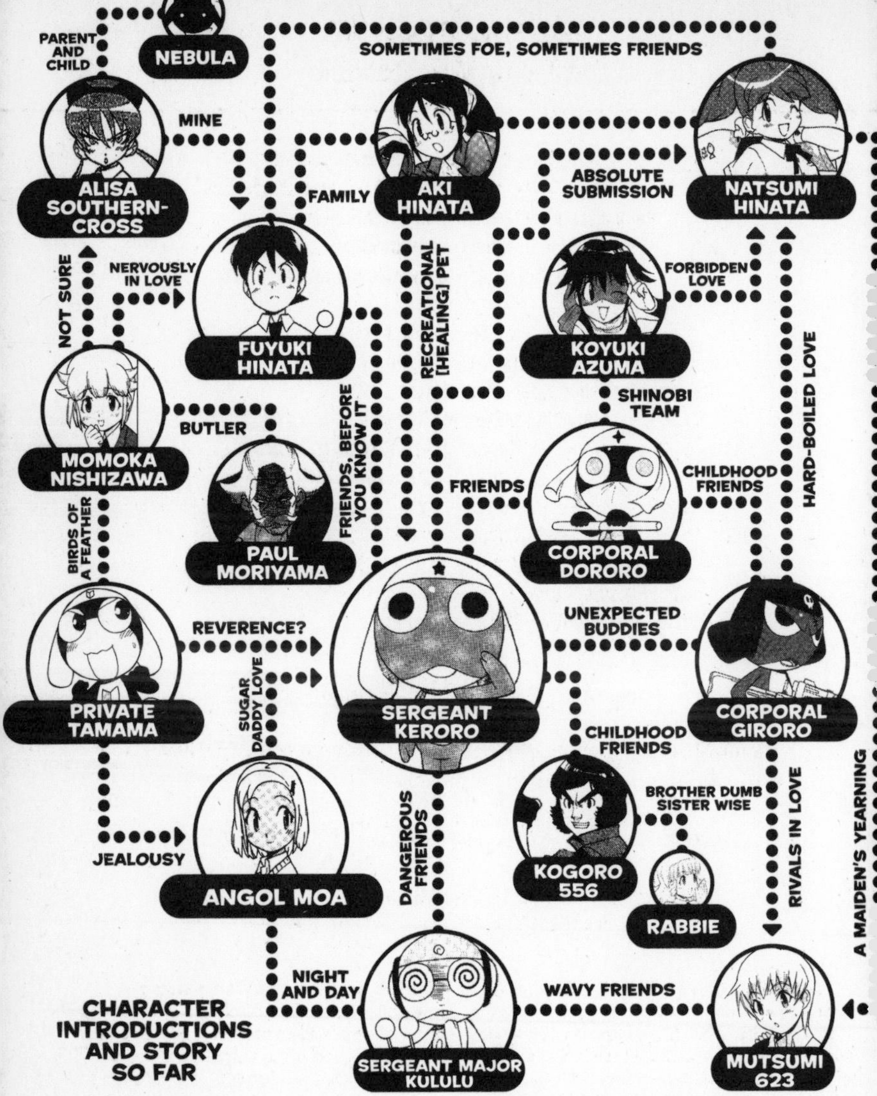
NEBULA
PARENT AND CHILD
SOMETIMES FOE, SOMETIMES FRIENDS
ALISA SOUTHERN-CROSS
MINE
AKI HINATA
FAMILY
NATSUMI HINATA
ABSOLUTE SUBMISSION
NOT SURE
NERVOUSLY IN LOVE
FUYUKI HINATA
RECREATIONAL [HEALING] PET
KOYUKI AZUMA
FORBIDDEN LOVE
HARD-BOILED LOVE
MOMOKA NISHIZAWA
BUTLER
FRIENDS, BEFORE YOU KNOW IT
SHINOBI TEAM
PAUL MORIYAMA
FRIENDS
CORPORAL DORORO
CHILDHOOD FRIENDS
BIRDS OF A FEATHER
PRIVATE TAMAMA
REVERENCE?
SUGAR DADDY LOVE
SERGEANT KERORO
UNEXPECTED BUDDIES
CORPORAL GIRORO
CHILDHOOD FRIENDS
KOGORO 556
BROTHER DUMB SISTER WISE
RABBIE
RIVALS IN LOVE
A MAIDEN'S YEARNING
JEALOUSY
ANGOL MOA
DANGEROUS FRIENDS
NIGHT AND DAY
SERGEANT MAJOR KULULU
WAVY FRIENDS
MUTSUMI 623
CHARACTER INTRODUCTIONS AND STORY SO FAR

AS CAPTAIN OF THE SPACE INVASION FORCE'S SPECIAL ADVANCE TEAM OF THE 58TH PLANET OF THE GAMMA STORM CLOUD SYSTEM, SGT. KERORO ENTERED THE HINATA FAMILY WHEN HIS PRE-ATTACK PREPARATION FOR THE INVASION OF EARTH RAN AFOUL VIA HIS EASY CAPTURE BY THE HINATA CHILDREN, FUYUKI AND NATSUMI. THANKS TO FUYUKI'S KINDNESS, OR RATHER HIS CURIOSITY, SGT. KERORO SOON BECAME A WARD OF THE HINATA HOME, WITH FREE ROOM AND BOARD IN EXCHANGE FOR HOUSEWORK. FROM THIS UNLIKELY BASE, HE AND HIS FOUR SUBORDINATES CONTINUE TO DEVISE THEIR STRATEGY FOR THE IMPENDING INVASION OF POKOPEN...OR NOT.

ON A RECENT SUMMER DAY, FUYUKI'S RESEARCH LED HIM TO ANOTHER BOY, WHOSE SITUATION WAS EERILY LIKE FUYUKI AND KERORO'S. AS OUR TALE BECOMES MORE AND MORE MYSTERIOUS, ANOTHER DAY WITH KERORO DAWNS!

There's more where that came from!

ENCOUNTER CXXVI
A NEW DAY DAWNS! KERORO = ONE BIG SOFTIE

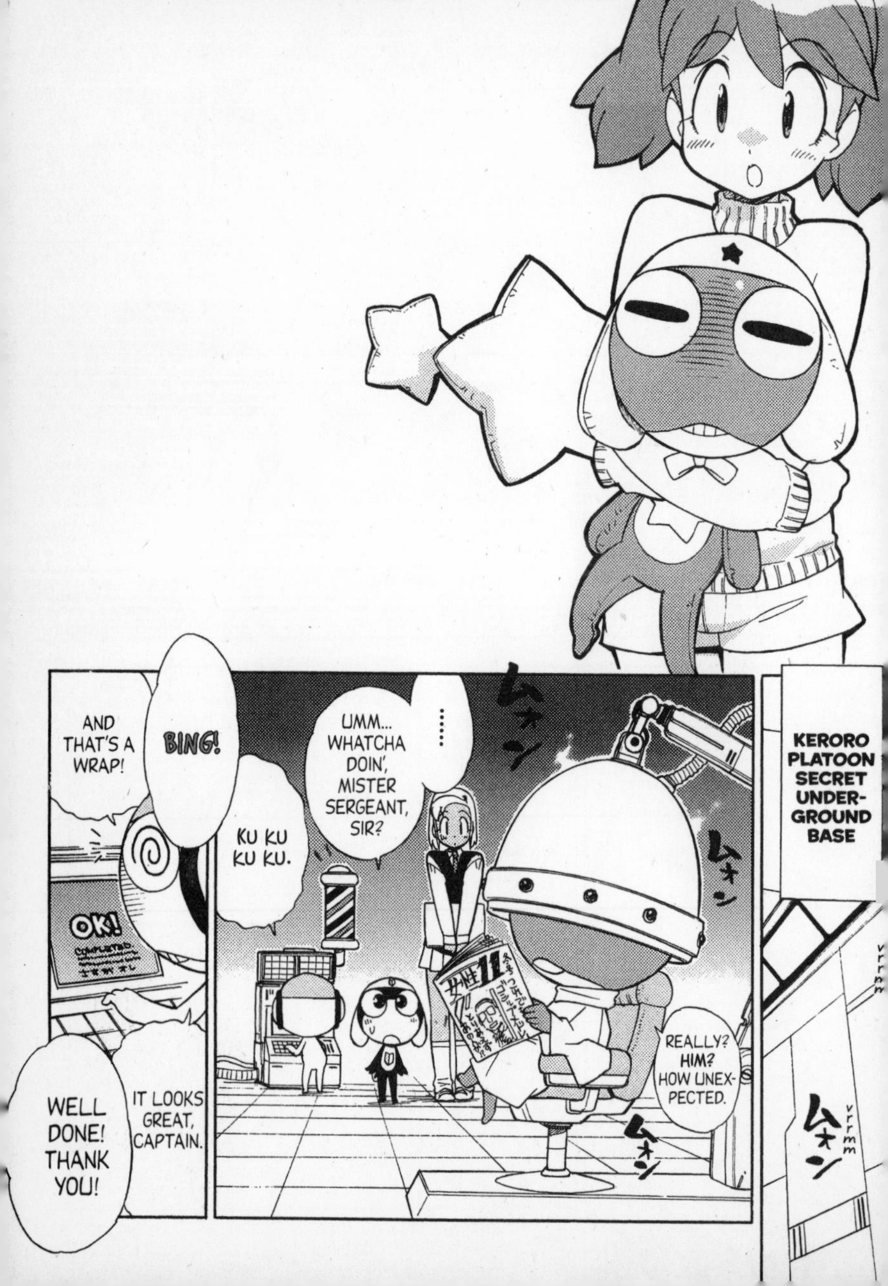
KERORO PLATOON SECRET UNDER-GROUND BASE
vrrrmm
REALLY? HIM? HOW UNEX-PECTED.
UMM... WHATCHA DOIN', MISTER SERGEANT, SIR?
......
KU KU KU KU.
BING!
AND THAT'S A WRAP!
OK!
COMPLETED
IT LOOKS GREAT, CAPTAIN.
WELL DONE! THANK YOU!

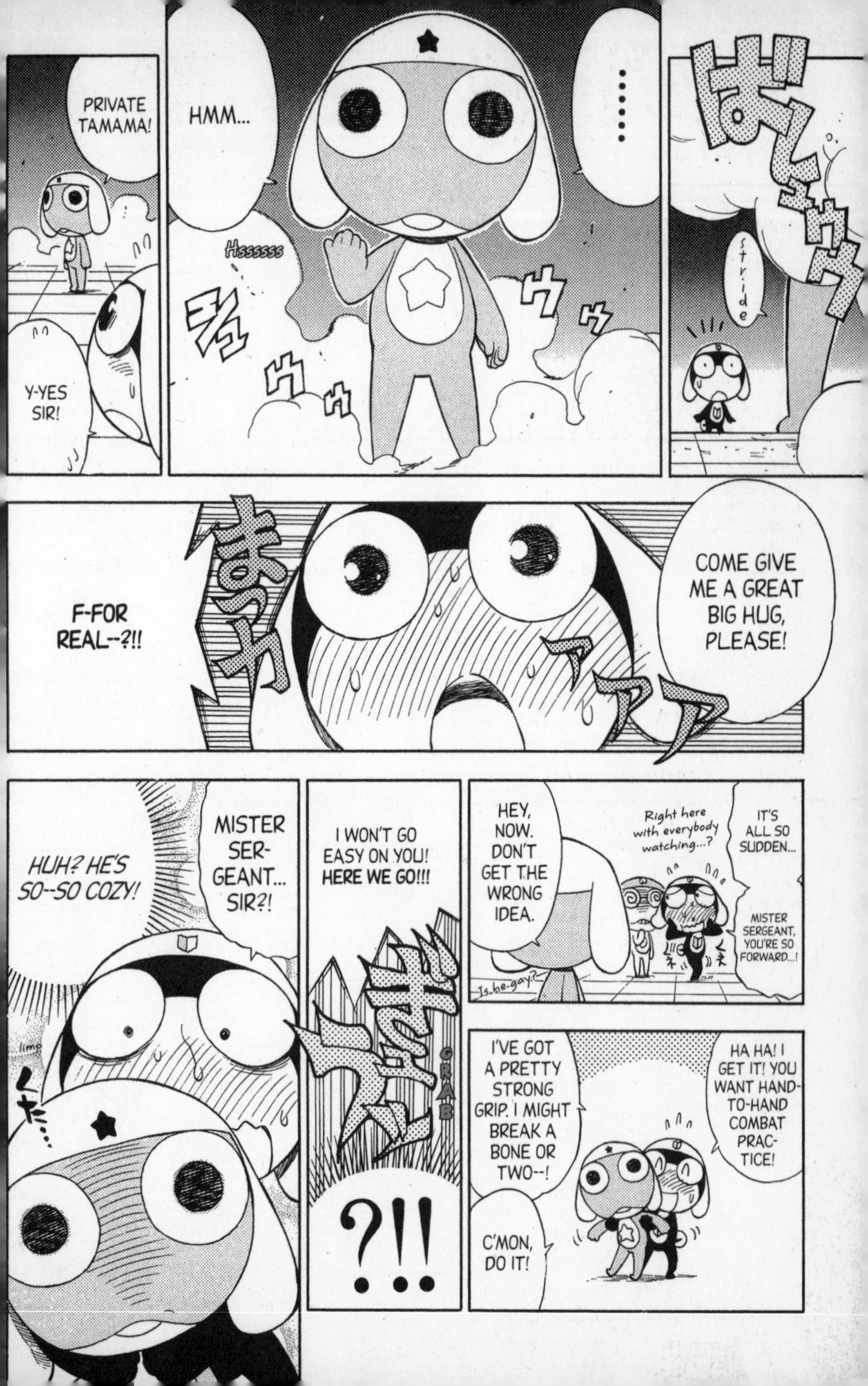
stride
......
HMM...
Hssssss
PRIVATE TAMAMA!
Y-YES SIR!
COME GIVE ME A GREAT BIG HUG, PLEASE!
F-FOR REAL--?!!
IT'S ALL SO SUDDEN...
Right here with everybody watching...?
MISTER SERGEANT, YOU'RE SO FORWARD...!
HEY, NOW. DON'T GET THE WRONG IDEA.
Is-he-gay?
HA HA! I GET IT! YOU WANT HAND-TO-HAND COMBAT PRAC-TICE!
I'VE GOT A PRETTY STRONG GRIP. I MIGHT BREAK A BONE OR TWO--!
C'MON, DO IT!
I WON'T GO EASY ON YOU! HERE WE GO!!!
GRAB
?!!
MISTER SER-GEANT... SIR?!
HUH? HE'S SO--SO COZY!
limp

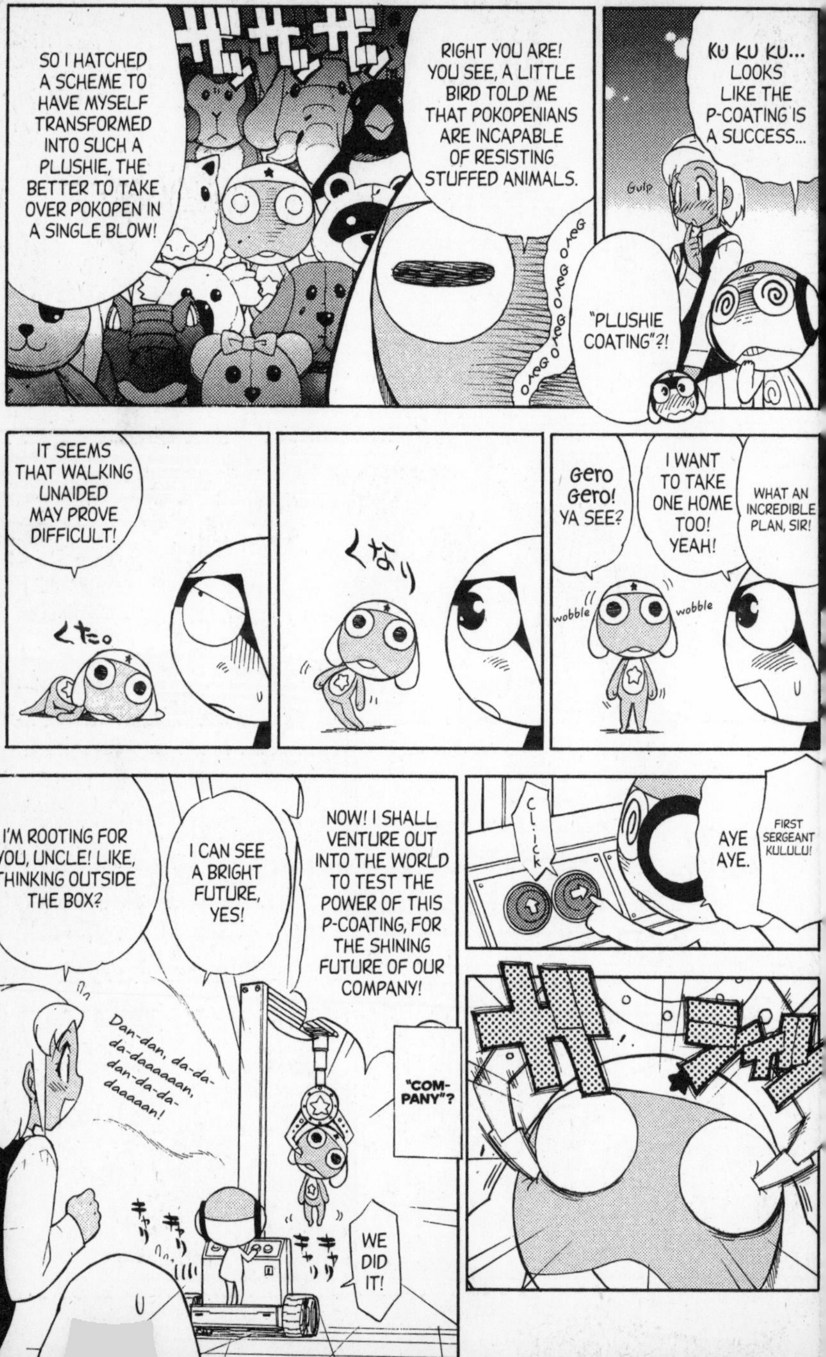
KU KU KU... LOOKS LIKE THE P-COATING IS A SUCCESS...
Gulp
"PLUSHIE COATING"?!
OHEG OHEG OHEG OHEG OHEG
RIGHT YOU ARE! YOU SEE, A LITTLE BIRD TOLD ME THAT POKOPENIANS ARE INCAPABLE OF RESISTING STUFFED ANIMALS.
SO I HATCHED A SCHEME TO HAVE MYSELF TRANSFORMED INTO SUCH A PLUSHIE, THE BETTER TO TAKE OVER POKOPEN IN A SINGLE BLOW!
WHAT AN INCREDIBLE PLAN, SIR!
I WANT TO TAKE ONE HOME TOO! YEAH!
Gero Gero! YA SEE?
wobble
wobble
くなり
IT SEEMS THAT WALKING UNAIDED MAY PROVE DIFFICULT!
くたっ
FIRST SERGEANT KULULU!
AYE AYE.
CLICK
NOW! I SHALL VENTURE OUT INTO THE WORLD TO TEST THE POWER OF THIS P-COATING, FOR THE SHINING FUTURE OF OUR COMPANY!
"COM-PANY"?
I CAN SEE A BRIGHT FUTURE, YES!
I'M ROOTING FOR YOU, UNCLE! LIKE, THINKING OUTSIDE THE BOX?
Dan-dan, da-da-da-daaaaaan, dan-da-da-daaaaan!
キャリ キャリ
キャリ キャリ
WE DID IT!

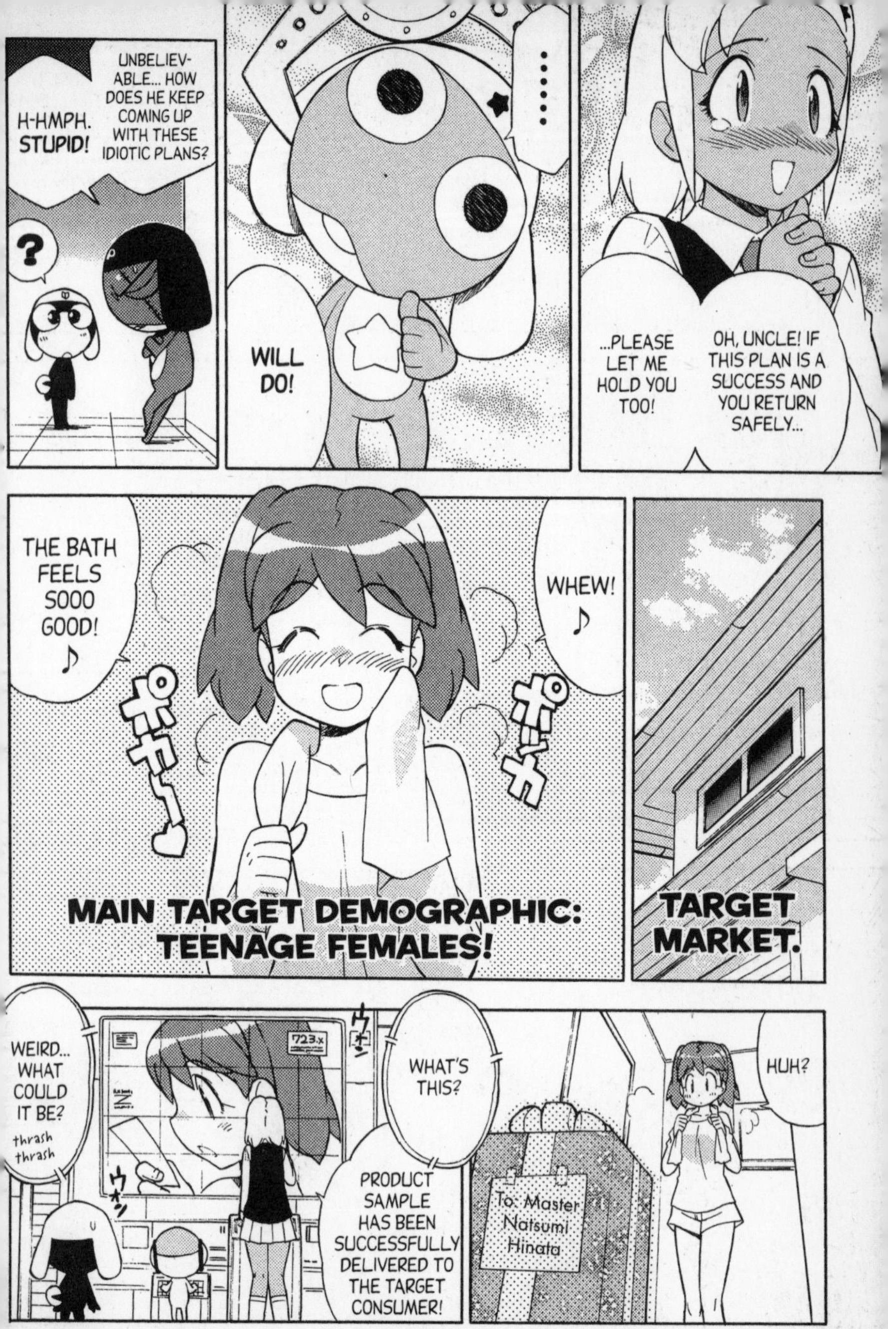
OH, UNCLE! IF THIS PLAN IS A SUCCESS AND YOU RETURN SAFELY...
...PLEASE LET ME HOLD YOU TOO!
......
WILL DO!
UNBELIEVABLE... HOW DOES HE KEEP COMING UP WITH THESE IDIOTIC PLANS?
H-HMPH. STUPID!
?
TARGET MARKET.
WHEW! ♪
THE BATH FEELS SOOO GOOD! ♪
MAIN TARGET DEMOGRAPHIC: TEENAGE FEMALES!
HUH?
To: Master Natsumi Hinata
WHAT'S THIS?
PRODUCT SAMPLE HAS BEEN SUCCESSFULLY DELIVERED TO THE TARGET CONSUMER!
WEIRD... WHAT COULD IT BE?
thrash thrash

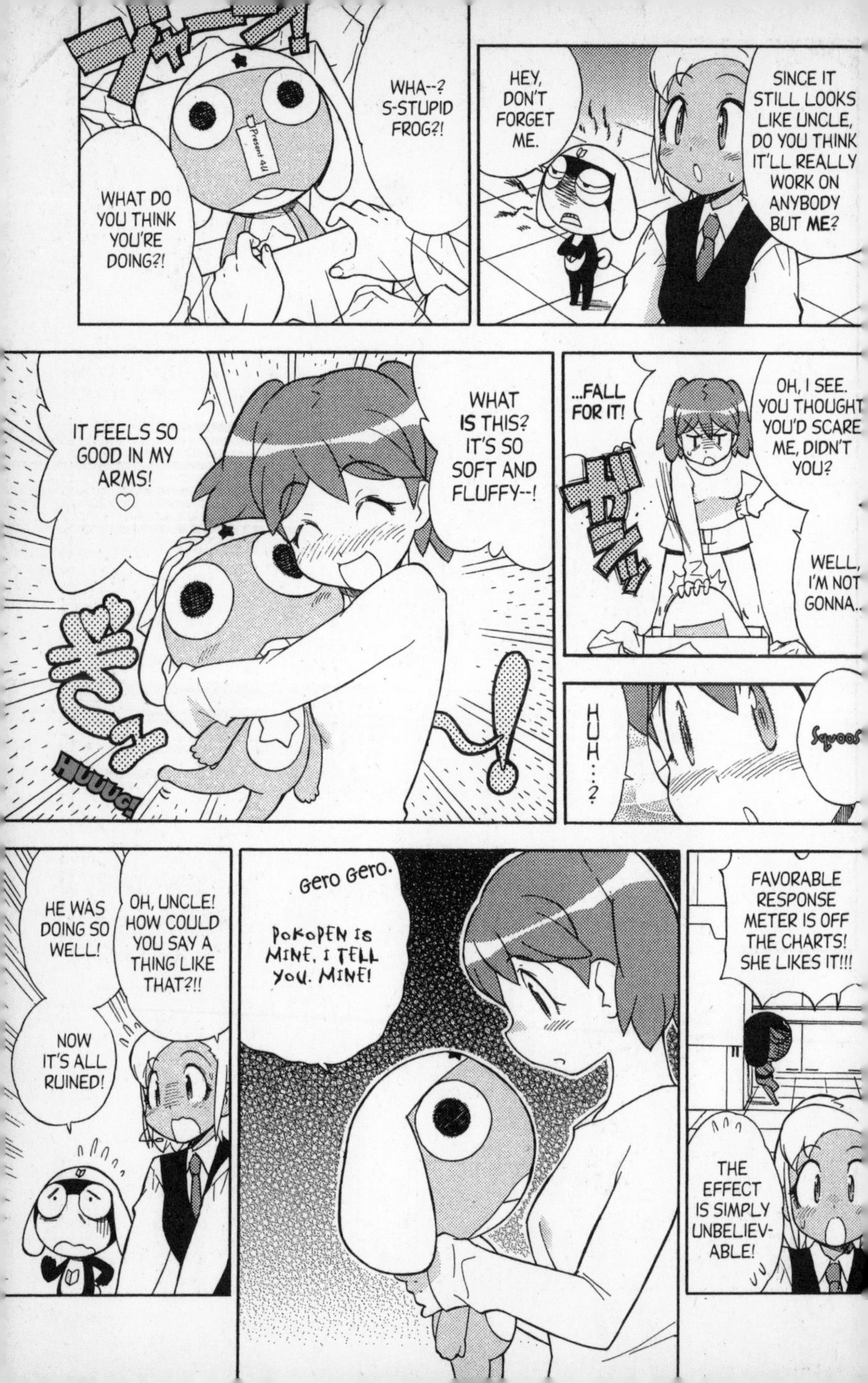
SINCE IT STILL LOOKS LIKE UNCLE, DO YOU THINK IT'LL REALLY WORK ON ANYBODY BUT ME?
HEY, DON'T FORGET ME.
WHA--? S-STUPID FROG?!
Present 4U
WHAT DO YOU THINK YOU'RE DOING?!
OH, I SEE. YOU THOUGHT YOU'D SCARE ME, DIDN'T YOU?
WELL, I'M NOT GONNA...
...FALL FOR IT!
Squoos
HUH...?
WHAT IS THIS? IT'S SO SOFT AND FLUFFY--!
IT FEELS SO GOOD IN MY ARMS!
HUUUG!
FAVORABLE RESPONSE METER IS OFF THE CHARTS! SHE LIKES IT!!!
THE EFFECT IS SIMPLY UNBELIEV-ABLE!
Gero Gero.
POKOPEN IS MINE, I TELL YOU. MINE!
OH, UNCLE! HOW COULD YOU SAY A THING LIKE THAT?!!
HE WAS DOING SO WELL!
NOW IT'S ALL RUINED!

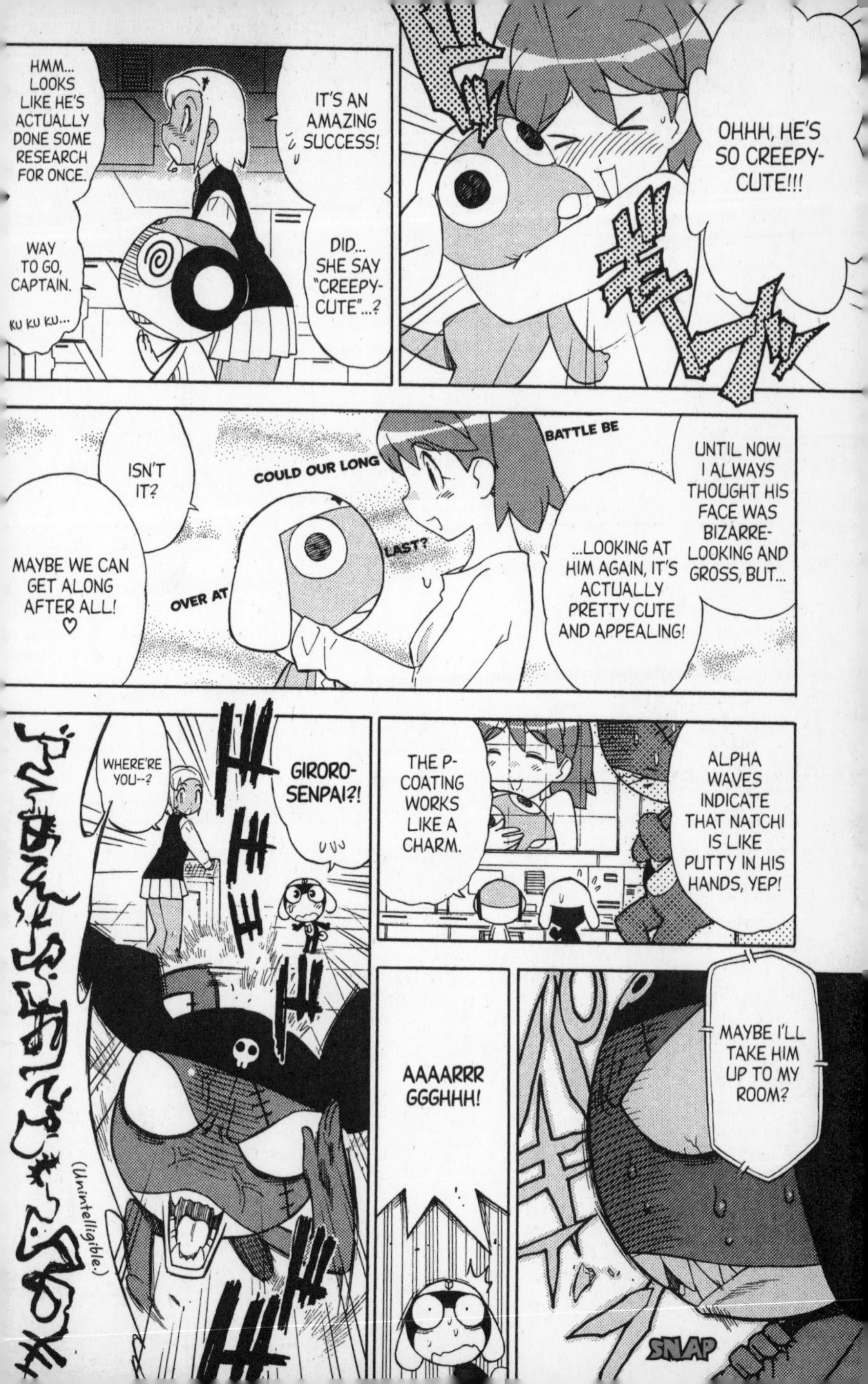
OHHH, HE'S SO CREEPY-CUTE!!!
IT'S AN AMAZING SUCCESS!
HMM... LOOKS LIKE HE'S ACTUALLY DONE SOME RESEARCH FOR ONCE.
DID... SHE SAY "CREEPY-CUTE"...?
WAY TO GO, CAPTAIN.
KU KU KU...
UNTIL NOW I ALWAYS THOUGHT HIS FACE WAS BIZARRE-LOOKING AND GROSS, BUT...
...LOOKING AT HIM AGAIN, IT'S ACTUALLY PRETTY CUTE AND APPEALING!
BATTLE BE
COULD OUR LONG
LAST?
OVER AT
ISN'T IT?
MAYBE WE CAN GET ALONG AFTER ALL! ♡
ALPHA WAVES INDICATE THAT NATCHI IS LIKE PUTTY IN HIS HANDS, YEP!
THE P-COATING WORKS LIKE A CHARM.
GIRORO-SENPAI?!
WHERE'RE YOU--?
(Unintelligible.)
MAYBE I'LL TAKE HIM UP TO MY ROOM?
AAAARRR GGGHHH!
SNAP

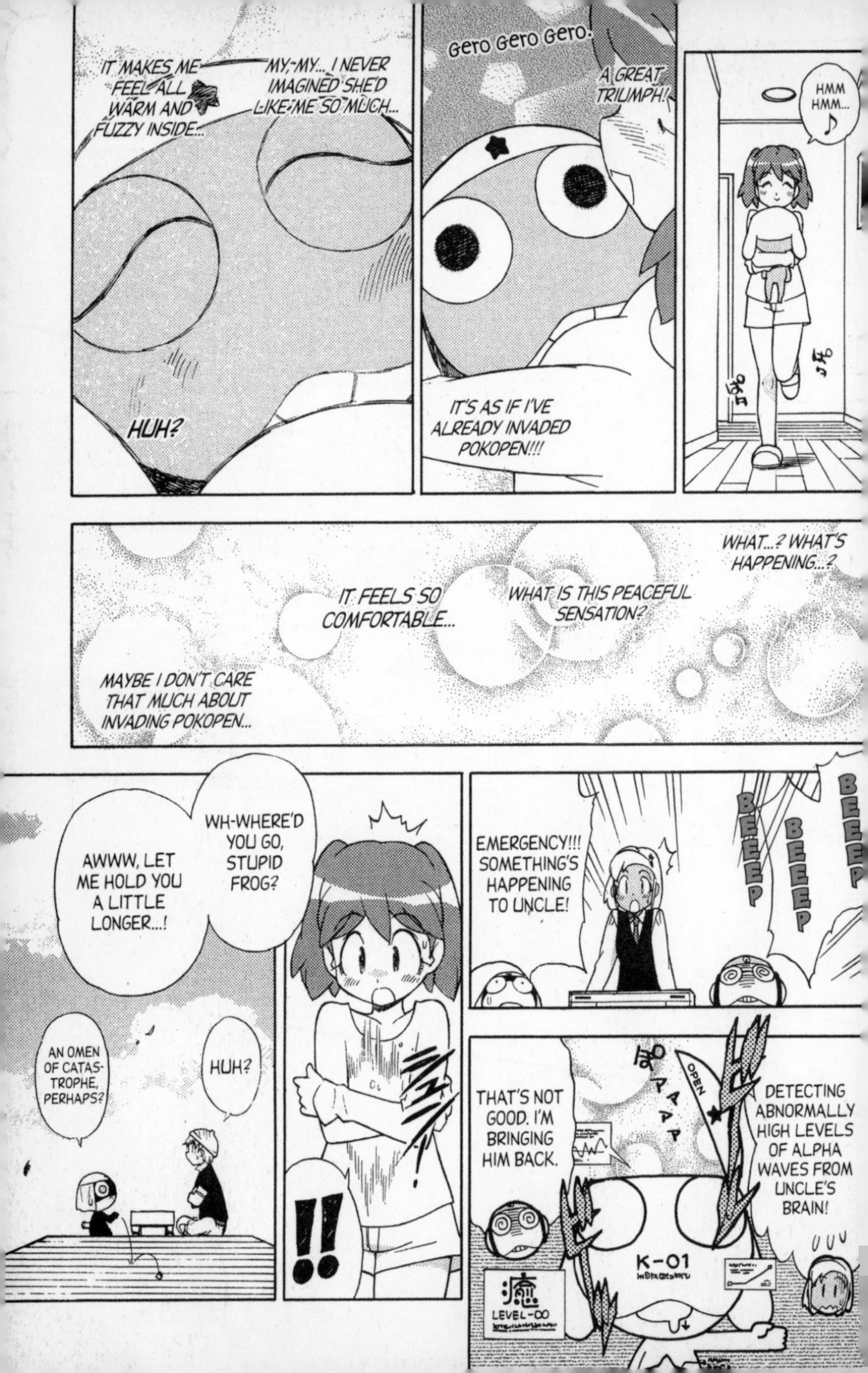
HMM HMM... ♪
Gero Gero Gero.
A GREAT TRIUMPH!
IT'S AS IF I'VE ALREADY INVADED POKOPEN!!!
MY, MY... I NEVER IMAGINED SHE'D LIKE ME SO MUCH...
IT MAKES ME FEEL ALL WARM AND FUZZY INSIDE...
HUH?
WHAT...? WHAT'S HAPPENING...?
WHAT IS THIS PEACEFUL SENSATION?
IT FEELS SO COMFORTABLE...
MAYBE I DON'T CARE THAT MUCH ABOUT INVADING POKOPEN...
BEEEP
BEEEP
BEEEP
EMERGENCY!!! SOMETHING'S HAPPENING TO UNCLE!
DETECTING ABNORMALLY HIGH LEVELS OF ALPHA WAVES FROM UNCLE'S BRAIN!
OPEN
THAT'S NOT GOOD. I'M BRINGING HIM BACK.
K-01
LEVEL-∞
WH-WHERE'D YOU GO, STUPID FROG?
!!
AWWW, LET ME HOLD YOU A LITTLE LONGER...!
HUH?
AN OMEN OF CATASTROPHE, PERHAPS?

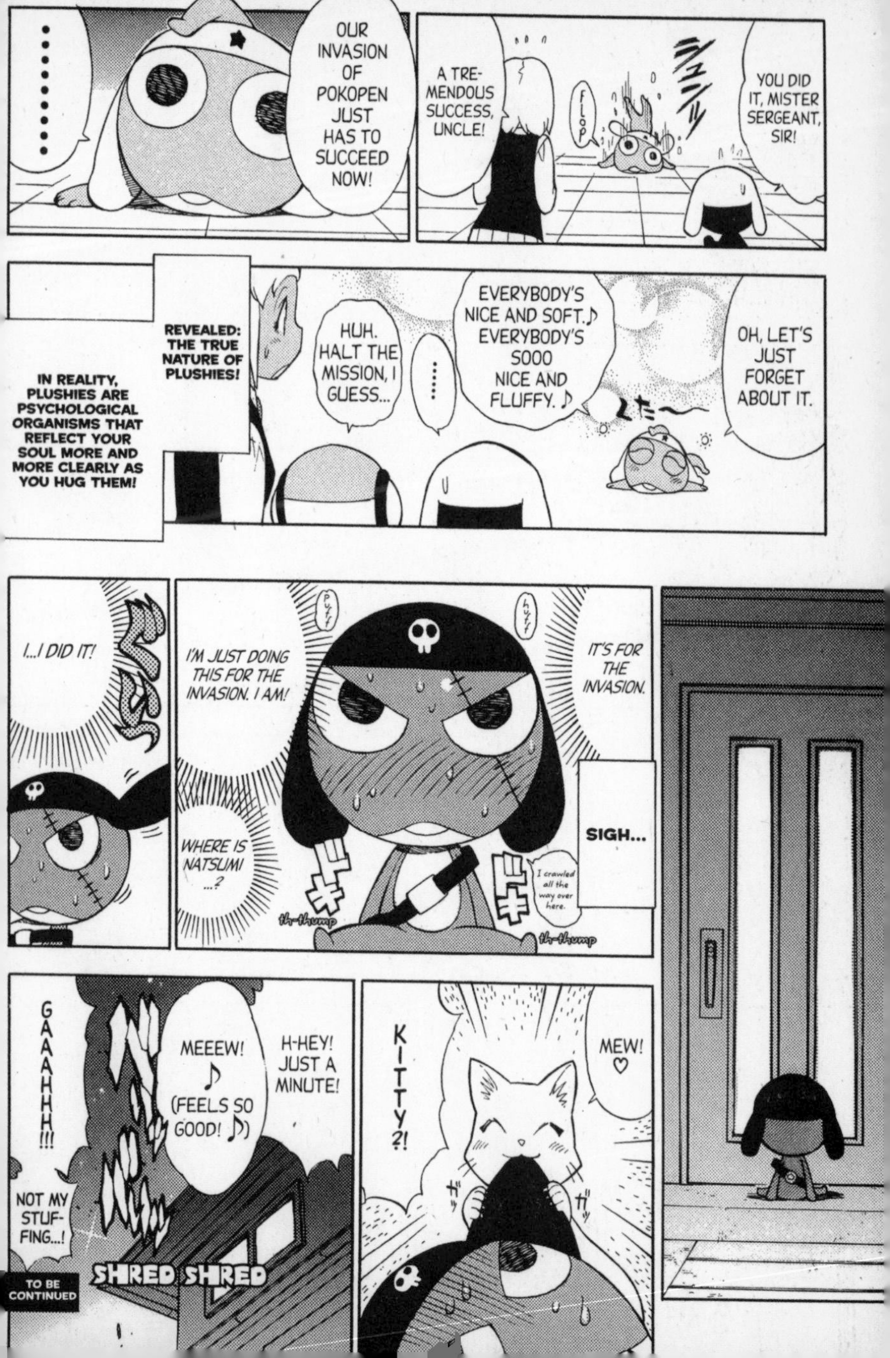
YOU DID IT, MISTER SERGEANT, SIR!
FLOP
A TREMENDOUS SUCCESS, UNCLE!
OUR INVASION OF POKOPEN JUST HAS TO SUCCEED NOW!
....
OH, LET'S JUST FORGET ABOUT IT.
EVERYBODY'S NICE AND SOFT.♪ EVERYBODY'S SOOO NICE AND FLUFFY.♪
......
HUH. HALT THE MISSION, I GUESS...
REVEALED: THE TRUE NATURE OF PLUSHIES!
IN REALITY, PLUSHIES ARE PSYCHOLOGICAL ORGANISMS THAT REFLECT YOUR SOUL MORE AND MORE CLEARLY AS YOU HUG THEM!
SIGH...
IT'S FOR THE INVASION.
huff
puff
I'M JUST DOING THIS FOR THE INVASION. I AM!
I crawled all the way over here.
WHERE IS NATSUMI ...?
th-thump
th-thump
I...I DID IT!
MEW! ♡
KITTY?!
H-HEY! JUST A MINUTE!
MEEEW! ♪ (FEELS SO GOOD! ♪)
GAAAHHH!!!
NOT MY STUF-FING...!
SHRED SHRED
TO BE CONTINUED

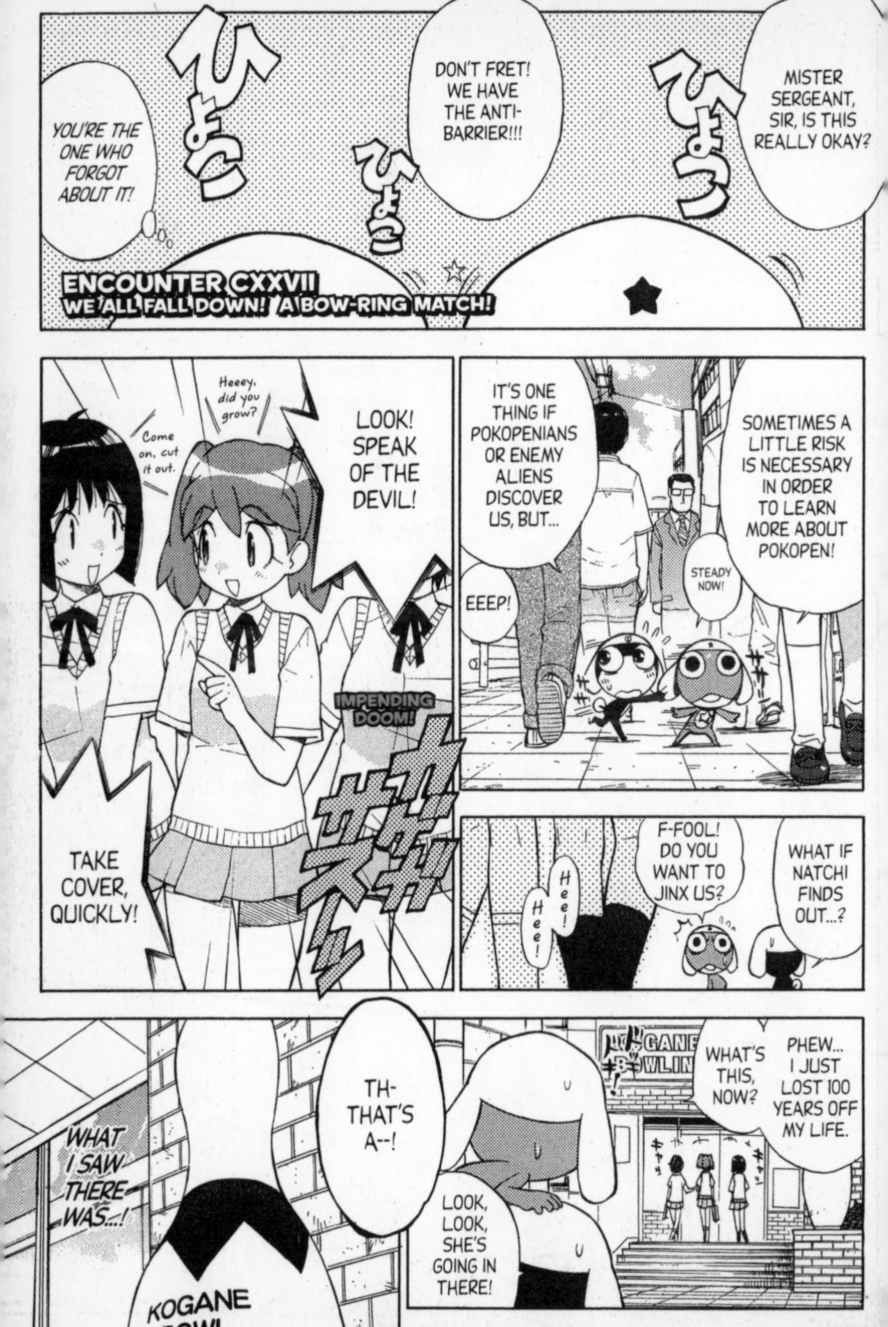

MISTER SERGEANT, SIR, IS THIS REALLY OKAY?
DON'T FRET! WE HAVE THE ANTI-BARRIER!!!
YOU'RE THE ONE WHO FORGOT ABOUT IT!
ENCOUNTER CXXVII
WE ALL FALL DOWN! A BOW-RING MATCH!
SOMETIMES A LITTLE RISK IS NECESSARY IN ORDER TO LEARN MORE ABOUT POKOPEN!
IT'S ONE THING IF POKOPENIANS OR ENEMY ALIENS DISCOVER US, BUT...
STEADY NOW!
EEEP!
WHAT IF NATCHI FINDS OUT...?
F-FOOL! DO YOU WANT TO JINX US?
Hee! Hee!
LOOK! SPEAK OF THE DEVIL!
Heeey, did you grow?
Come on, cut it out.
IMPENDING DOOM!
TAKE COVER, QUICKLY!
PHEW... I JUST LOST 100 YEARS OFF MY LIFE.
WHAT'S THIS, NOW?
LOOK, LOOK, SHE'S GOING IN THERE!
TH-THAT'S A--!
WHAT I SAW THERE WAS...!
KOGANE BOWL

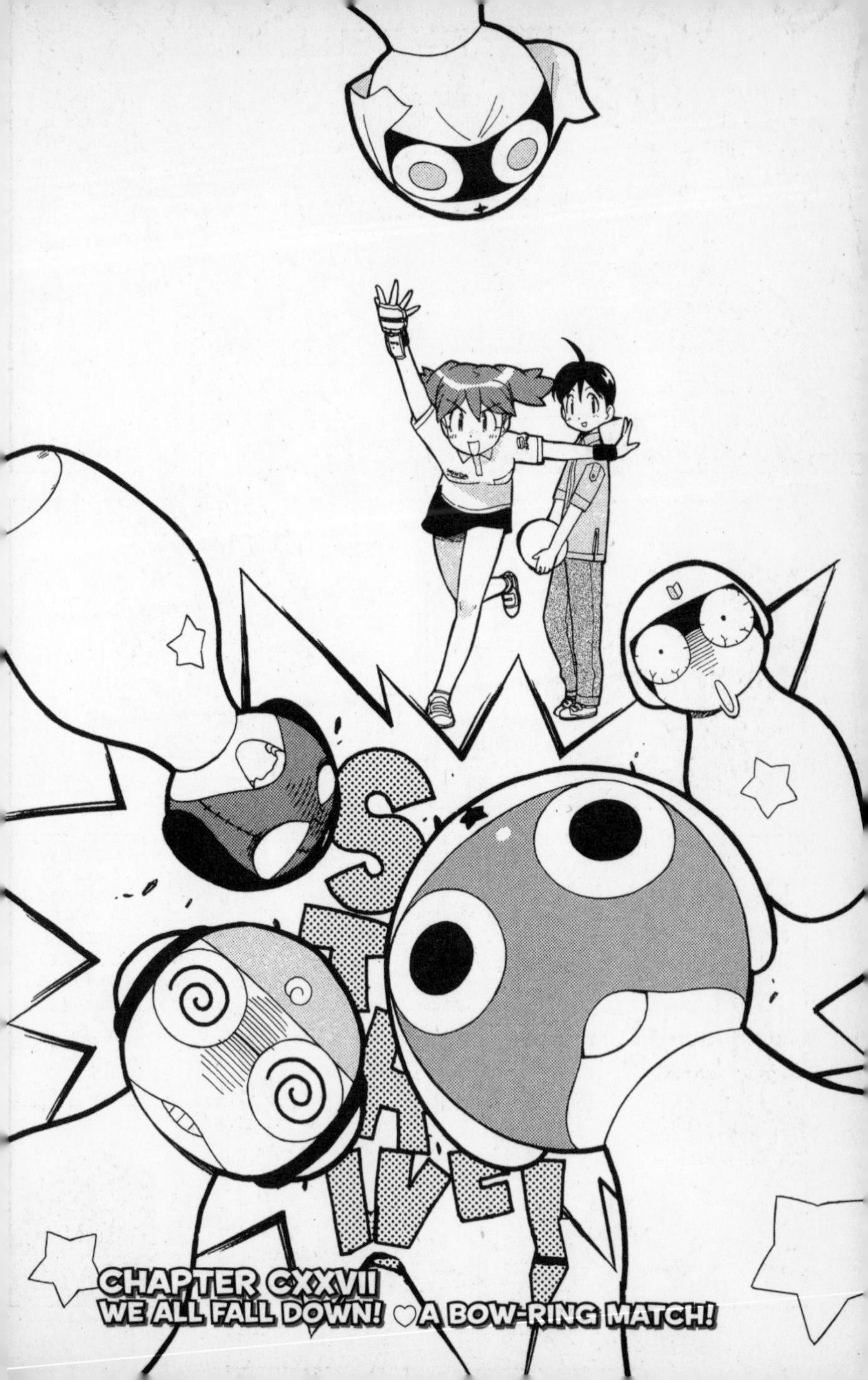

CHAPTER CXXVII
WE ALL FALL DOWN! ♡A BOW-RING MATCH!

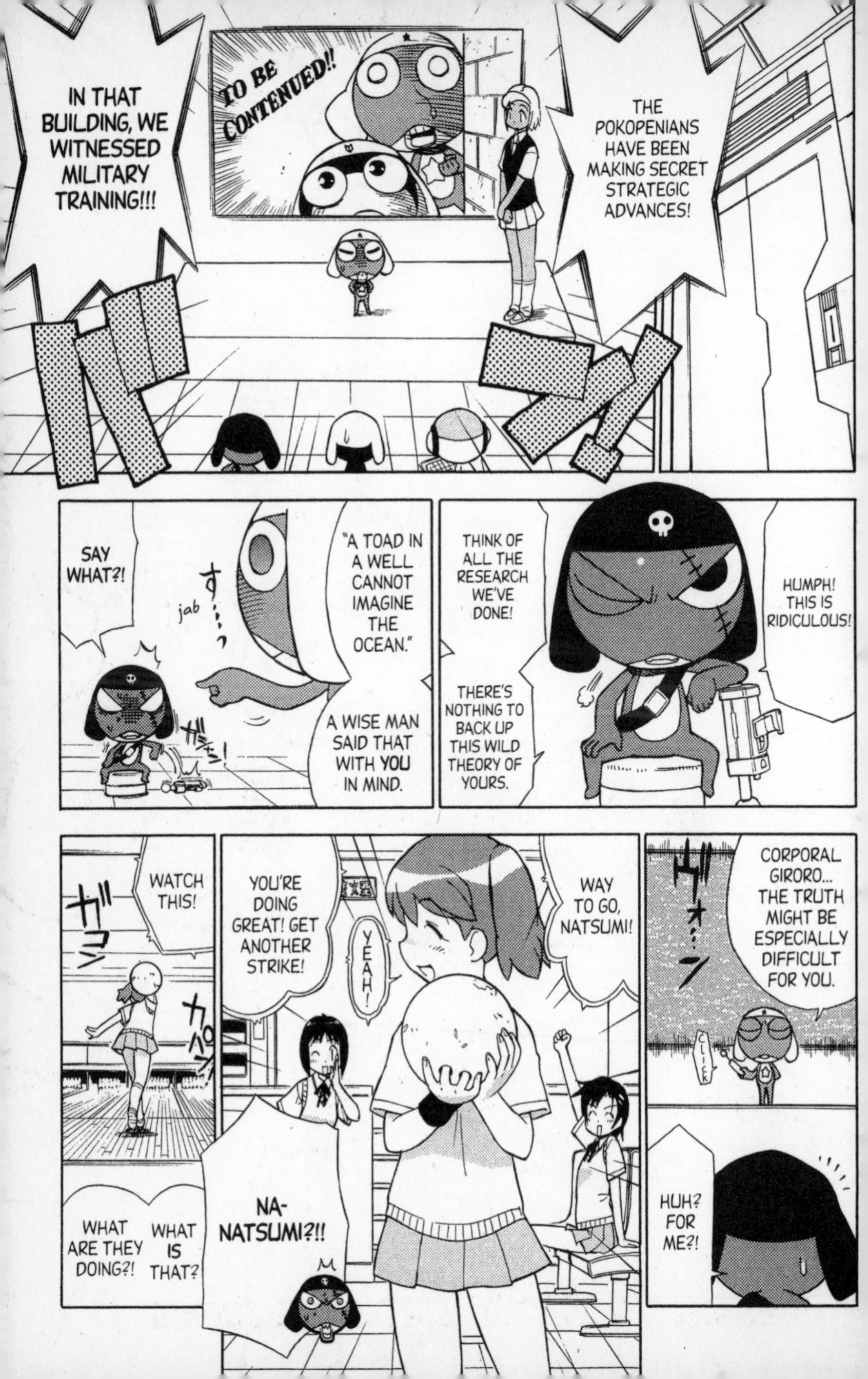
THE POKOPENIANS HAVE BEEN MAKING SECRET STRATEGIC ADVANCES!
TO BE CONTENUED!!
IN THAT BUILDING, WE WITNESSED MILITARY TRAINING!!!
HUMPH! THIS IS RIDICULOUS!
THINK OF ALL THE RESEARCH WE'VE DONE!
THERE'S NOTHING TO BACK UP THIS WILD THEORY OF YOURS.
"A TOAD IN A WELL CANNOT IMAGINE THE OCEAN."
A WISE MAN SAID THAT WITH YOU IN MIND.
jab
SAY WHAT?!
CORPORAL GIRORO... THE TRUTH MIGHT BE ESPECIALLY DIFFICULT FOR YOU.
CLICK
HUH? FOR ME?!
WAY TO GO, NATSUMI!
YEAH!
YOU'RE DOING GREAT! GET ANOTHER STRIKE!
NA-NATSUMI?!!
WATCH THIS!
WHAT IS THAT?
WHAT ARE THEY DOING?!

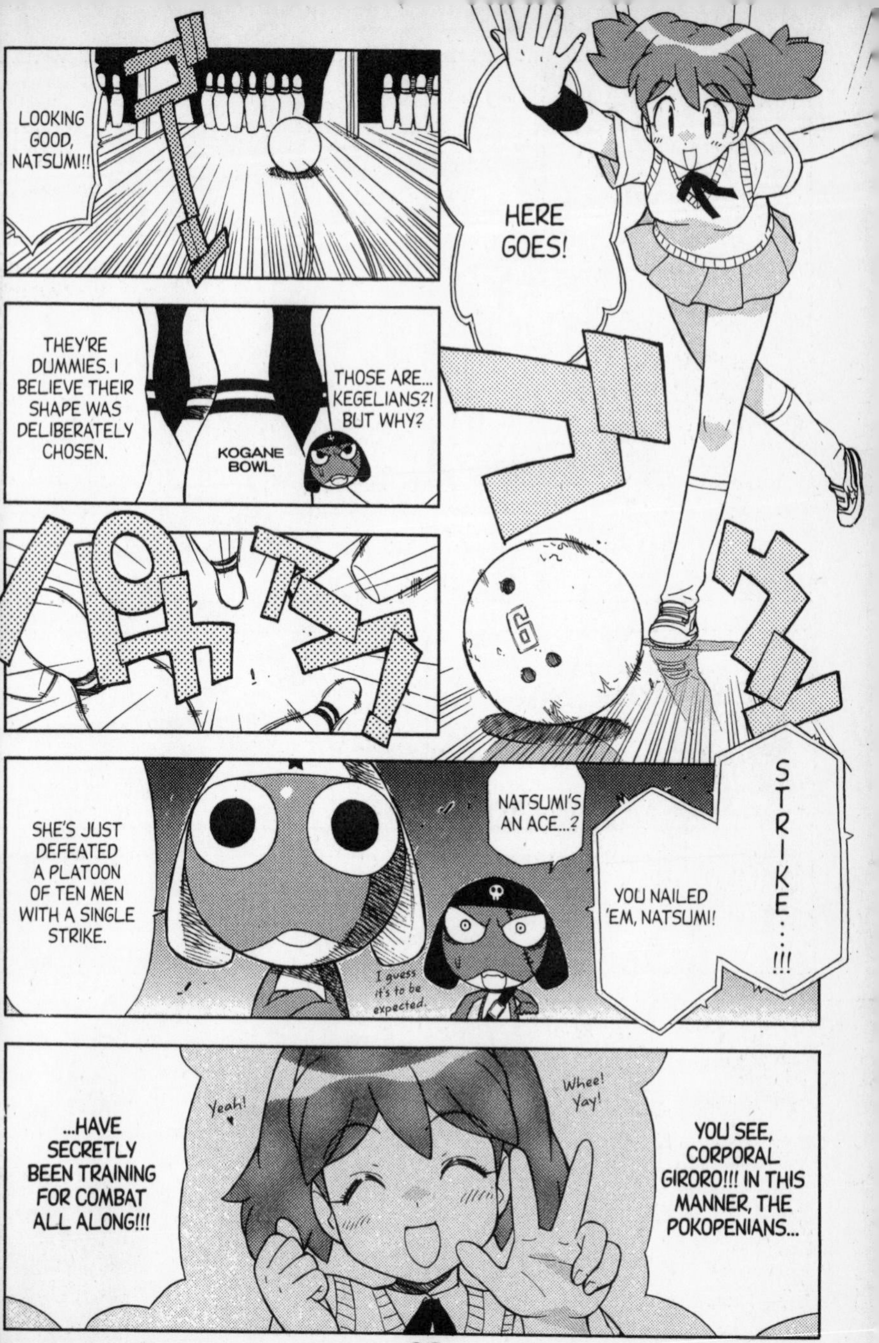
HERE GOES!
LOOKING GOOD, NATSUMI!!
THOSE ARE... KEGELIANS?! BUT WHY?
KOGANE BOWL
THEY'RE DUMMIES. I BELIEVE THEIR SHAPE WAS DELIBERATELY CHOSEN.
STRIKE...!!!
YOU NAILED 'EM, NATSUMI!
NATSUMI'S AN ACE...?
I guess it's to be expected.
SHE'S JUST DEFEATED A PLATOON OF TEN MEN WITH A SINGLE STRIKE.
YOU SEE, CORPORAL GIRORO!!! IN THIS MANNER, THE POKOPENIANS...
Whee! Yay!
Yeah!
...HAVE SECRETLY BEEN TRAINING FOR COMBAT ALL ALONG!!!

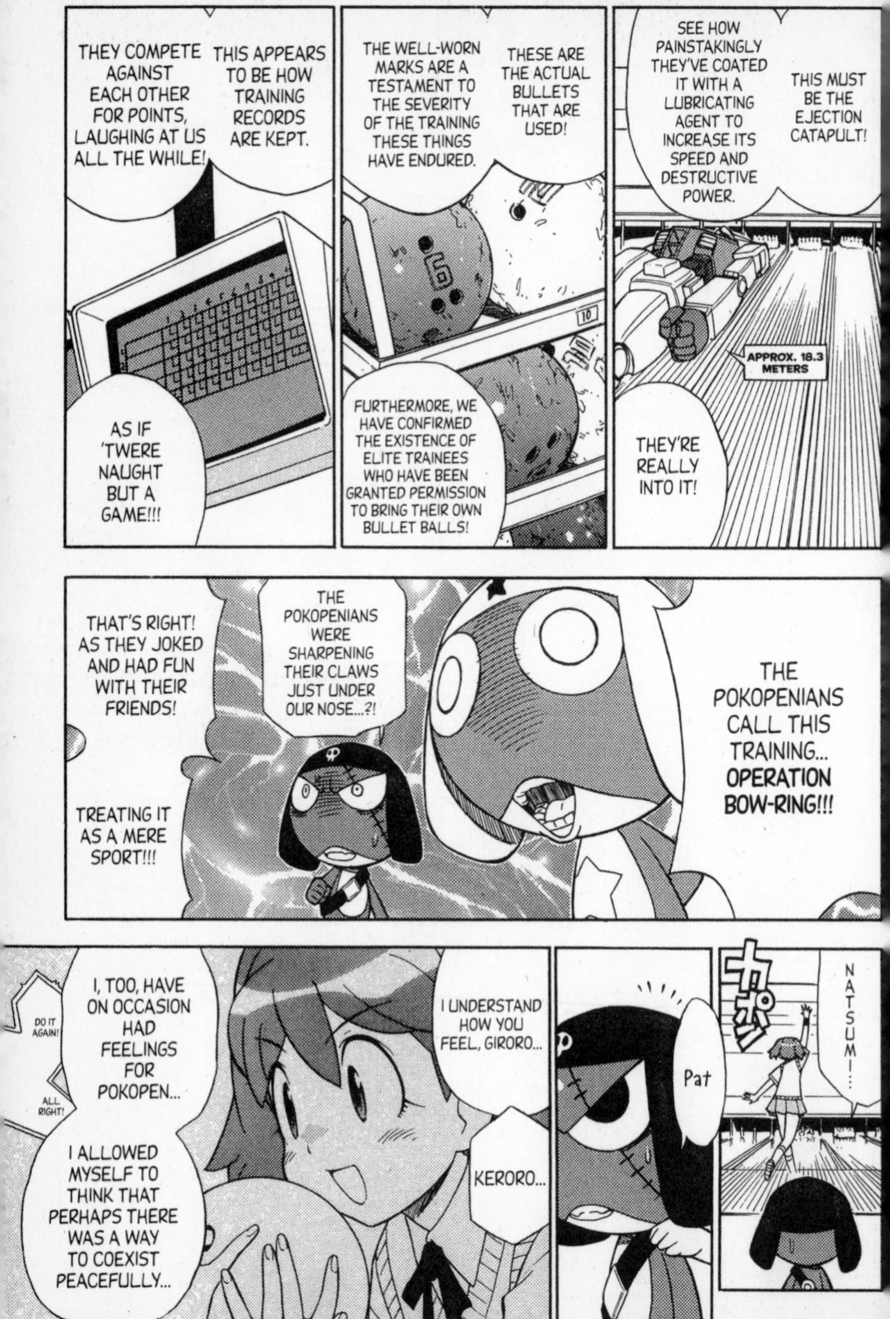
SEE HOW PAINSTAKINGLY THEY'VE COATED IT WITH A LUBRICATING AGENT TO INCREASE ITS SPEED AND DESTRUCTIVE POWER.
THIS MUST BE THE EJECTION CATAPULT!
APPROX. 18.3 METERS
THEY'RE REALLY INTO IT!
THESE ARE THE ACTUAL BULLETS THAT ARE USED!
THE WELL-WORN MARKS ARE A TESTAMENT TO THE SEVERITY OF THE TRAINING THESE THINGS HAVE ENDURED.
FURTHERMORE, WE HAVE CONFIRMED THE EXISTENCE OF ELITE TRAINEES WHO HAVE BEEN GRANTED PERMISSION TO BRING THEIR OWN BULLET BALLS!
THIS APPEARS TO BE HOW TRAINING RECORDS ARE KEPT.
THEY COMPETE AGAINST EACH OTHER FOR POINTS, LAUGHING AT US ALL THE WHILE!
AS IF 'TWERE NAUGHT BUT A GAME!!!
THE POKOPENIANS CALL THIS TRAINING... OPERATION BOW-RING!!!
THE POKOPENIANS WERE SHARPENING THEIR CLAWS JUST UNDER OUR NOSE...?!
THAT'S RIGHT! AS THEY JOKED AND HAD FUN WITH THEIR FRIENDS!
TREATING IT AS A MERE SPORT!!!
NATSUMI...
Pat
I UNDERSTAND HOW YOU FEEL, GIRORO...
KERORO...
I, TOO, HAVE ON OCCASION HAD FEELINGS FOR POKOPEN...
DO IT AGAIN!
ALL RIGHT!
I ALLOWED MYSELF TO THINK THAT PERHAPS THERE WAS A WAY TO COEXIST PEACEFULLY...

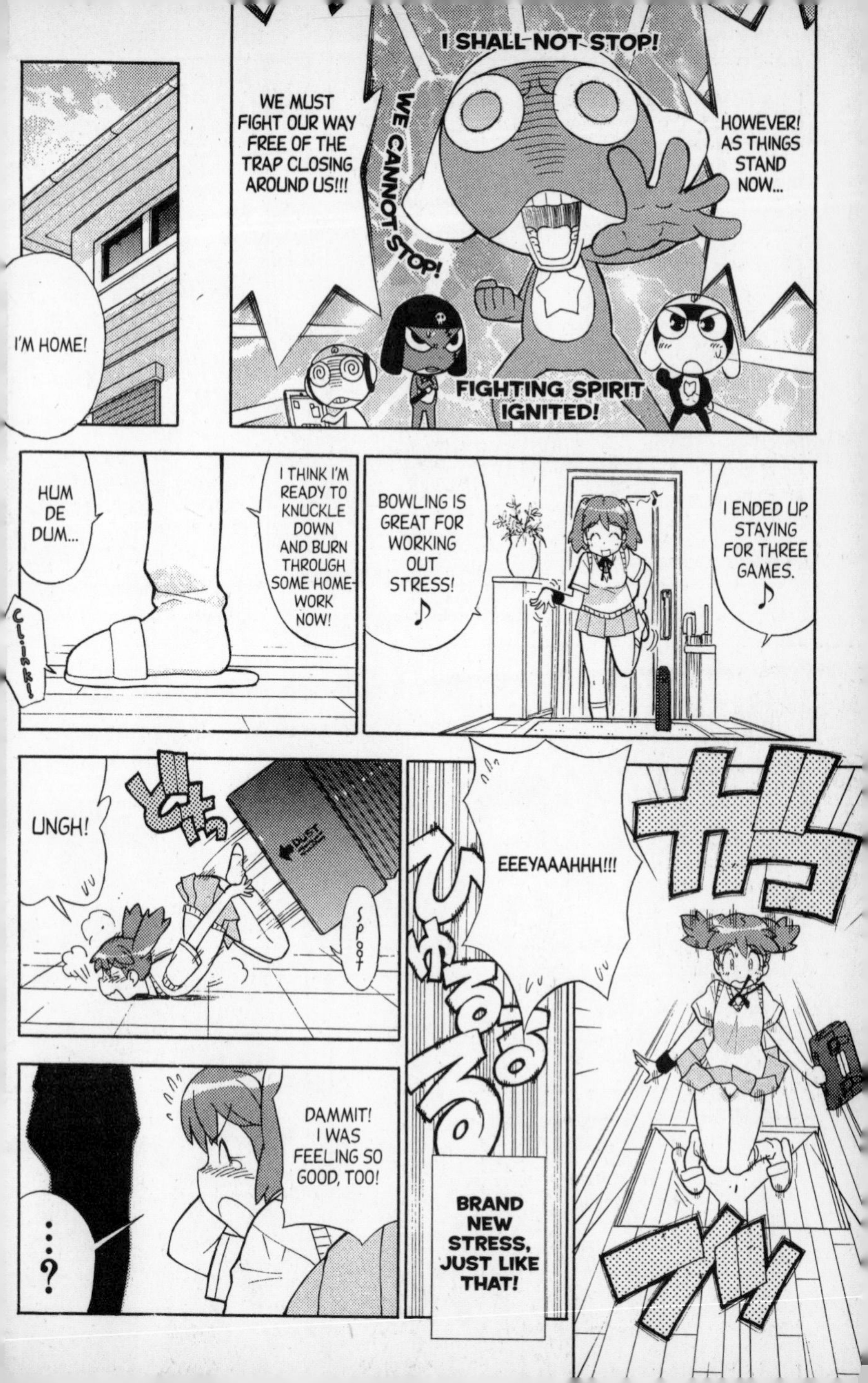
HOWEVER! AS THINGS STAND NOW...
I SHALL NOT STOP!
WE MUST FIGHT OUR WAY FREE OF THE TRAP CLOSING AROUND US!!!
WE CANNOT STOP!
FIGHTING SPIRIT IGNITED!
I'M HOME!
I ENDED UP STAYING FOR THREE GAMES. ♪
BOWLING IS GREAT FOR WORKING OUT STRESS! ♪
I THINK I'M READY TO KNUCKLE DOWN AND BURN THROUGH SOME HOME-WORK NOW!
HUM DE DUM...
CLINK!
EEEYAAAHHH!!!
UNGH!
SPLOOT
DAMMIT! I WAS FEELING SO GOOD, TOO!
BRAND NEW STRESS, JUST LIKE THAT!
...?

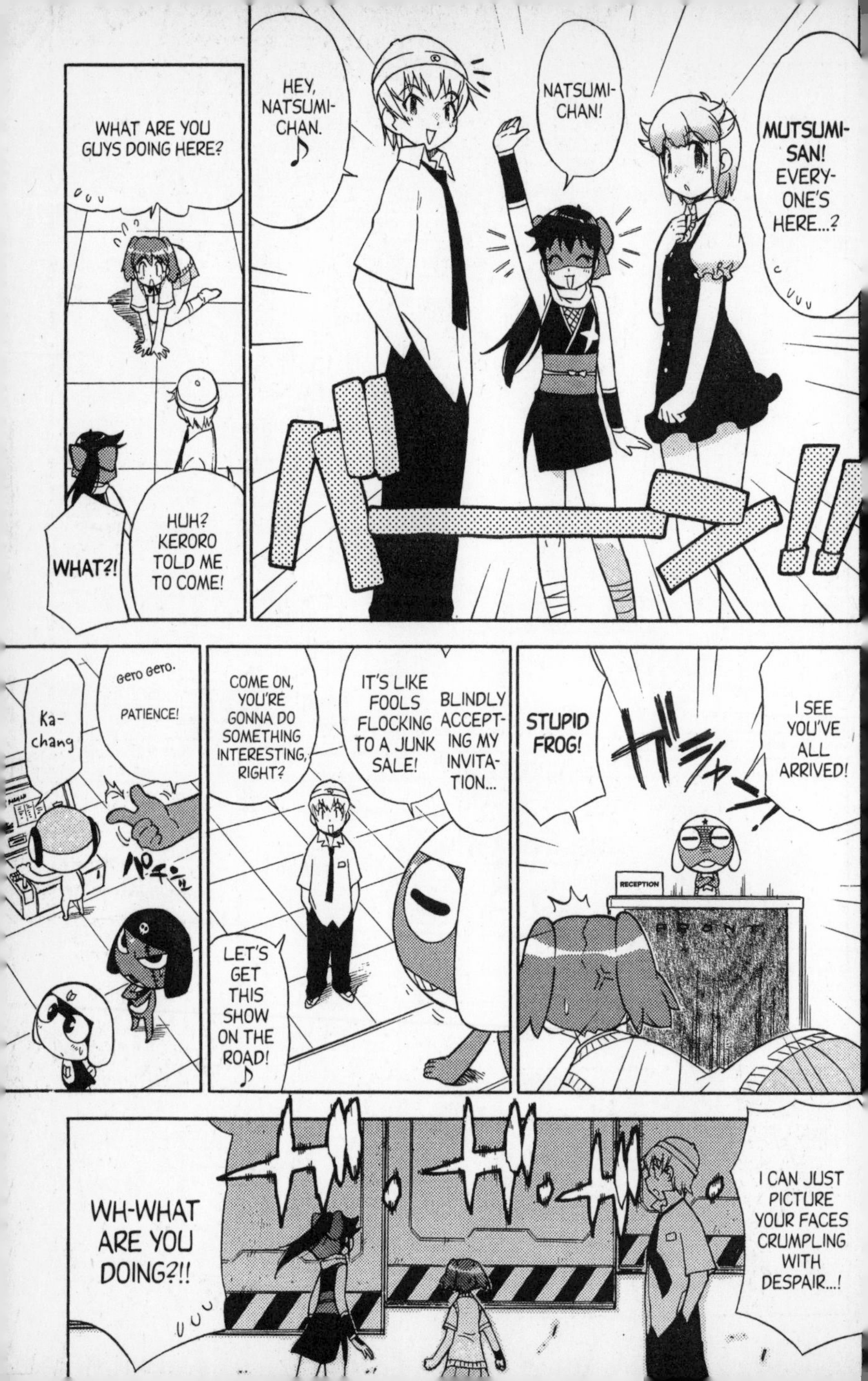
MUTSUMI-SAN! EVERY-ONE'S HERE...?
NATSUMI-CHAN!
HEY, NATSUMI-CHAN. ♪
WHAT ARE YOU GUYS DOING HERE?
HUH? KERORO TOLD ME TO COME!
WHAT?!
I SEE YOU'VE ALL ARRIVED!
STUPID FROG!
RECEPTION
BLINDLY ACCEPT-ING MY INVITA-TION...
IT'S LIKE FOOLS FLOCKING TO A JUNK SALE!
COME ON, YOU'RE GONNA DO SOMETHING INTERESTING, RIGHT?
LET'S GET THIS SHOW ON THE ROAD! ♪
Gero Gero.
PATIENCE!
Ka-chang
I CAN JUST PICTURE YOUR FACES CRUMPLING WITH DESPAIR...!
WH-WHAT ARE YOU DOING?!!

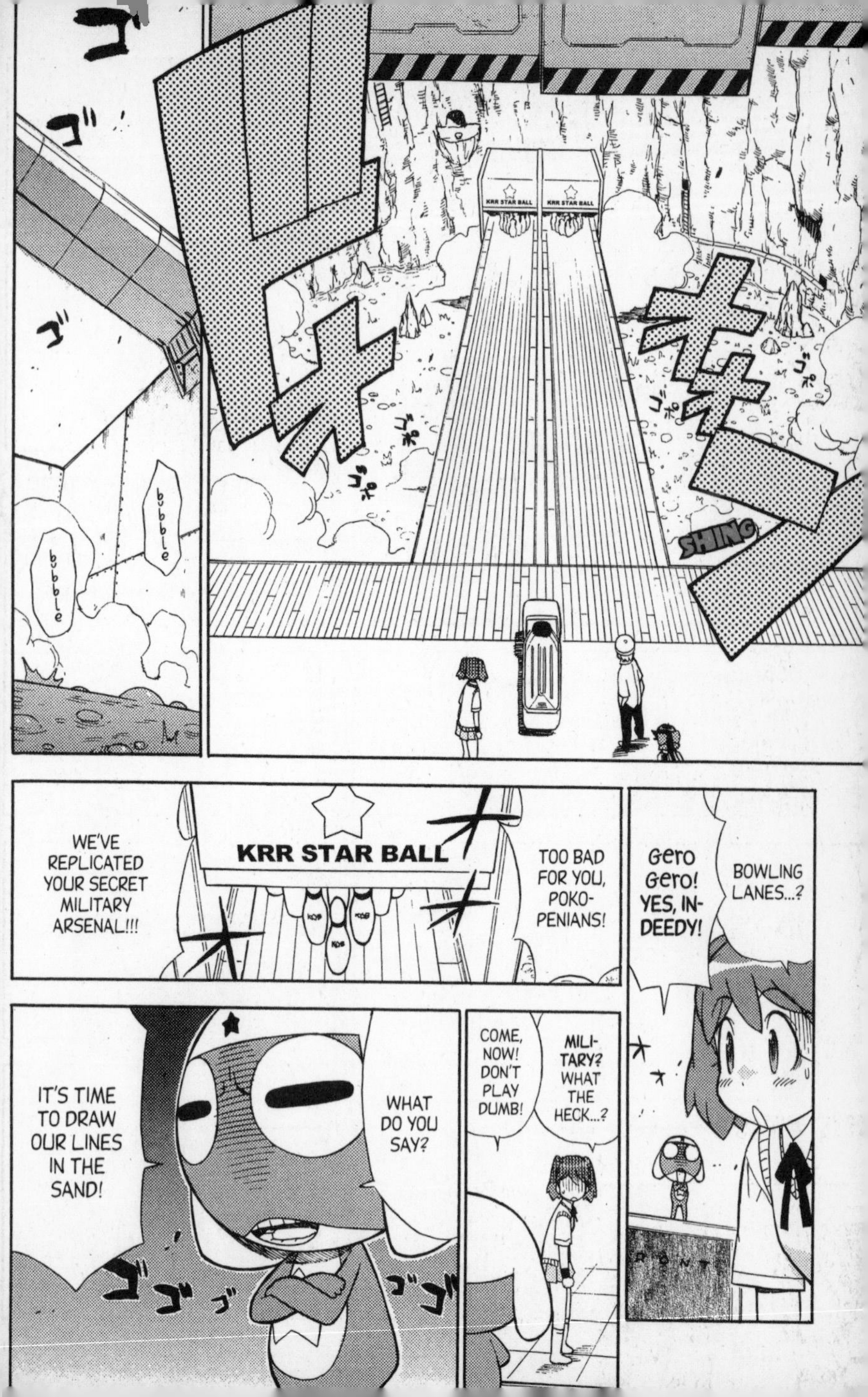
SHING
bubble
bubble
KRR STAR BALL
KRR STAR BALL
BOWLING LANES...?
Gero Gero! YES, INDEEDY!
TOO BAD FOR YOU, POKO-PENIANS!
WE'VE REPLICATED YOUR SECRET MILITARY ARSENAL!!!
KRR STAR BALL
MILITARY? WHAT THE HECK...?
COME, NOW! DON'T PLAY DUMB!
WHAT DO YOU SAY?
IT'S TIME TO DRAW OUR LINES IN THE SAND!

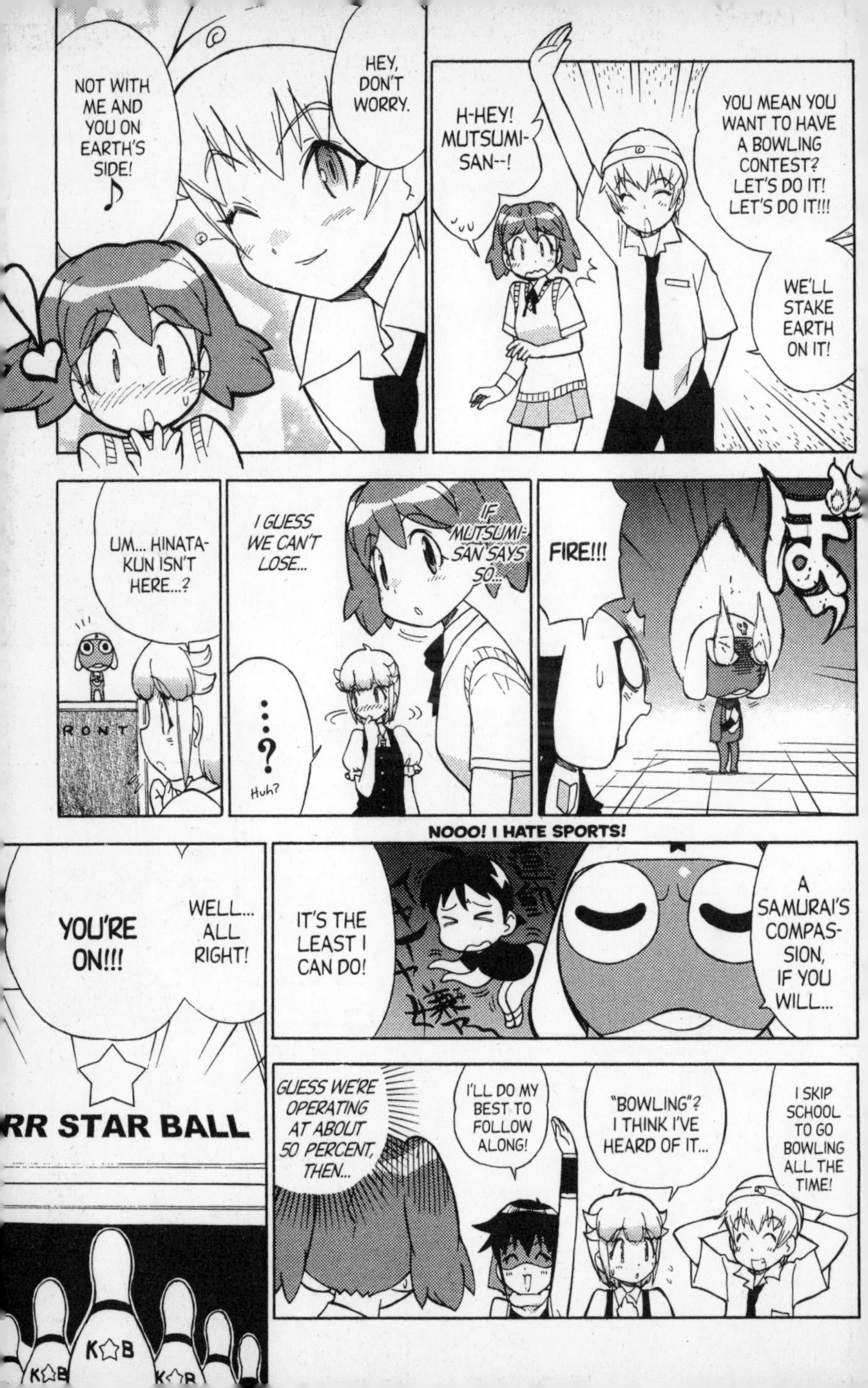
YOU MEAN YOU WANT TO HAVE A BOWLING CONTEST? LET'S DO IT! LET'S DO IT!!!
WE'LL STAKE EARTH ON IT!
H-HEY! MUTSUMI-SAN--!
HEY, DON'T WORRY.
NOT WITH ME AND YOU ON EARTH'S SIDE! ♪
ほ
FIRE!!!
NOOO! I HATE SPORTS!
IF MUTSUMI-SAN SAYS SO...
I GUESS WE CAN'T LOSE...
...?
Huh?
UM... HINATA-KUN ISN'T HERE...?
RONT
A SAMURAI'S COMPASSION, IF YOU WILL...
IT'S THE LEAST I CAN DO!
I SKIP SCHOOL TO GO BOWLING ALL THE TIME!
"BOWLING"? I THINK I'VE HEARD OF IT...
I'LL DO MY BEST TO FOLLOW ALONG!
GUESS WE'RE OPERATING AT ABOUT 50 PERCENT, THEN...
WELL... ALL RIGHT!
YOU'RE ON!!!
RR STAR BALL
K☆B

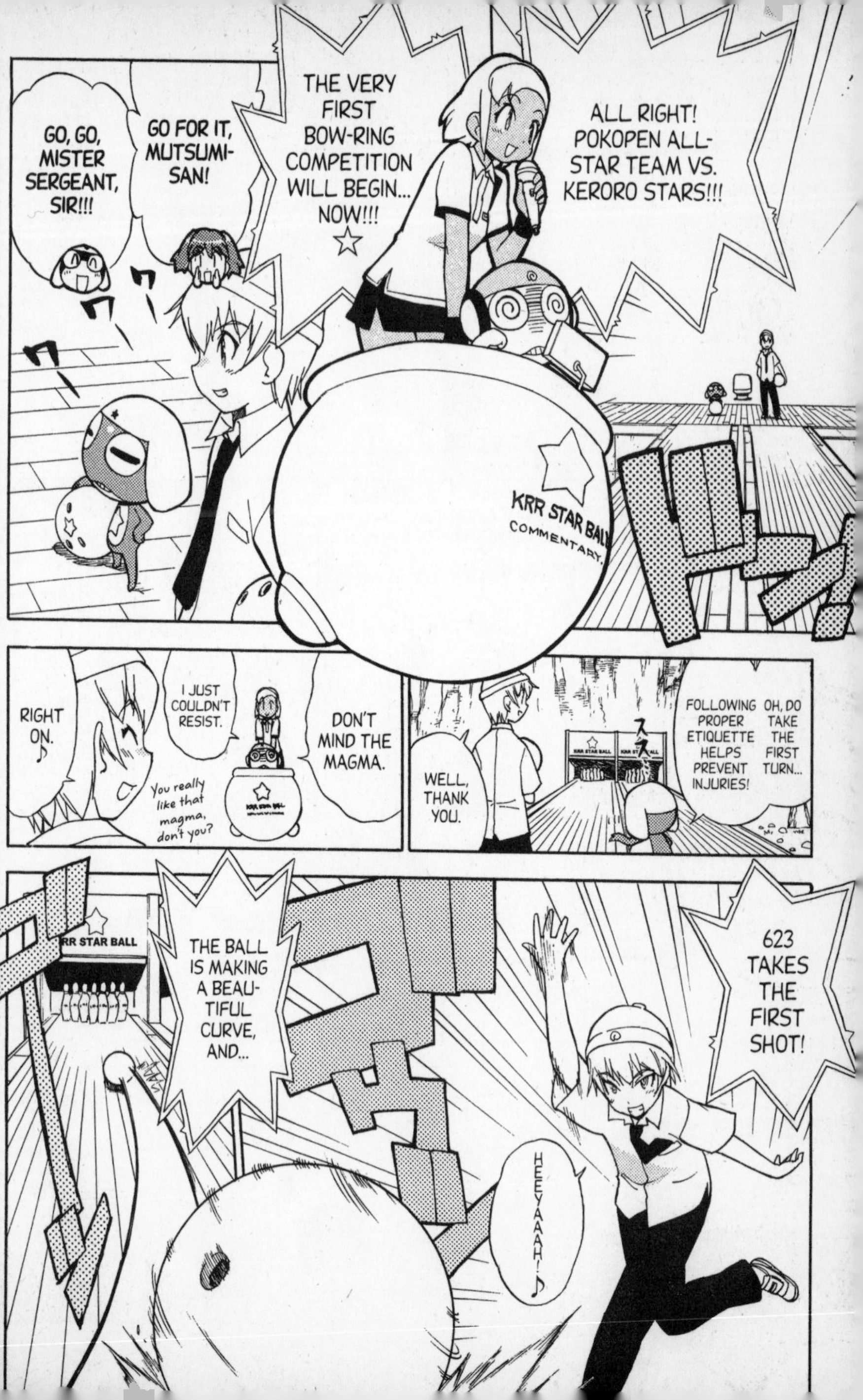
ALL RIGHT! POKOPEN ALL-STAR TEAM VS. KERORO STARS!!!
THE VERY FIRST BOW-RING COMPETITION WILL BEGIN... NOW!!! ☆
GO FOR IT, MUTSUMI-SAN!
GO, GO, MISTER SERGEANT, SIR!!!
KRR STAR BALL
COMMENTARY
OH, DO TAKE THE FIRST TURN...
FOLLOWING PROPER ETIQUETTE HELPS PREVENT INJURIES!
WELL, THANK YOU.
DON'T MIND THE MAGMA.
I JUST COULDN'T RESIST.
RIGHT ON. ♪
You really like that magma, don't you?
623 TAKES THE FIRST SHOT!
HEEYAAAH!♪
THE BALL IS MAKING A BEAU-TIFUL CURVE, AND...
KRR STAR BALL

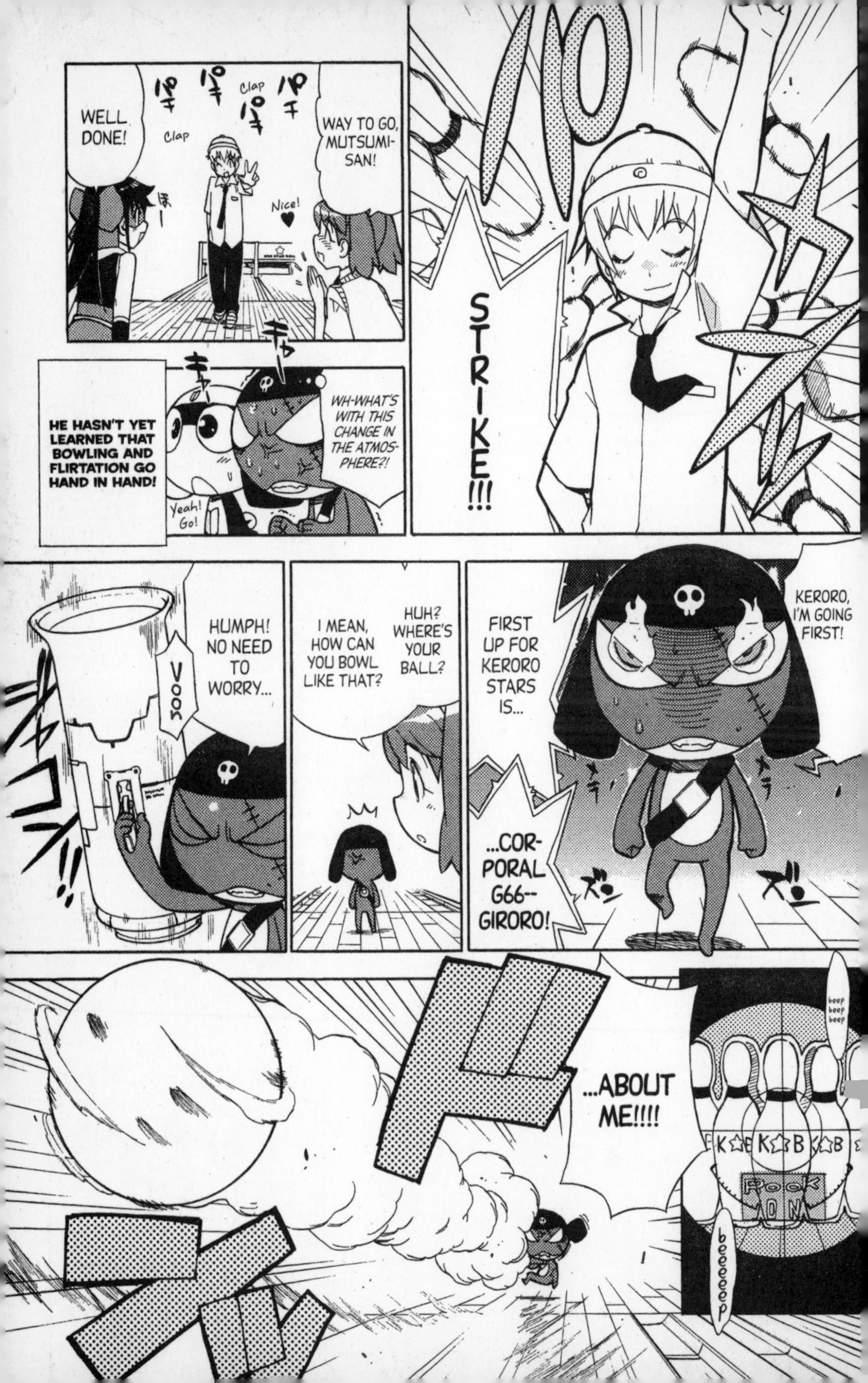
STRIKE!!!
WAY TO GO, MUTSUMI-SAN!
Clap
Clap
WELL DONE!
Nice!
WH-WHAT'S WITH THIS CHANGE IN THE ATMOSPHERE?!
Yeah! Go!
HE HASN'T YET LEARNED THAT BOWLING AND FLIRTATION GO HAND IN HAND!
KERORO, I'M GOING FIRST!
FIRST UP FOR KERORO STARS IS...
...COR-PORAL G66-- GIRORO!
HUH? WHERE'S YOUR BALL?
I MEAN, HOW CAN YOU BOWL LIKE THAT?
HUMPH! NO NEED TO WORRY...
Voon
beep beep beep
K☆B K☆B K☆B
ROCK ON
beeeeeep
...ABOUT ME!!!!

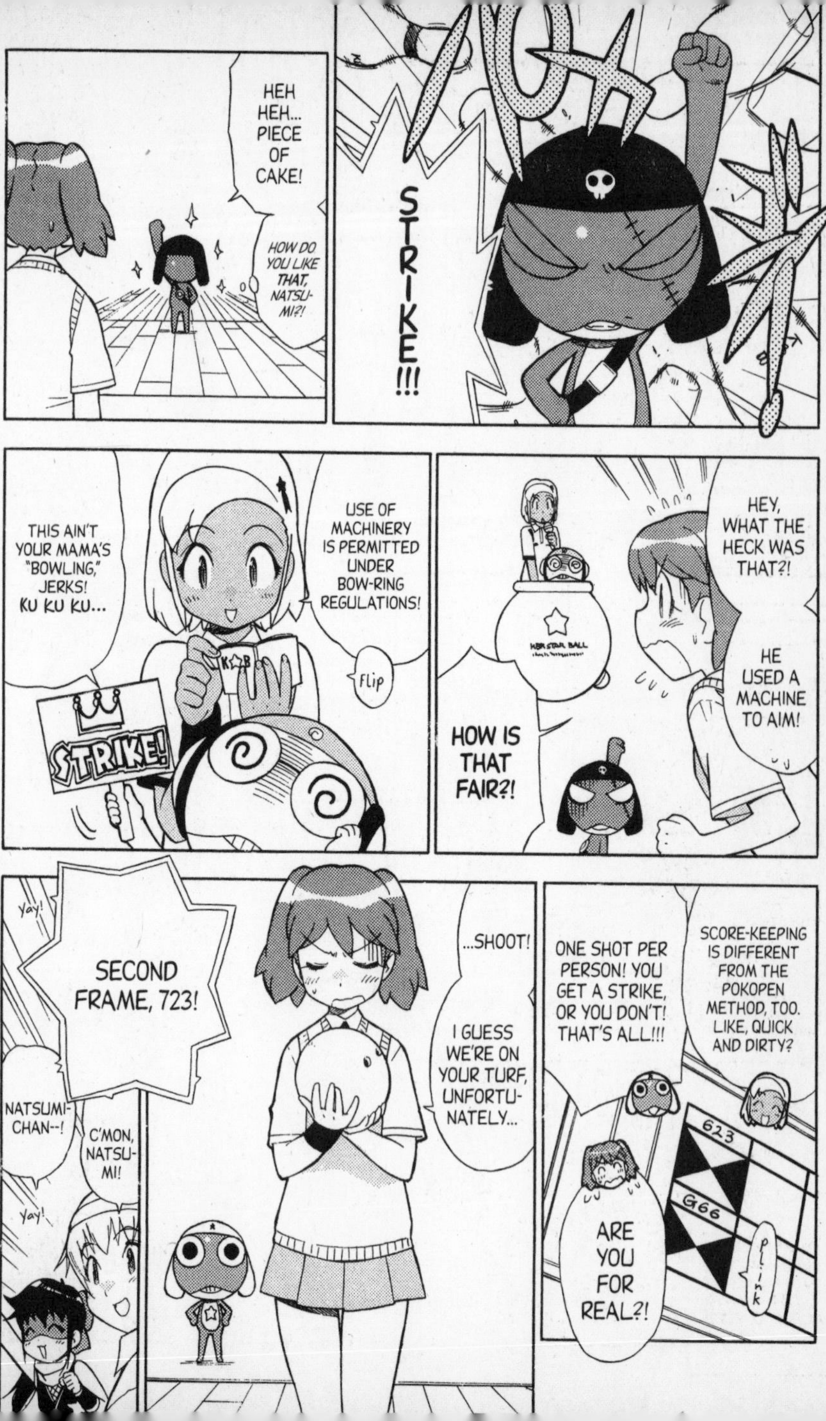
STRIKE!!!
HEH HEH... PIECE OF CAKE!
HOW DO YOU LIKE THAT, NATSUMI?!
HEY, WHAT THE HECK WAS THAT?!
HE USED A MACHINE TO AIM!
HOW IS THAT FAIR?!
KBR STAR BALL
USE OF MACHINERY IS PERMITTED UNDER BOW-RING REGULATIONS!
Flip
THIS AIN'T YOUR MAMA'S "BOWLING," JERKS! KU KU KU...
STRIKE!
SCORE-KEEPING IS DIFFERENT FROM THE POKOPEN METHOD, TOO. LIKE, QUICK AND DIRTY?
ONE SHOT PER PERSON! YOU GET A STRIKE, OR YOU DON'T! THAT'S ALL!!!
623
G66
Plink
ARE YOU FOR REAL?!
...SHOOT!
I GUESS WE'RE ON YOUR TURF, UNFORTUNATELY...
SECOND FRAME, 723!
Yay!
NATSUMI-CHAN--!
C'MON, NATSUMI!
Yay!

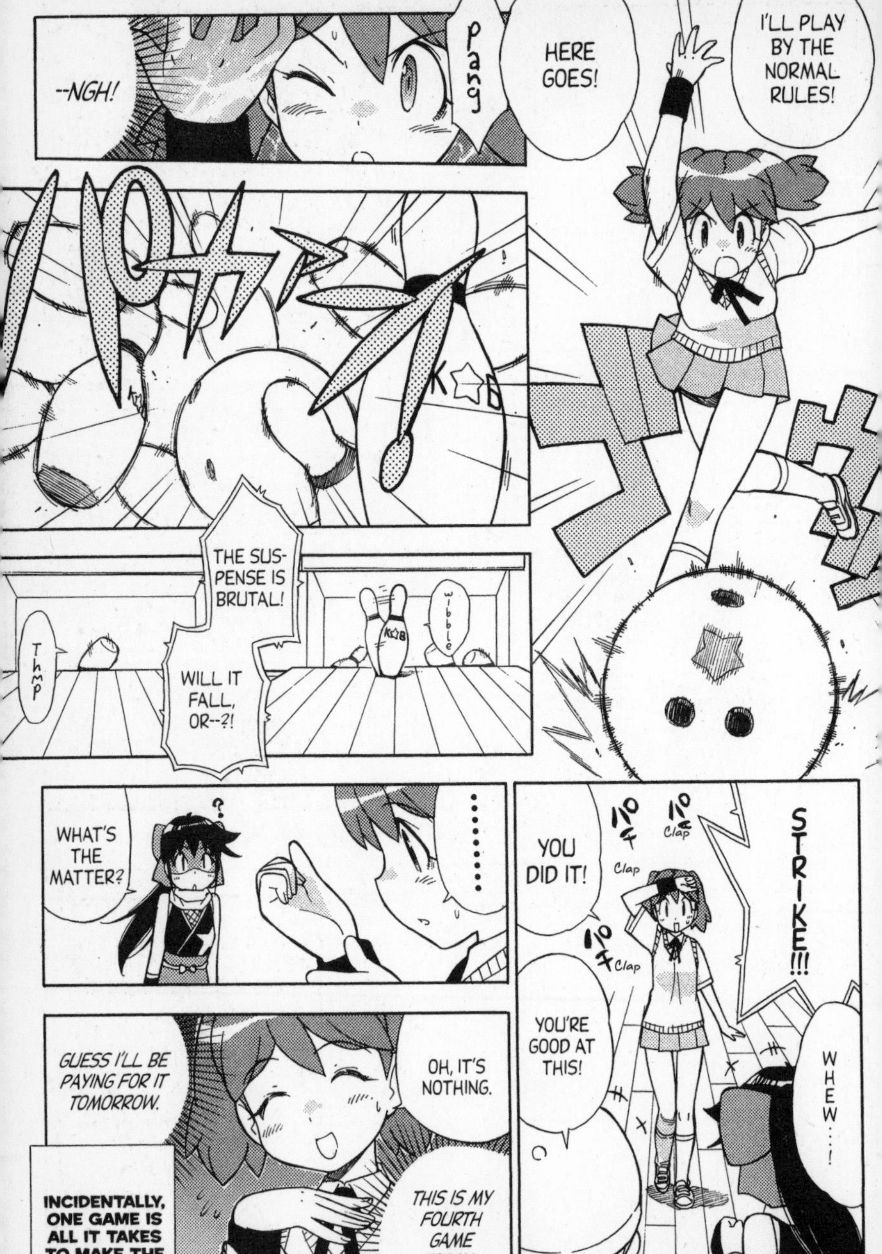
I'LL PLAY BY THE NORMAL RULES!
HERE GOES!
pang
--NGH!
THE SUSPENSE IS BRUTAL!
WILL IT FALL, OR--?!
wibble
Thmp
STRIKE!!!
Clap
Clap
YOU DID IT!
Clap
YOU'RE GOOD AT THIS!
WHEW...!
....
?
WHAT'S THE MATTER?
OH, IT'S NOTHING.
THIS IS MY FOURTH GAME TODAY...
GUESS I'LL BE PAYING FOR IT TOMORROW.
INCIDENTALLY, ONE GAME IS ALL IT TAKES TO MAKE THE AUTHOR SORE!

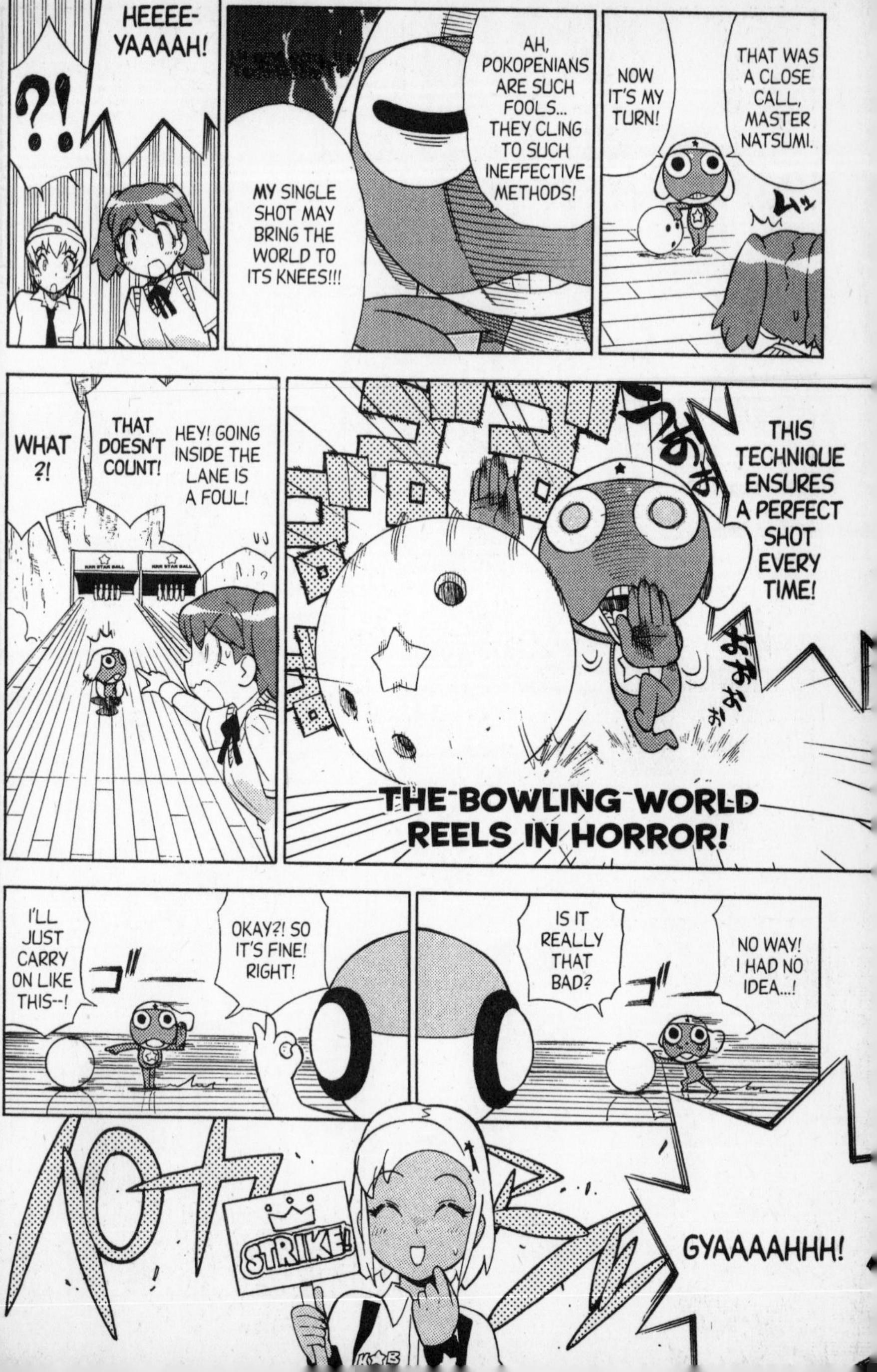
THAT WAS A CLOSE CALL, MASTER NATSUMI.
NOW IT'S MY TURN!
AH, POKOPENIANS ARE SUCH FOOLS... THEY CLING TO SUCH INEFFECTIVE METHODS!
MY SINGLE SHOT MAY BRING THE WORLD TO ITS KNEES!!!
HEEEE-YAAAAH!
?!
THIS TECHNIQUE ENSURES A PERFECT SHOT EVERY TIME!
THE BOWLING WORLD REELS IN HORROR!
HEY! GOING INSIDE THE LANE IS A FOUL!
THAT DOESN'T COUNT!
WHAT ?!
NO WAY! I HAD NO IDEA...!
IS IT REALLY THAT BAD?
OKAY?! SO IT'S FINE! RIGHT!
I'LL JUST CARRY ON LIKE THIS--!
STRIKE!
GYAAAAHHH!

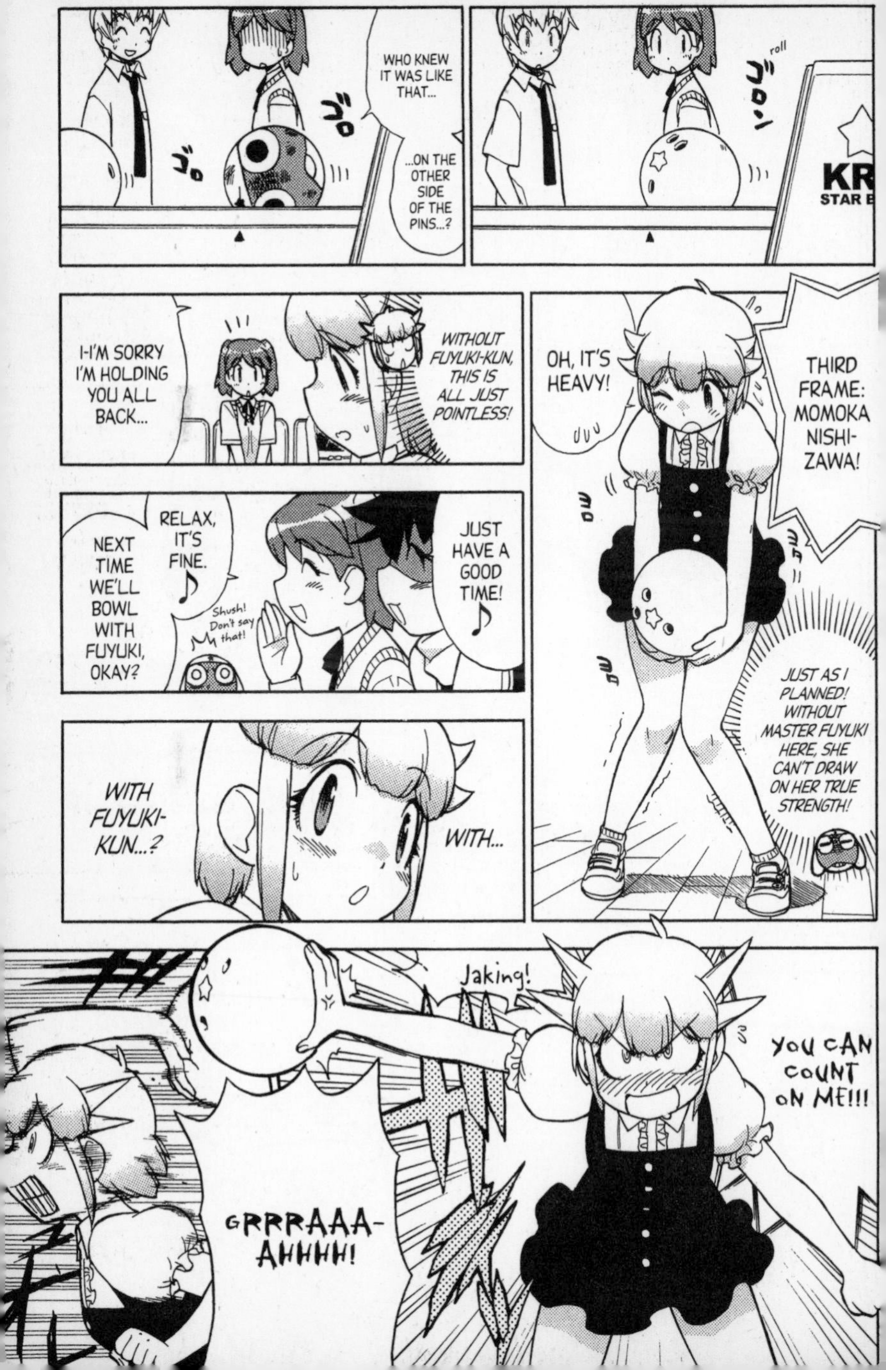
roll
KR
STAR B
WHO KNEW IT WAS LIKE THAT...
...ON THE OTHER SIDE OF THE PINS...?
THIRD FRAME: MOMOKA NISHI-ZAWA!
OH, IT'S HEAVY!
JUST AS I PLANNED! WITHOUT MASTER FUYUKI HERE, SHE CAN'T DRAW ON HER TRUE STRENGTH!
WITHOUT FUYUKI-KUN, THIS IS ALL JUST POINTLESS!
I-I'M SORRY I'M HOLDING YOU ALL BACK...
JUST HAVE A GOOD TIME! ♪
RELAX, IT'S FINE. ♪
NEXT TIME WE'LL BOWL WITH FUYUKI, OKAY?
Shush! Don't say that!
WITH...
WITH FUYUKI-KUN...?
YOU CAN COUNT ON ME!!!
Jaking!
GRRRAAA-AHHHH!

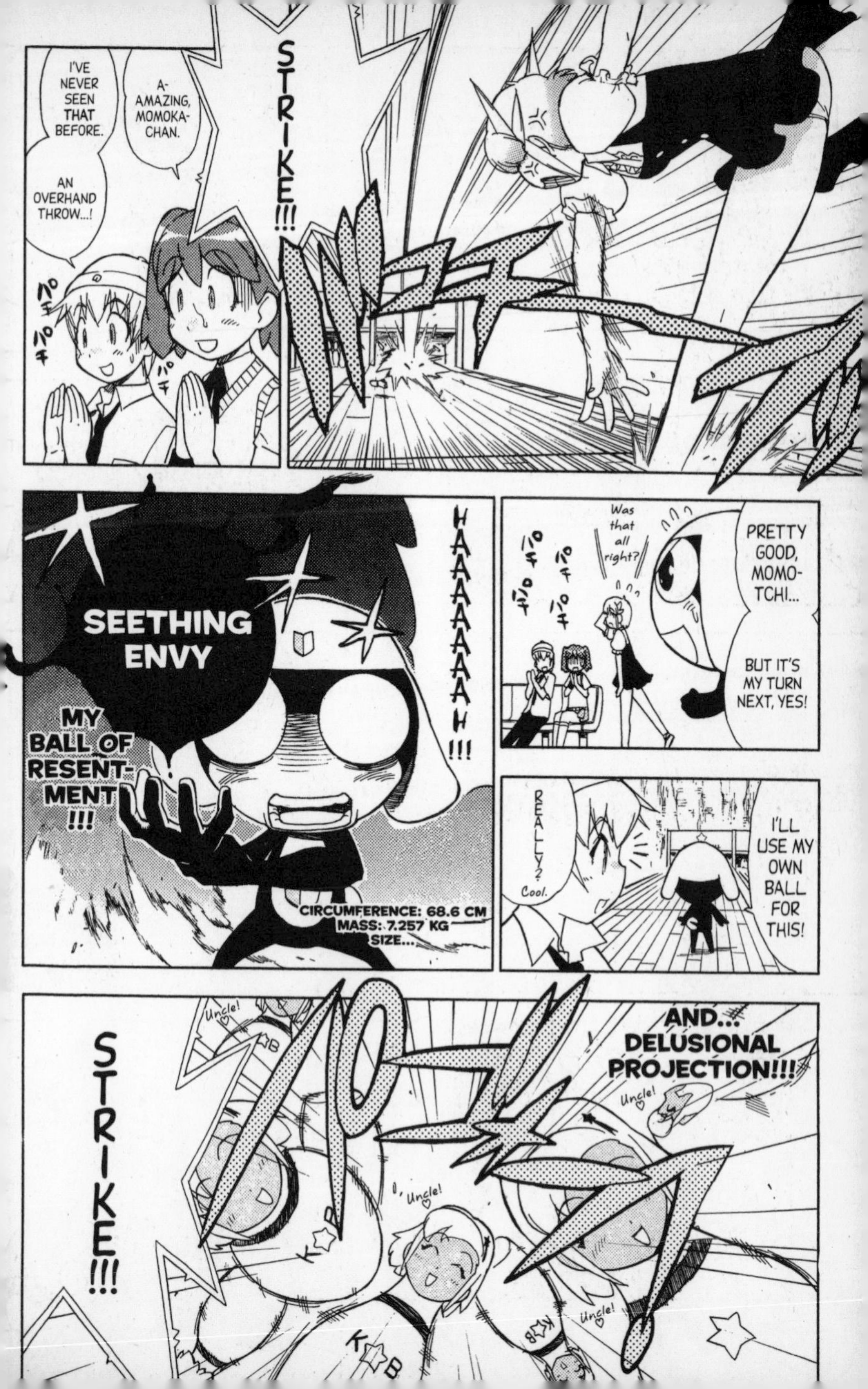
STRIKE!!!
A-AMAZING, MOMOKA-CHAN.
I'VE NEVER SEEN THAT BEFORE.
AN OVERHAND THROW...!
PRETTY GOOD, MOMOTCHI...
BUT IT'S MY TURN NEXT, YES!
Was that all right?
I'LL USE MY OWN BALL FOR THIS!
REALLY? Cool.
HAAAAAAAAH!!!
SEETHING ENVY
MY BALL OF RESENTMENT!!!
CIRCUMFERENCE: 68.6 CM
MASS: 7.257 KG
SIZE...
AND... DELUSIONAL PROJECTION!!!
Uncle!
Uncle!
Uncle!
Uncle!
STRIKE!!!

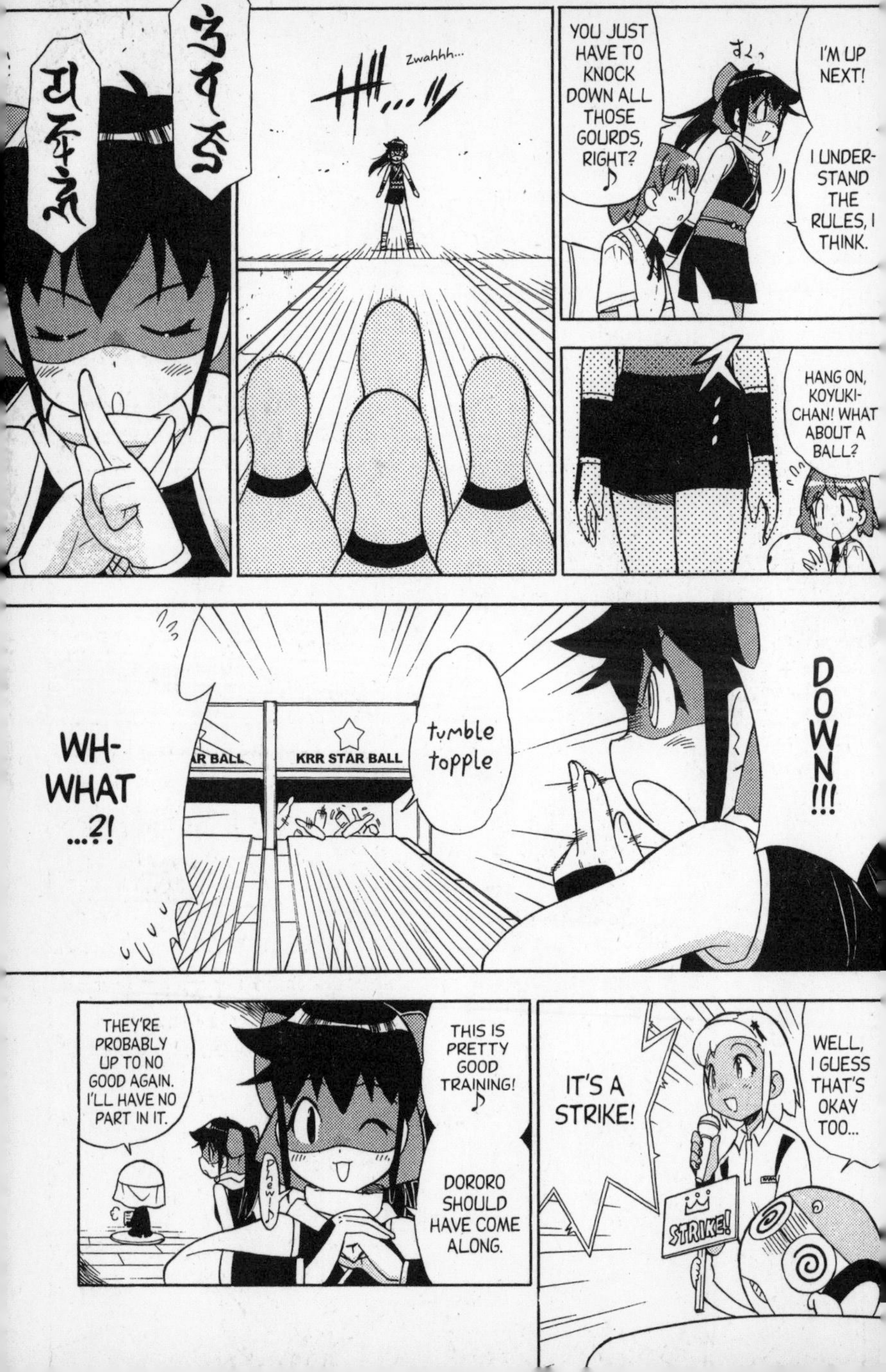
I'M UP NEXT!
I UNDERSTAND THE RULES, I THINK.
YOU JUST HAVE TO KNOCK DOWN ALL THOSE GOURDS, RIGHT? ♪
HANG ON, KOYUKI-CHAN! WHAT ABOUT A BALL?
Zwahhh...
DOWN!!!
tumble topple
KRR STAR BALL
WH-WHAT ...?!
WELL, I GUESS THAT'S OKAY TOO...
IT'S A STRIKE!
STRIKE!
THIS IS PRETTY GOOD TRAINING! ♪
DORORO SHOULD HAVE COME ALONG.
Phew♪
THEY'RE PROBABLY UP TO NO GOOD AGAIN. I'LL HAVE NO PART IN IT.

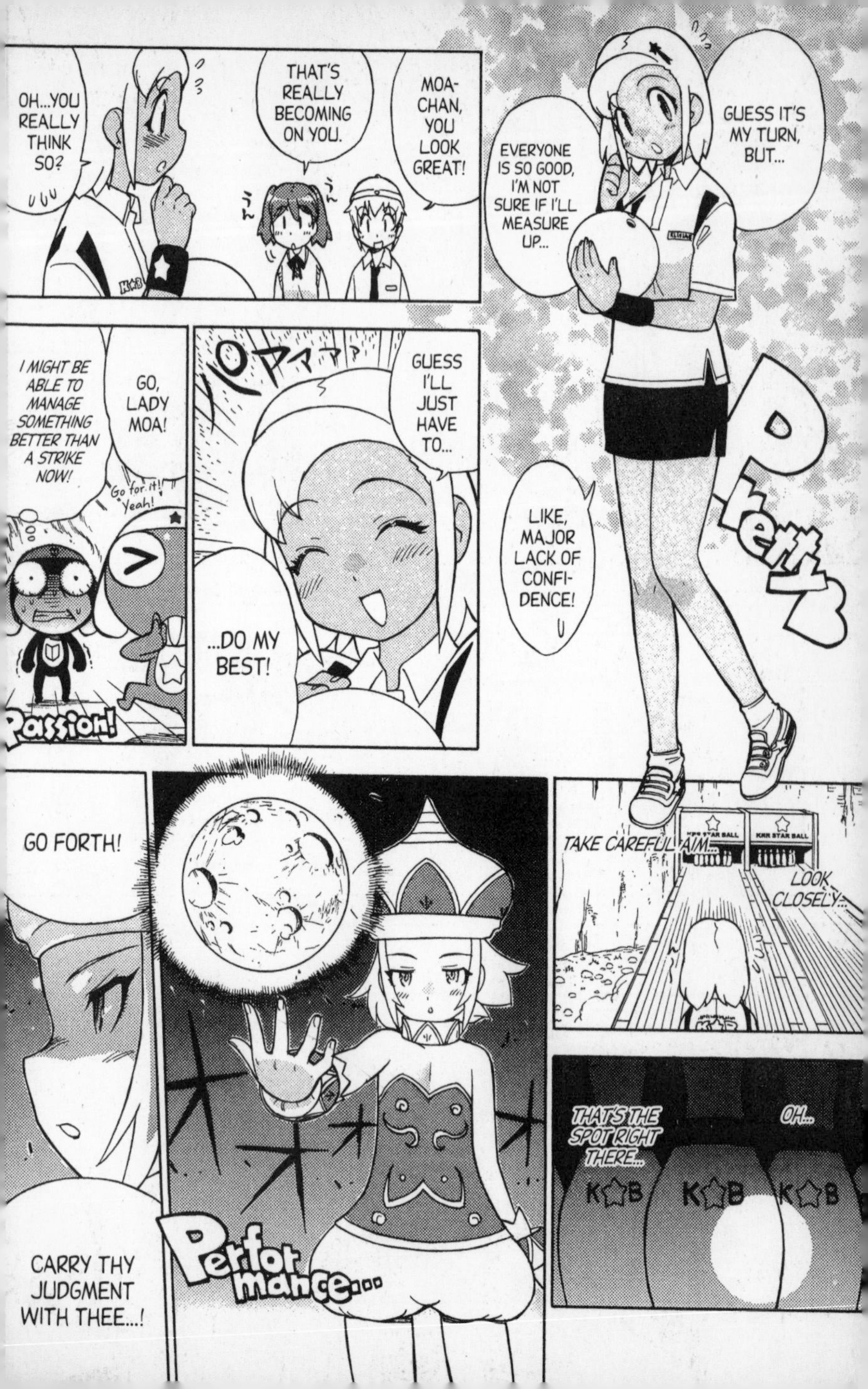
GUESS IT'S MY TURN, BUT...
EVERYONE IS SO GOOD, I'M NOT SURE IF I'LL MEASURE UP...
LIKE, MAJOR LACK OF CONFIDENCE!
Pretty
MOA-CHAN, YOU LOOK GREAT!
THAT'S REALLY BECOMING ON YOU.
OH...YOU REALLY THINK SO?
GUESS I'LL JUST HAVE TO...
...DO MY BEST!
GO, LADY MOA!
I MIGHT BE ABLE TO MANAGE SOMETHING BETTER THAN A STRIKE NOW!
Go for it!! Yeah!
Passion!
TAKE CAREFUL AIM...
LOOK CLOSELY...
OH...
THAT'S THE SPOT RIGHT THERE...
K☆B K☆B K☆B
GO FORTH!
Perfotmance...
CARRY THY JUDGMENT WITH THEE...!

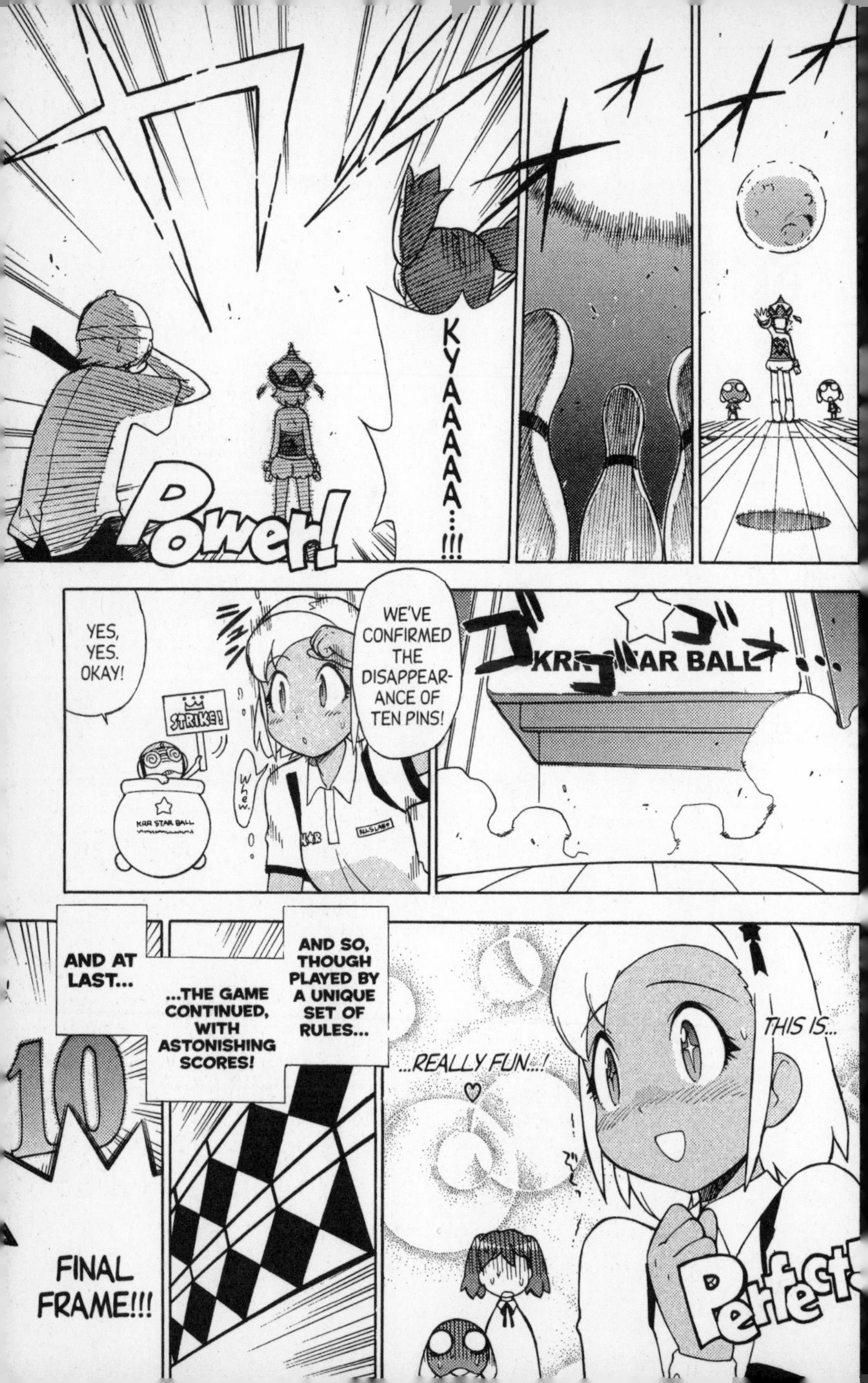
KYAAAAAA...!!!
Power!
WE'VE CONFIRMED THE DISAPPEARANCE OF TEN PINS!
Whew.
STRIKE!
KRR STAR BALL
YES, YES. OKAY!
AND SO, THOUGH PLAYED BY A UNIQUE SET OF RULES...
...THE GAME CONTINUED, WITH ASTONISHING SCORES!
AND AT LAST...
10
FINAL FRAME!!!
THIS IS...
...REALLY FUN...!
Perfect

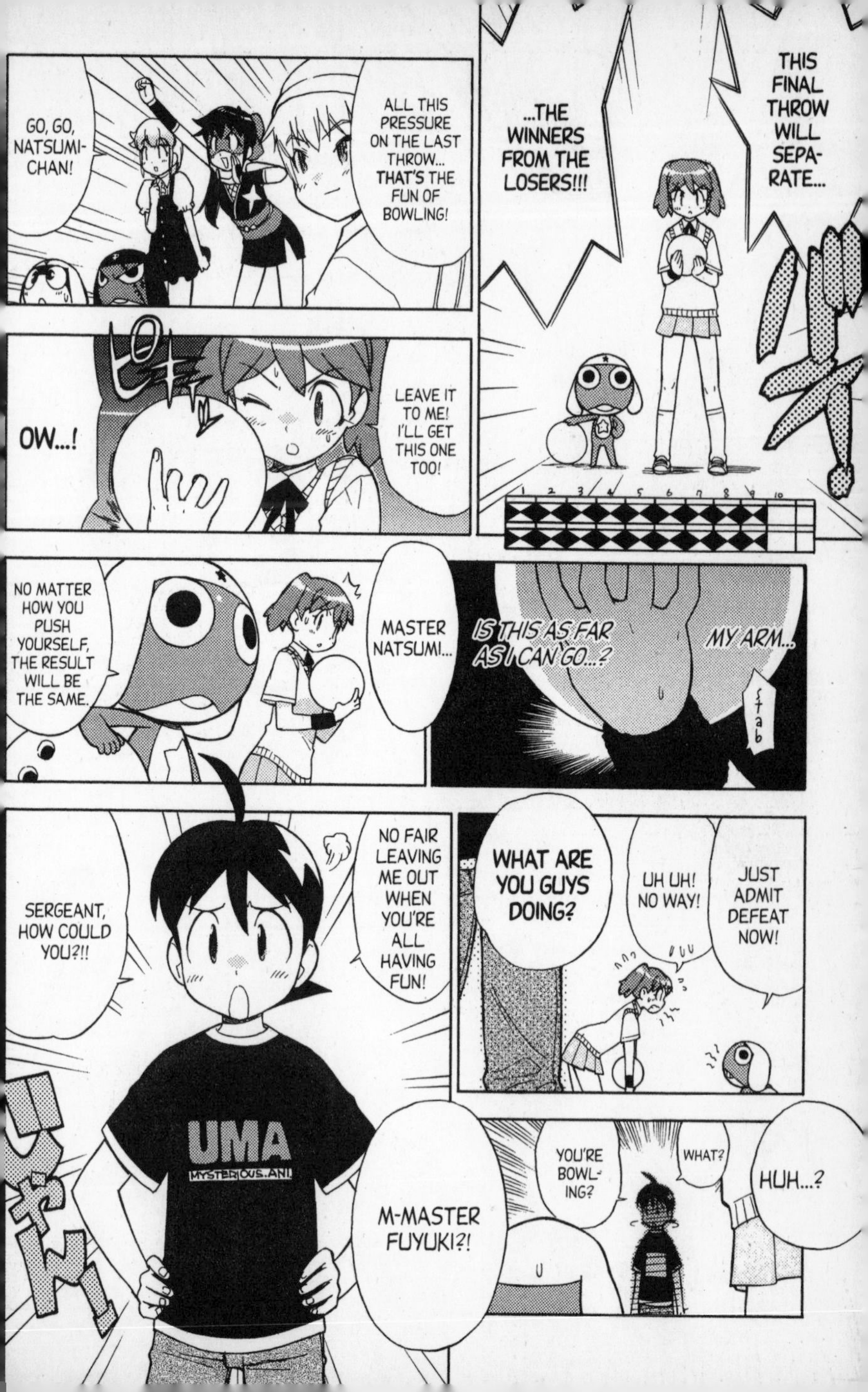

THIS FINAL THROW WILL SEPA-RATE...
...THE WINNERS FROM THE LOSERS!!!
ALL THIS PRESSURE ON THE LAST THROW... THAT'S THE FUN OF BOWLING!
GO, GO, NATSUMI-CHAN!
LEAVE IT TO ME! I'LL GET THIS ONE TOO!
OW...!
MY ARM...
IS THIS AS FAR AS I CAN GO...?
stab
MASTER NATSUMI...
NO MATTER HOW YOU PUSH YOURSELF, THE RESULT WILL BE THE SAME.
JUST ADMIT DEFEAT NOW!
UH UH! NO WAY!
WHAT ARE YOU GUYS DOING?
HUH...?
WHAT?
YOU'RE BOWL-ING?
M-MASTER FUYUKI?!
NO FAIR LEAVING ME OUT WHEN YOU'RE ALL HAVING FUN!
SERGEANT, HOW COULD YOU?!!
UMA
MYSTERIOUS.ANI.

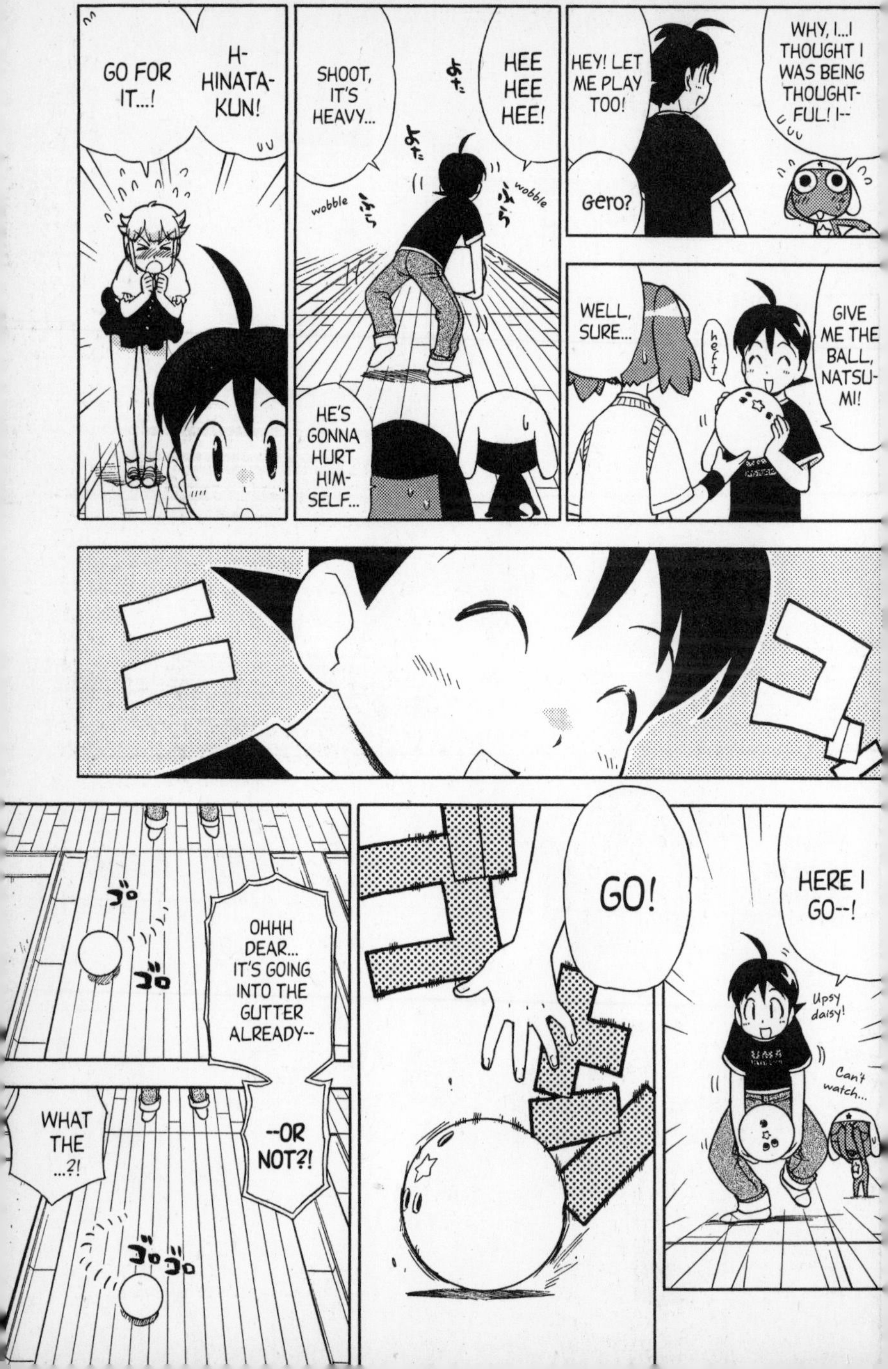
WHY, I...I THOUGHT I WAS BEING THOUGHT-FUL! I--
HEY! LET ME PLAY TOO!
Gero?
GIVE ME THE BALL, NATSU-MI!
heft
WELL, SURE...
HEE HEE HEE!
SHOOT, IT'S HEAVY...
wobble
wobble
HE'S GONNA HURT HIM-SELF...
H-HINATA-KUN!
GO FOR IT...!
HERE I GO--!
Upsy daisy!
Can't watch...
GO!
OHHH DEAR... IT'S GOING INTO THE GUTTER ALREADY--
--OR NOT?!
WHAT THE ...?!

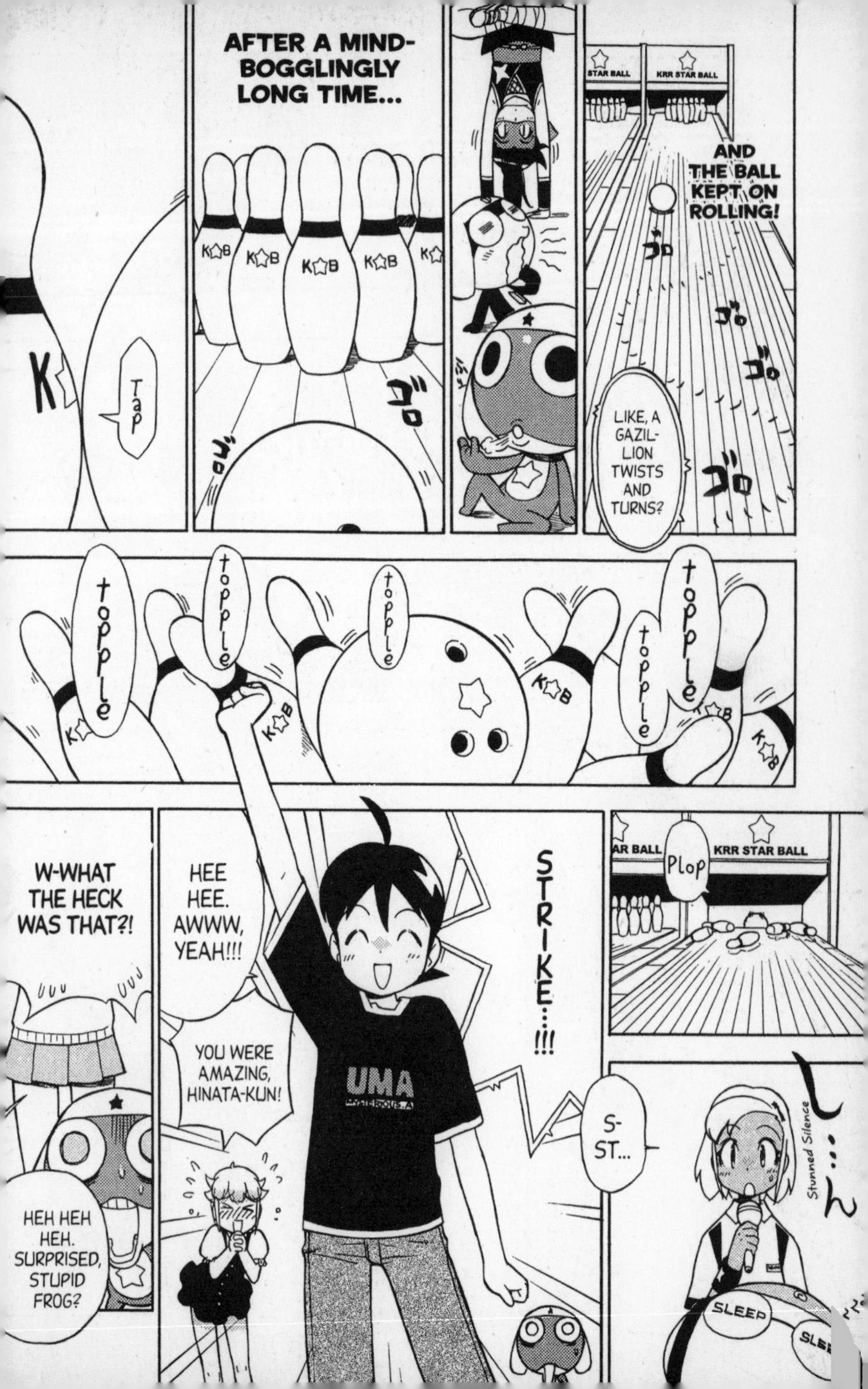
AND THE BALL KEPT ON ROLLING!
ゴロ
ゴロ
ゴロ
ゴロ
LIKE, A GAZIL-LION TWISTS AND TURNS?
AFTER A MIND-BOGGLINGLY LONG TIME...
ゴロ
ゴロ
Tap
topple
topple
topple
topple
topple
Plop
KRR STAR BALL
S-ST...
Stunned Silence
STRIKE...!!!
UMA
YOU WERE AMAZING, HINATA-KUN!
HEE HEE. AWWW, YEAH!!!
W-WHAT THE HECK WAS THAT?!
HEH HEH HEH. SURPRISED, STUPID FROG?
SLEEP

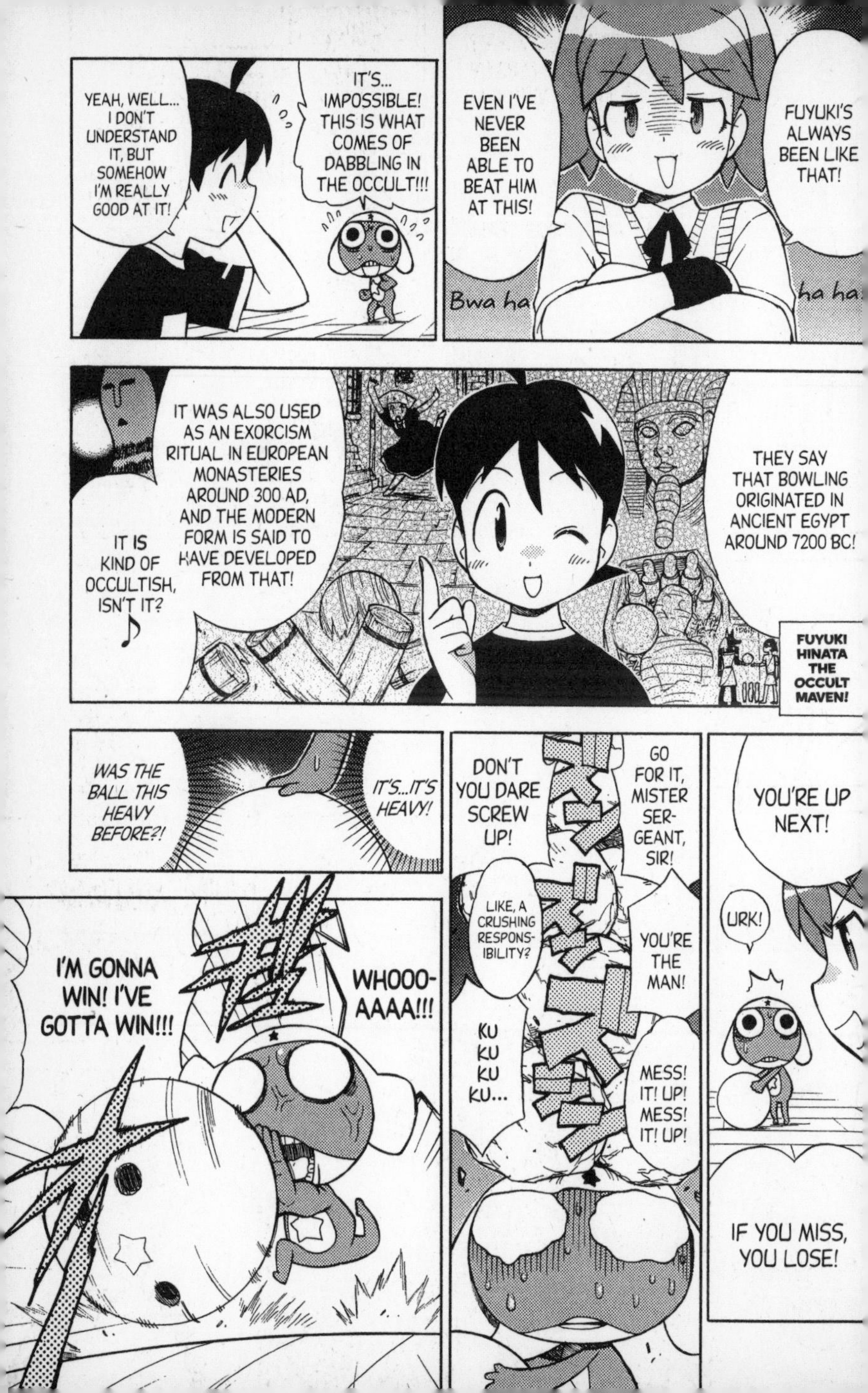
FUYUKI'S ALWAYS BEEN LIKE THAT!
EVEN I'VE NEVER BEEN ABLE TO BEAT HIM AT THIS!
Bwa ha ha ha
IT'S... IMPOSSIBLE! THIS IS WHAT COMES OF DABBLING IN THE OCCULT!!!
YEAH, WELL... I DON'T UNDERSTAND IT, BUT SOMEHOW I'M REALLY GOOD AT IT!
THEY SAY THAT BOWLING ORIGINATED IN ANCIENT EGYPT AROUND 7200 BC!
FUYUKI HINATA THE OCCULT MAVEN!
IT WAS ALSO USED AS AN EXORCISM RITUAL IN EUROPEAN MONASTERIES AROUND 300 AD, AND THE MODERN FORM IS SAID TO HAVE DEVELOPED FROM THAT!
IT IS KIND OF OCCULTISH, ISN'T IT? ♪
YOU'RE UP NEXT!
URK!
IF YOU MISS, YOU LOSE!
GO FOR IT, MISTER SER-GEANT, SIR!
DON'T YOU DARE SCREW UP!
YOU'RE THE MAN!
LIKE, A CRUSHING RESPONS-IBILITY?
MESS! IT! UP! MESS! IT! UP!
KU KU KU KU...
IT'S...IT'S HEAVY!
WAS THE BALL THIS HEAVY BEFORE?!
WHOOO-AAAA!!!
I'M GONNA WIN! I'VE GOTTA WIN!!!

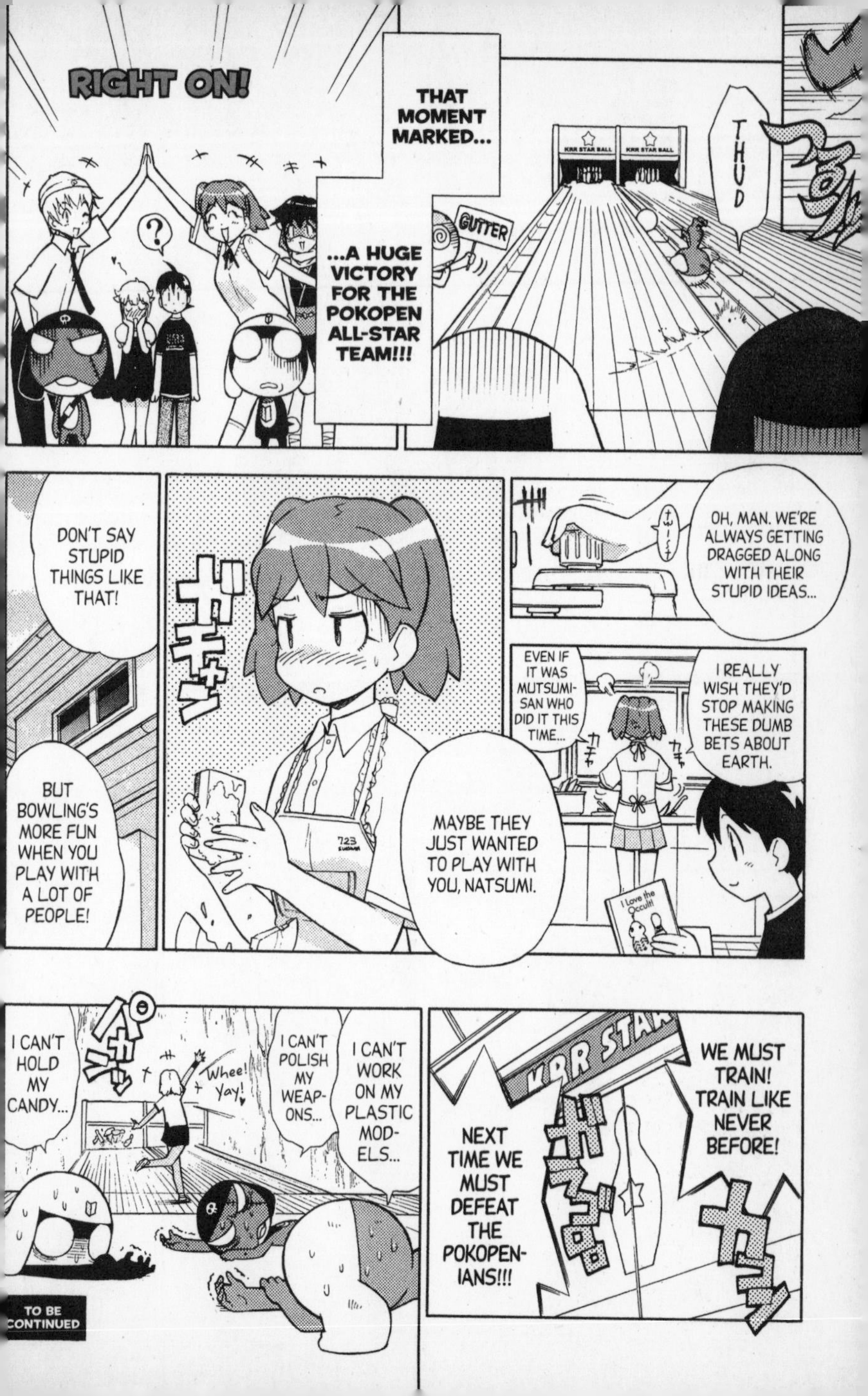
THUD
KRR STAR BALL
GUTTER
THAT MOMENT MARKED...
...A HUGE VICTORY FOR THE POKOPEN ALL-STAR TEAM!!!
RIGHT ON!
OH, MAN. WE'RE ALWAYS GETTING DRAGGED ALONG WITH THEIR STUPID IDEAS...
I REALLY WISH THEY'D STOP MAKING THESE DUMB BETS ABOUT EARTH.
EVEN IF IT WAS MUTSUMI-SAN WHO DID IT THIS TIME...
I Love the Occult!
MAYBE THEY JUST WANTED TO PLAY WITH YOU, NATSUMI.
DON'T SAY STUPID THINGS LIKE THAT!
BUT BOWLING'S MORE FUN WHEN YOU PLAY WITH A LOT OF PEOPLE!
KRR STAR
WE MUST TRAIN! TRAIN LIKE NEVER BEFORE!
NEXT TIME WE MUST DEFEAT THE POKOPEN-IANS!!!
I CAN'T WORK ON MY PLASTIC MOD-ELS...
I CAN'T POLISH MY WEAP-ONS...
I CAN'T HOLD MY CANDY...
Whee! Yay!
TO BE CONTINUED

Flump

ENCOUNTER CXXVIII
COME, COME, COME CHEW GUM!

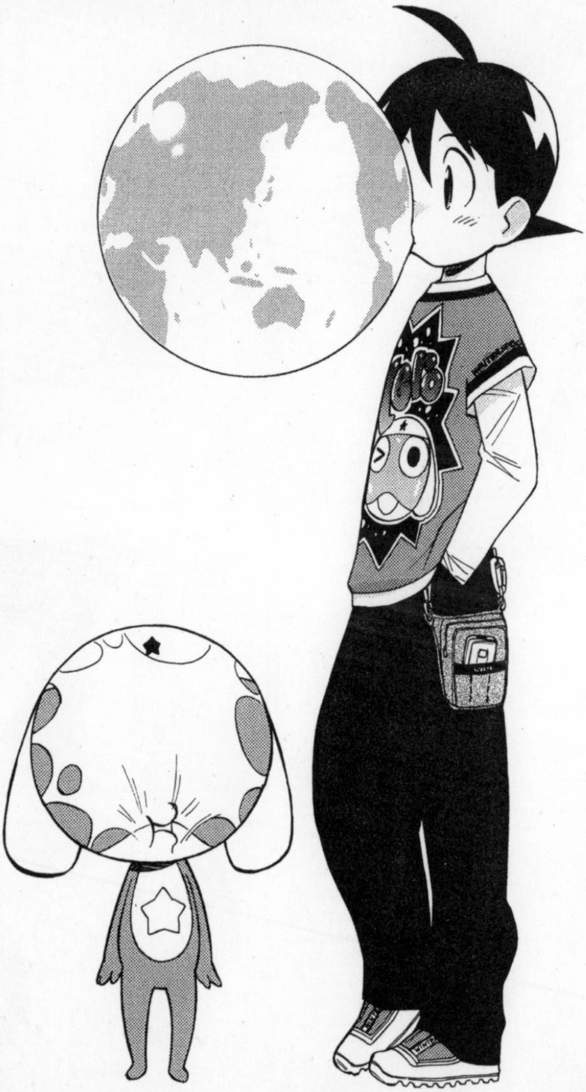

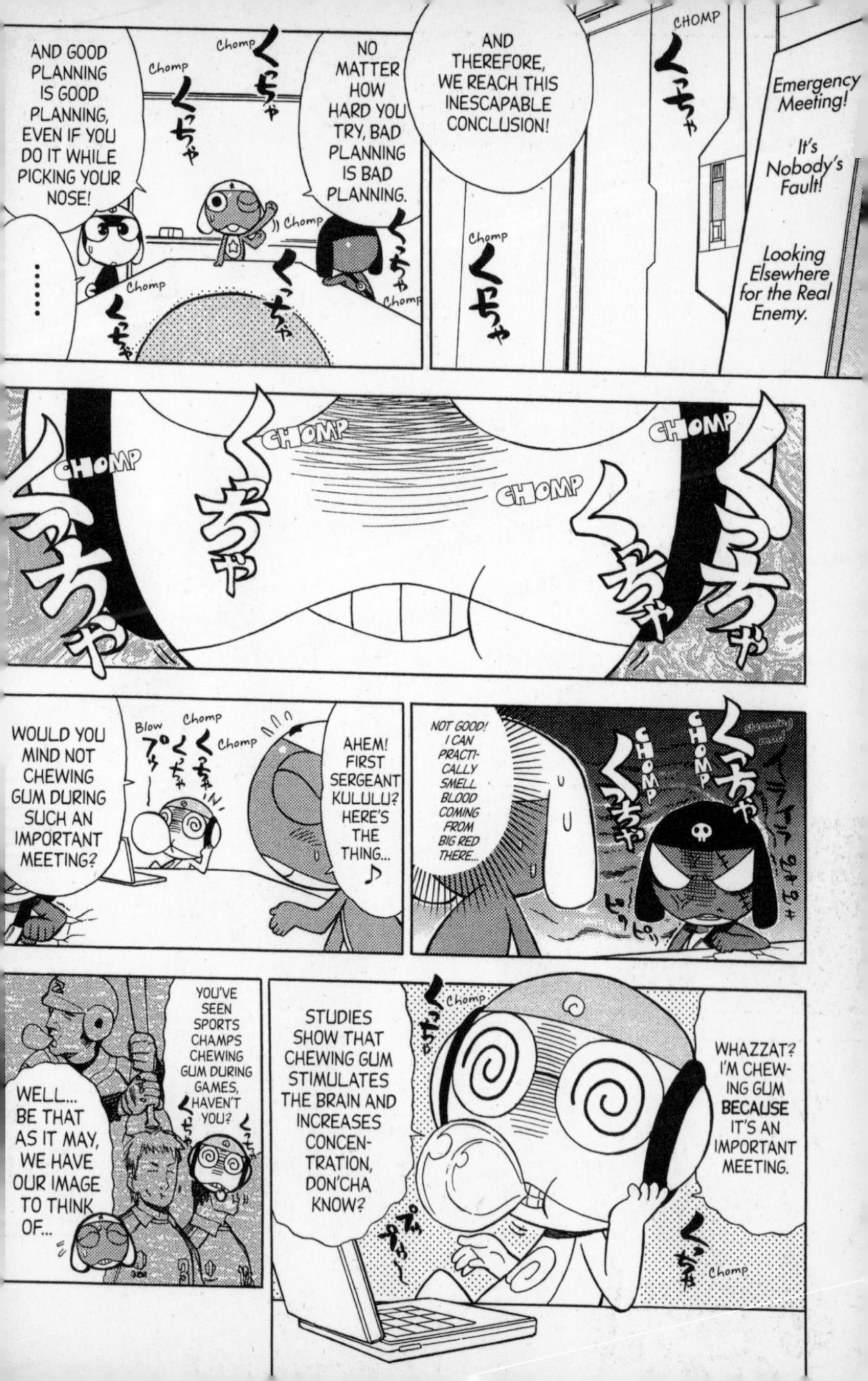
Emergency Meeting!
It's Nobody's Fault!
Looking Elsewhere for the Real Enemy.
CHOMP
Chomp
AND THEREFORE, WE REACH THIS INESCAPABLE CONCLUSION!
NO MATTER HOW HARD YOU TRY, BAD PLANNING IS BAD PLANNING.
Chomp
Chomp
AND GOOD PLANNING IS GOOD PLANNING, EVEN IF YOU DO IT WHILE PICKING YOUR NOSE!
Chomp
Chomp
Chomp
......
CHOMP
CHOMP
CHOMP
CHOMP
CHOMP
CHOMP
NOT GOOD! I CAN PRACTICALLY SMELL BLOOD COMING FROM BIG RED THERE...
AHEM! FIRST SERGEANT KULULU? HERE'S THE THING... ♪
Chomp
Chomp
Blow
WOULD YOU MIND NOT CHEWING GUM DURING SUCH AN IMPORTANT MEETING?
Chomp
WHAZZAT? I'M CHEWING GUM BECAUSE IT'S AN IMPORTANT MEETING.
STUDIES SHOW THAT CHEWING GUM STIMULATES THE BRAIN AND INCREASES CONCENTRATION, DON'CHA KNOW?
Chomp
YOU'VE SEEN SPORTS CHAMPS CHEWING GUM DURING GAMES, HAVEN'T YOU?
WELL... BE THAT AS IT MAY, WE HAVE OUR IMAGE TO THINK OF...

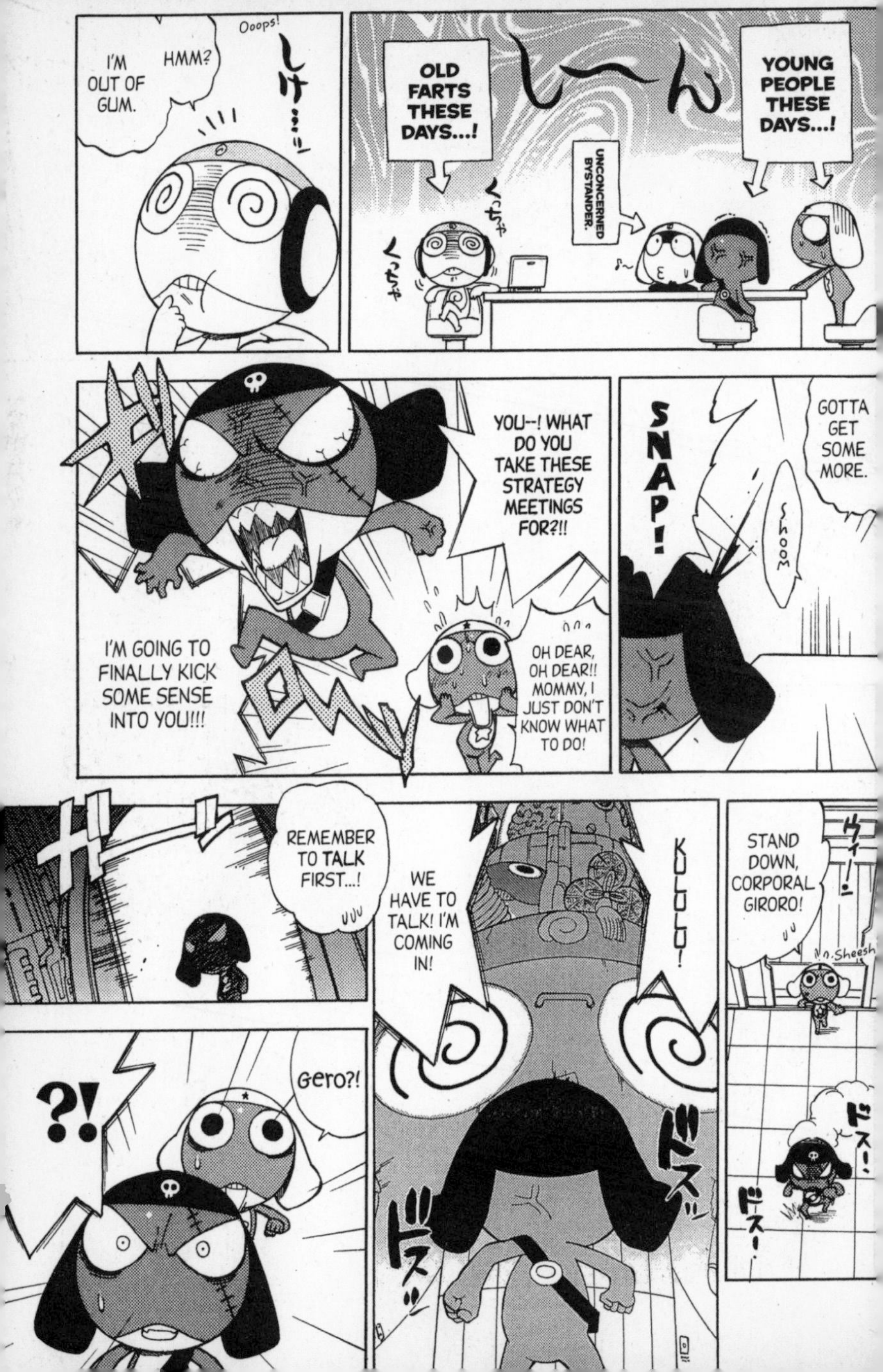
YOUNG PEOPLE THESE DAYS...!
UNCONCERNED BYSTANDER.
しーん
OLD FARTS THESE DAYS...!
くっちゃ
くっちゃ
HMM?
Ooops!
しけ…
I'M OUT OF GUM.
GOTTA GET SOME MORE.
~shoom
SNAP!!
YOU--! WHAT DO YOU TAKE THESE STRATEGY MEETINGS FOR?!!
OH DEAR, OH DEAR!! MOMMY, I JUST DON'T KNOW WHAT TO DO!
I'M GOING TO FINALLY KICK SOME SENSE INTO YOU!!!
ヴィー!
STAND DOWN, CORPORAL GIRORO!
N..Sheesh
ドスー
ドスー
KULULU!
WE HAVE TO TALK! I'M COMING IN!
REMEMBER TO TALK FIRST...!
ガー
ドスッ
ドスッ
Gero?!
?!

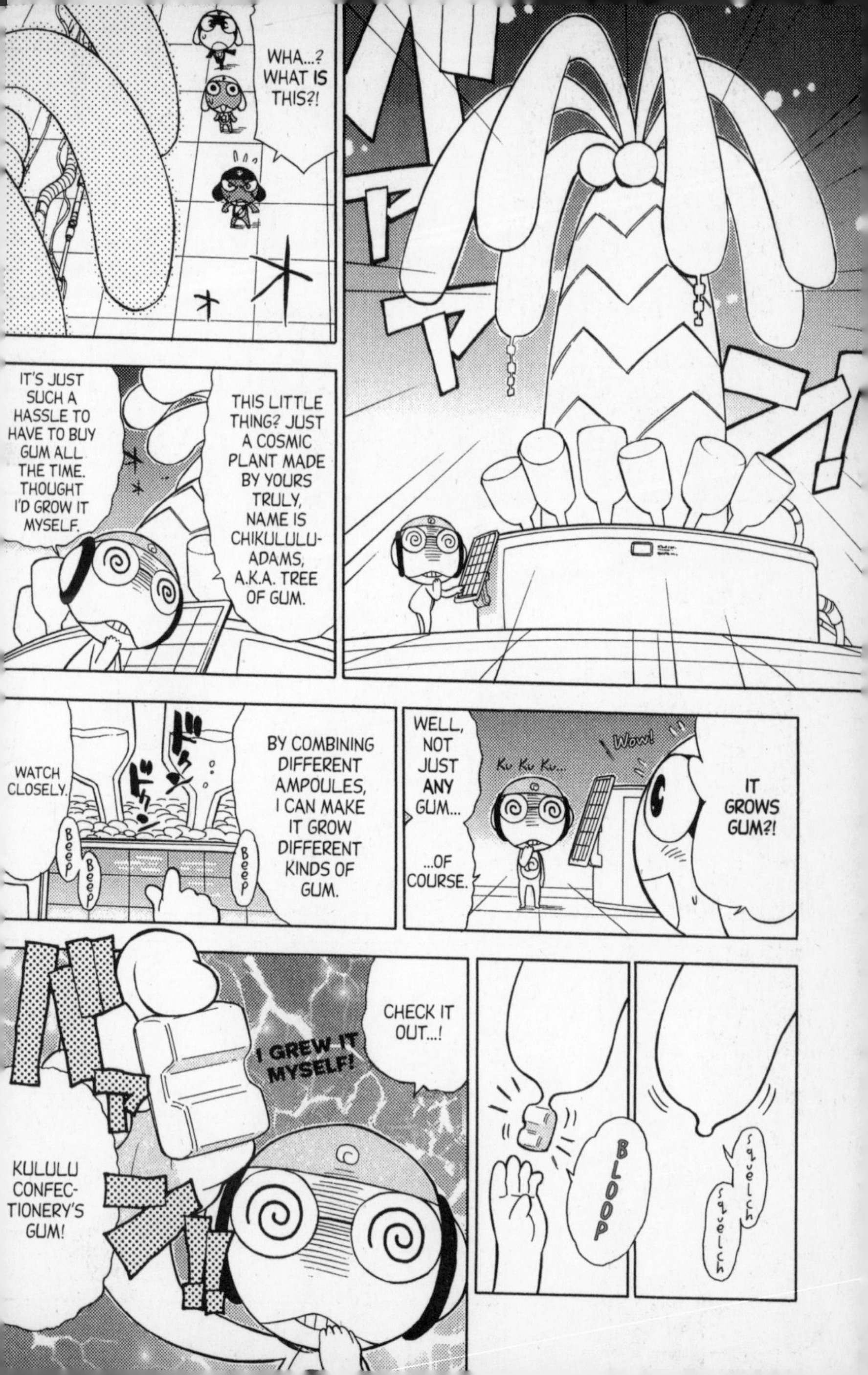
WHA...? WHAT IS THIS?!
THIS LITTLE THING? JUST A COSMIC PLANT MADE BY YOURS TRULY, NAME IS CHIKULULU-ADAMS, A.K.A. TREE OF GUM.
IT'S JUST SUCH A HASSLE TO HAVE TO BUY GUM ALL THE TIME. THOUGHT I'D GROW IT MYSELF.
IT GROWS GUM?!
Wow!
Ku Ku Ku...
WELL, NOT JUST ANY GUM...
...OF COURSE.
BY COMBINING DIFFERENT AMPOULES, I CAN MAKE IT GROW DIFFERENT KINDS OF GUM.
Beep
Beep
Beep
WATCH CLOSELY.
squelch
squelch
BLOOP
CHECK IT OUT...!
I GREW IT MYSELF!
KULULU CONFEC-TIONERY'S GUM!

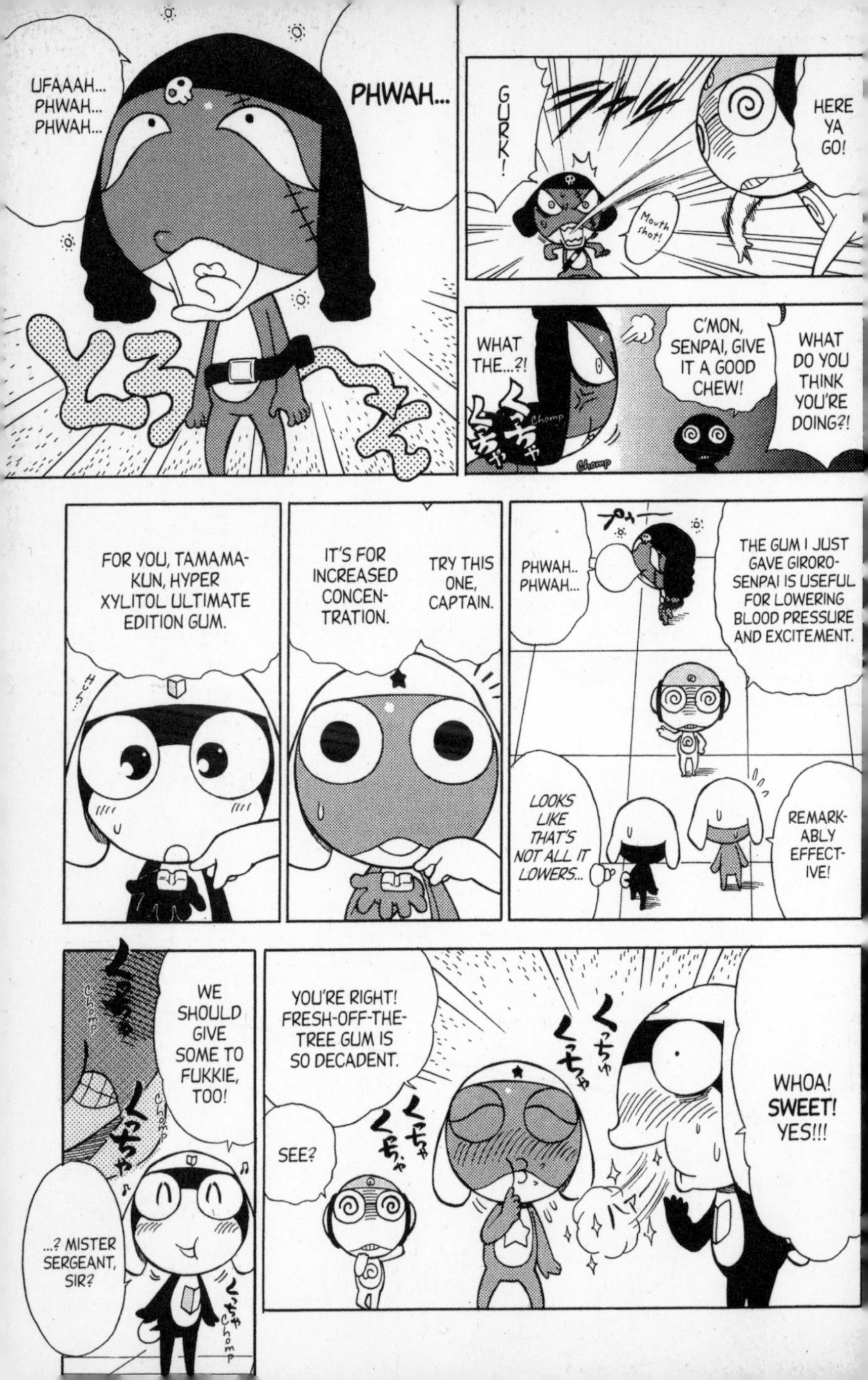
HERE YA GO!
GURK!
Mouth shot!
WHAT DO YOU THINK YOU'RE DOING?!
C'MON, SENPAI, GIVE IT A GOOD CHEW!
WHAT THE...?!
Chomp
Chomp
UFAAAH... PHWAH... PHWAH...
PHWAH...
THE GUM I JUST GAVE GIRORO-SENPAI IS USEFUL FOR LOWERING BLOOD PRESSURE AND EXCITEMENT.
PHWAH.. PHWAH...
REMARKABLY EFFECTIVE!
LOOKS LIKE THAT'S NOT ALL IT LOWERS...
TRY THIS ONE, CAPTAIN.
IT'S FOR INCREASED CONCENTRATION.
FOR YOU, TAMAMA-KUN, HYPER XYLITOL ULTIMATE EDITION GUM.
WHOA! SWEET! YES!!!
YOU'RE RIGHT! FRESH-OFF-THE-TREE GUM IS SO DECADENT.
SEE?
WE SHOULD GIVE SOME TO FUKKIE, TOO!
Chomp
Chomp
...? MISTER SERGEANT, SIR?
Chomp

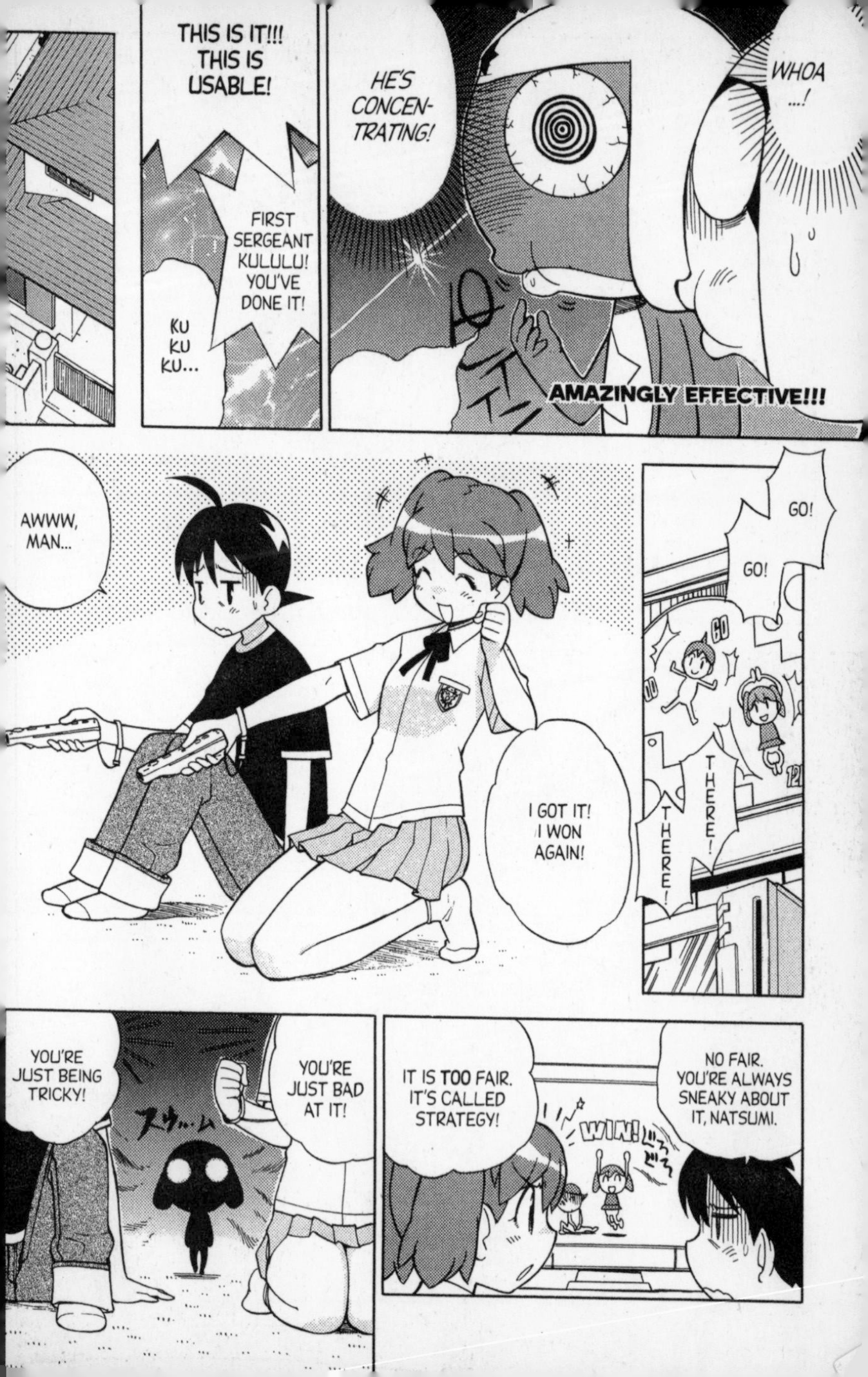
WHOA ...!
HE'S CONCEN-TRATING!
AMAZINGLY EFFECTIVE!!!
THIS IS IT!!! THIS IS USABLE!
FIRST SERGEANT KULULU! YOU'VE DONE IT!
KU KU KU...
GO!
GO!
THERE!
THERE!
I GOT IT! I WON AGAIN!
AWWW, MAN...
NO FAIR. YOU'RE ALWAYS SNEAKY ABOUT IT, NATSUMI.
WIN!
IT IS TOO FAIR. IT'S CALLED STRATEGY!
YOU'RE JUST BAD AT IT!
YOU'RE JUST BEING TRICKY!

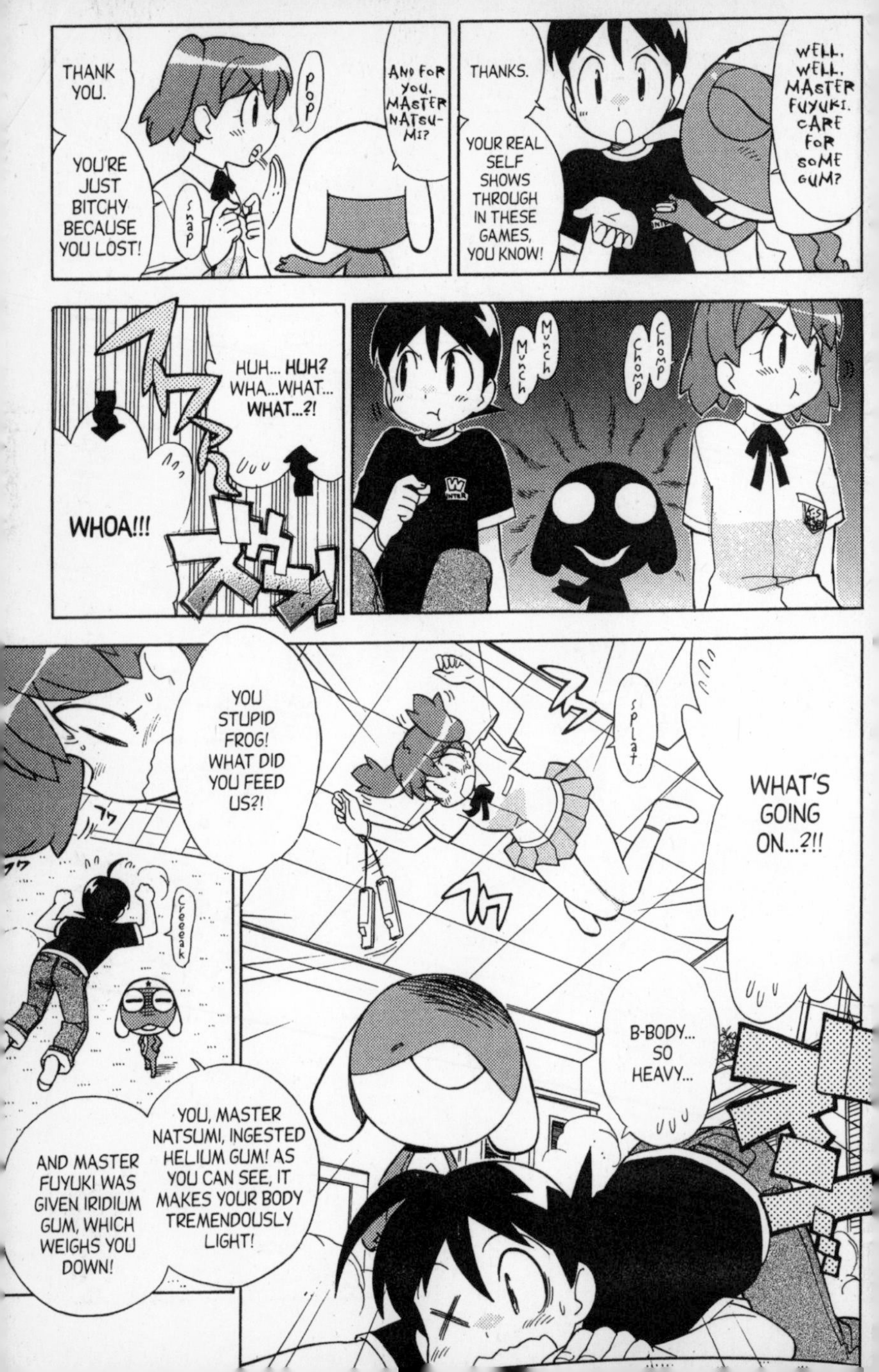
WELL, WELL. MASTER FUYUKI. CARE FOR SOME GUM?
THANKS.
YOUR REAL SELF SHOWS THROUGH IN THESE GAMES, YOU KNOW!
AND FOR YOU, MASTER NATSUMI?
pop
THANK YOU.
snap
YOU'RE JUST BITCHY BECAUSE YOU LOST!
Chomp Chomp
Munch Munch
HUH... HUH? WHA...WHAT... WHAT...?!
WHOA!!!
WHAT'S GOING ON...?!!
splat
YOU STUPID FROG! WHAT DID YOU FEED US?!
B-BODY... SO HEAVY...
Creeeak
YOU, MASTER NATSUMI, INGESTED HELIUM GUM! AS YOU CAN SEE, IT MAKES YOUR BODY TREMENDOUSLY LIGHT!
AND MASTER FUYUKI WAS GIVEN IRIDIUM GUM, WHICH WEIGHS YOU DOWN!

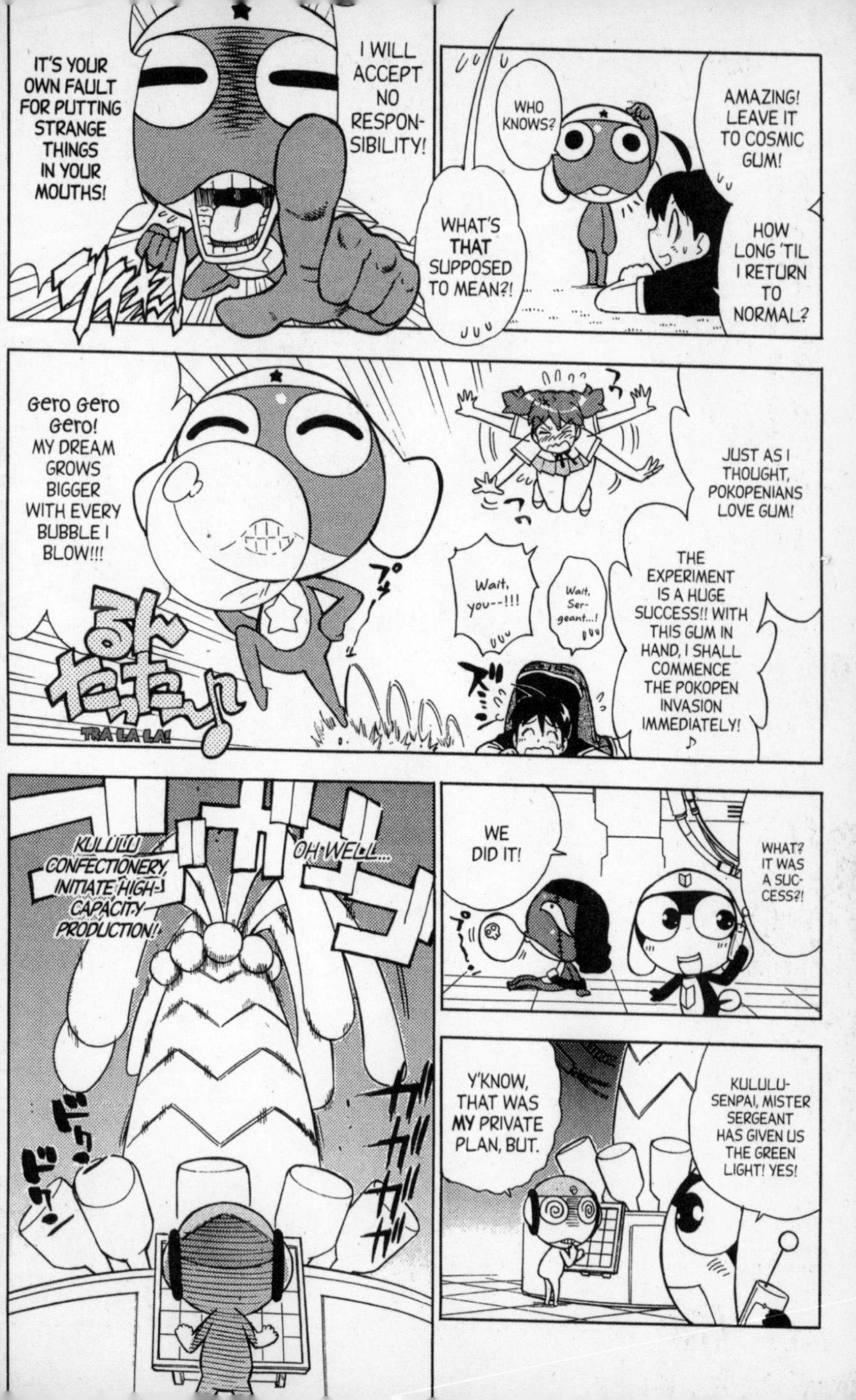
AMAZING! LEAVE IT TO COSMIC GUM!
WHO KNOWS?
HOW LONG 'TIL I RETURN TO NORMAL?
WHAT'S THAT SUPPOSED TO MEAN?!
I WILL ACCEPT NO RESPON-SIBILITY!
IT'S YOUR OWN FAULT FOR PUTTING STRANGE THINGS IN YOUR MOUTHS!
JUST AS I THOUGHT, POKOPENIANS LOVE GUM!
THE EXPERIMENT IS A HUGE SUCCESS!! WITH THIS GUM IN HAND, I SHALL COMMENCE THE POKOPEN INVASION IMMEDIATELY! ♪
Wait, Ser-geant...!
Wait, you--!!!
Gero Gero Gero! MY DREAM GROWS BIGGER WITH EVERY BUBBLE I BLOW!!!
TRA-LA-LA!
WHAT? IT WAS A SUC-CESS?!
WE DID IT!
KULULU-SENPAI, MISTER SERGEANT HAS GIVEN US THE GREEN LIGHT! YES!
Y'KNOW, THAT WAS MY PRIVATE PLAN, BUT.
KULULU CONFECTIONERY, INITIATE HIGH-CAPACITY PRODUCTION!
OH WELL...

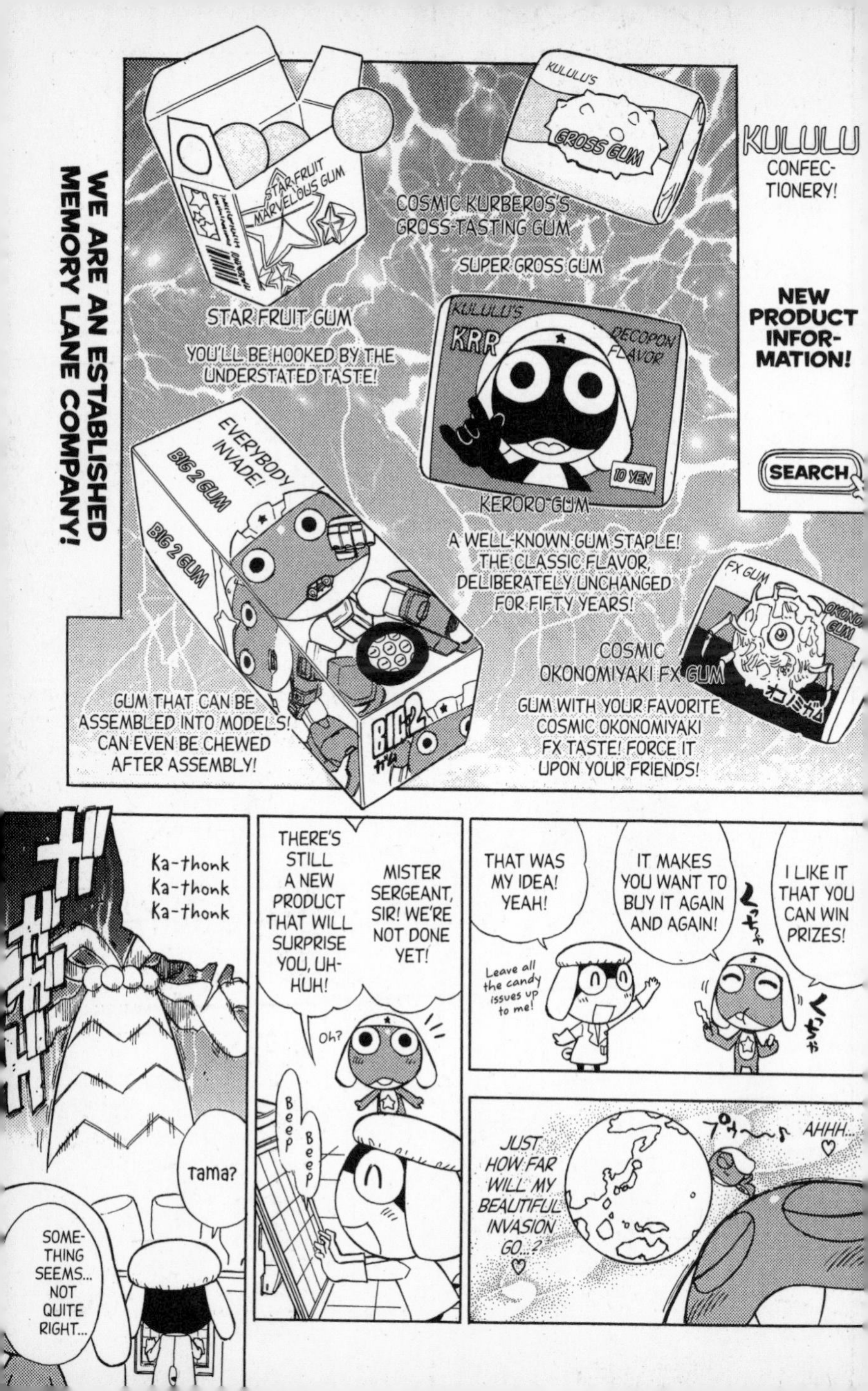
KULULU
CONFECTIONERY!
NEW PRODUCT INFORMATION!
SEARCH
WE ARE AN ESTABLISHED MEMORY LANE COMPANY!
KULULU'S
GROSS GUM
COSMIC KURBEROS'S GROSS-TASTING GUM
SUPER GROSS GUM
STAR FRUIT MARVELOUS GUM
STAR FRUIT GUM
YOU'LL BE HOOKED BY THE UNDERSTATED TASTE!
KULULU'S
KRR
DECOPON FLAVOR
10 YEN
KERORO GUM
A WELL-KNOWN GUM STAPLE! THE CLASSIC FLAVOR, DELIBERATELY UNCHANGED FOR FIFTY YEARS!
FX GUM
OKONO GUM
COSMIC OKONOMIYAKI FX GUM
GUM WITH YOUR FAVORITE COSMIC OKONOMIYAKI FX TASTE! FORCE IT UPON YOUR FRIENDS!
EVERYBODY INVADE!
BIG 2 GUM
BIG 2 GUM
BIG 2
GUM THAT CAN BE ASSEMBLED INTO MODELS! CAN EVEN BE CHEWED AFTER ASSEMBLY!
I LIKE IT THAT YOU CAN WIN PRIZES!
IT MAKES YOU WANT TO BUY IT AGAIN AND AGAIN!
THAT WAS MY IDEA! YEAH!
Leave all the candy issues up to me!
AHHH... ♡
JUST HOW FAR WILL MY BEAUTIFUL INVASION GO...? ♡
MISTER SERGEANT, SIR! WE'RE NOT DONE YET!
THERE'S STILL A NEW PRODUCT THAT WILL SURPRISE YOU, UH-HUH!
Oh?
Beep
Beep
Ka-thonk
Ka-thonk
Ka-thonk
Tama?
SOMETHING SEEMS... NOT QUITE RIGHT...

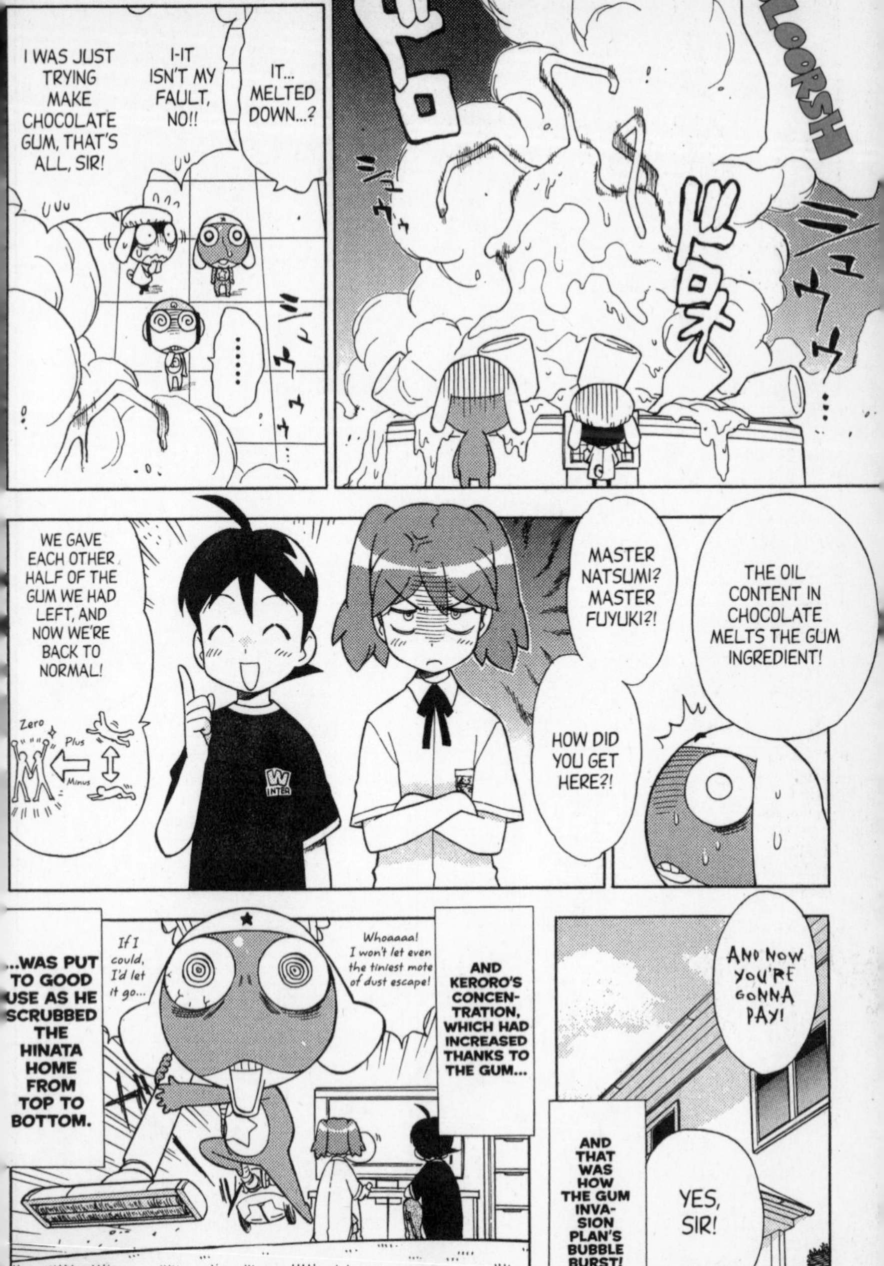
BLOORSH
IT... MELTED DOWN...?
I-IT ISN'T MY FAULT, NO!!
I WAS JUST TRYING MAKE CHOCOLATE GUM, THAT'S ALL, SIR!
......
THE OIL CONTENT IN CHOCOLATE MELTS THE GUM INGREDIENT!
MASTER NATSUMI? MASTER FUYUKI?!
HOW DID YOU GET HERE?!
WE GAVE EACH OTHER HALF OF THE GUM WE HAD LEFT, AND NOW WE'RE BACK TO NORMAL!
Zero
Plus
Minus
INTER
AND NOW YOU'RE GONNA PAY!
YES, SIR!
AND THAT WAS HOW THE GUM INVA-SION PLAN'S BUBBLE BURST!
AND KERORO'S CONCEN-TRATION, WHICH HAD INCREASED THANKS TO THE GUM...
Whoaaaa! I won't let even the tiniest mote of dust escape!
If I could, I'd let it go...
...WAS PUT TO GOOD USE AS HE SCRUBBED THE HINATA HOME FROM TOP TO BOTTOM.
TO BE CONTINUED

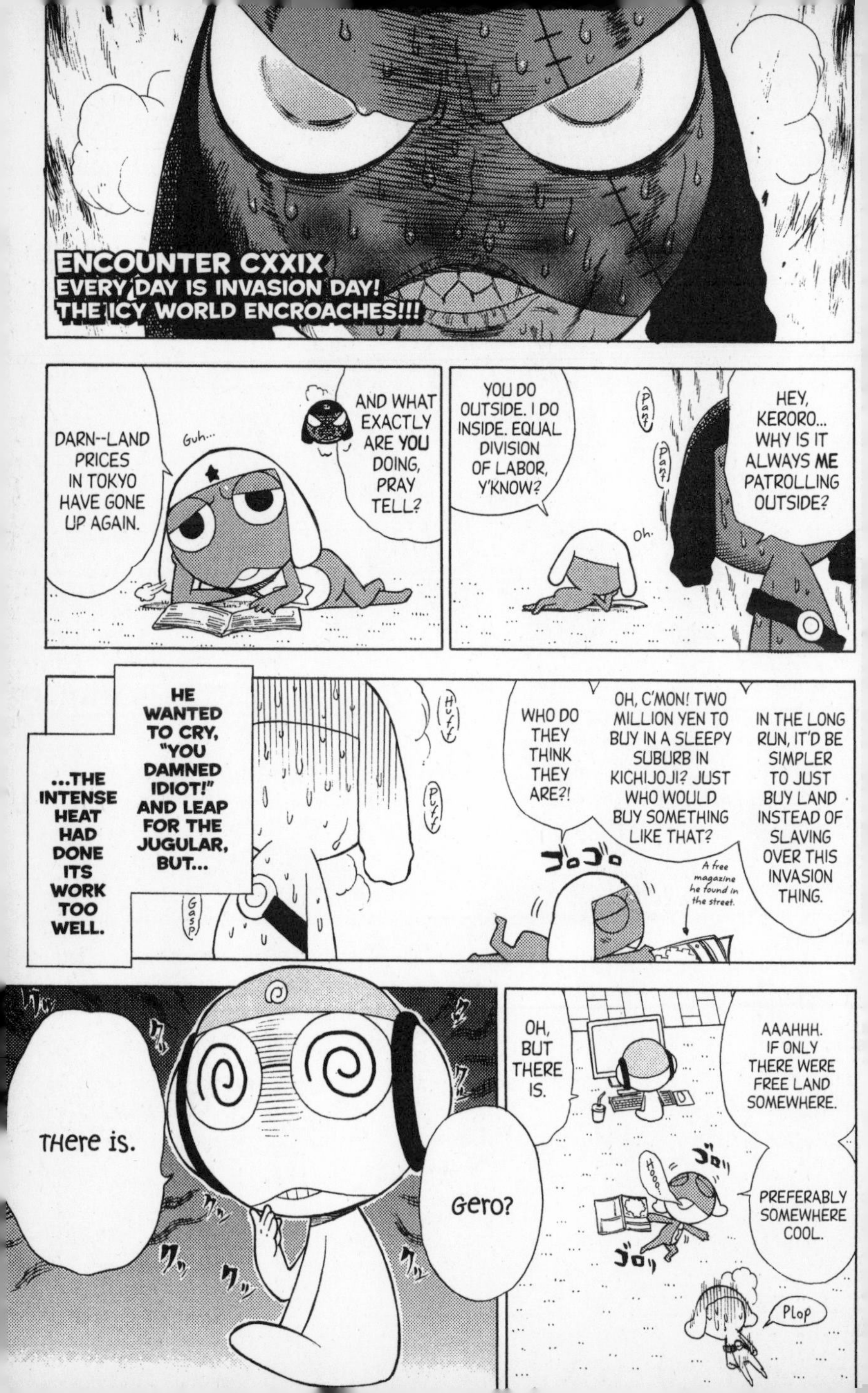
ENCOUNTER CXXIX
EVERY DAY IS INVASION DAY! THE ICY WORLD ENCROACHES!!!
HEY, KERORO... WHY IS IT ALWAYS ME PATROLLING OUTSIDE?
Pant
Pant
YOU DO OUTSIDE. I DO INSIDE. EQUAL DIVISION OF LABOR, Y'KNOW?
Oh.
AND WHAT EXACTLY ARE YOU DOING, PRAY TELL?
DARN--LAND PRICES IN TOKYO HAVE GONE UP AGAIN.
Guh...
IN THE LONG RUN, IT'D BE SIMPLER TO JUST BUY LAND INSTEAD OF SLAVING OVER THIS INVASION THING.
OH, C'MON! TWO MILLION YEN TO BUY IN A SLEEPY SUBURB IN KICHIJOJI? JUST WHO WOULD BUY SOMETHING LIKE THAT?
WHO DO THEY THINK THEY ARE?!
A free magazine he found in the street.
Huff
Puff
Gasp
HE WANTED TO CRY, "YOU DAMNED IDIOT!" AND LEAP FOR THE JUGULAR, BUT...
...THE INTENSE HEAT HAD DONE ITS WORK TOO WELL.
AAAHHH. IF ONLY THERE WERE FREE LAND SOMEWHERE.
OH, BUT THERE IS.
Hooo...
PREFERABLY SOMEWHERE COOL.
Plop
There is.
Gero?

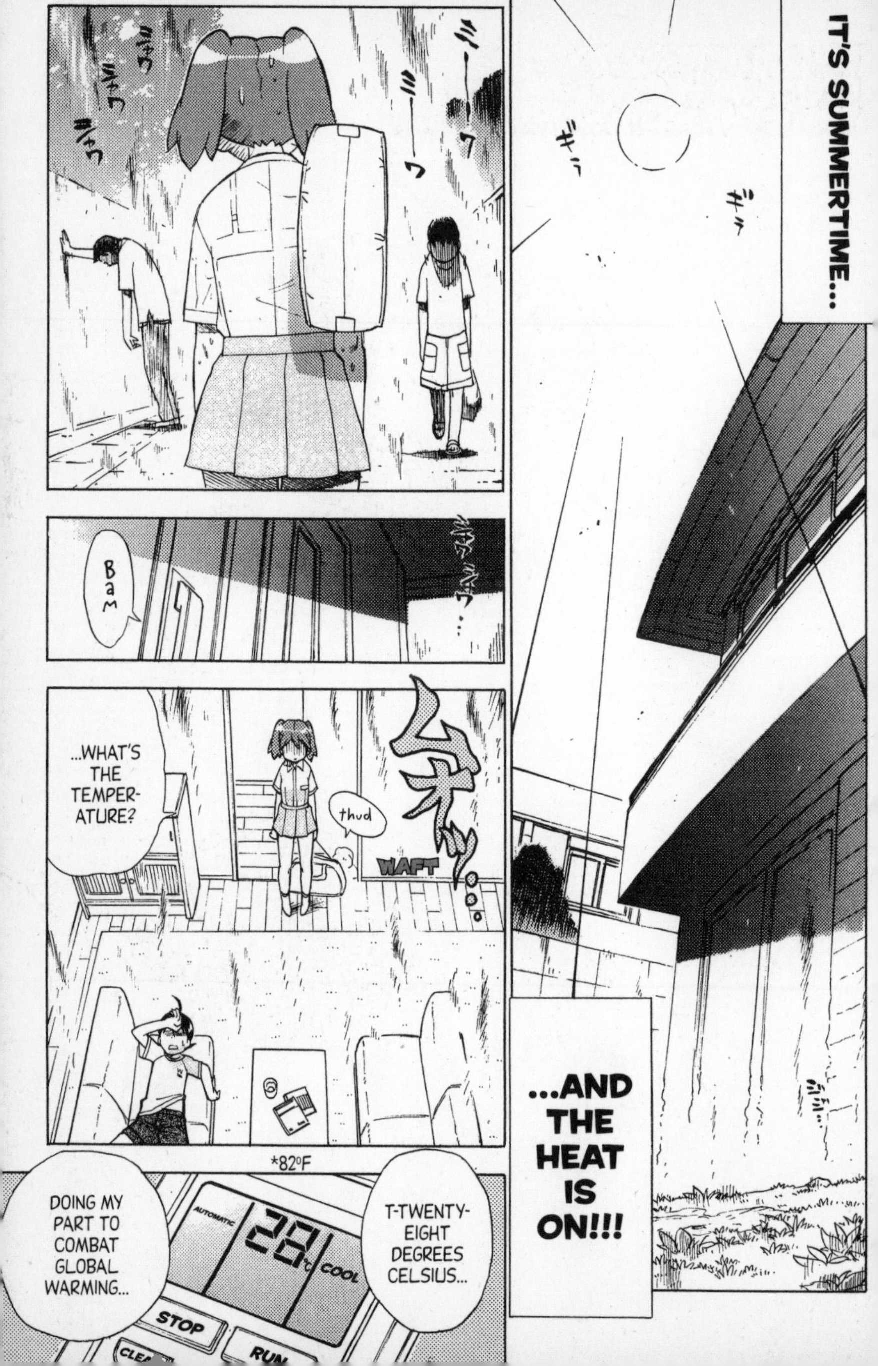
IT'S SUMMERTIME...
...AND THE HEAT IS ON!!!
Bam
...WHAT'S THE TEMPER-ATURE?
thud
WAFT
T-TWENTY-EIGHT DEGREES CELSIUS...
DOING MY PART TO COMBAT GLOBAL WARMING...
AUTOMATIC
28°C
COOL
STOP
RUN
*82°F

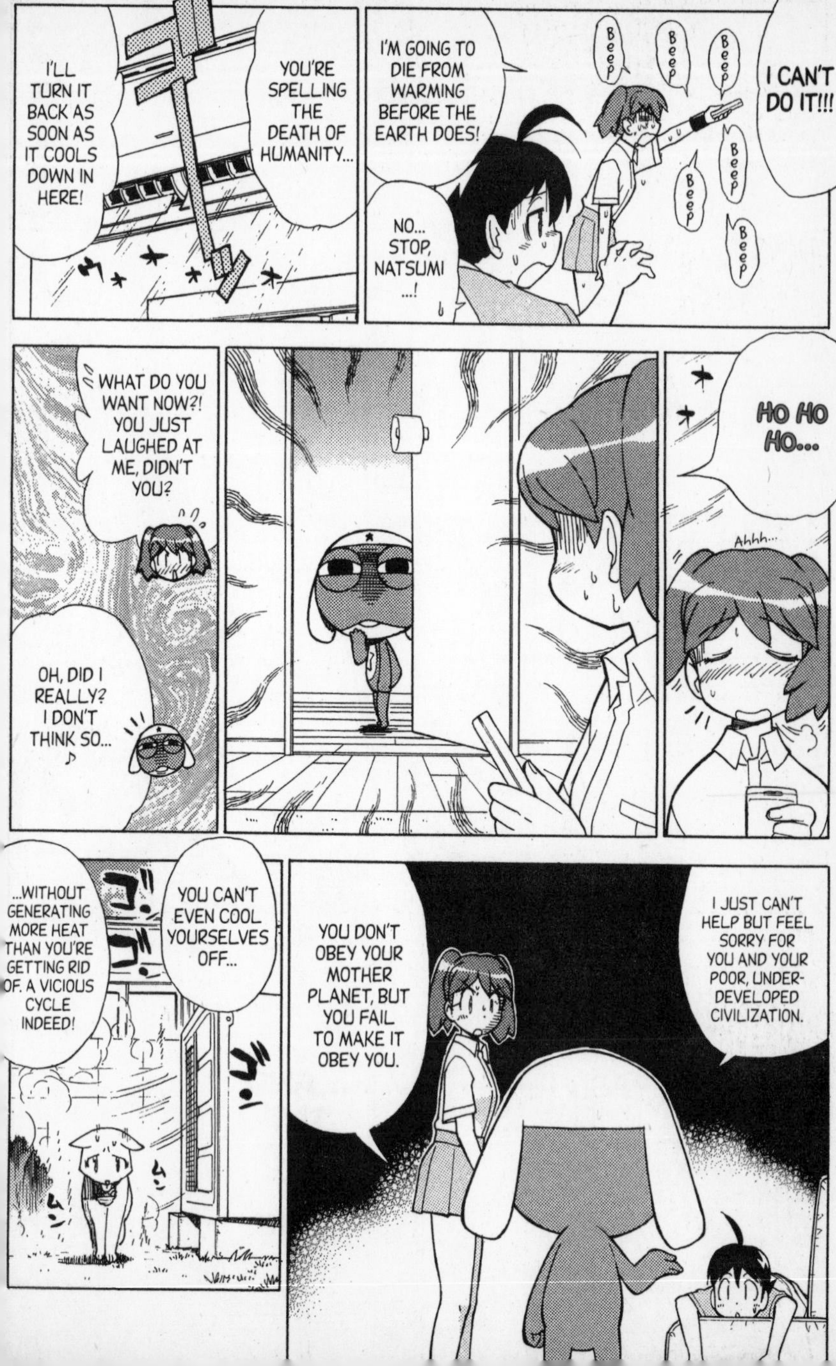
I CAN'T DO IT!!!
Beep
Beep
Beep
Beep
Beep
Beep
I'M GOING TO DIE FROM WARMING BEFORE THE EARTH DOES!
NO... STOP, NATSUMI ...!
YOU'RE SPELLING THE DEATH OF HUMANITY...
I'LL TURN IT BACK AS SOON AS IT COOLS DOWN IN HERE!
HO HO HO...
Ahhh...
WHAT DO YOU WANT NOW?! YOU JUST LAUGHED AT ME, DIDN'T YOU?
OH, DID I REALLY? I DON'T THINK SO... ♪
I JUST CAN'T HELP BUT FEEL SORRY FOR YOU AND YOUR POOR, UNDER-DEVELOPED CIVILIZATION.
YOU DON'T OBEY YOUR MOTHER PLANET, BUT YOU FAIL TO MAKE IT OBEY YOU.
YOU CAN'T EVEN COOL YOURSELVES OFF...
...WITHOUT GENERATING MORE HEAT THAN YOU'RE GETTING RID OF. A VICIOUS CYCLE INDEED!

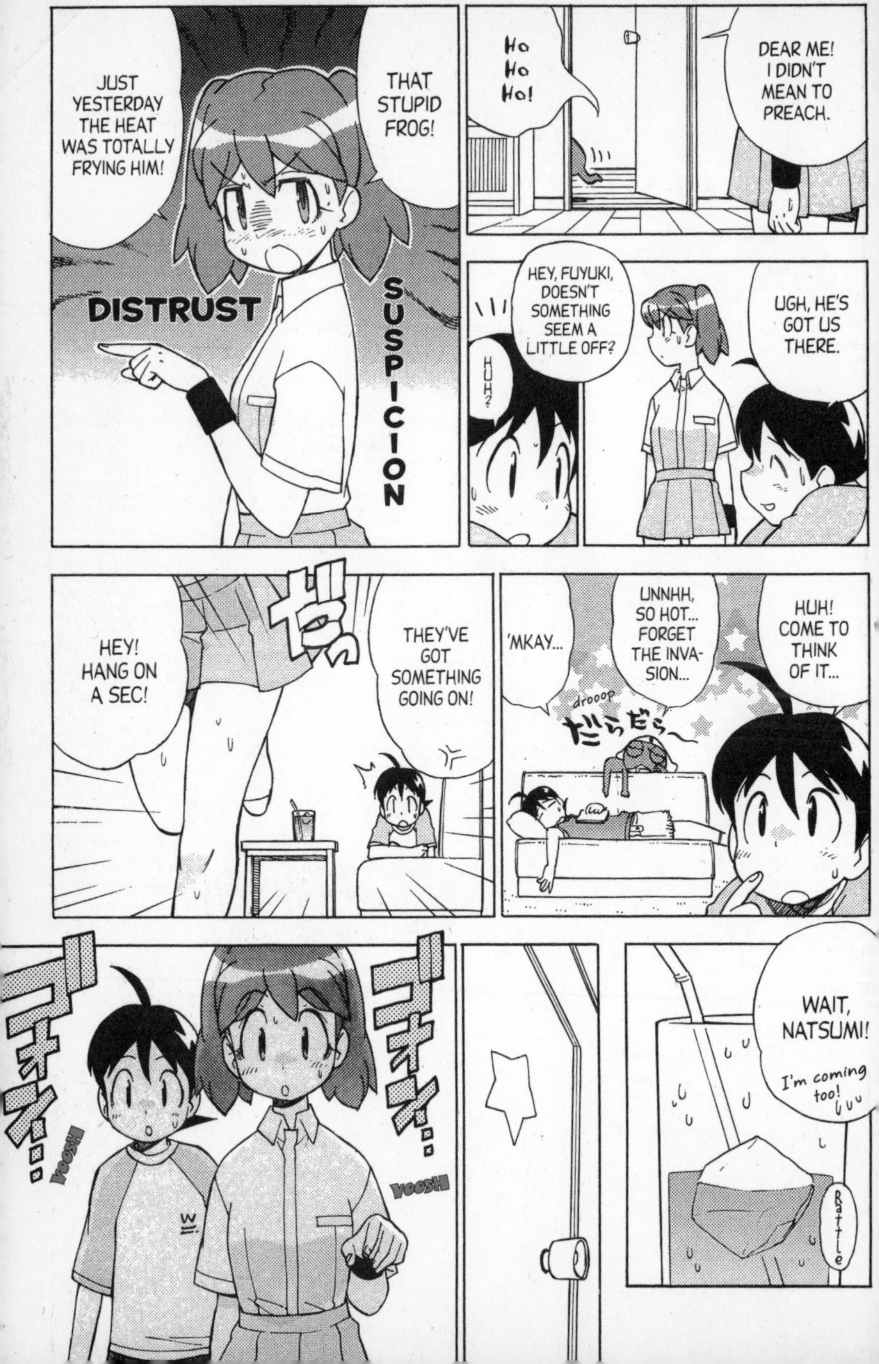
DEAR ME! I DIDN'T MEAN TO PREACH.
Ho Ho Ho!
UGH, HE'S GOT US THERE.
HEY, FUYUKI, DOESN'T SOMETHING SEEM A LITTLE OFF?
HUH?
THAT STUPID FROG!
JUST YESTERDAY THE HEAT WAS TOTALLY FRYING HIM!
DISTRUST
SUSPICION
HUH! COME TO THINK OF IT...
UNNHH, SO HOT... FORGET THE INVA-SION...
'MKAY...
droop
だらだら〜
THEY'VE GOT SOMETHING GOING ON!
だっ
HEY! HANG ON A SEC!
WAIT, NATSUMI!
I'm coming too!
Rattle
VOOSH
VOOSH

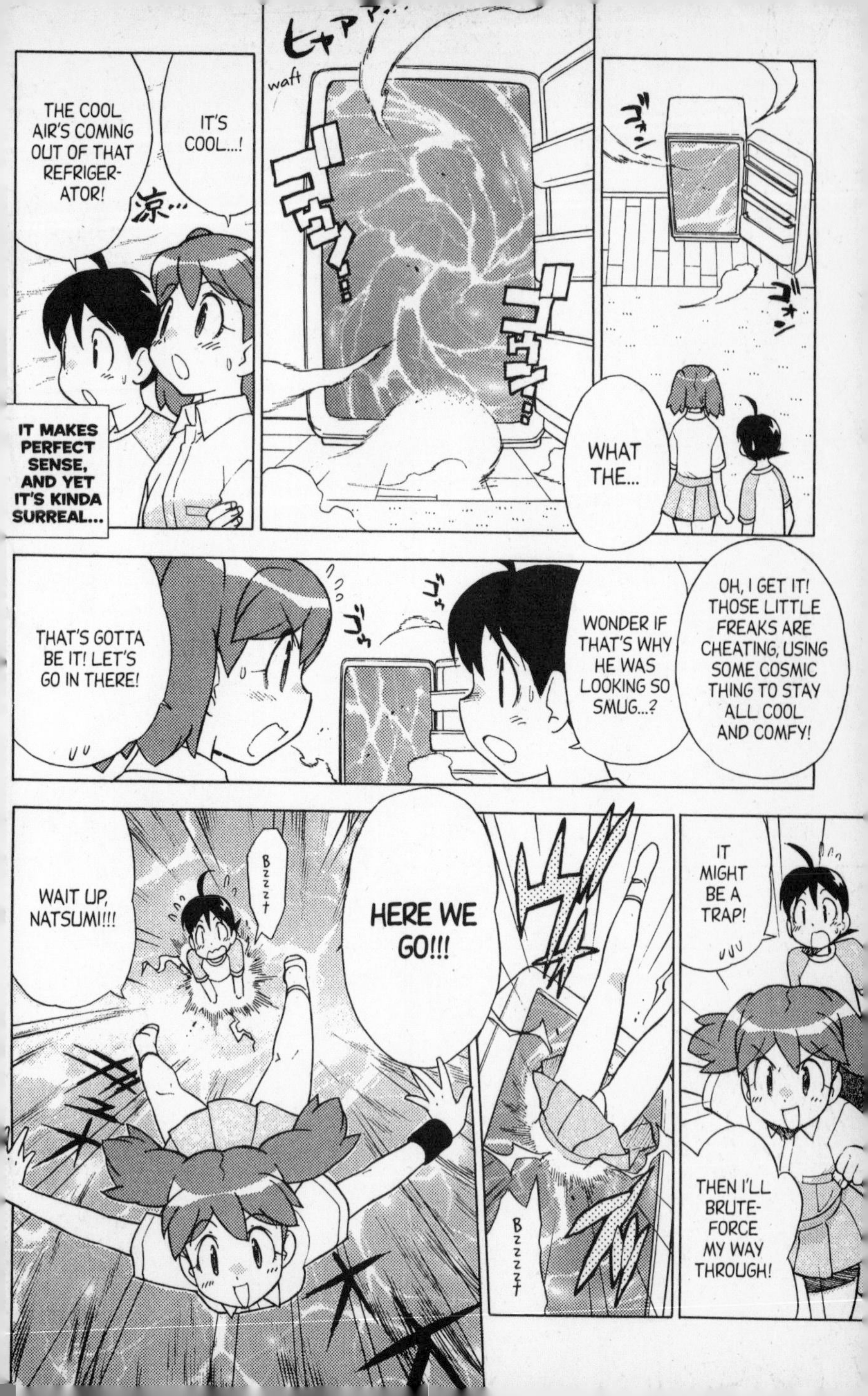
WHAT THE...
waft
IT'S COOL...!
THE COOL AIR'S COMING OUT OF THAT REFRIGER-ATOR!
IT MAKES PERFECT SENSE, AND YET IT'S KINDA SURREAL...
OH, I GET IT! THOSE LITTLE FREAKS ARE CHEATING, USING SOME COSMIC THING TO STAY ALL COOL AND COMFY!
WONDER IF THAT'S WHY HE WAS LOOKING SO SMUG...?
THAT'S GOTTA BE IT! LET'S GO IN THERE!
IT MIGHT BE A TRAP!
THEN I'LL BRUTE-FORCE MY WAY THROUGH!
Bzzzt
HERE WE GO!!!
Bzzzt
WAIT UP, NATSUMI!!!

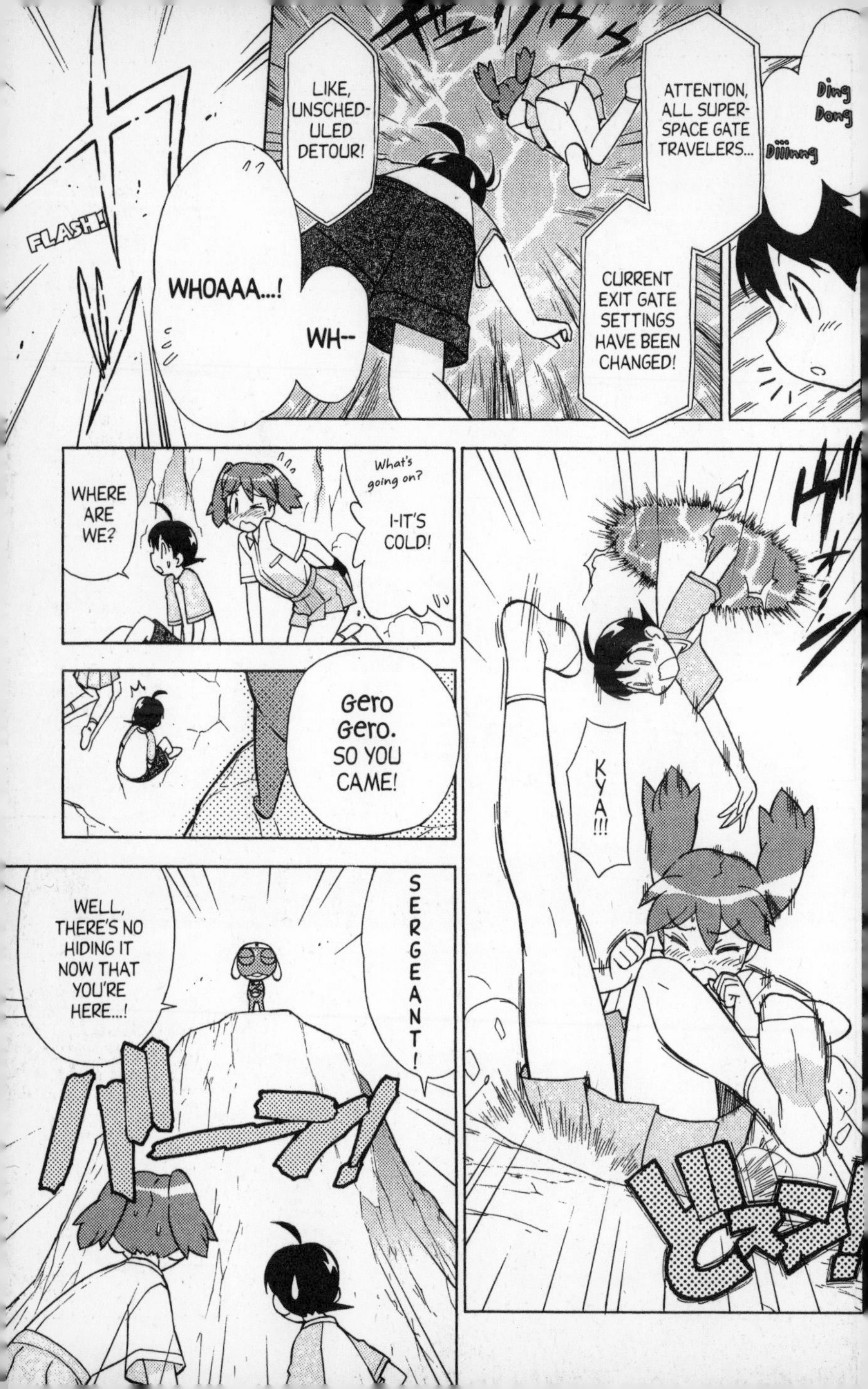
Ding Dong
Diiinng
ATTENTION, ALL SUPER-SPACE GATE TRAVELERS...
CURRENT EXIT GATE SETTINGS HAVE BEEN CHANGED!
LIKE, UNSCHED-ULED DETOUR!
WHOAAA...!
WH--
FLASH!
What's going on?
I-IT'S COLD!
WHERE ARE WE?
Gero Gero. SO YOU CAME!
WELL, THERE'S NO HIDING IT NOW THAT YOU'RE HERE...!
SERGEANT!
KYA!!!

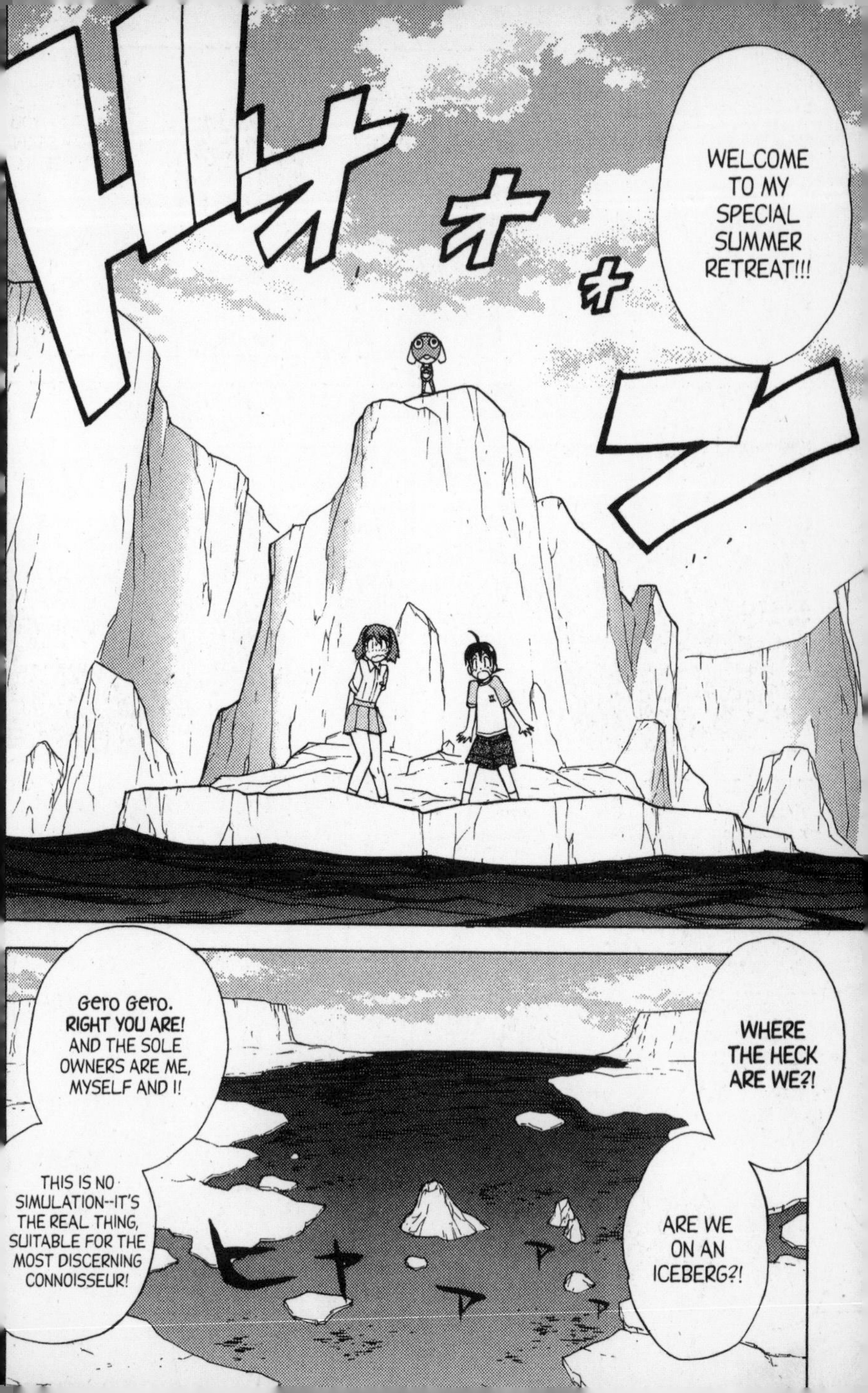
WELCOME TO MY SPECIAL SUMMER RETREAT!!!
WHERE THE HECK ARE WE?!
ARE WE ON AN ICEBERG?!
Gero Gero. RIGHT YOU ARE! AND THE SOLE OWNERS ARE ME, MYSELF AND I!
THIS IS NO SIMULATION--IT'S THE REAL THING, SUITABLE FOR THE MOST DISCERNING CONNOISSEUR!

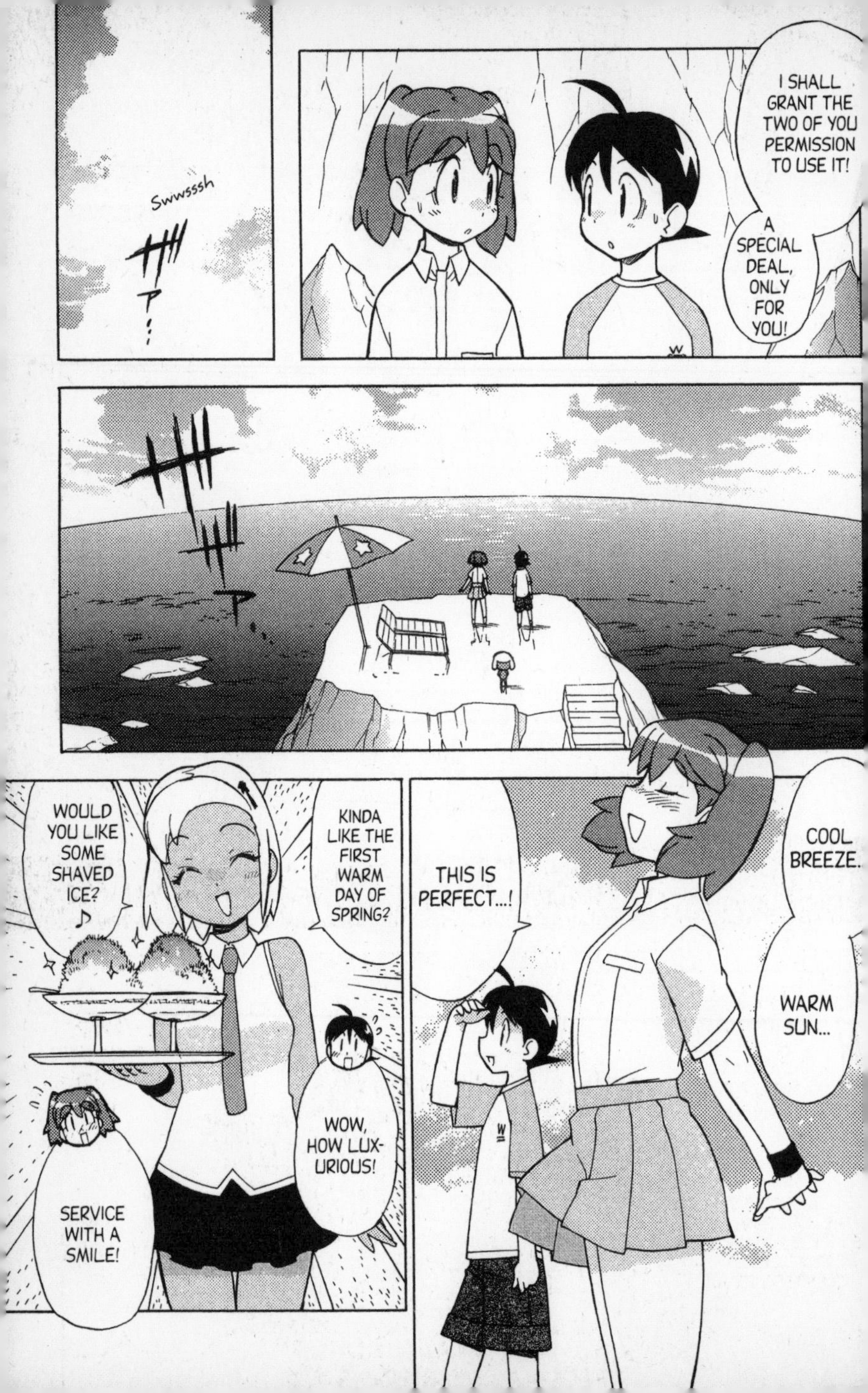
I SHALL GRANT THE TWO OF YOU PERMISSION TO USE IT!
A SPECIAL DEAL, ONLY FOR YOU!
Swwsssh
COOL BREEZE...
WARM SUN...
THIS IS PERFECT...!
KINDA LIKE THE FIRST WARM DAY OF SPRING?
WOW, HOW LUX-URIOUS!
WOULD YOU LIKE SOME SHAVED ICE? ♪
SERVICE WITH A SMILE!

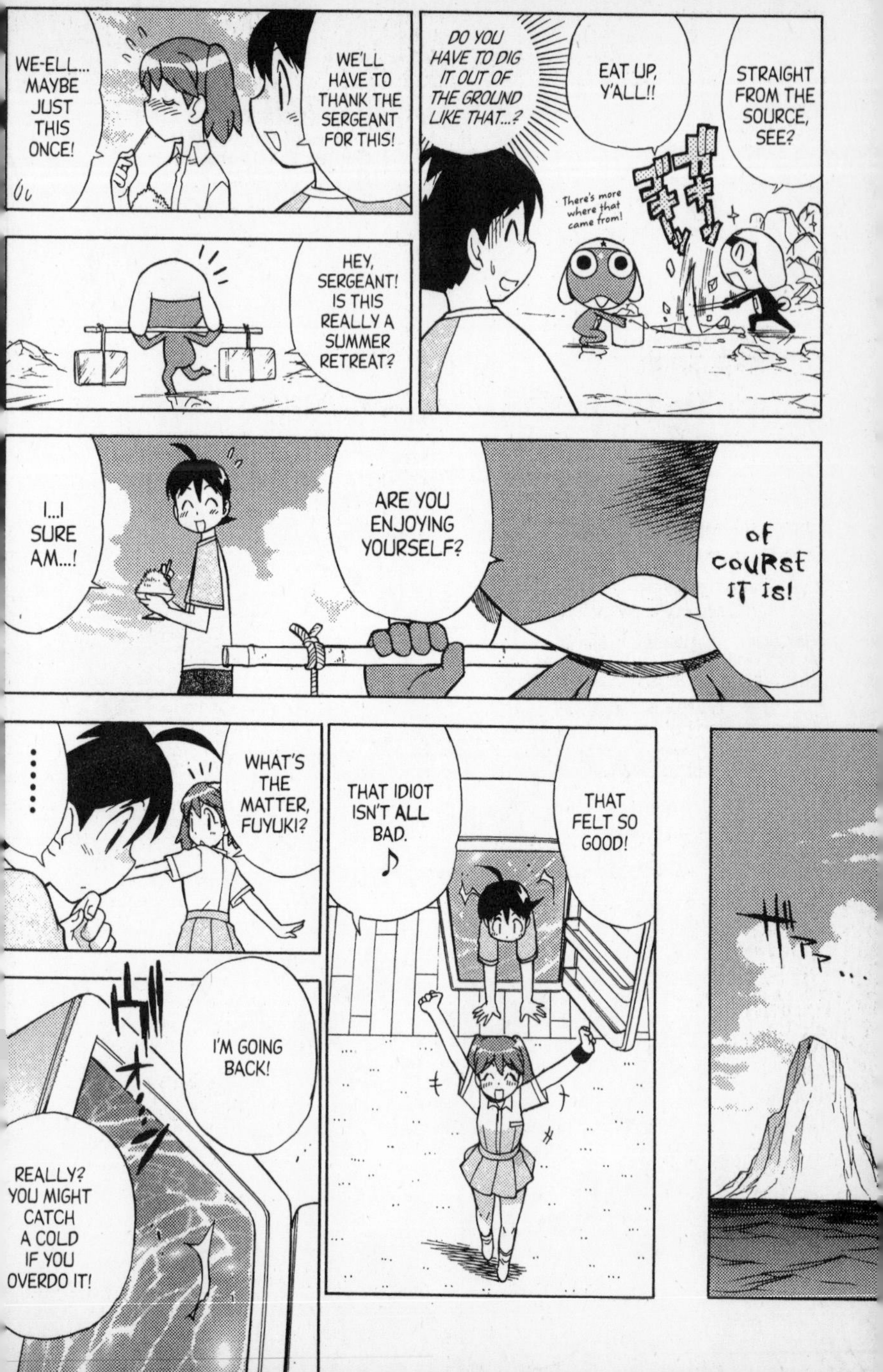
STRAIGHT FROM THE SOURCE, SEE?
EAT UP, Y'ALL!!
DO YOU HAVE TO DIG IT OUT OF THE GROUND LIKE THAT...?
There's more where that came from!
WE'LL HAVE TO THANK THE SERGEANT FOR THIS!
WE-ELL... MAYBE JUST THIS ONCE!
HEY, SERGEANT! IS THIS REALLY A SUMMER RETREAT?
of course it is!
ARE YOU ENJOYING YOURSELF?
I...I SURE AM...!
THAT FELT SO GOOD!
THAT IDIOT ISN'T ALL BAD. ♪
WHAT'S THE MATTER, FUYUKI?
......
I'M GOING BACK!
REALLY? YOU MIGHT CATCH A COLD IF YOU OVERDO IT!

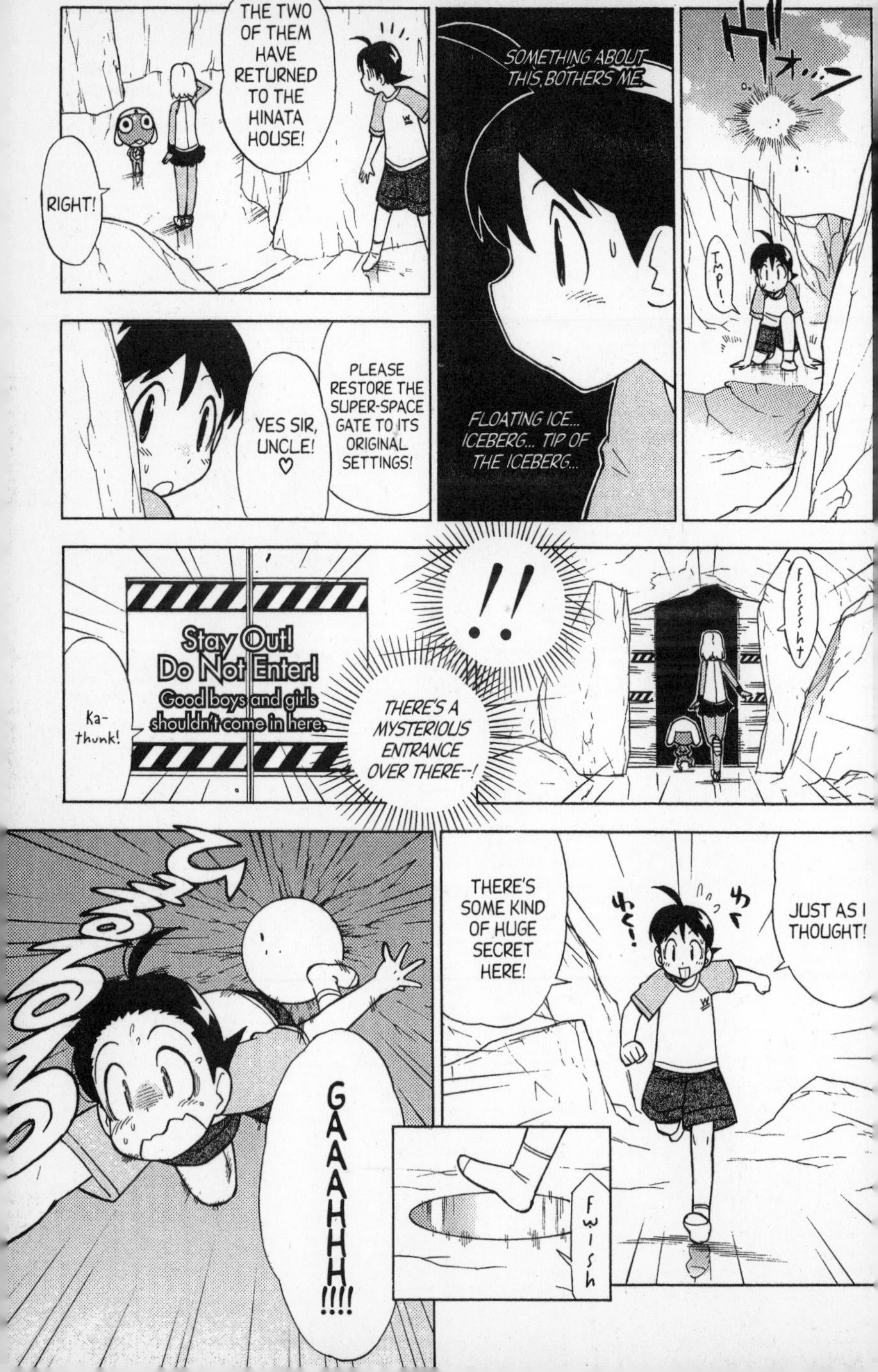
Tmp!
SOMETHING ABOUT THIS BOTHERS ME.
FLOATING ICE... ICEBERG... TIP OF THE ICEBERG...
THE TWO OF THEM HAVE RETURNED TO THE HINATA HOUSE!
RIGHT!
PLEASE RESTORE THE SUPER-SPACE GATE TO ITS ORIGINAL SETTINGS!
YES SIR, UNCLE! ♡
Fssssht
!!
THERE'S A MYSTERIOUS ENTRANCE OVER THERE--!
Stay Out!
Do Not Enter!
Good boys and girls shouldn't come in here.
Ka-thunk!
JUST AS I THOUGHT!
THERE'S SOME KIND OF HUGE SECRET HERE!
Fwish
GAAAHHH!!!!

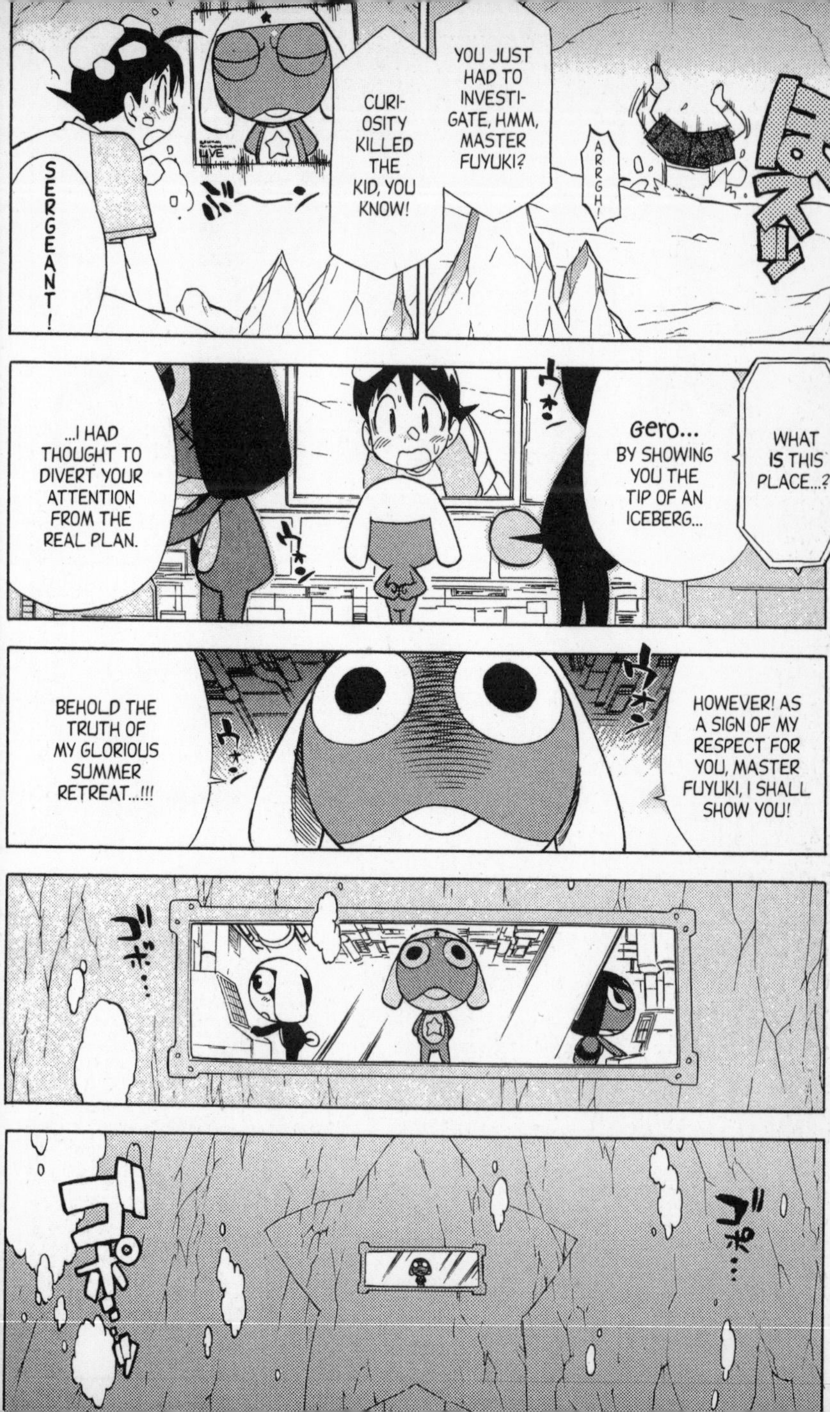
ぼすっ!
ARRGH!
YOU JUST HAD TO INVESTI-GATE, HMM, MASTER FUYUKI?
CURI-OSITY KILLED THE KID, YOU KNOW!
ぶーーん
SERGEANT!
WHAT IS THIS PLACE...?!
Gero... BY SHOWING YOU THE TIP OF AN ICEBERG...
ウォ
...I HAD THOUGHT TO DIVERT YOUR ATTENTION FROM THE REAL PLAN.
HOWEVER! AS A SIGN OF MY RESPECT FOR YOU, MASTER FUYUKI, I SHALL SHOW YOU!
BEHOLD THE TRUTH OF MY GLORIOUS SUMMER RETREAT...!!!
ゴボ...
ゴポ...
ゴポ...

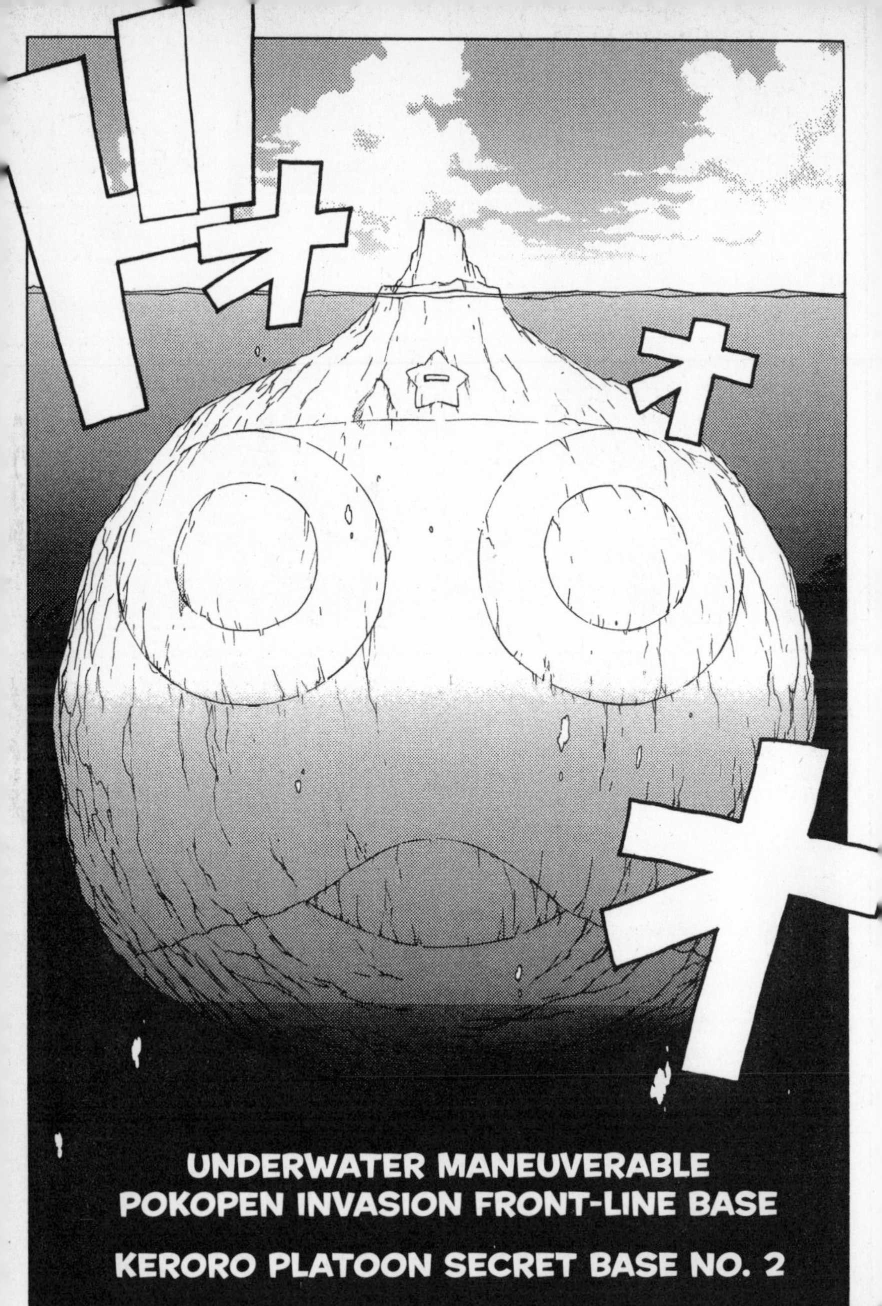
ドオオオ
UNDERWATER MANEUVERABLE
POKOPEN INVASION FRONT-LINE BASE
KERORO PLATOON SECRET BASE NO. 2

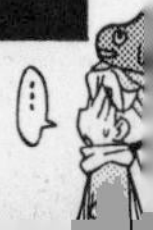
...

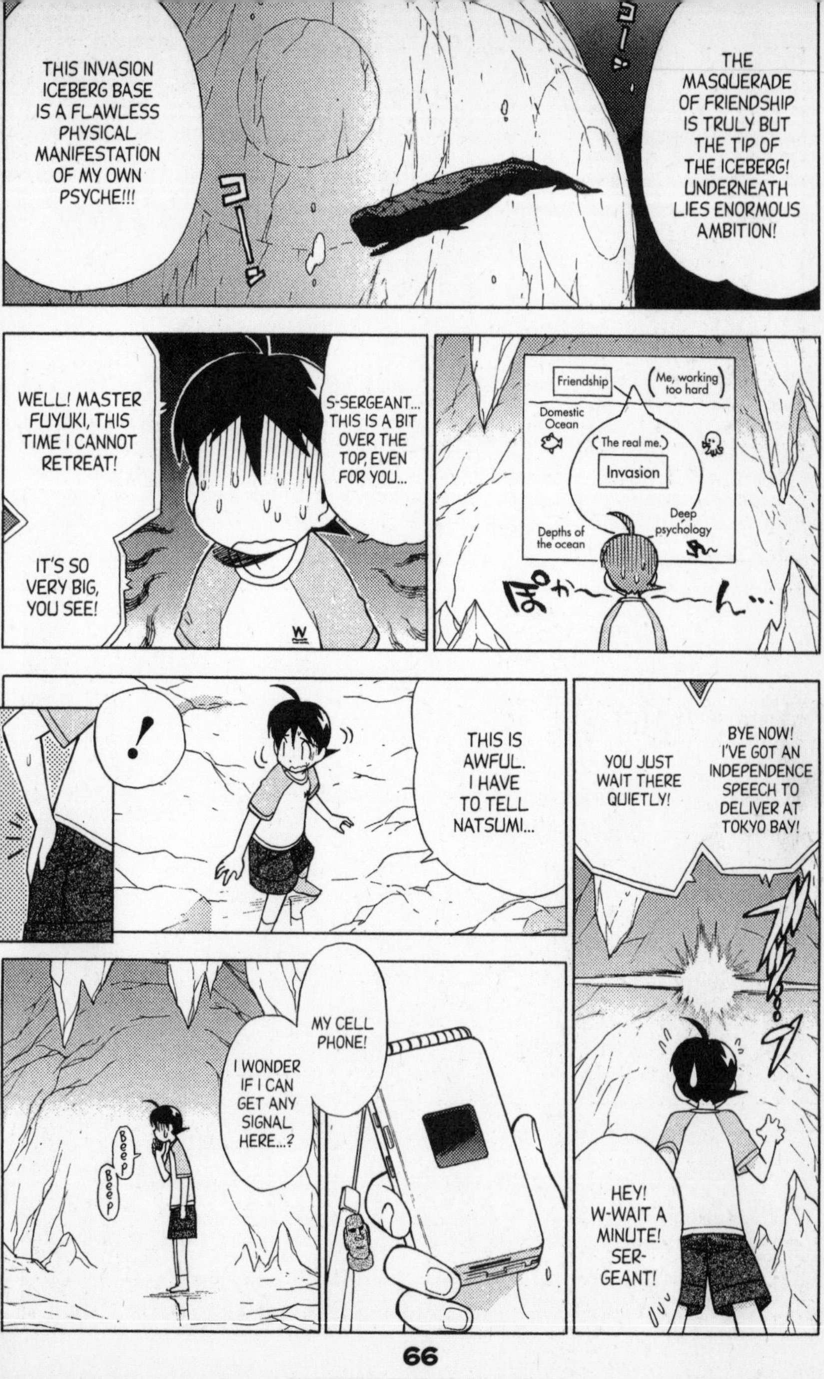
THE MASQUERADE OF FRIENDSHIP IS TRULY BUT THE TIP OF THE ICEBERG! UNDERNEATH LIES ENORMOUS AMBITION!
THIS INVASION ICEBERG BASE IS A FLAWLESS PHYSICAL MANIFESTATION OF MY OWN PSYCHE!!!
Friendship
(Me, working too hard)
Domestic Ocean
(The real me.)
Invasion
Deep psychology
Depths of the ocean
S-SERGEANT... THIS IS A BIT OVER THE TOP, EVEN FOR YOU...
WELL! MASTER FUYUKI, THIS TIME I CANNOT RETREAT!
IT'S SO VERY BIG, YOU SEE!
BYE NOW! I'VE GOT AN INDEPENDENCE SPEECH TO DELIVER AT TOKYO BAY!
YOU JUST WAIT THERE QUIETLY!
THIS IS AWFUL. I HAVE TO TELL NATSUMI...
!
HEY! W-WAIT A MINUTE! SER- GEANT!
MY CELL PHONE!
I WONDER IF I CAN GET ANY SIGNAL HERE...?
Beep Beep

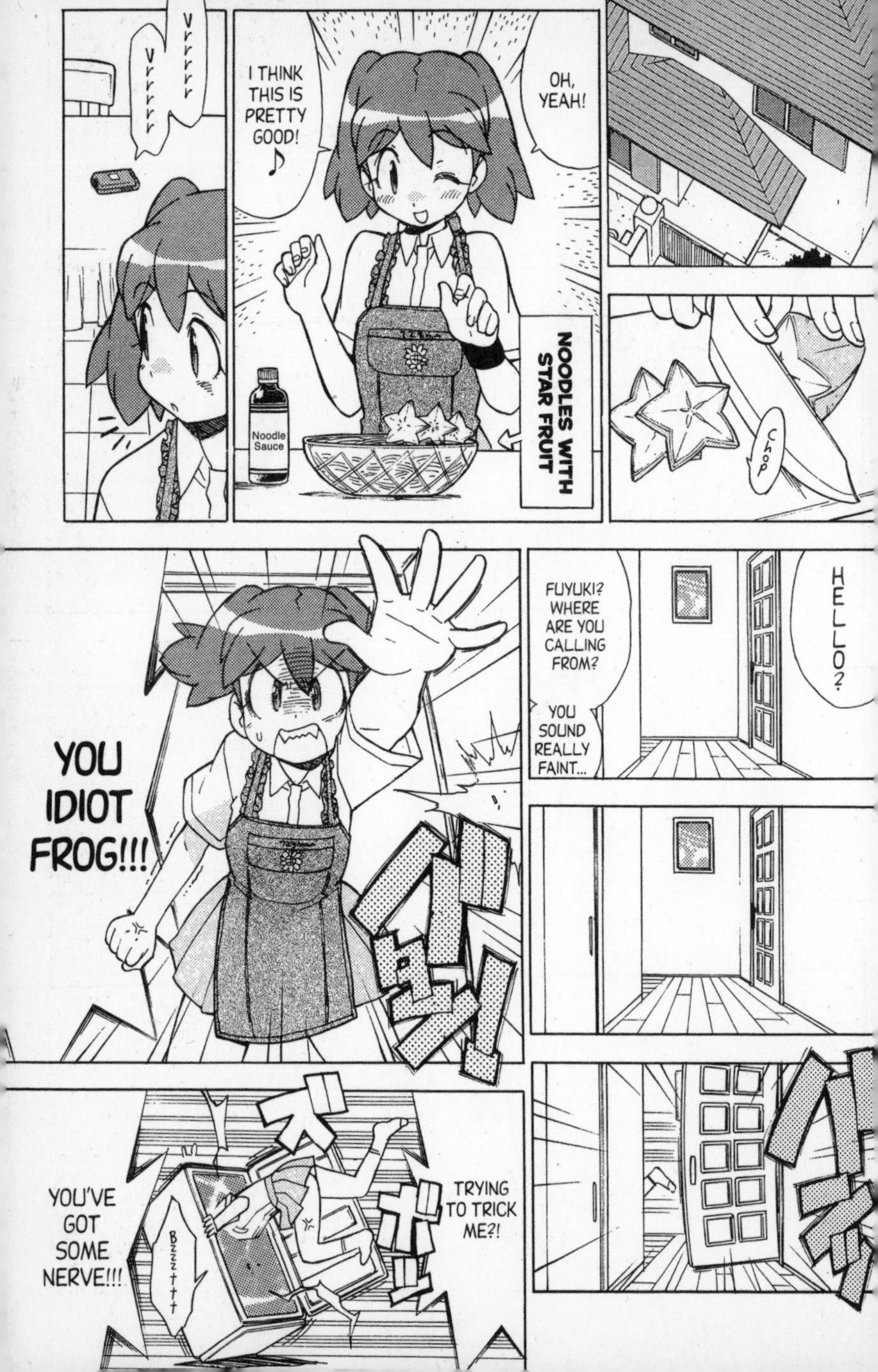
Chop
OH, YEAH!
I THINK THIS IS PRETTY GOOD! ♪
NOODLES WITH STAR FRUIT
Noodle Sauce
Vrrrrr
Vrrrrr
HELLO?
FUYUKI? WHERE ARE YOU CALLING FROM?
YOU SOUND REALLY FAINT...
YOU IDIOT FROG!!!
TRYING TO TRICK ME?!
Bzzttt
YOU'VE GOT SOME NERVE!!!

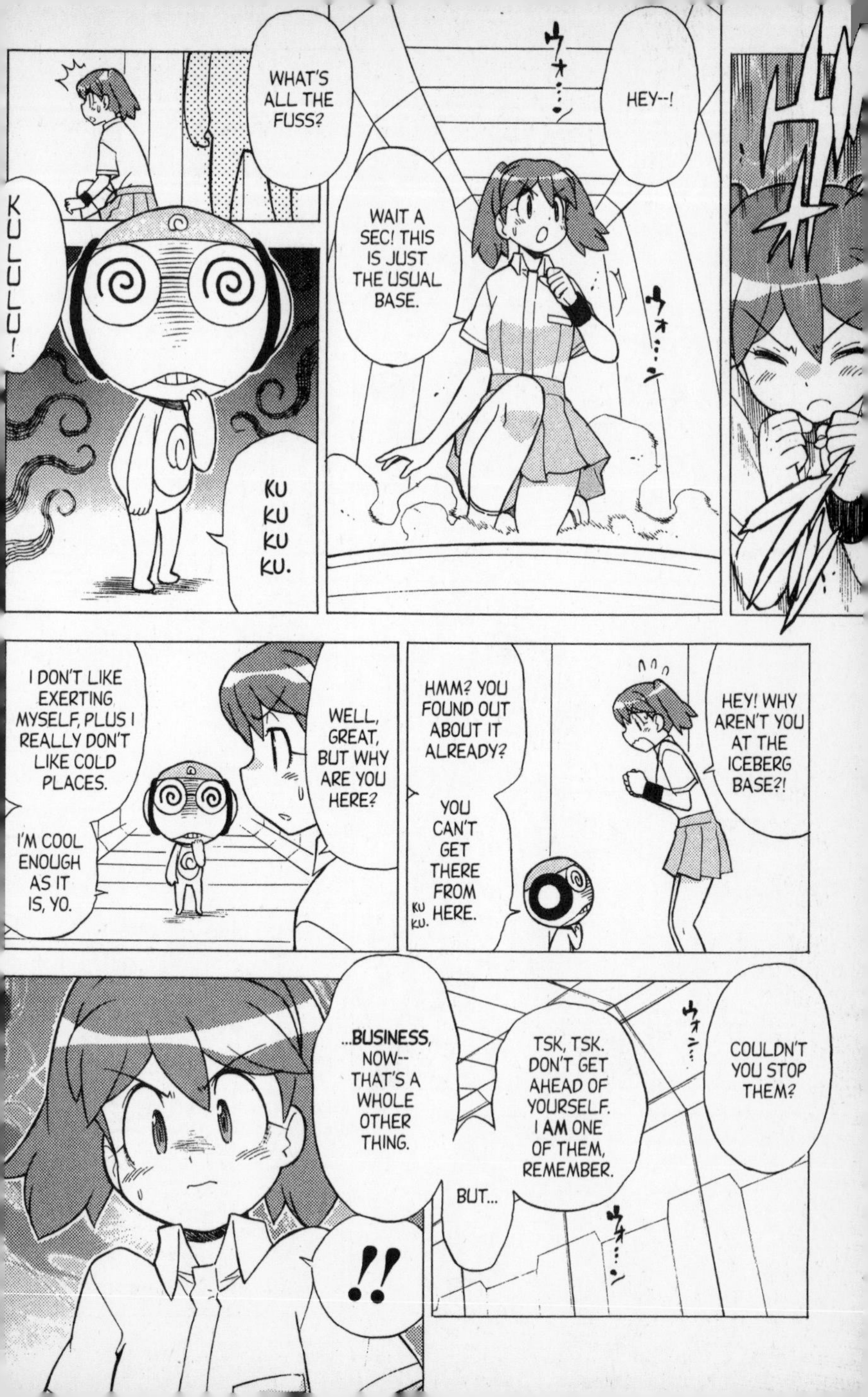

ウォ…ン
HEY--!
WAIT A SEC! THIS IS JUST THE USUAL BASE.
ウォ…ン
WHAT'S ALL THE FUSS?
KULULULU!
KU KU KU KU.
HEY! WHY AREN'T YOU AT THE ICEBERG BASE?!
HMM? YOU FOUND OUT ABOUT IT ALREADY?
YOU CAN'T GET THERE FROM HERE.
KU KU.
WELL, GREAT, BUT WHY ARE YOU HERE?
I DON'T LIKE EXERTING MYSELF, PLUS I REALLY DON'T LIKE COLD PLACES.
I'M COOL ENOUGH AS IT IS, YO.
ウォン…
COULDN'T YOU STOP THEM?
TSK, TSK. DON'T GET AHEAD OF YOURSELF. I AM ONE OF THEM, REMEMBER.
ウォ…ン
BUT...
...BUSINESS, NOW-- THAT'S A WHOLE OTHER THING.
!!

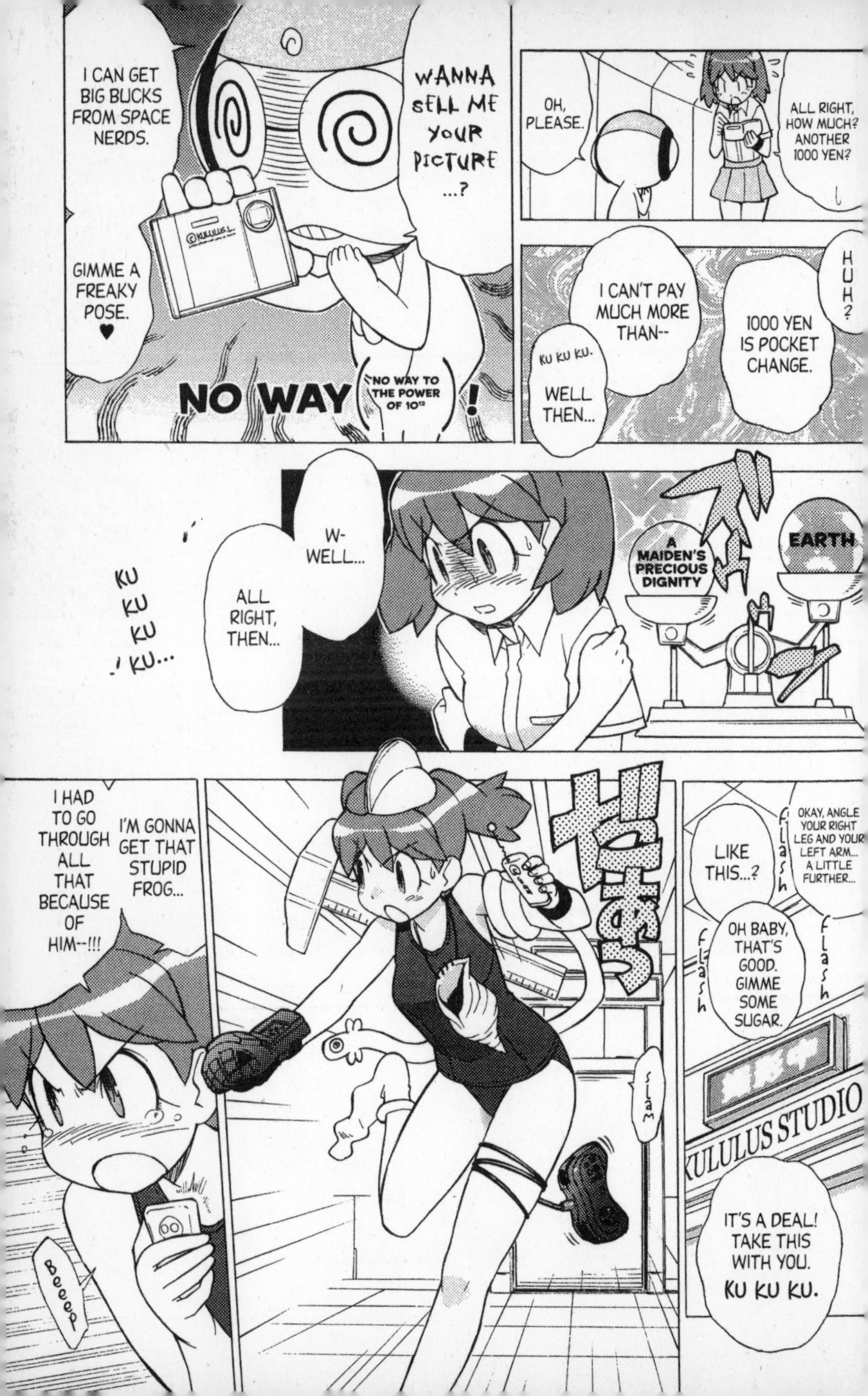

ALL RIGHT, HOW MUCH? ANOTHER 1000 YEN?
OH, PLEASE.
WANNA SELL ME YOUR PICTURE ...?
I CAN GET BIG BUCKS FROM SPACE NERDS.
GIMME A FREAKY POSE. ♥
HUH?
1000 YEN IS POCKET CHANGE.
I CAN'T PAY MUCH MORE THAN--
KU KU KU.
WELL THEN...
NO WAY (NO WAY TO THE POWER OF 10¹²)!
EARTH
A MAIDEN'S PRECIOUS DIGNITY
W- WELL...
ALL RIGHT, THEN...
KU KU KU KU...
OKAY, ANGLE YOUR RIGHT LEG AND YOUR LEFT ARM... A LITTLE FURTHER...
LIKE THIS...?
flash
OH BABY, THAT'S GOOD. GIMME SOME SUGAR.
flash
flash
KULULUS STUDIO
IT'S A DEAL! TAKE THIS WITH YOU. KU KU KU.
slam
I'M GONNA GET THAT STUPID FROG...
I HAD TO GO THROUGH ALL THAT BECAUSE OF HIM--!!!
Beeep

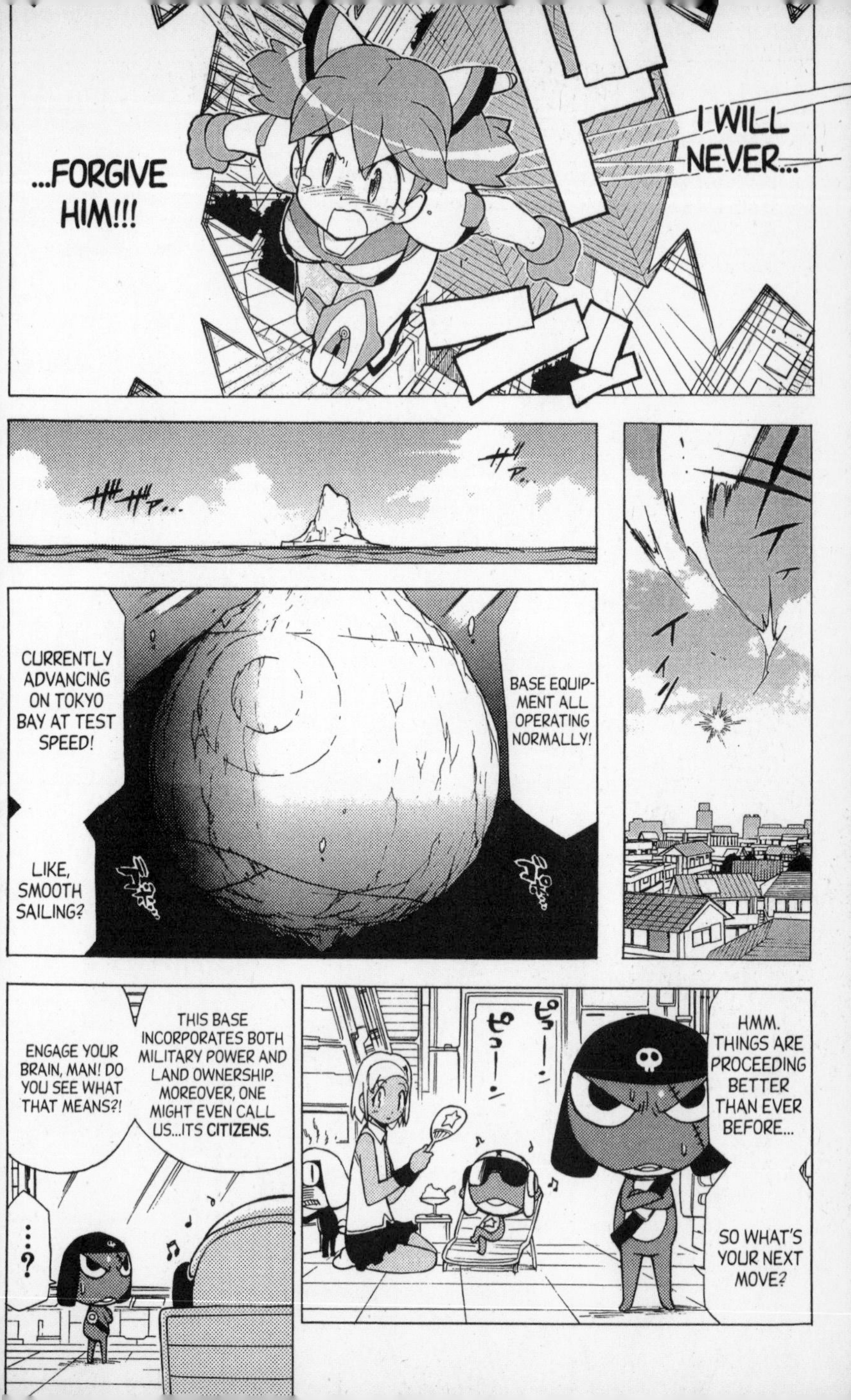
I WILL NEVER...
...FORGIVE HIM!!!
CURRENTLY ADVANCING ON TOKYO BAY AT TEST SPEED!
BASE EQUIPMENT ALL OPERATING NORMALLY!
LIKE, SMOOTH SAILING?
HMM. THINGS ARE PROCEEDING BETTER THAN EVER BEFORE...
SO WHAT'S YOUR NEXT MOVE?
THIS BASE INCORPORATES BOTH MILITARY POWER AND LAND OWNERSHIP. MOREOVER, ONE MIGHT EVEN CALL US...ITS CITIZENS.
ENGAGE YOUR BRAIN, MAN! DO YOU SEE WHAT THAT MEANS?!
...?

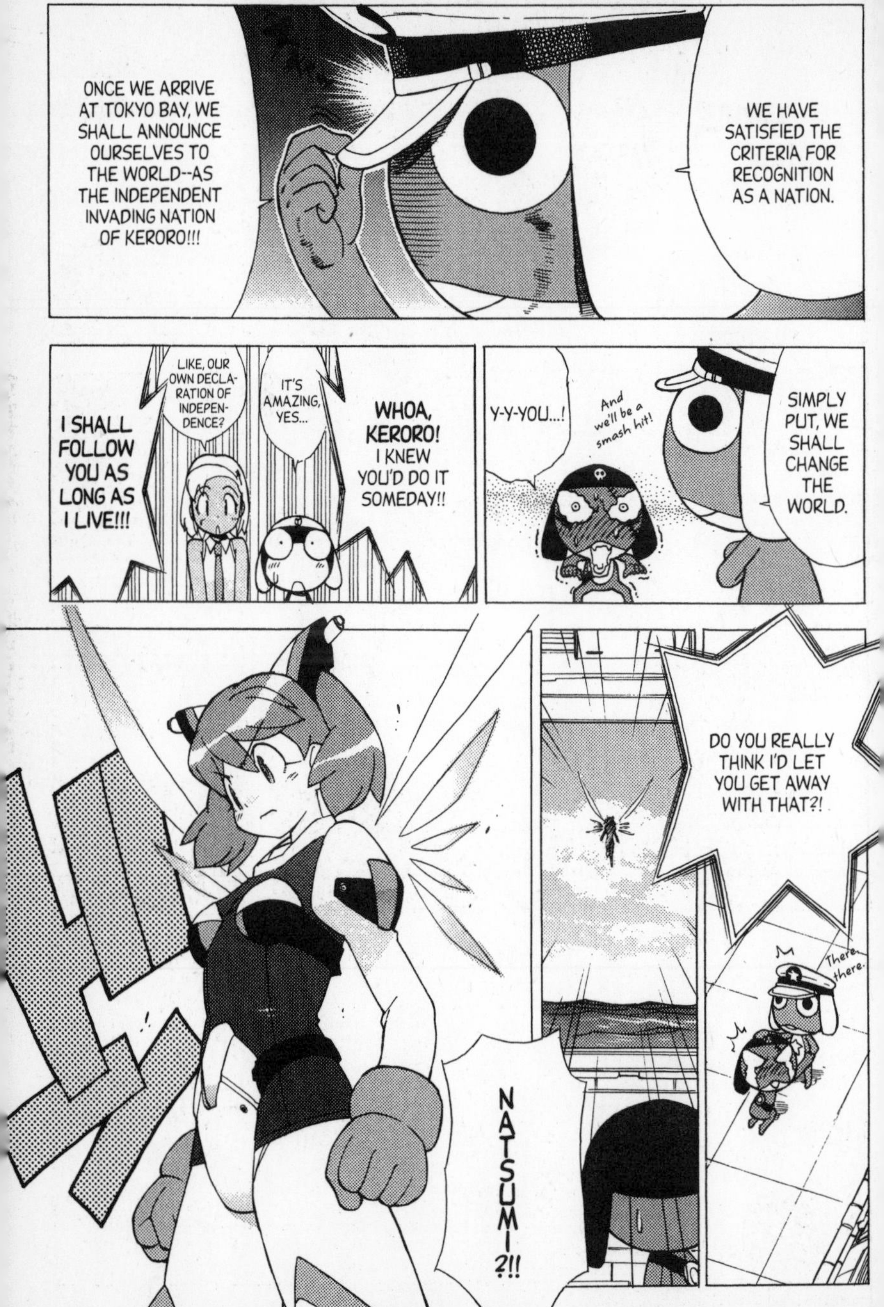
WE HAVE SATISFIED THE CRITERIA FOR RECOGNITION AS A NATION.
ONCE WE ARRIVE AT TOKYO BAY, WE SHALL ANNOUNCE OURSELVES TO THE WORLD--AS THE INDEPENDENT INVADING NATION OF KERORO!!!
SIMPLY PUT, WE SHALL CHANGE THE WORLD.
And we'll be a smash hit!
Y-Y-YOU...!
WHOA, KERORO! I KNEW YOU'D DO IT SOMEDAY!!
IT'S AMAZING, YES...
LIKE, OUR OWN DECLARATION OF INDEPENDENCE?
I SHALL FOLLOW YOU AS LONG AS I LIVE!!!
DO YOU REALLY THINK I'D LET YOU GET AWAY WITH THAT?!
There there.
NATSUMI?!!

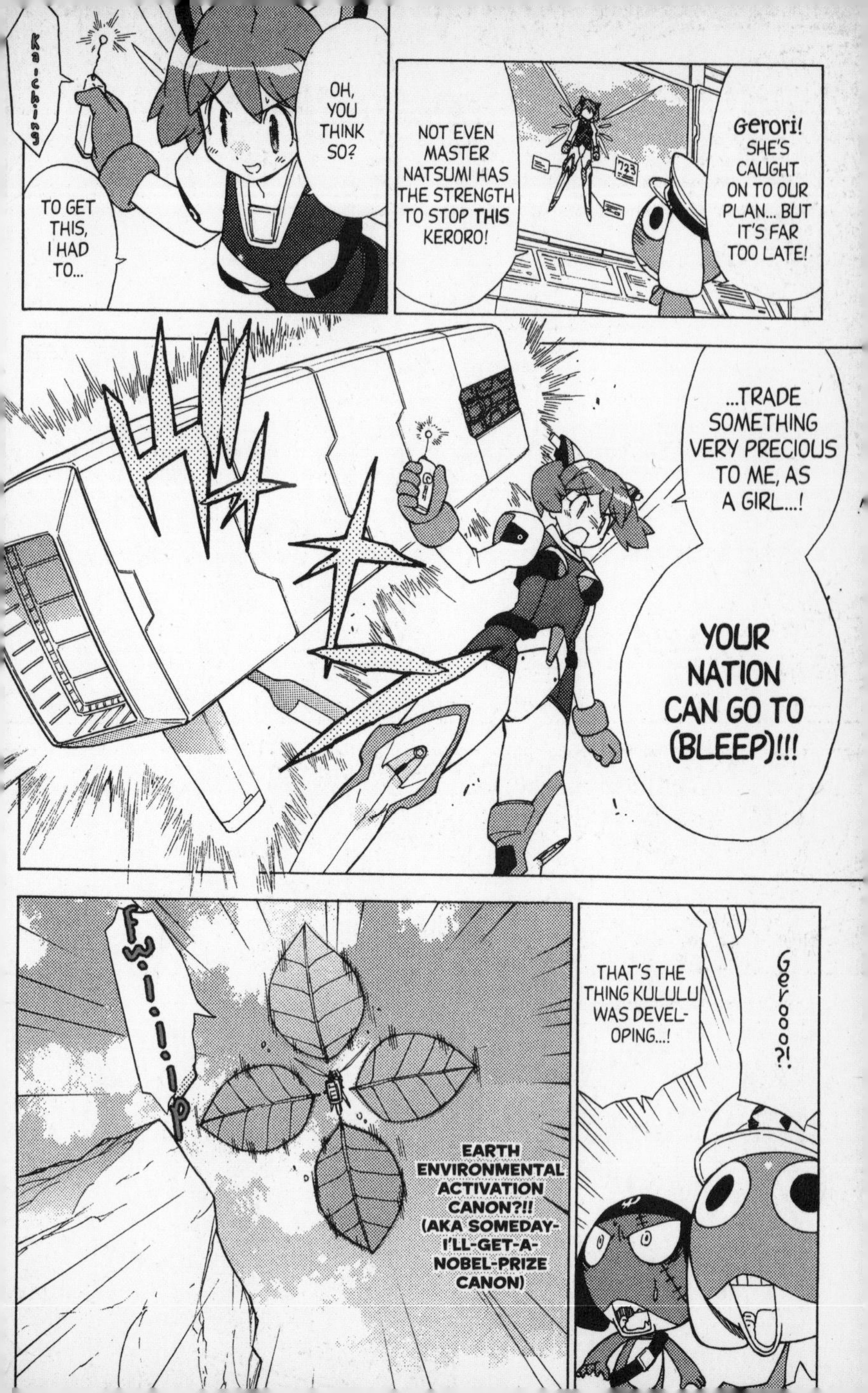
Gerori! SHE'S CAUGHT ON TO OUR PLAN... BUT IT'S FAR TOO LATE!
NOT EVEN MASTER NATSUMI HAS THE STRENGTH TO STOP THIS KERORO!
OH, YOU THINK SO?
Ka-ching
TO GET THIS, I HAD TO...
...TRADE SOMETHING VERY PRECIOUS TO ME, AS A GIRL...!
YOUR NATION CAN GO TO (BLEEP)!!!
THAT'S THE THING KULULU WAS DEVEL-OPING...!
Gerooo?!
Fw-l-l-p
EARTH ENVIRONMENTAL ACTIVATION CANON?!! (AKA SOMEDAY-I'LL-GET-A-NOBEL-PRIZE CANON)

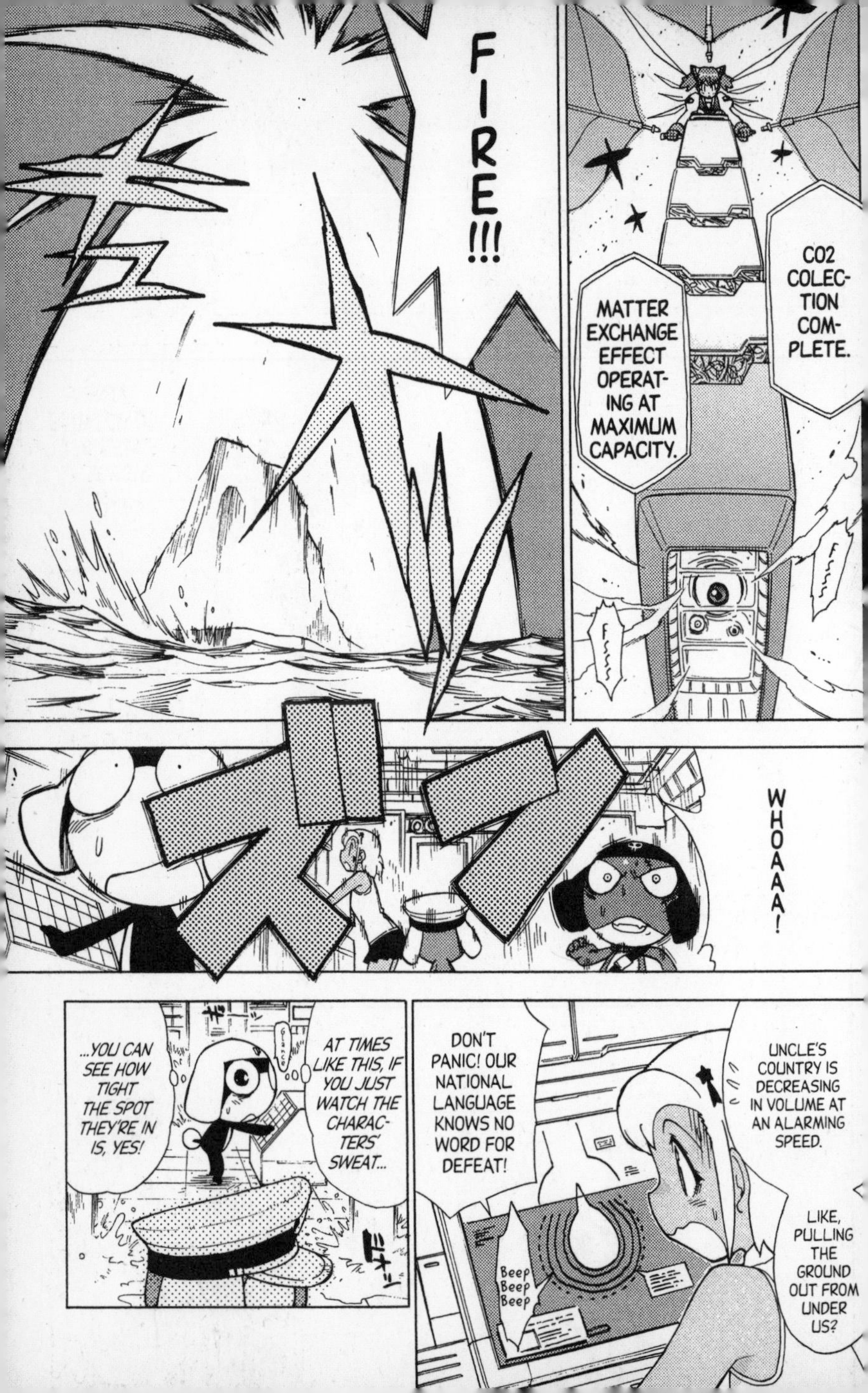
CO2 COLEC-TION COM-PLETE.
MATTER EXCHANGE EFFECT OPERAT-ING AT MAXIMUM CAPACITY.
Fsss
Fsss
FIRE!!!
WHOAAA!
UNCLE'S COUNTRY IS DECREASING IN VOLUME AT AN ALARMING SPEED.
LIKE, PULLING THE GROUND OUT FROM UNDER US?
DON'T PANIC! OUR NATIONAL LANGUAGE KNOWS NO WORD FOR DEFEAT!
Beep Beep Beep
AT TIMES LIKE THIS, IF YOU JUST WATCH THE CHARAC-TERS' SWEAT...
...YOU CAN SEE HOW TIGHT THE SPOT THEY'RE IN IS, YES!

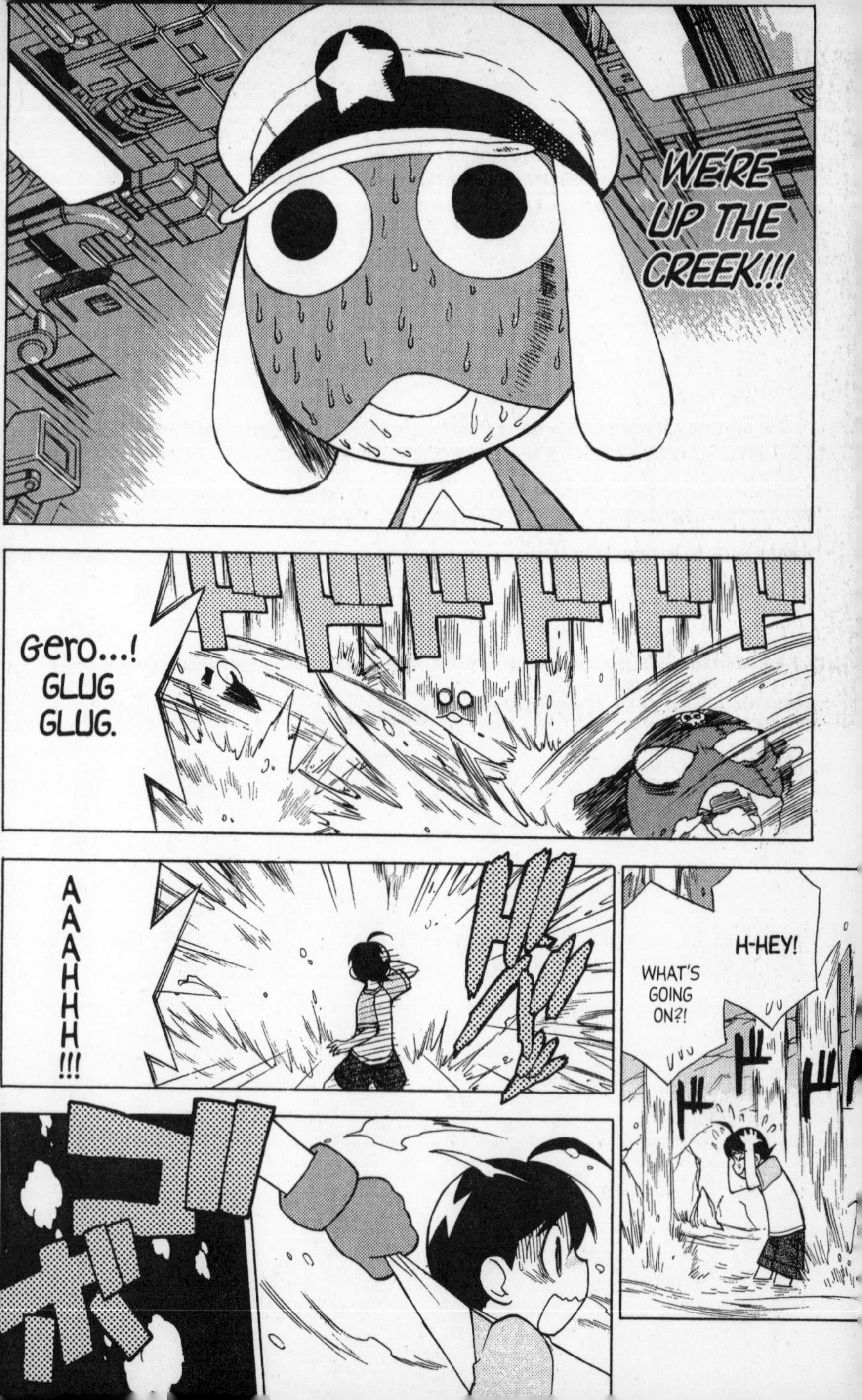
WE'RE UP THE CREEK!!!
Gero...! GLUG GLUG.
H-HEY!
WHAT'S GOING ON?!
AAAHHH!!!

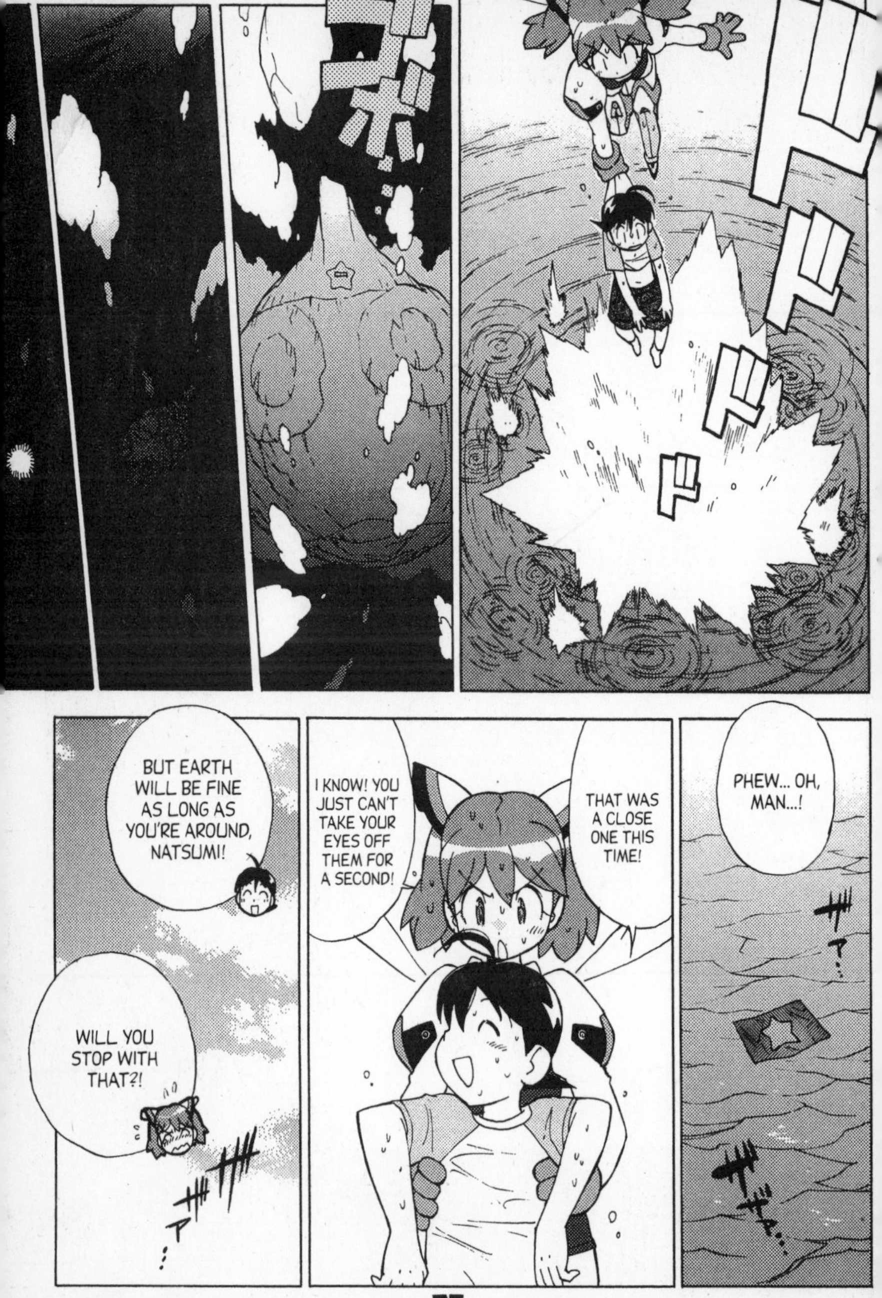
PHEW... OH, MAN...!
THAT WAS A CLOSE ONE THIS TIME!
I KNOW! YOU JUST CAN'T TAKE YOUR EYES OFF THEM FOR A SECOND!
BUT EARTH WILL BE FINE AS LONG AS YOU'RE AROUND, NATSUMI!
WILL YOU STOP WITH THAT?!

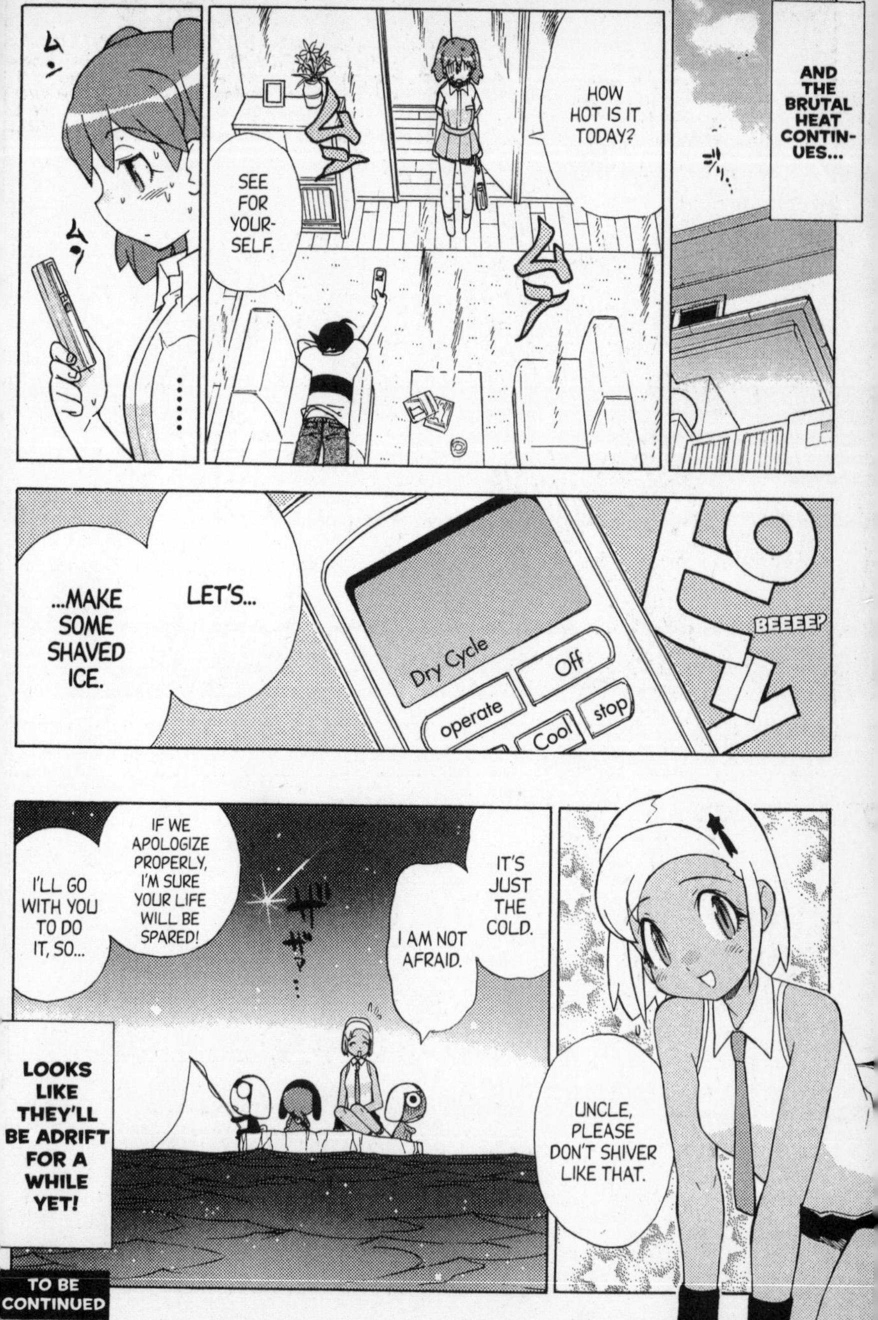
AND THE BRUTAL HEAT CONTIN-UES...
HOW HOT IS IT TODAY?
SEE FOR YOUR-SELF.
......
LET'S...
...MAKE SOME SHAVED ICE.
BEEEEP
Dry Cycle
Off
operate
Cool
stop
UNCLE, PLEASE DON'T SHIVER LIKE THAT.
IT'S JUST THE COLD.
I AM NOT AFRAID.
IF WE APOLOGIZE PROPERLY, I'M SURE YOUR LIFE WILL BE SPARED!
I'LL GO WITH YOU TO DO IT, SO...
LOOKS LIKE THEY'LL BE ADRIFT FOR A WHILE YET!
TO BE CONTINUED

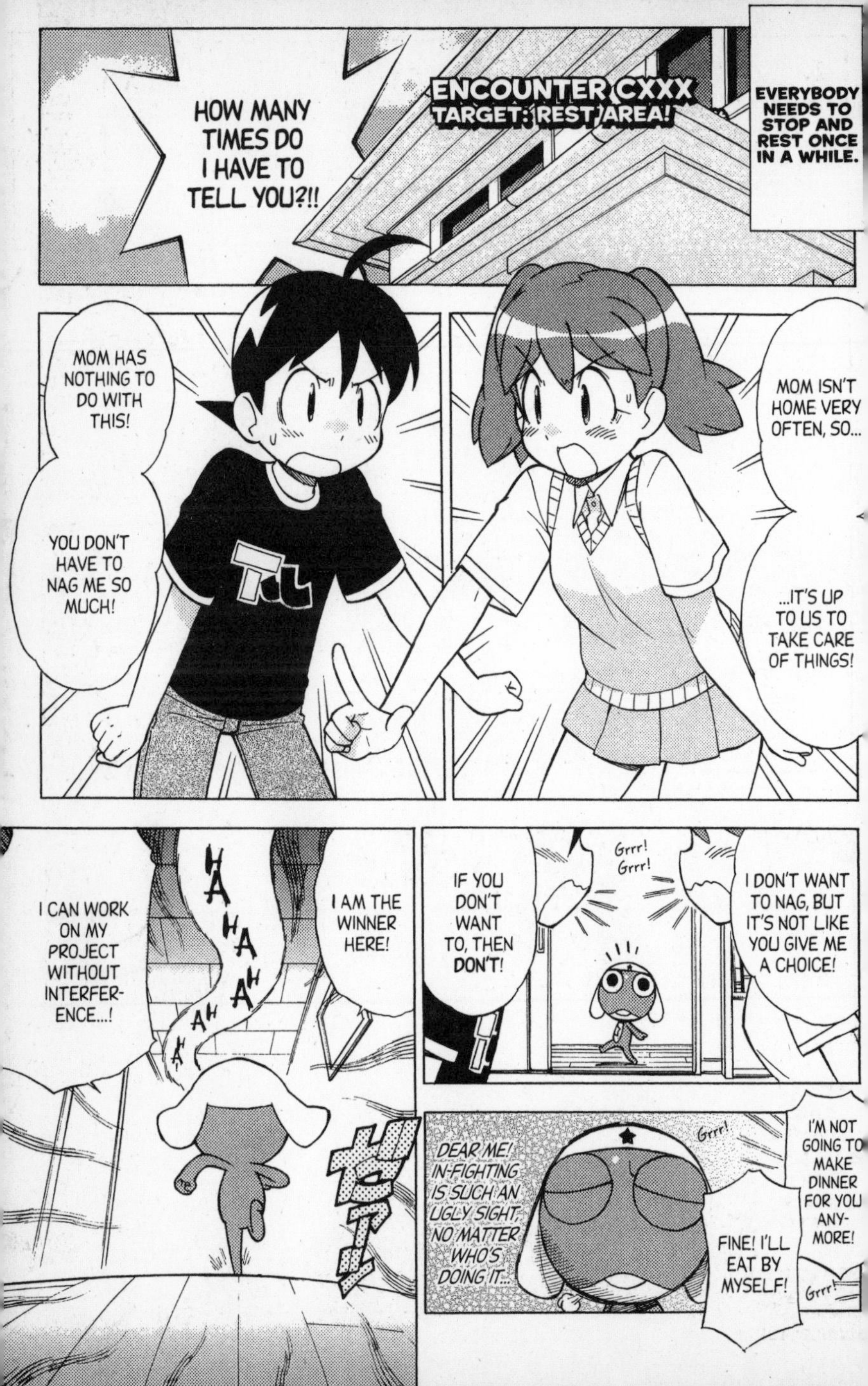
EVERYBODY NEEDS TO STOP AND REST ONCE IN A WHILE.
ENCOUNTER CXXX
TARGET: REST AREA!
HOW MANY TIMES DO I HAVE TO TELL YOU?!!
MOM ISN'T HOME VERY OFTEN, SO...
...IT'S UP TO US TO TAKE CARE OF THINGS!
MOM HAS NOTHING TO DO WITH THIS!
YOU DON'T HAVE TO NAG ME SO MUCH!
I DON'T WANT TO NAG, BUT IT'S NOT LIKE YOU GIVE ME A CHOICE!
Grrr! Grrr!
IF YOU DON'T WANT TO, THEN DON'T!
I'M NOT GOING TO MAKE DINNER FOR YOU ANY-MORE!
Grrr!
FINE! I'LL EAT BY MYSELF!
Grrr!
DEAR ME! IN-FIGHTING IS SUCH AN UGLY SIGHT, NO MATTER WHO'S DOING IT...
I AM THE WINNER HERE!
I CAN WORK ON MY PROJECT WITHOUT INTERFER-ENCE...!
HA HA HA AH AH AH

ENCOUNTER GXXX
TARGET: REST AREA!

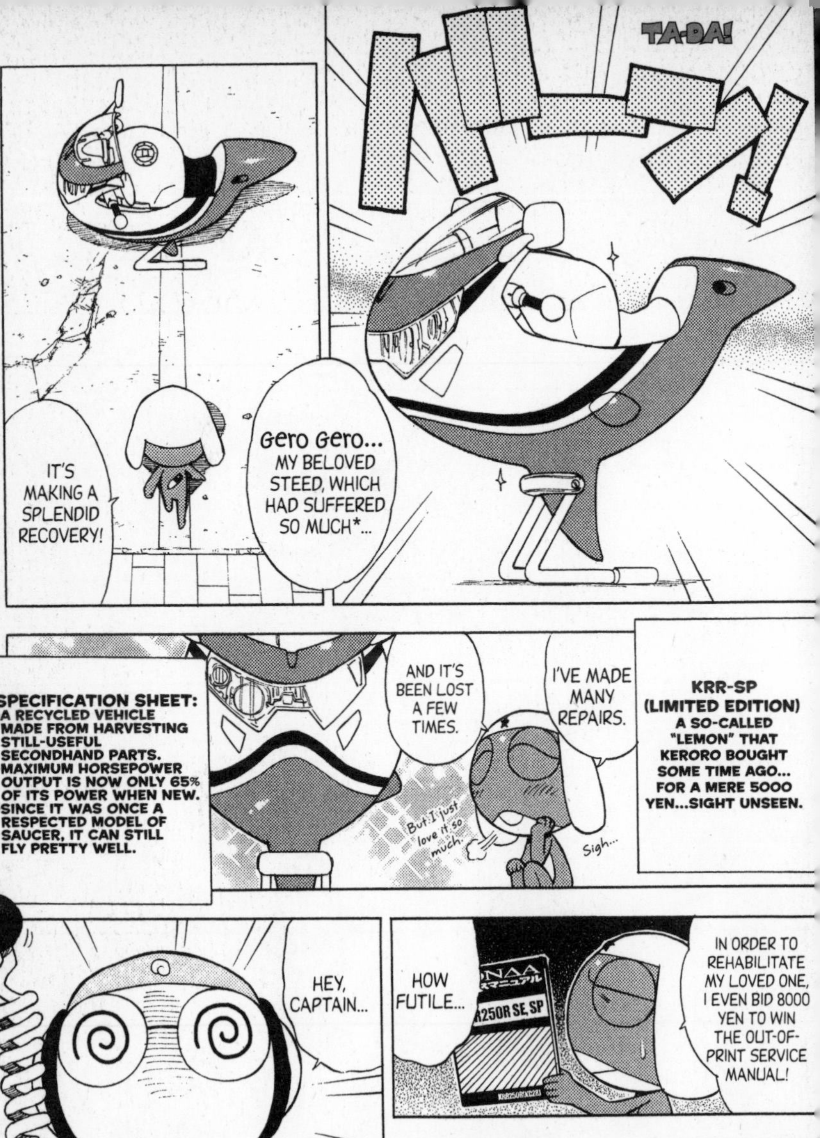
TA-DA!
Gero Gero... MY BELOVED STEED, WHICH HAD SUFFERED SO MUCH*...
IT'S MAKING A SPLENDID RECOVERY!
KRR-SP (LIMITED EDITION) A SO-CALLED "LEMON" THAT KERORO BOUGHT SOME TIME AGO... FOR A MERE 5000 YEN...SIGHT UNSEEN.
I'VE MADE MANY REPAIRS.
AND IT'S BEEN LOST A FEW TIMES.
But I just love it so much.
Sigh...
SPECIFICATION SHEET:
•A RECYCLED VEHICLE MADE FROM HARVESTING STILL-USEFUL SECONDHAND PARTS.
•MAXIMUM HORSEPOWER OUTPUT IS NOW ONLY 65% OF ITS POWER WHEN NEW.
•SINCE IT WAS ONCE A RESPECTED MODEL OF SAUCER, IT CAN STILL FLY PRETTY WELL.
IN ORDER TO REHABILITATE MY LOVED ONE, I EVEN BID 8000 YEN TO WIN THE OUT-OF-PRINT SERVICE MANUAL!
HOW FUTILE...
R250R SE, SP
ALL I NEED TO DO NOW IS WAIT FOR THE LAST PART TO ARRIVE!
CAN'T WAIT. CAN'T WAIT...! ♪
KU KU KU KU.
HEY, CAPTAIN...
I'VE GOT THAT ANTI-GRAVITY SUSPENSION YOU ORDERED.
KU KU KU.
PARTS DEALER!
sproing
sproing

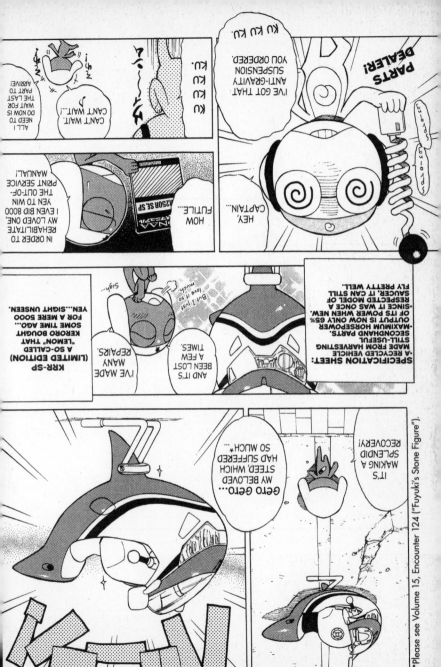

*Please see Volume 15, Encounter 124 ("Fuyuki's Stone Figure").

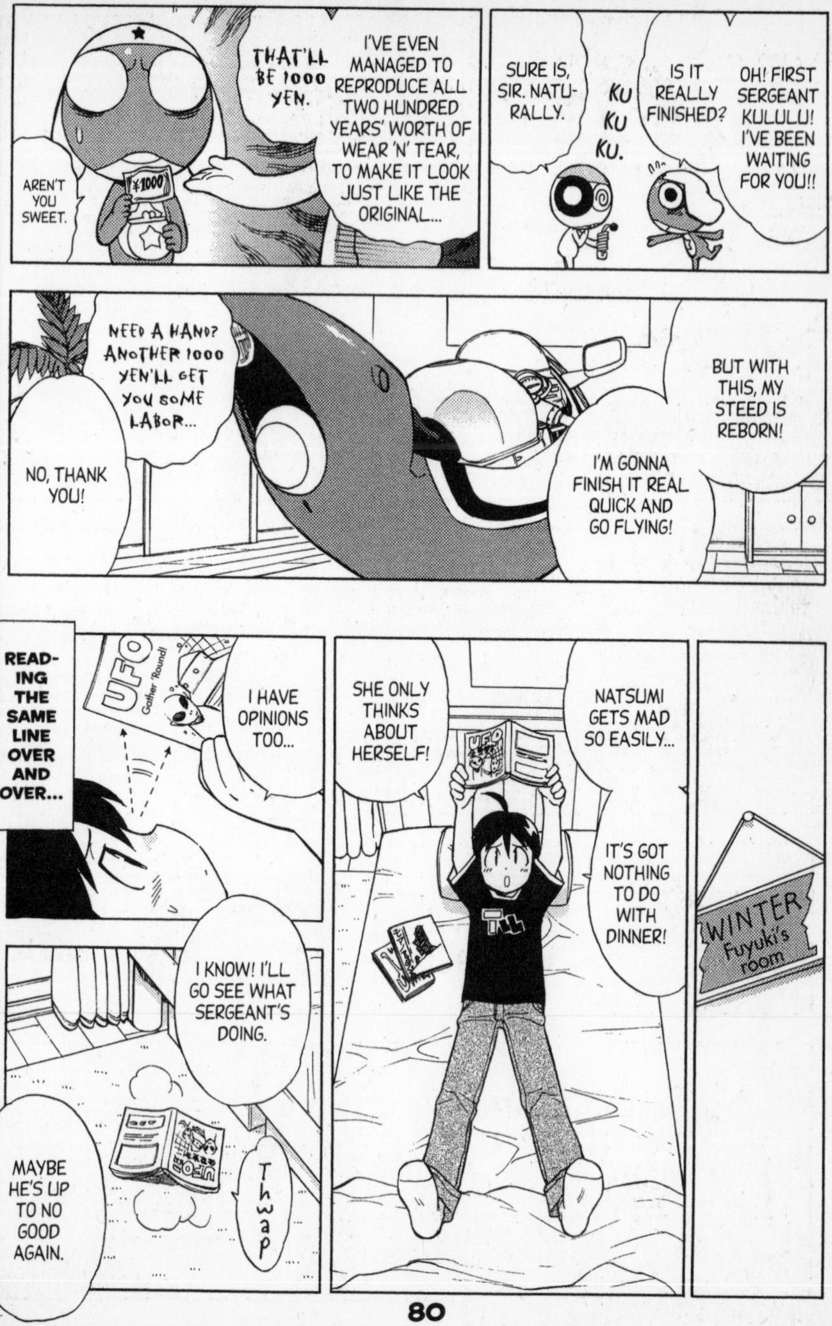
OH! FIRST SERGEANT KULULU! I'VE BEEN WAITING FOR YOU!!
IS IT REALLY FINISHED?
KU KU KU.
SURE IS, SIR. NATU-RALLY.
I'VE EVEN MANAGED TO REPRODUCE ALL TWO HUNDRED YEARS' WORTH OF WEAR 'N' TEAR, TO MAKE IT LOOK JUST LIKE THE ORIGINAL...
THAT'LL BE 1000 YEN.
¥1000
AREN'T YOU SWEET.
BUT WITH THIS, MY STEED IS REBORN!
I'M GONNA FINISH IT REAL QUICK AND GO FLYING!
NEED A HAND? ANOTHER 1000 YEN'LL GET YOU SOME LABOR...
NO, THANK YOU!
WINTER
Fuyuki's room
NATSUMI GETS MAD SO EASILY...
SHE ONLY THINKS ABOUT HERSELF!
IT'S GOT NOTHING TO DO WITH DINNER!
UFO
I HAVE OPINIONS TOO...
UFO
Gather 'Round!
READ-ING THE SAME LINE OVER AND OVER...
I KNOW! I'LL GO SEE WHAT SERGEANT'S DOING.
Thwap
UFO
MAYBE HE'S UP TO NO GOOD AGAIN.

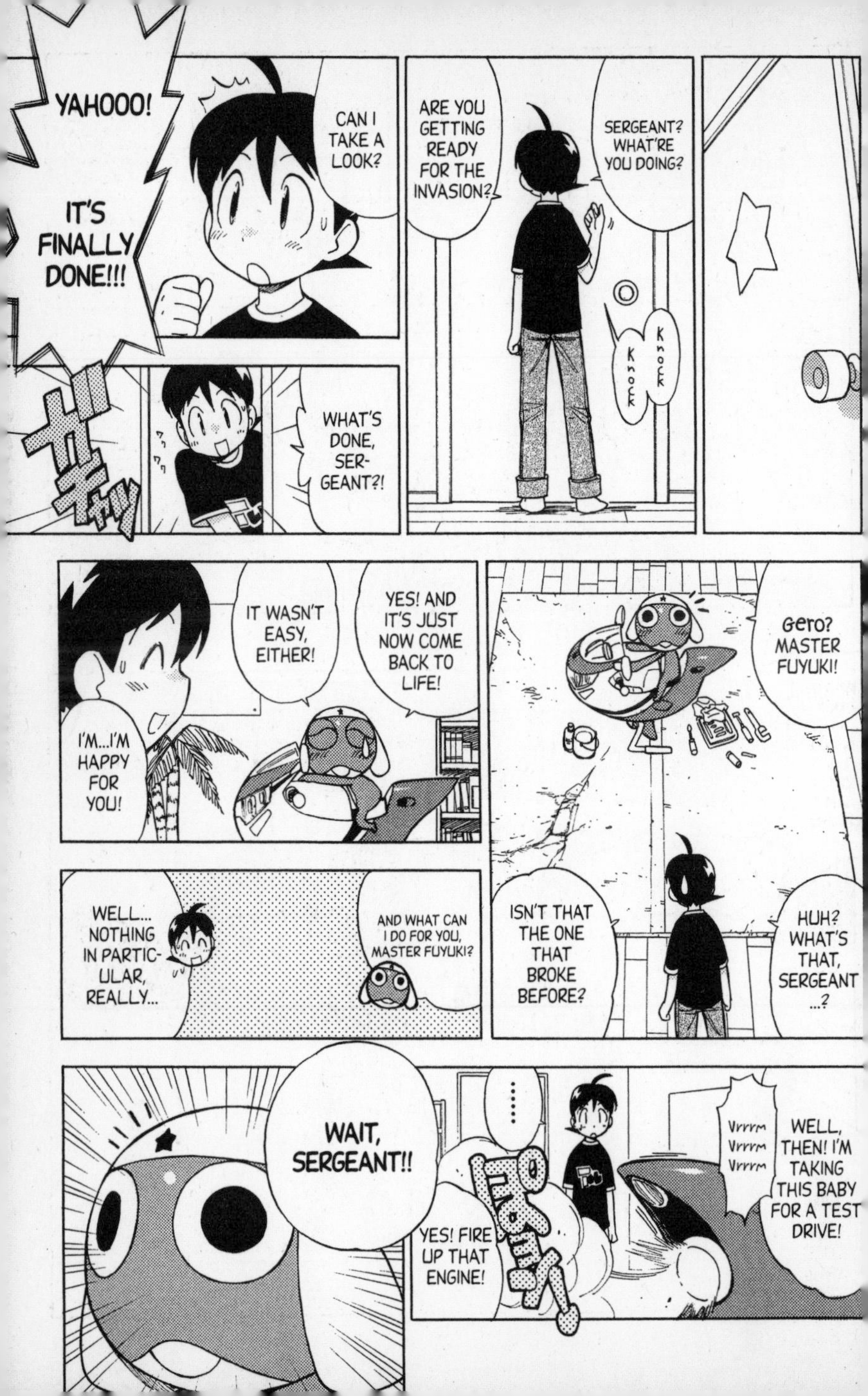
SERGEANT? WHAT'RE YOU DOING?
Knock Knock
ARE YOU GETTING READY FOR THE INVASION?
CAN I TAKE A LOOK?
YAHOOO!
IT'S FINALLY DONE!!!
WHAT'S DONE, SER-GEANT?!
Gero? MASTER FUYUKI!
HUH? WHAT'S THAT, SERGEANT ...?
ISN'T THAT THE ONE THAT BROKE BEFORE?
YES! AND IT'S JUST NOW COME BACK TO LIFE!
IT WASN'T EASY, EITHER!
I'M...I'M HAPPY FOR YOU!
AND WHAT CAN I DO FOR YOU, MASTER FUYUKI?
WELL... NOTHING IN PARTIC-ULAR, REALLY...
WELL, THEN! I'M TAKING THIS BABY FOR A TEST DRIVE!
Vrrrm Vrrrm Vrrrm
YES! FIRE UP THAT ENGINE!
......
WAIT, SERGEANT!!

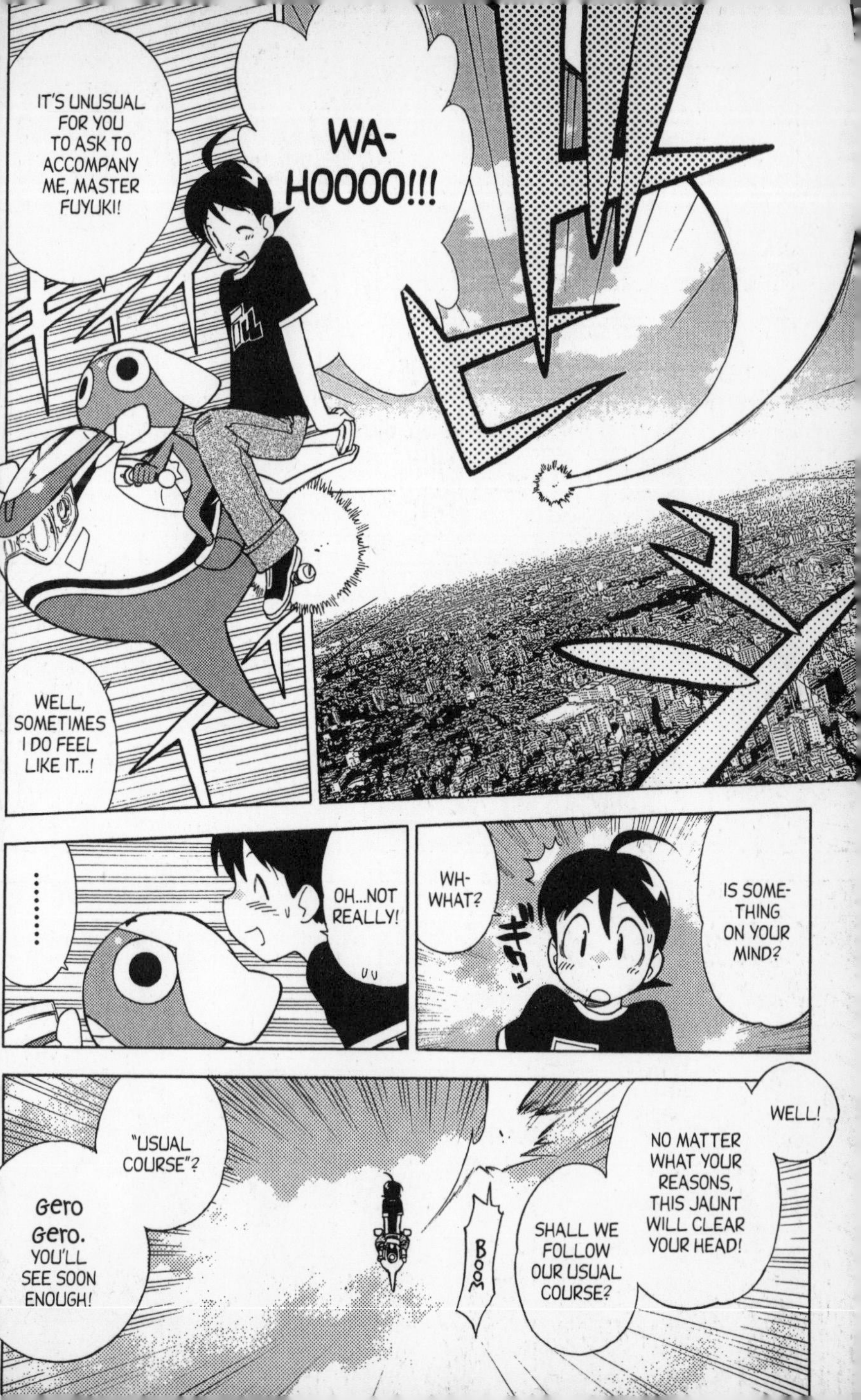
WA-HOOOO!!!
IT'S UNUSUAL FOR YOU TO ASK TO ACCOMPANY ME, MASTER FUYUKI!
WELL, SOMETIMES I DO FEEL LIKE IT...!
IS SOME-THING ON YOUR MIND?
WH-WHAT?
OH...NOT REALLY!
....
WELL!
NO MATTER WHAT YOUR REASONS, THIS JAUNT WILL CLEAR YOUR HEAD!
SHALL WE FOLLOW OUR USUAL COURSE?
BOOM
"USUAL COURSE"?
Gero Gero. YOU'LL SEE SOON ENOUGH!

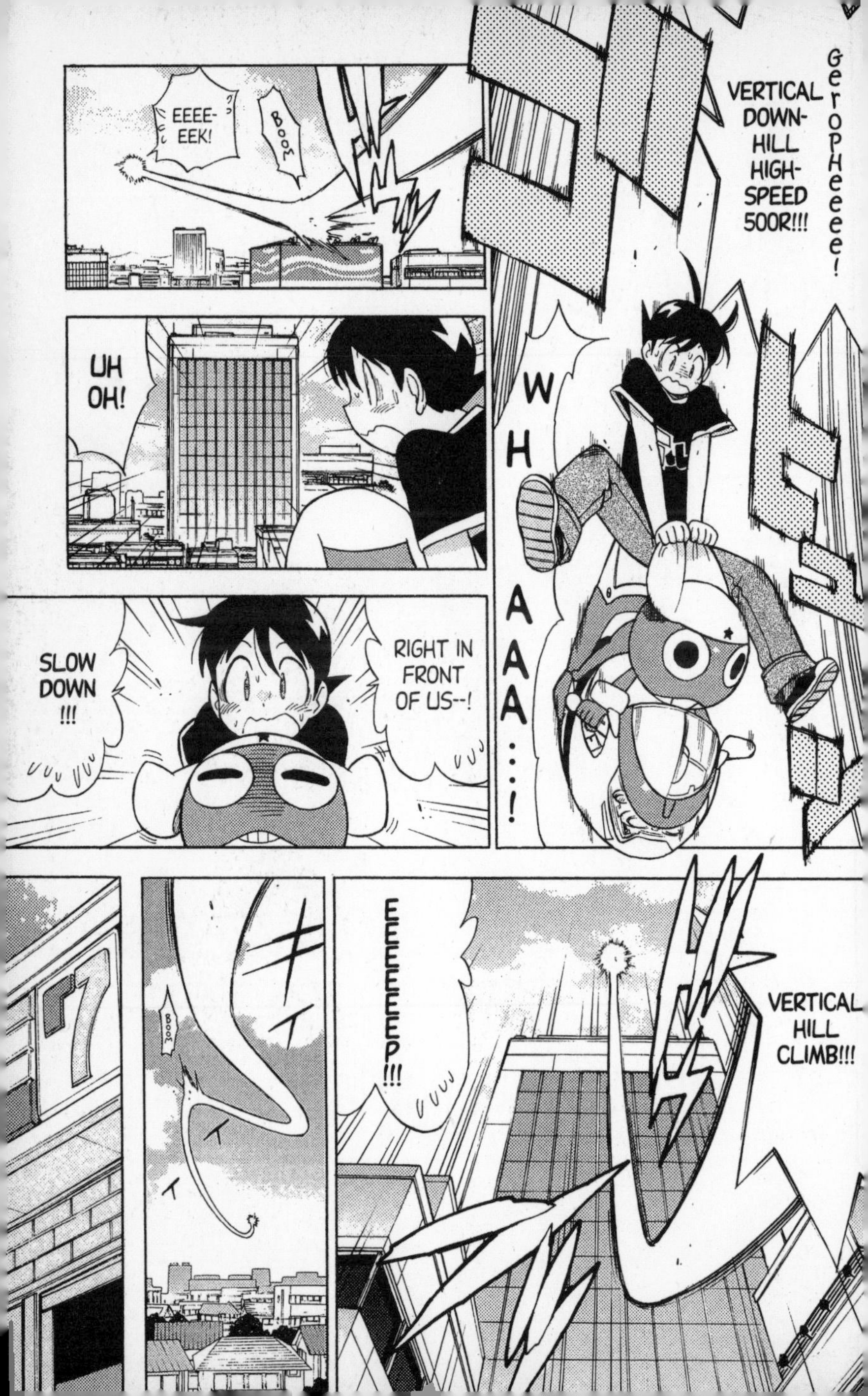
Geropheeee!
VERTICAL DOWN-HILL HIGH-SPEED 500R!!!
WHAAA...!
BOOM
EEEE-EEK!
UH OH!
RIGHT IN FRONT OF US--!
SLOW DOWN!!!
VERTICAL HILL CLIMB!!!
EEEEEEP!!!
BOOM

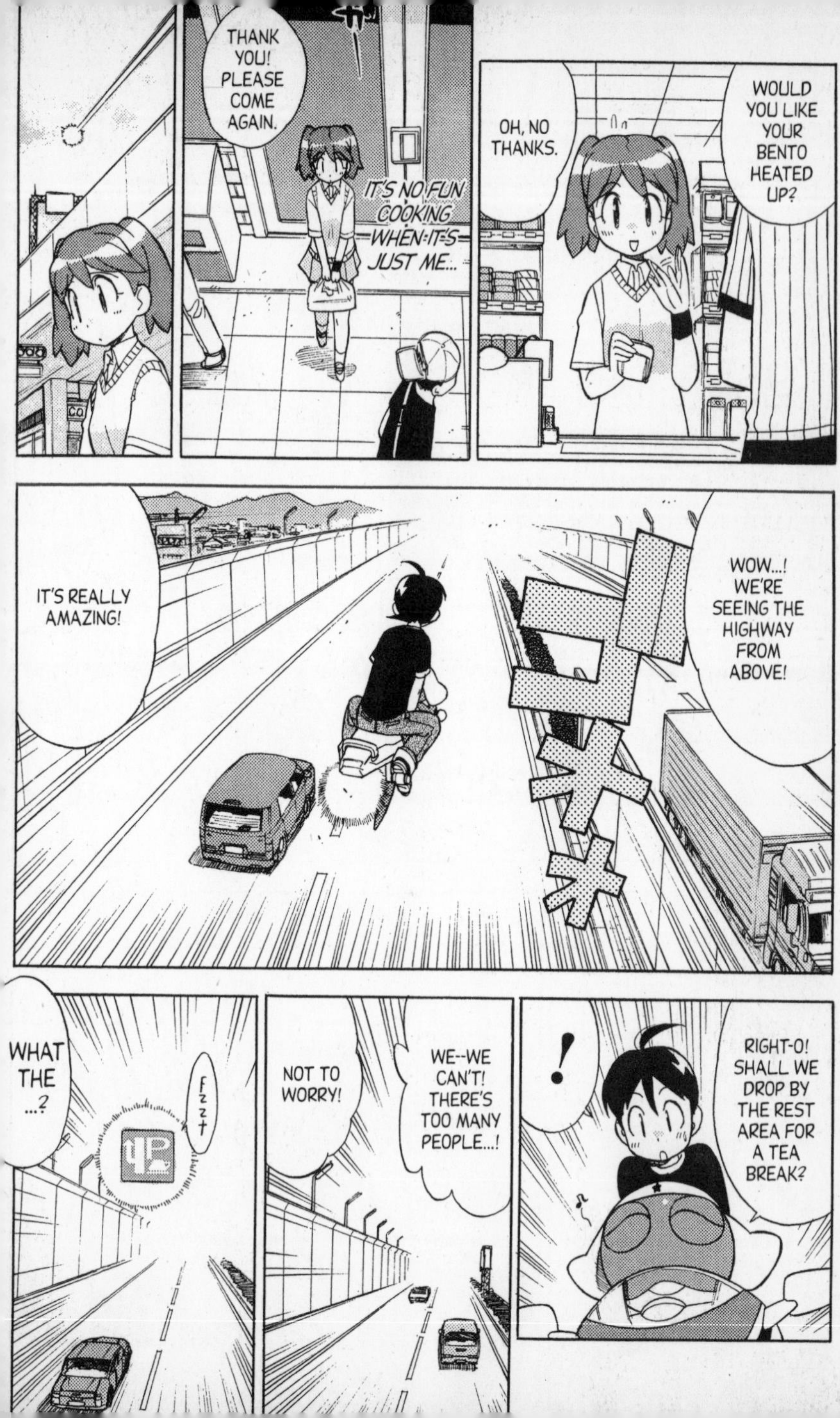
WOULD YOU LIKE YOUR BENTO HEATED UP?
OH, NO THANKS.
THANK YOU! PLEASE COME AGAIN.
IT'S NO FUN COOKING WHEN IT'S JUST ME...
WOW...! WE'RE SEEING THE HIGHWAY FROM ABOVE!
IT'S REALLY AMAZING!
RIGHT-O! SHALL WE DROP BY THE REST AREA FOR A TEA BREAK?
!
WE--WE CAN'T! THERE'S TOO MANY PEOPLE...!
NOT TO WORRY!
fzzt
WHAT THE ...?

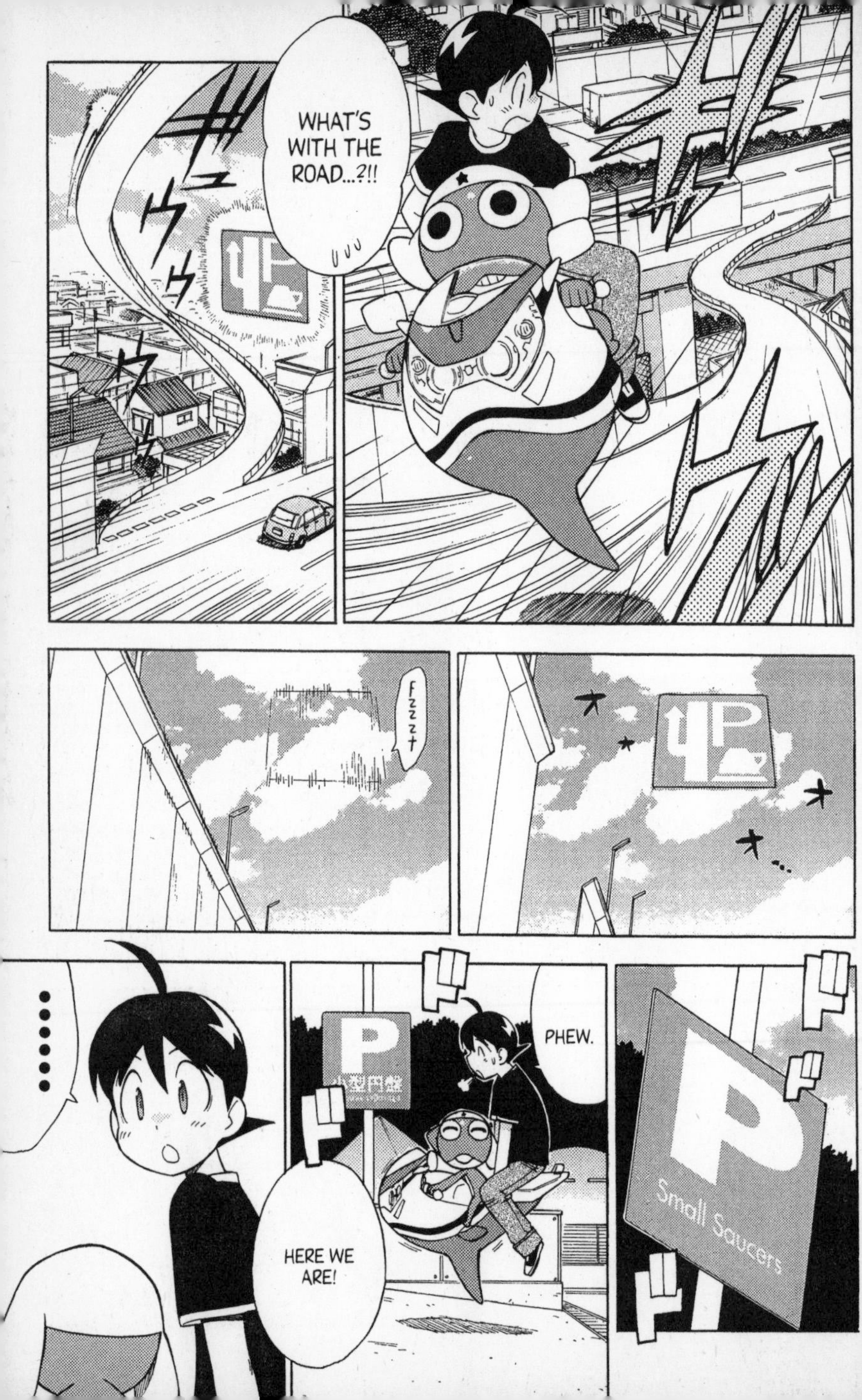
WHAT'S WITH THE ROAD...?!!
FZZZT
P
Small Saucers
PHEW.
P
HERE WE ARE!
......

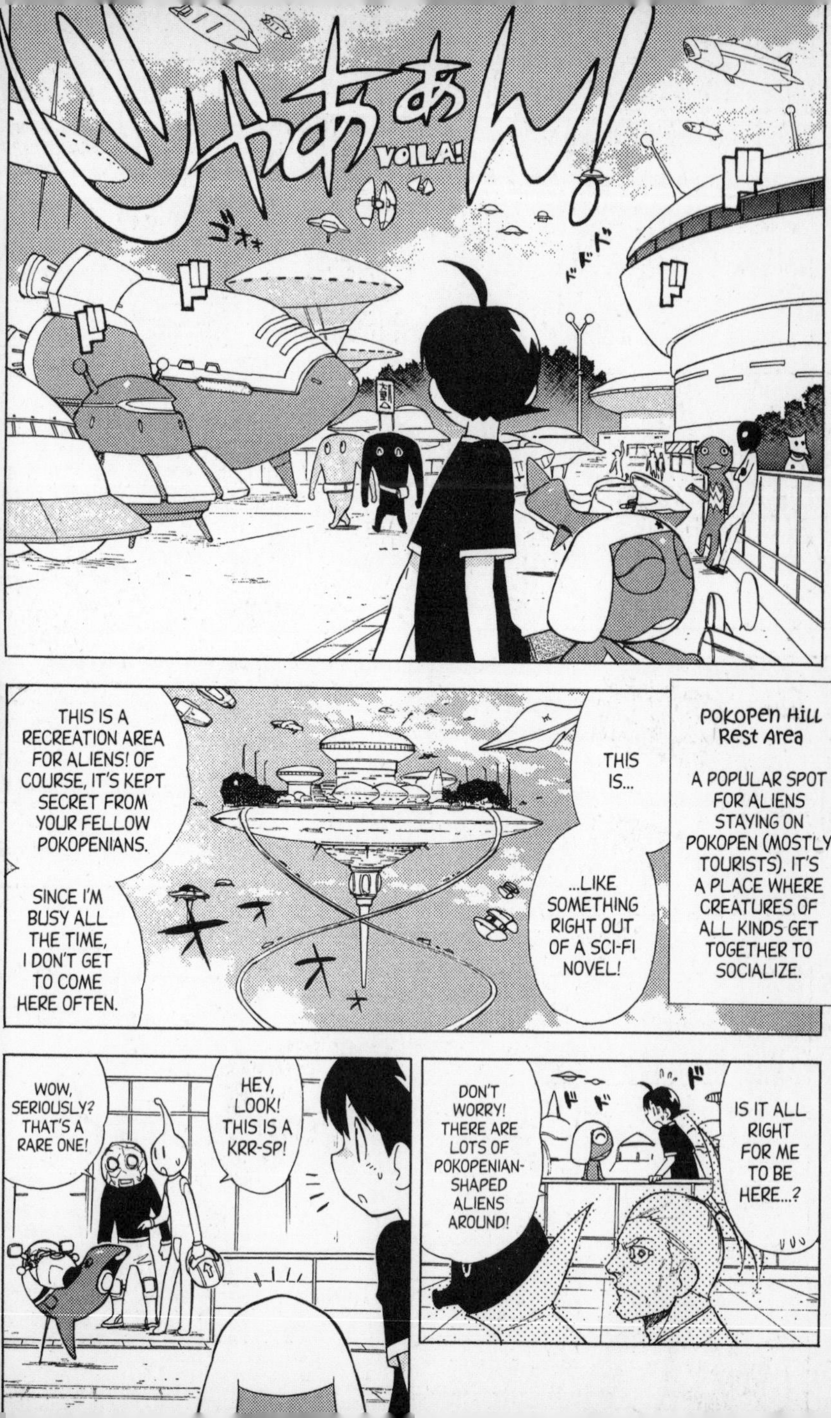
VOILA!
Pokopen Hill Rest Area
A POPULAR SPOT FOR ALIENS STAYING ON POKOPEN (MOSTLY TOURISTS). IT'S A PLACE WHERE CREATURES OF ALL KINDS GET TOGETHER TO SOCIALIZE.
THIS IS...
...LIKE SOMETHING RIGHT OUT OF A SCI-FI NOVEL!
THIS IS A RECREATION AREA FOR ALIENS! OF COURSE, IT'S KEPT SECRET FROM YOUR FELLOW POKOPENIANS.
SINCE I'M BUSY ALL THE TIME, I DON'T GET TO COME HERE OFTEN.
IS IT ALL RIGHT FOR ME TO BE HERE...?
DON'T WORRY! THERE ARE LOTS OF POKOPENIAN-SHAPED ALIENS AROUND!
HEY, LOOK! THIS IS A KRR-SP!
WOW, SERIOUSLY? THAT'S A RARE ONE!

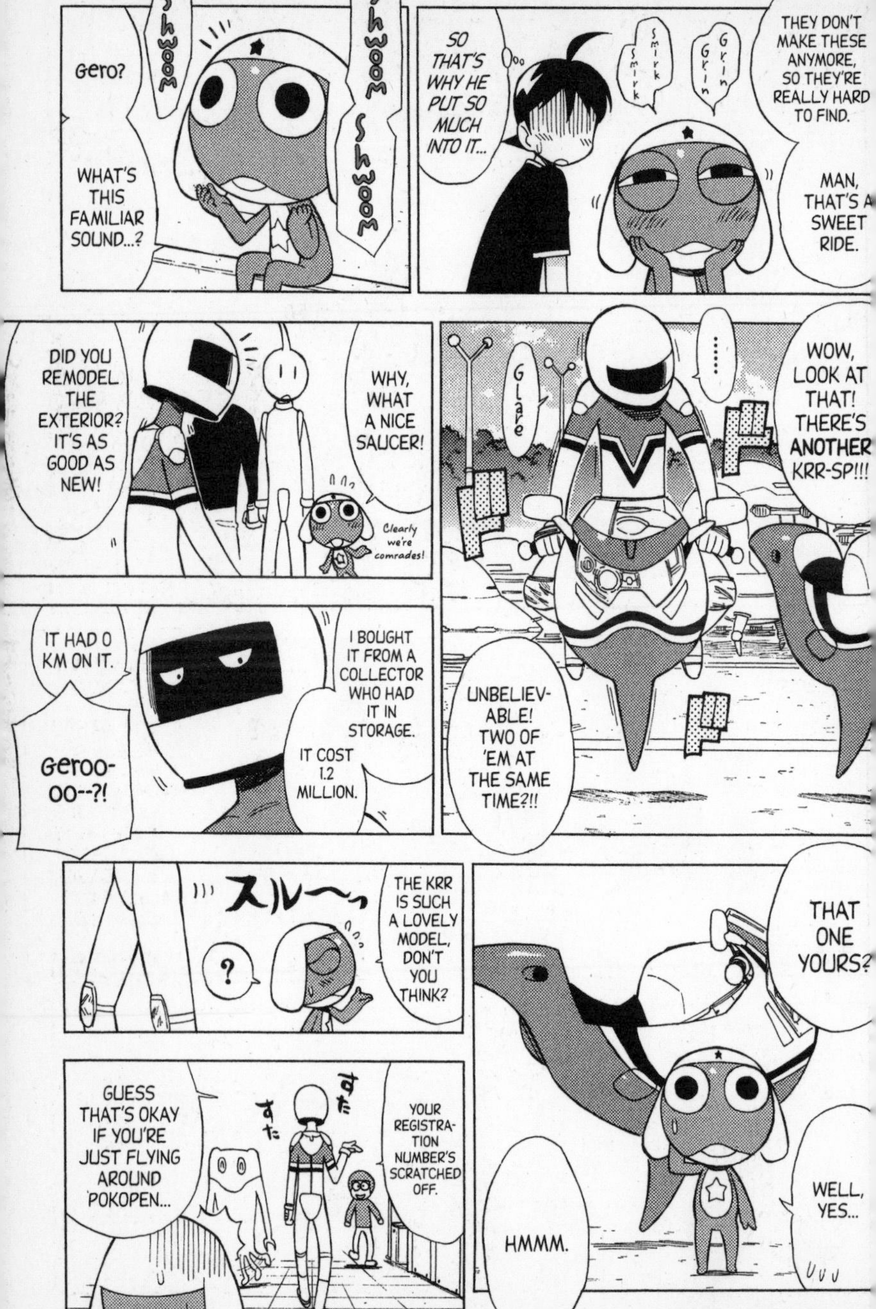
THEY DON'T MAKE THESE ANYMORE, SO THEY'RE REALLY HARD TO FIND.
MAN, THAT'S A SWEET RIDE.
Grin Grin
Smirk Smirk
SO THAT'S WHY HE PUT SO MUCH INTO IT...
Shwoom Shwoom
Shwoom
Gero?
WHAT'S THIS FAMILIAR SOUND...?
WOW, LOOK AT THAT! THERE'S ANOTHER KRR-SP!!!
......
Glare
UNBELIEV-ABLE! TWO OF 'EM AT THE SAME TIME?!!
DID YOU REMODEL THE EXTERIOR? IT'S AS GOOD AS NEW!
WHY, WHAT A NICE SAUCER!
Clearly we're comrades!
I BOUGHT IT FROM A COLLECTOR WHO HAD IT IN STORAGE.
IT COST 1.2 MILLION.
IT HAD 0 KM ON IT.
Geroo-oo--?!
THAT ONE YOURS?
WELL, YES...
HMMM.
THE KRR IS SUCH A LOVELY MODEL, DON'T YOU THINK?
スルー～っ
?
すた すた
YOUR REGISTRA-TION NUMBER'S SCRATCHED OFF.
GUESS THAT'S OKAY IF YOU'RE JUST FLYING AROUND POKOPEN...

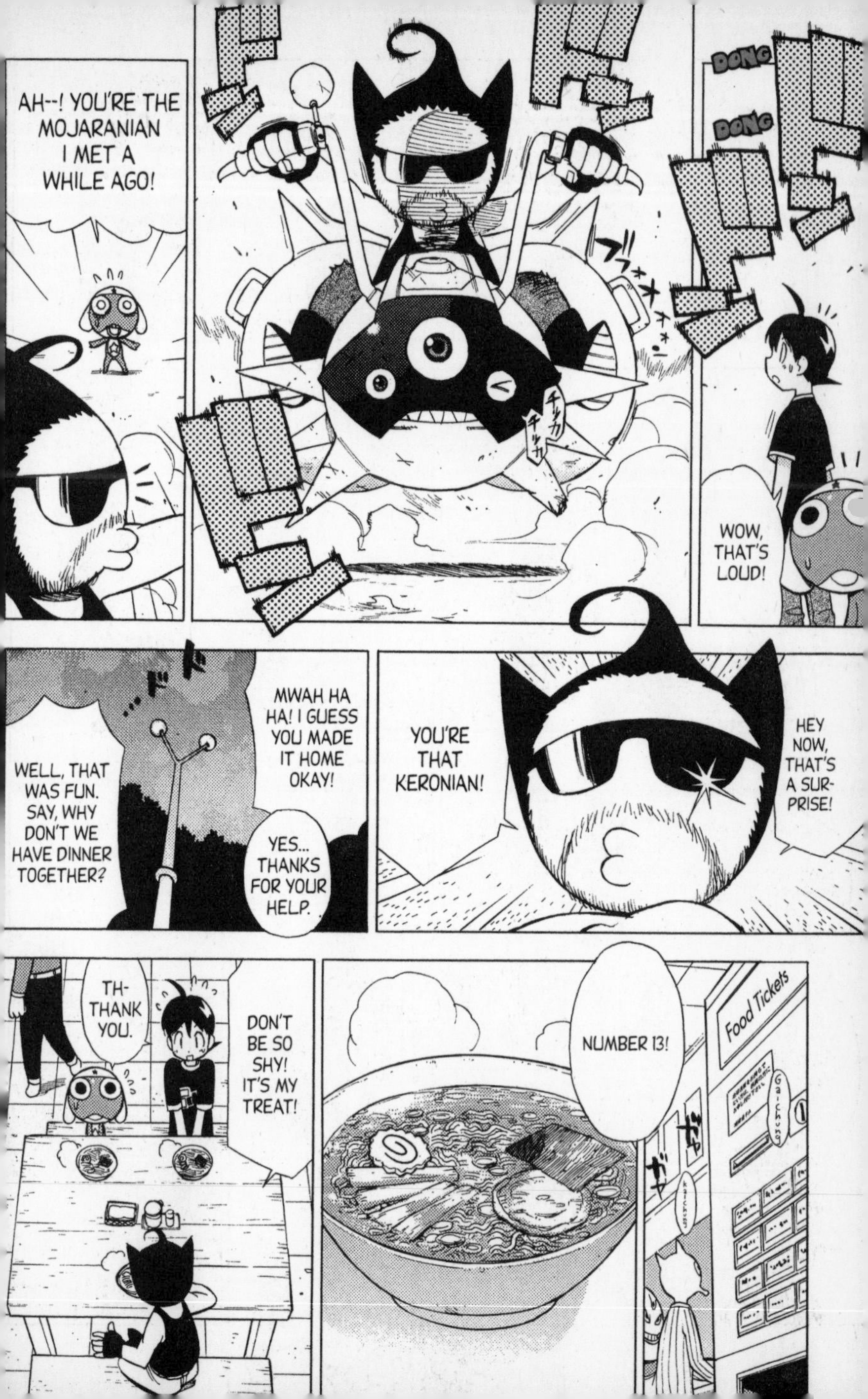
DONG
DONG
WOW, THAT'S LOUD!
AH--! YOU'RE THE MOJARANIAN I MET A WHILE AGO!
HEY NOW, THAT'S A SUR-PRISE!
YOU'RE THAT KERONIAN!
MWAH HA HA! I GUESS YOU MADE IT HOME OKAY!
YES... THANKS FOR YOUR HELP.
WELL, THAT WAS FUN. SAY, WHY DON'T WE HAVE DINNER TOGETHER?
Food Tickets
NUMBER 13!
DON'T BE SO SHY! IT'S MY TREAT!
TH-THANK YOU.

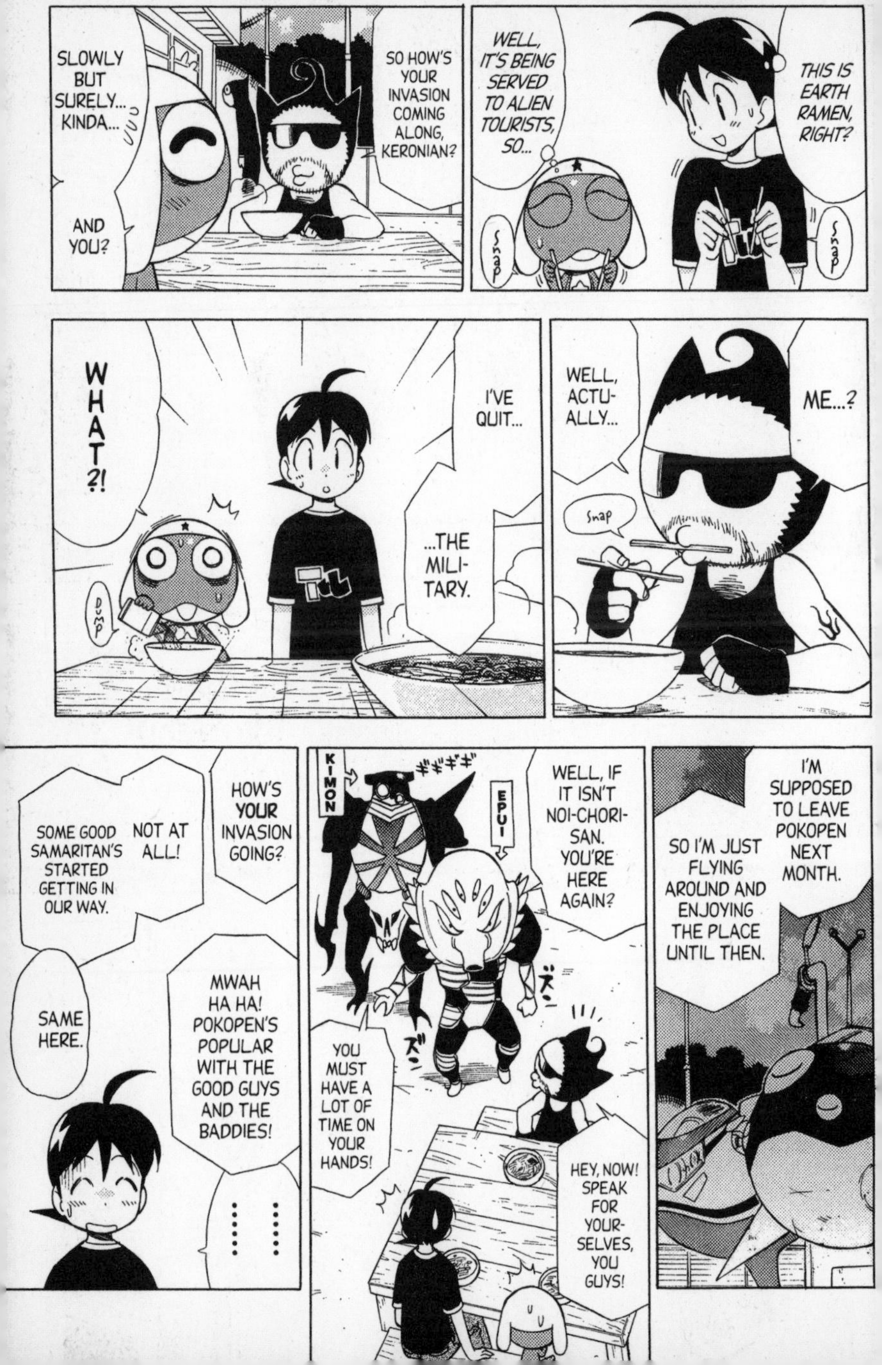
THIS IS EARTH RAMEN, RIGHT?
Snap
WELL, IT'S BEING SERVED TO ALIEN TOURISTS, SO...
Snap
SO HOW'S YOUR INVASION COMING ALONG, KERONIAN?
SLOWLY BUT SURELY... KINDA...
AND YOU?
ME...?
Snap
WELL, ACTU-ALLY...
I'VE QUIT...
...THE MILI-TARY.
WHAT?!
DUMP
I'M SUPPOSED TO LEAVE POKOPEN NEXT MONTH.
SO I'M JUST FLYING AROUND AND ENJOYING THE PLACE UNTIL THEN.
KIMON
EPUI
WELL, IF IT ISN'T NOI-CHORI-SAN. YOU'RE HERE AGAIN?
YOU MUST HAVE A LOT OF TIME ON YOUR HANDS!
HEY, NOW! SPEAK FOR YOUR-SELVES, YOU GUYS!
HOW'S YOUR INVASION GOING?
NOT AT ALL!
SOME GOOD SAMARITAN'S STARTED GETTING IN OUR WAY.
MWAH HA HA! POKOPEN'S POPULAR WITH THE GOOD GUYS AND THE BADDIES!
SAME HERE.
......
......

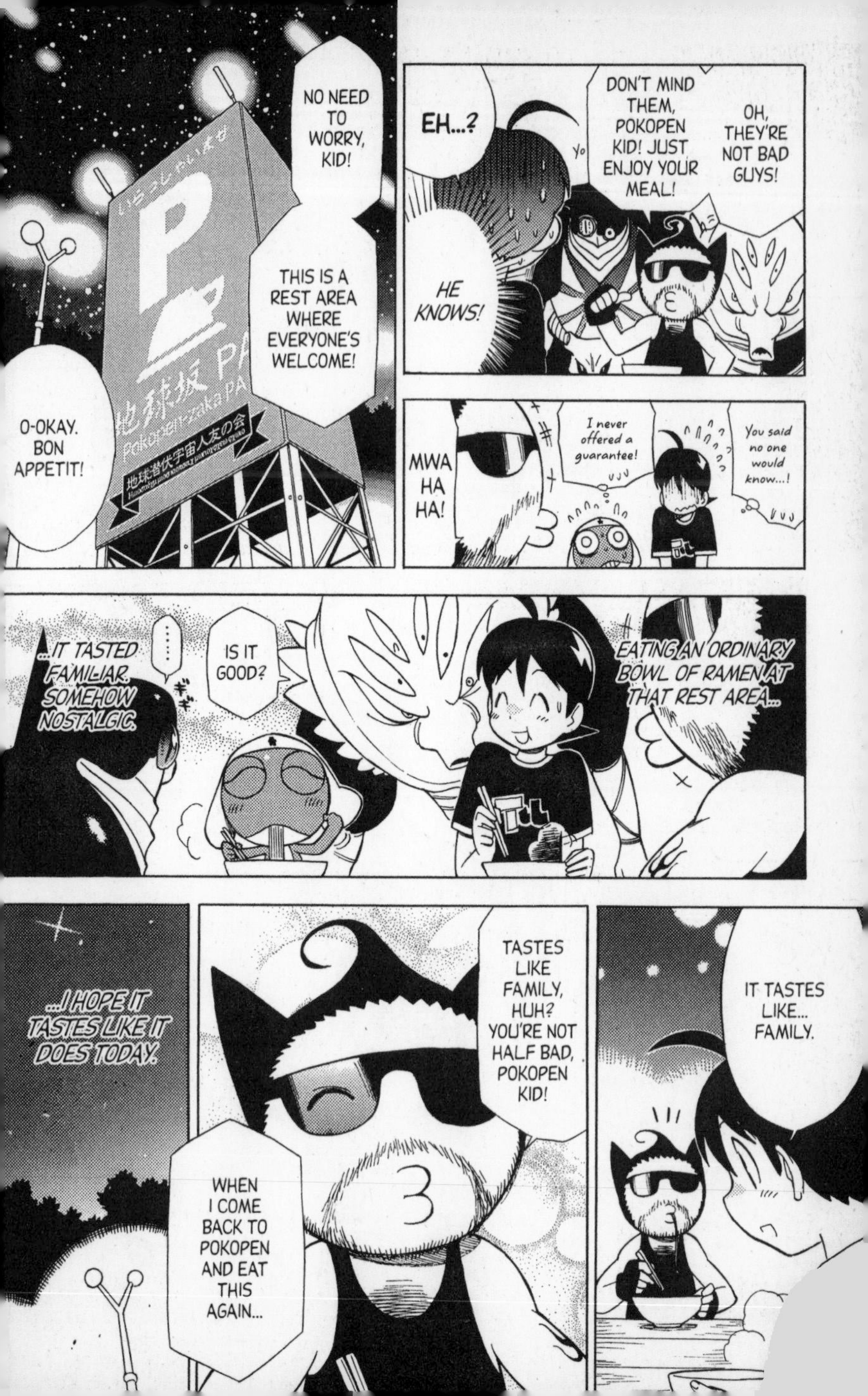
OH, THEY'RE NOT BAD GUYS!
DON'T MIND THEM, POKOPEN KID! JUST ENJOY YOUR MEAL!
Yo
EH...?
HE KNOWS!
You said no one would know...!
I never offered a guarantee!
MWA HA HA!
NO NEED TO WORRY, KID!
THIS IS A REST AREA WHERE EVERYONE'S WELCOME!
いらっしゃいませ
P
地球坂 PA
Pokopen-zaka PA
地球潜伏宇宙人友の会
O-OKAY. BON APPETIT!
EATING AN ORDINARY BOWL OF RAMEN AT THAT REST AREA...
IS IT GOOD?
ギギ
......
...IT TASTED FAMILIAR. SOMEHOW NOSTALGIC.
IT TASTES LIKE... FAMILY.
TASTES LIKE FAMILY, HUH? YOU'RE NOT HALF BAD, POKOPEN KID!
WHEN I COME BACK TO POKOPEN AND EAT THIS AGAIN...
...I HOPE IT TASTES LIKE IT DOES TODAY.

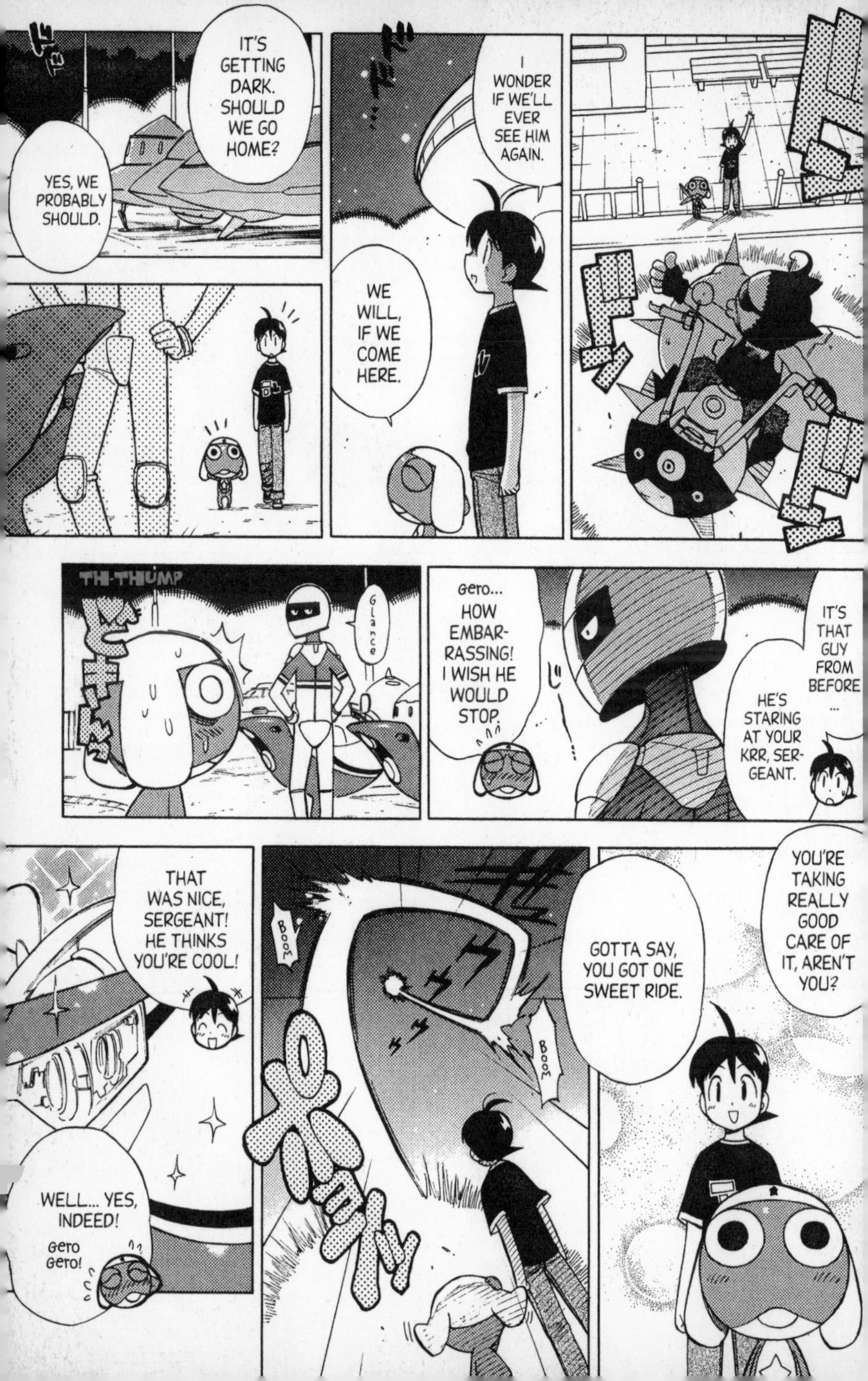
I WONDER IF WE'LL EVER SEE HIM AGAIN.
WE WILL, IF WE COME HERE.
IT'S GETTING DARK. SHOULD WE GO HOME?
YES, WE PROBABLY SHOULD.
IT'S THAT GUY FROM BEFORE ...
HE'S STARING AT YOUR KRR, SERGEANT.
Gero... HOW EMBARRASSING! I WISH HE WOULD STOP.
TH-THUMP
Glance
YOU'RE TAKING REALLY GOOD CARE OF IT, AREN'T YOU?
GOTTA SAY, YOU GOT ONE SWEET RIDE.
BOOM
BOOM
THAT WAS NICE, SERGEANT! HE THINKS YOU'RE COOL!
WELL... YES, INDEED!
Gero Gero!

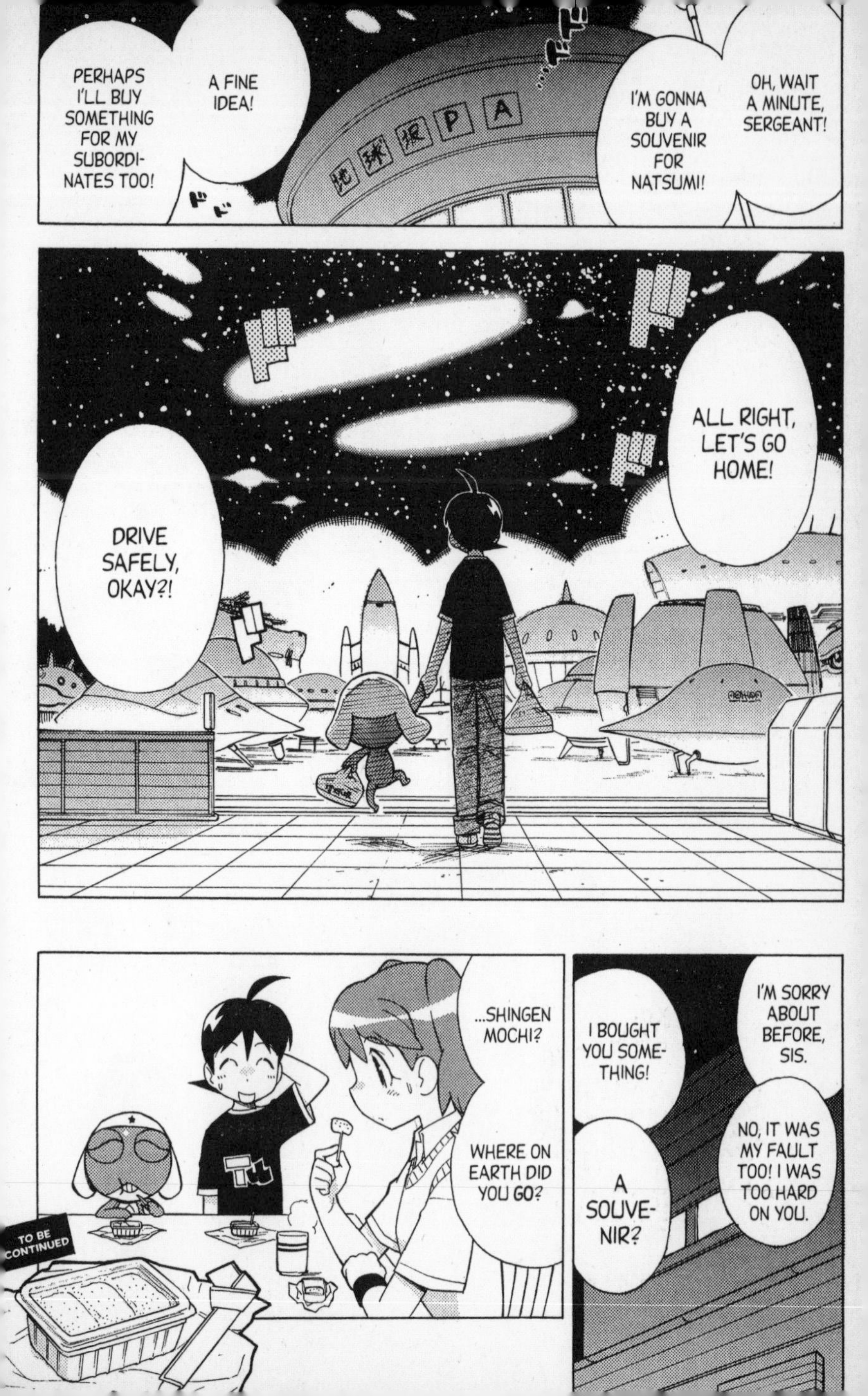
OH, WAIT A MINUTE, SERGEANT!
I'M GONNA BUY A SOUVENIR FOR NATSUMI!
A FINE IDEA!
PERHAPS I'LL BUY SOMETHING FOR MY SUBORDI-NATES TOO!
ALL RIGHT, LET'S GO HOME!
DRIVE SAFELY, OKAY?!
I'M SORRY ABOUT BEFORE, SIS.
NO, IT WAS MY FAULT TOO! I WAS TOO HARD ON YOU.
I BOUGHT YOU SOME-THING!
A SOUVE-NIR?
...SHINGEN MOCHI?
WHERE ON EARTH DID YOU GO?
TO BE CONTINUED

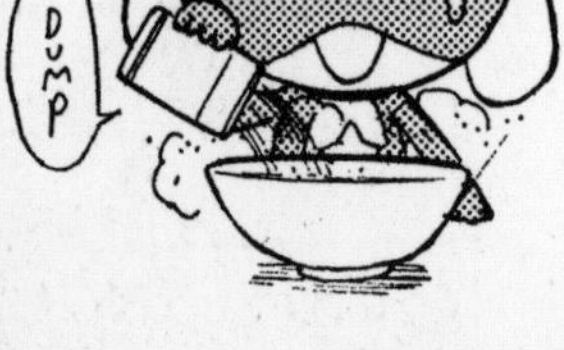
DUMP

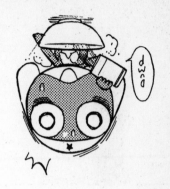

ENCOUNTER CXXXI
THE ULTIMATE SPIRIT PHOTO CONTEST?!

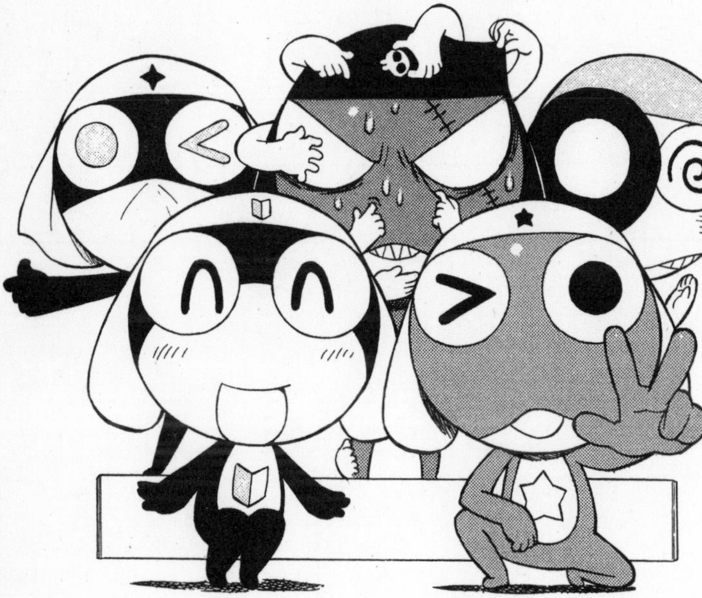

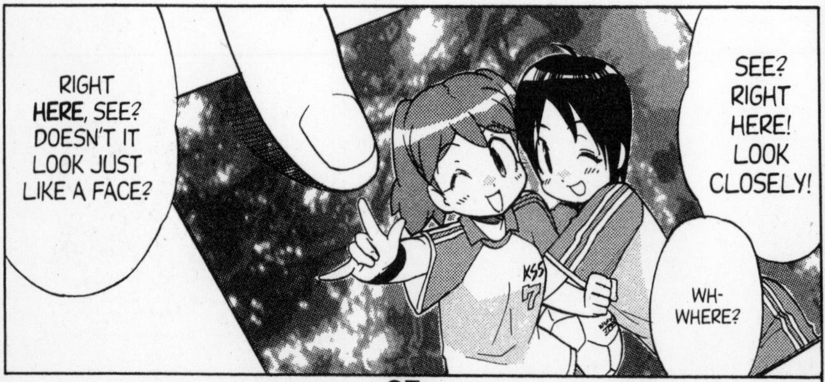
SEE? RIGHT HERE! LOOK CLOSELY!
RIGHT HERE, SEE? DOESN'T IT LOOK JUST LIKE A FACE?
WH- WHERE?

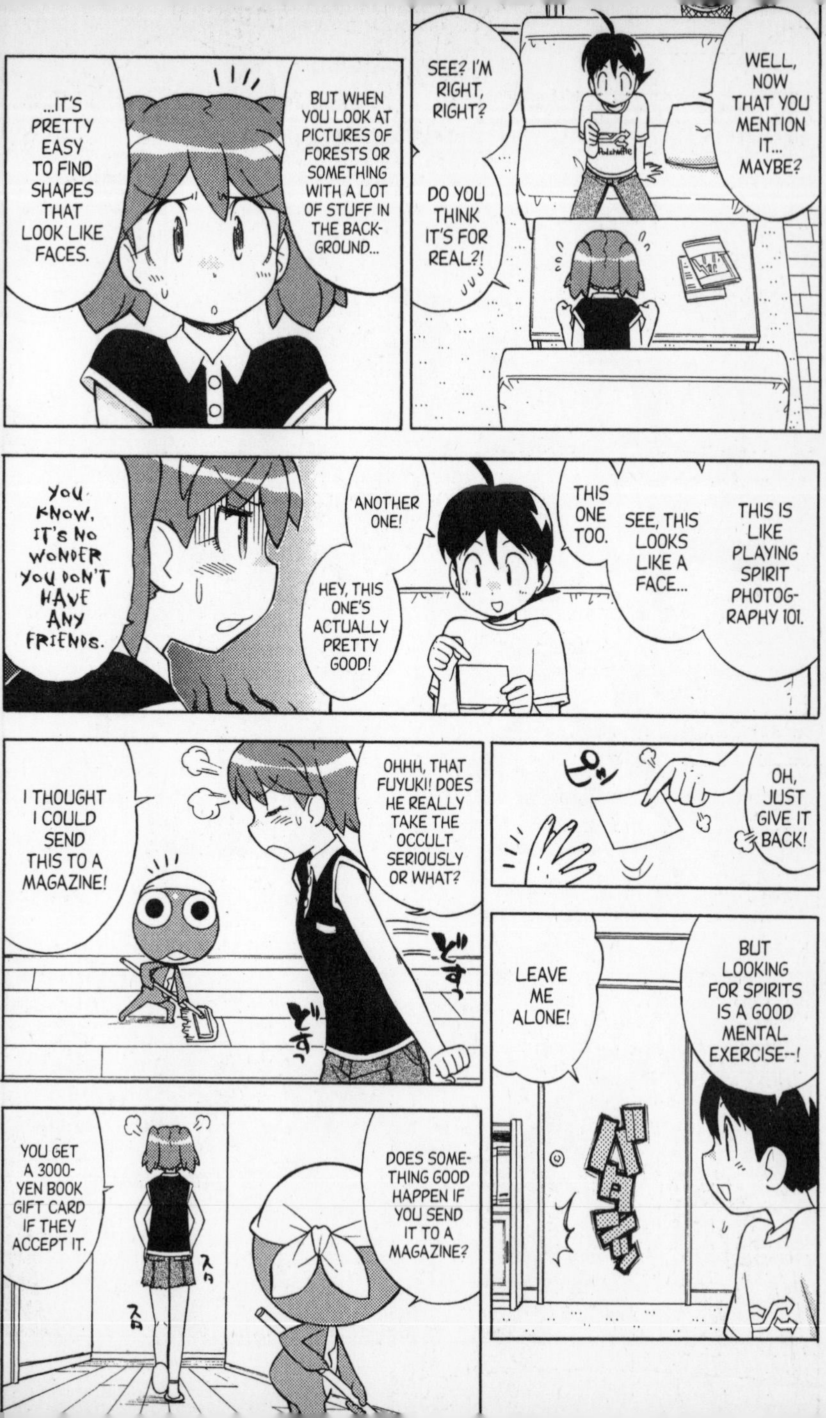
WELL, NOW THAT YOU MENTION IT... MAYBE?
SEE? I'M RIGHT, RIGHT?
DO YOU THINK IT'S FOR REAL?!
BUT WHEN YOU LOOK AT PICTURES OF FORESTS OR SOMETHING WITH A LOT OF STUFF IN THE BACK-GROUND...
...IT'S PRETTY EASY TO FIND SHAPES THAT LOOK LIKE FACES.
THIS IS LIKE PLAYING SPIRIT PHOTOG-RAPHY 101.
SEE, THIS LOOKS LIKE A FACE...
THIS ONE TOO.
ANOTHER ONE!
HEY, THIS ONE'S ACTUALLY PRETTY GOOD!
YOU KNOW, IT'S NO WONDER YOU DON'T HAVE ANY FRIENDS.
OH, JUST GIVE IT BACK!
OHHH, THAT FUYUKI! DOES HE REALLY TAKE THE OCCULT SERIOUSLY OR WHAT?
I THOUGHT I COULD SEND THIS TO A MAGAZINE!
BUT LOOKING FOR SPIRITS IS A GOOD MENTAL EXERCISE--!
LEAVE ME ALONE!
DOES SOME-THING GOOD HAPPEN IF YOU SEND IT TO A MAGAZINE?
YOU GET A 3000-YEN BOOK GIFT CARD IF THEY ACCEPT IT.

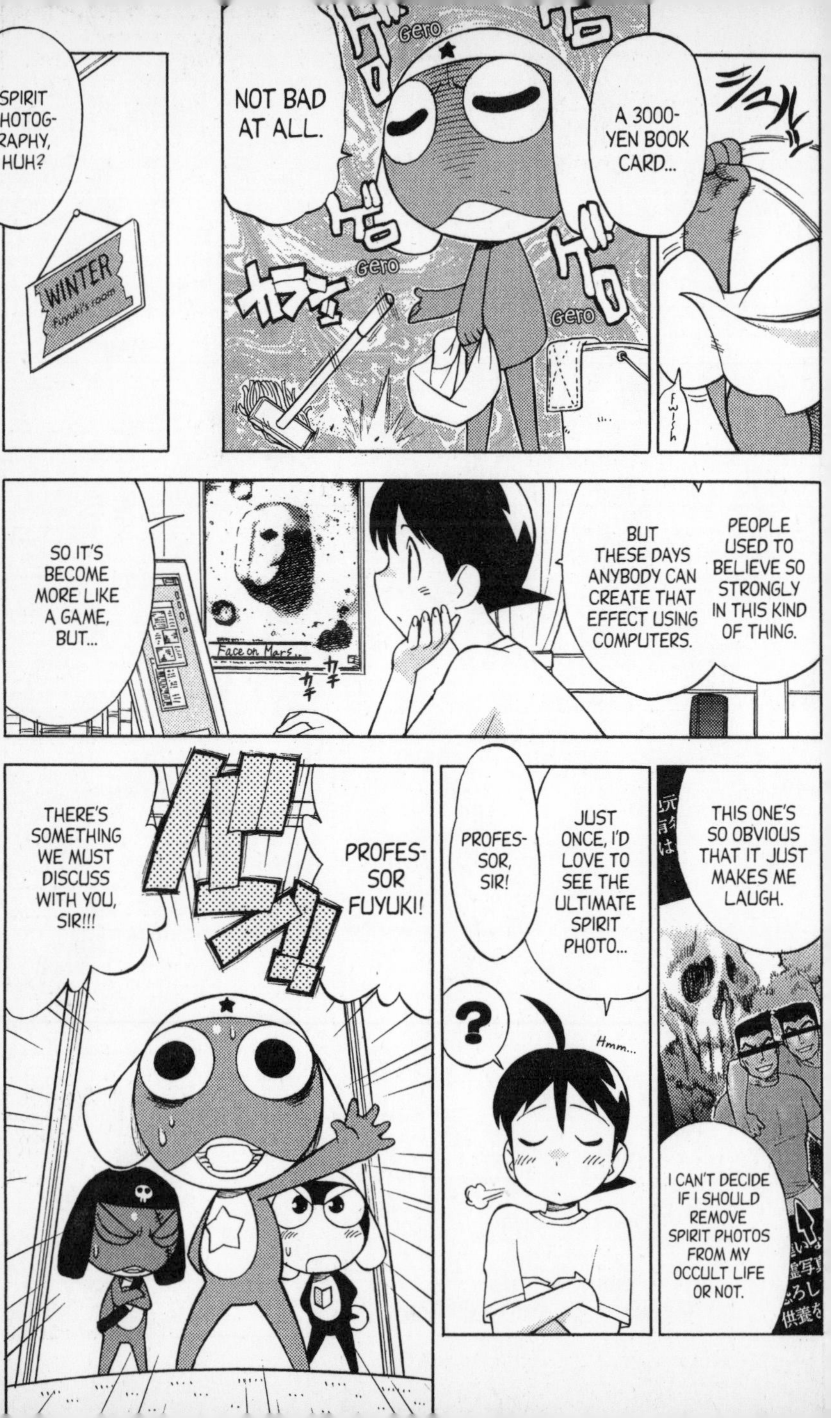
A 3000-
YEN BOOK
CARD...
Fwish
Gero
Gero
NOT BAD
AT ALL.
Gero
SPIRIT
PHOTOG-
RAPHY,
HUH?
WINTER
Fuyuki's room
PEOPLE
USED TO
BELIEVE SO
STRONGLY
IN THIS KIND
OF THING.
BUT
THESE DAYS
ANYBODY CAN
CREATE THAT
EFFECT USING
COMPUTERS.
Face on Mars...
SO IT'S
BECOME
MORE LIKE
A GAME,
BUT...
THIS ONE'S
SO OBVIOUS
THAT IT JUST
MAKES ME
LAUGH.
I CAN'T DECIDE
IF I SHOULD
REMOVE
SPIRIT PHOTOS
FROM MY
OCCULT LIFE
OR NOT.
JUST
ONCE, I'D
LOVE TO
SEE THE
ULTIMATE
SPIRIT
PHOTO...
PROFES-
SOR,
SIR!
?
Hmm...
PROFES-
SOR
FUYUKI!
THERE'S
SOMETHING
WE MUST
DISCUSS
WITH YOU,
SIR!!!

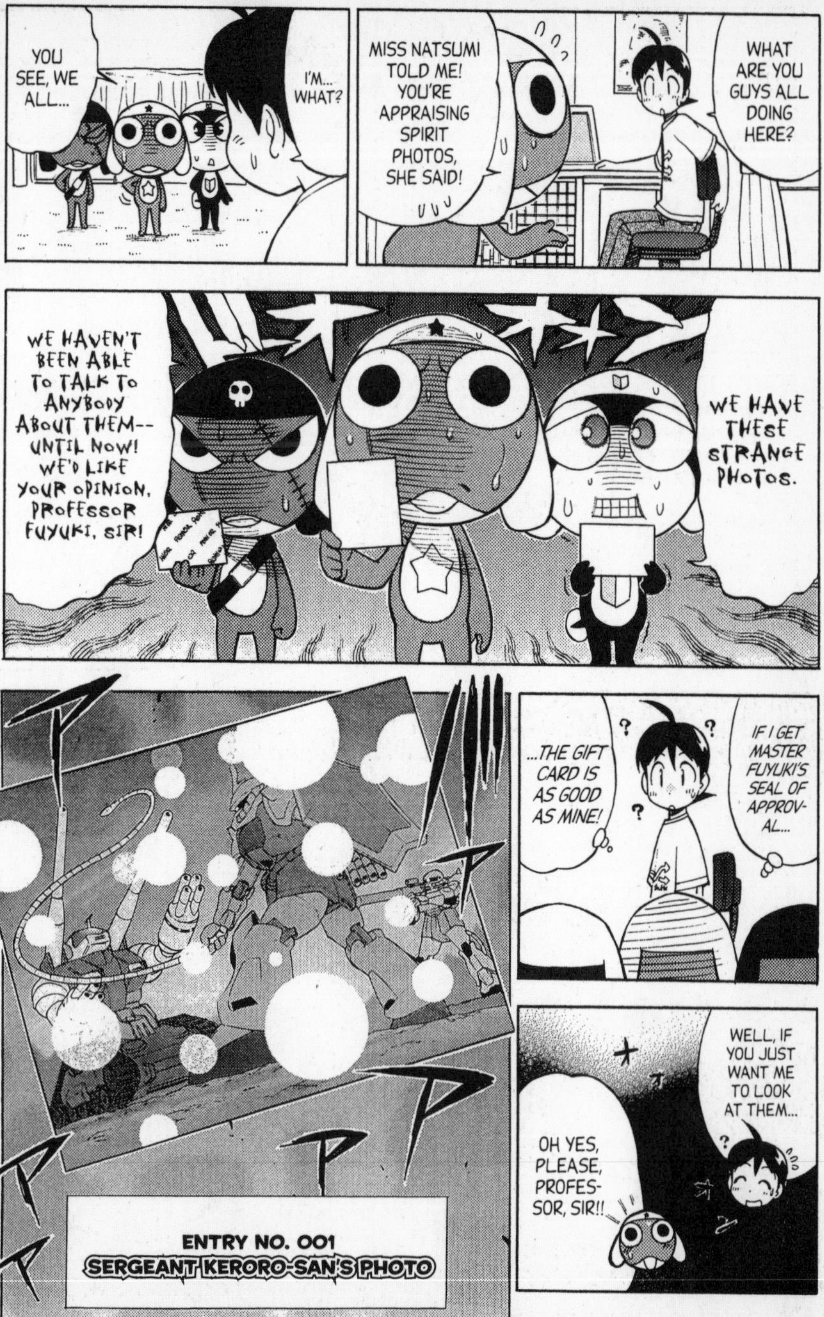
WHAT ARE YOU GUYS ALL DOING HERE?
MISS NATSUMI TOLD ME! YOU'RE APPRAISING SPIRIT PHOTOS, SHE SAID!
I'M... WHAT?
YOU SEE, WE ALL...
WE HAVE THESE STRANGE PHOTOS.
WE HAVEN'T BEEN ABLE TO TALK TO ANYBODY ABOUT THEM-- UNTIL NOW! WE'D LIKE YOUR OPINION, PROFESSOR FUYUKI, SIR!
IF I GET MASTER FUYUKI'S SEAL OF APPROV-AL...
...THE GIFT CARD IS AS GOOD AS MINE!
WELL, IF YOU JUST WANT ME TO LOOK AT THEM...
OH YES, PLEASE, PROFES-SOR, SIR!!
ENTRY NO. 001
SERGEANT KERORO-SAN'S PHOTO

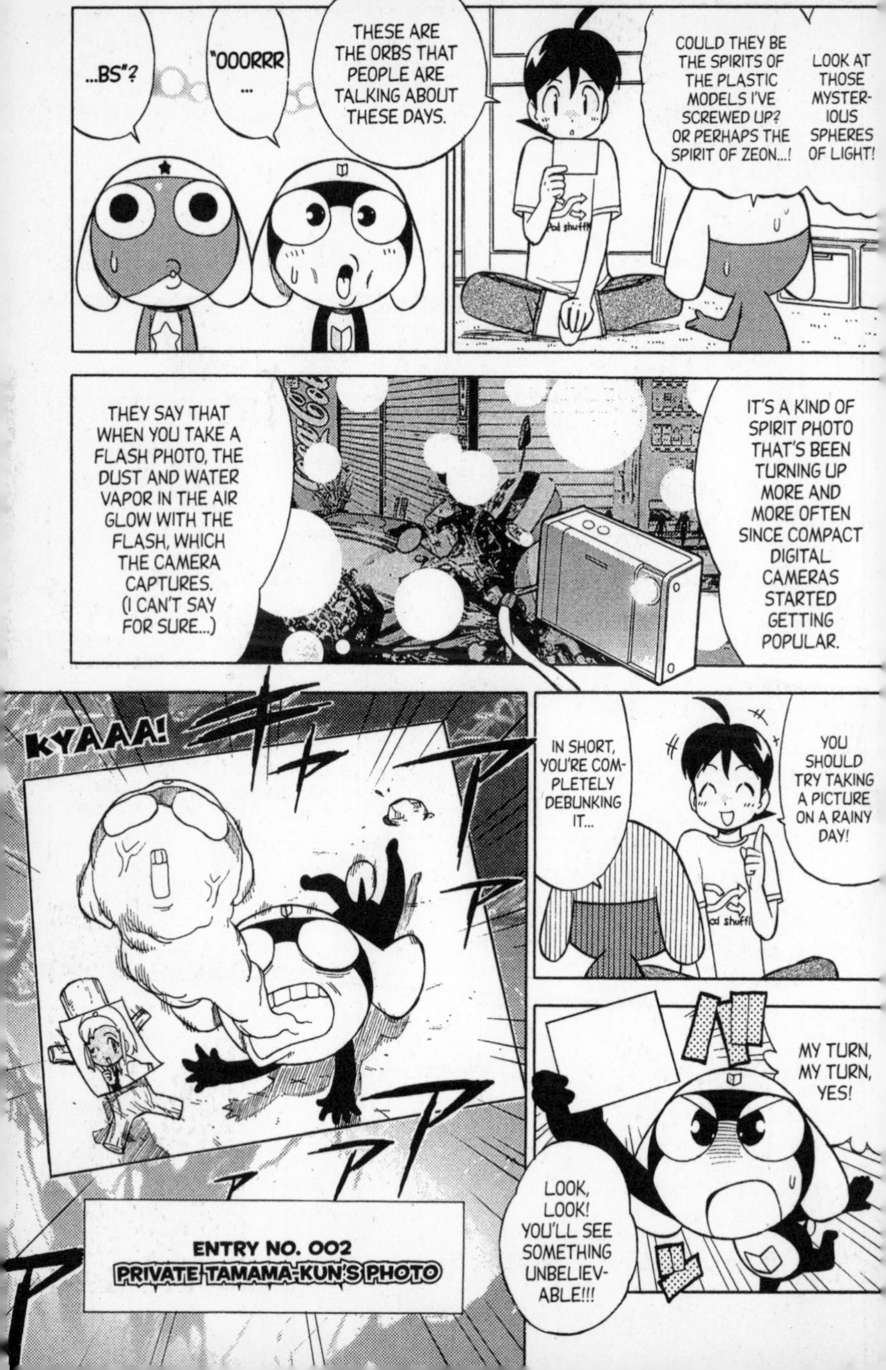
LOOK AT THOSE MYSTER-IOUS SPHERES OF LIGHT!
COULD THEY BE THE SPIRITS OF THE PLASTIC MODELS I'VE SCREWED UP? OR PERHAPS THE SPIRIT OF ZEON...!
THESE ARE THE ORBS THAT PEOPLE ARE TALKING ABOUT THESE DAYS.
"OOORRR ...
...BS"?
IT'S A KIND OF SPIRIT PHOTO THAT'S BEEN TURNING UP MORE AND MORE OFTEN SINCE COMPACT DIGITAL CAMERAS STARTED GETTING POPULAR.
THEY SAY THAT WHEN YOU TAKE A FLASH PHOTO, THE DUST AND WATER VAPOR IN THE AIR GLOW WITH THE FLASH, WHICH THE CAMERA CAPTURES. (I CAN'T SAY FOR SURE...)
YOU SHOULD TRY TAKING A PICTURE ON A RAINY DAY!
IN SHORT, YOU'RE COM-PLETELY DEBUNKING IT...
MY TURN, MY TURN, YES!
LOOK, LOOK! YOU'LL SEE SOMETHING UNBELIEV-ABLE!!!
KYAAA!
ENTRY NO. 002
PRIVATE TAMAMA-KUN'S PHOTO

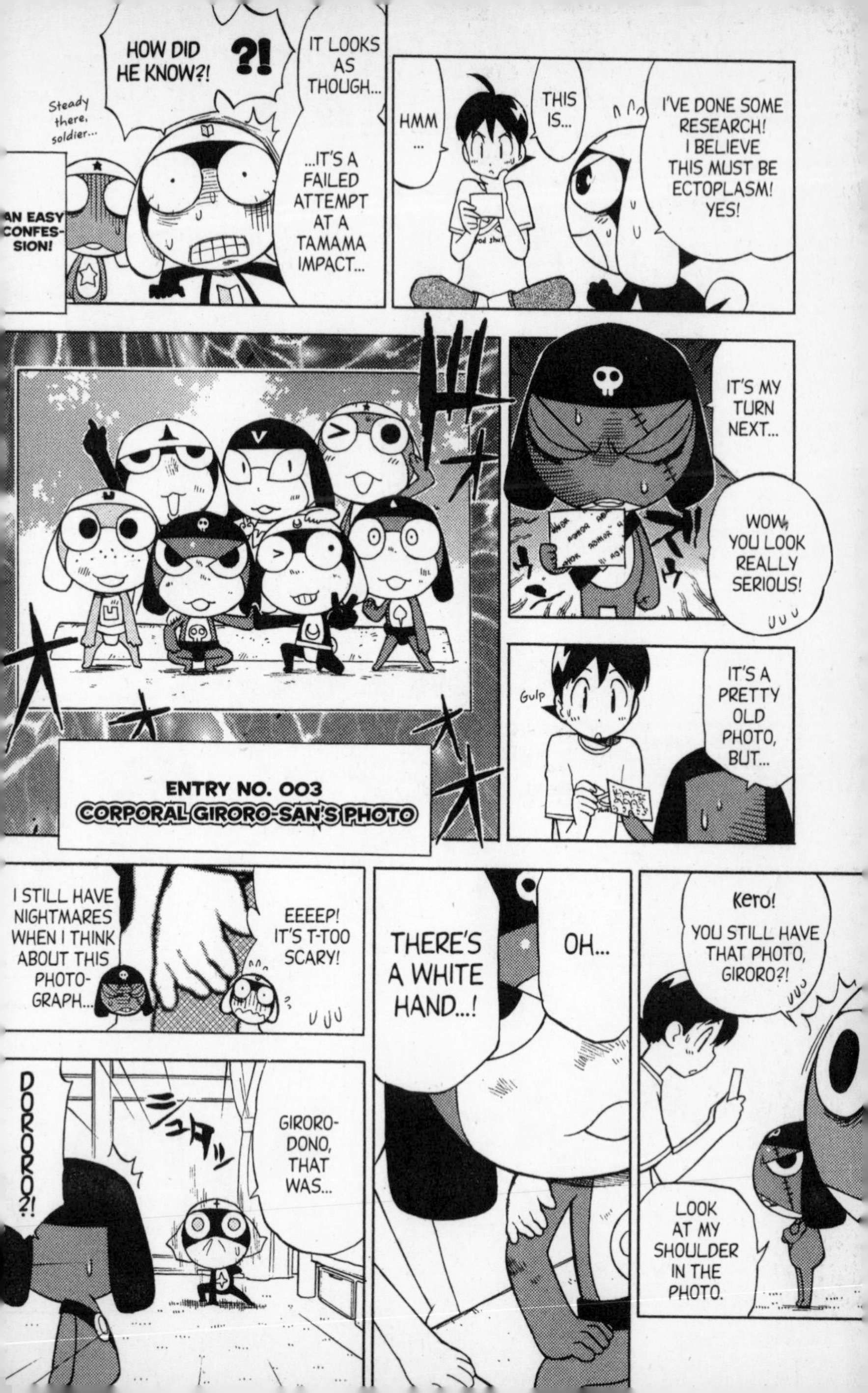

I'VE DONE SOME RESEARCH! I BELIEVE THIS MUST BE ECTOPLASM! YES!
THIS IS...
HMM...
IT LOOKS AS THOUGH...
...IT'S A FAILED ATTEMPT AT A TAMAMA IMPACT...
HOW DID HE KNOW?!
?!
Steady there, soldier...
AN EASY CONFESSION!
IT'S MY TURN NEXT...
WOW, YOU LOOK REALLY SERIOUS!
IT'S A PRETTY OLD PHOTO, BUT...
Gulp
ENTRY NO. 003
CORPORAL GIRORO-SAN'S PHOTO
Kero!
YOU STILL HAVE THAT PHOTO, GIRORO?!
LOOK AT MY SHOULDER IN THE PHOTO.
OH...
THERE'S A WHITE HAND...!
EEEEP! IT'S T-TOO SCARY!
I STILL HAVE NIGHTMARES WHEN I THINK ABOUT THIS PHOTOGRAPH...
GIRORO-DONO, THAT WAS...
DORORO?!

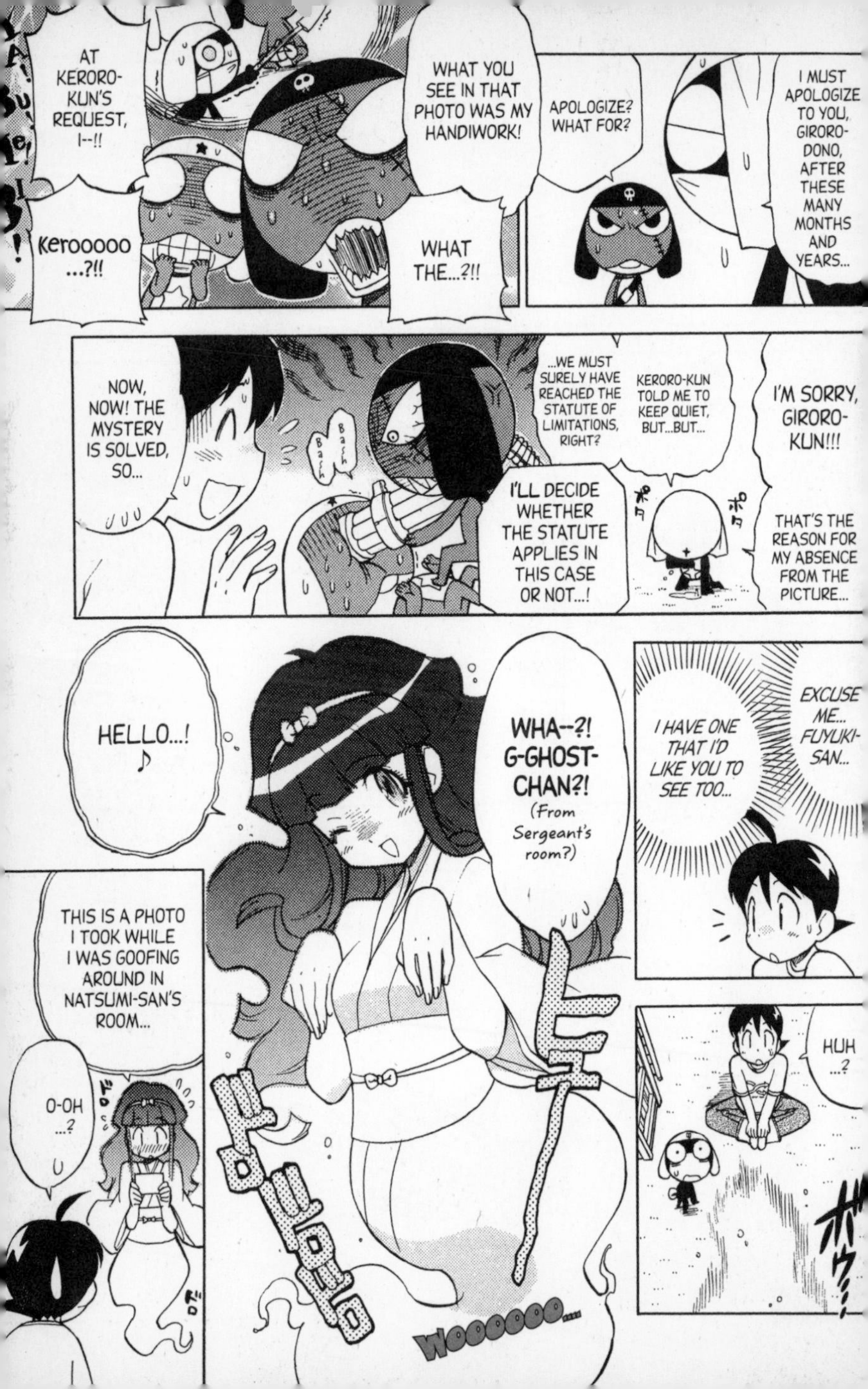
I MUST APOLOGIZE TO YOU, GIRORO-DONO, AFTER THESE MANY MONTHS AND YEARS...
APOLOGIZE? WHAT FOR?
WHAT YOU SEE IN THAT PHOTO WAS MY HANDIWORK!
WHAT THE...?!!
AT KERORO-KUN'S REQUEST, I--!!
Kerooooo...?!!
I'M SORRY, GIRORO-KUN!!!
THAT'S THE REASON FOR MY ABSENCE FROM THE PICTURE...
KERORO-KUN TOLD ME TO KEEP QUIET, BUT...BUT...
...WE MUST SURELY HAVE REACHED THE STATUTE OF LIMITATIONS, RIGHT?
I'LL DECIDE WHETHER THE STATUTE APPLIES IN THIS CASE OR NOT...!
Bash Bash
NOW, NOW! THE MYSTERY IS SOLVED, SO...
EXCUSE ME... FUYUKI-SAN...
I HAVE ONE THAT I'D LIKE YOU TO SEE TOO...
HUH...?
WHA--?! G-GHOST-CHAN?!
(From Sergeant's room?)
HELLO...! ♪
THIS IS A PHOTO I TOOK WHILE I WAS GOOFING AROUND IN NATSUMI-SAN'S ROOM...
O-OH...?
WOOOOOO...

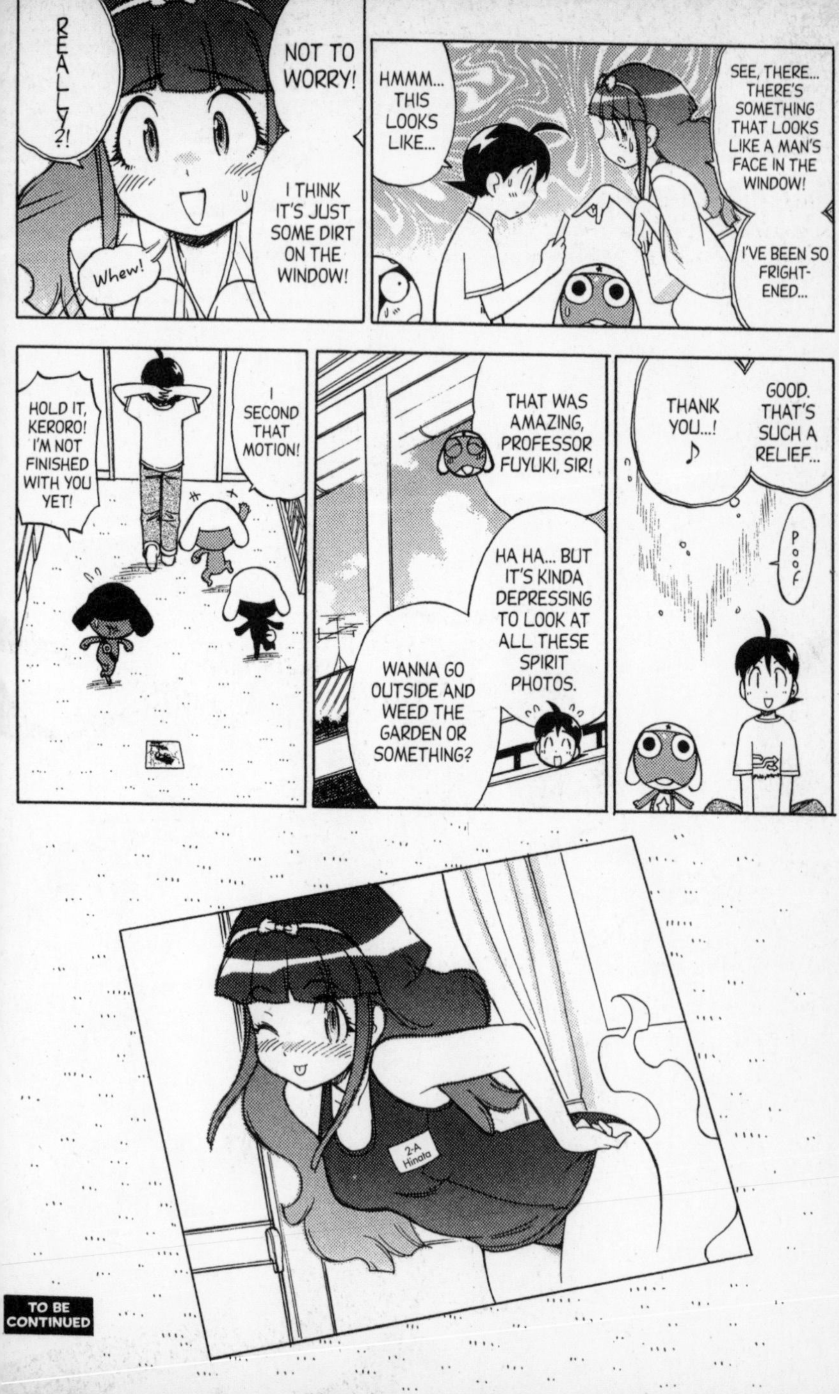
SEE, THERE... THERE'S SOMETHING THAT LOOKS LIKE A MAN'S FACE IN THE WINDOW!
I'VE BEEN SO FRIGHT-ENED...
HMMM... THIS LOOKS LIKE...
NOT TO WORRY!
I THINK IT'S JUST SOME DIRT ON THE WINDOW!
REALLY?!
Whew!
GOOD. THAT'S SUCH A RELIEF...
THANK YOU...! ♪
Poof
THAT WAS AMAZING, PROFESSOR FUYUKI, SIR!
HA HA... BUT IT'S KINDA DEPRESSING TO LOOK AT ALL THESE SPIRIT PHOTOS.
WANNA GO OUTSIDE AND WEED THE GARDEN OR SOMETHING?
I SECOND THAT MOTION!
HOLD IT, KERORO! I'M NOT FINISHED WITH YOU YET!
2-A Hinata
TO BE CONTINUED

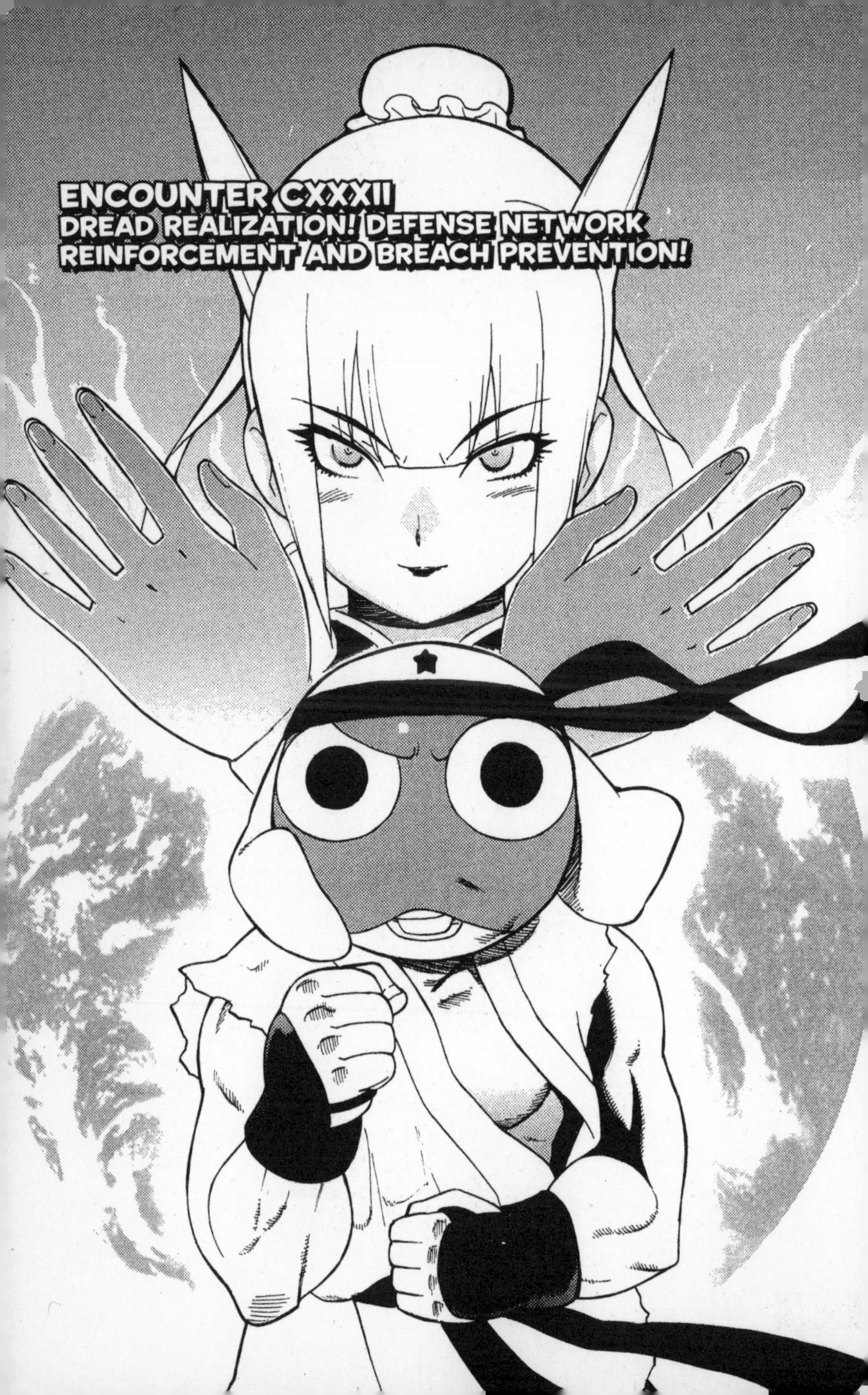
ENCOUNTER CXXXII
DREAD REALIZATION! DEFENSE NETWORK REINFORCEMENT AND BREACH PREVENTION!

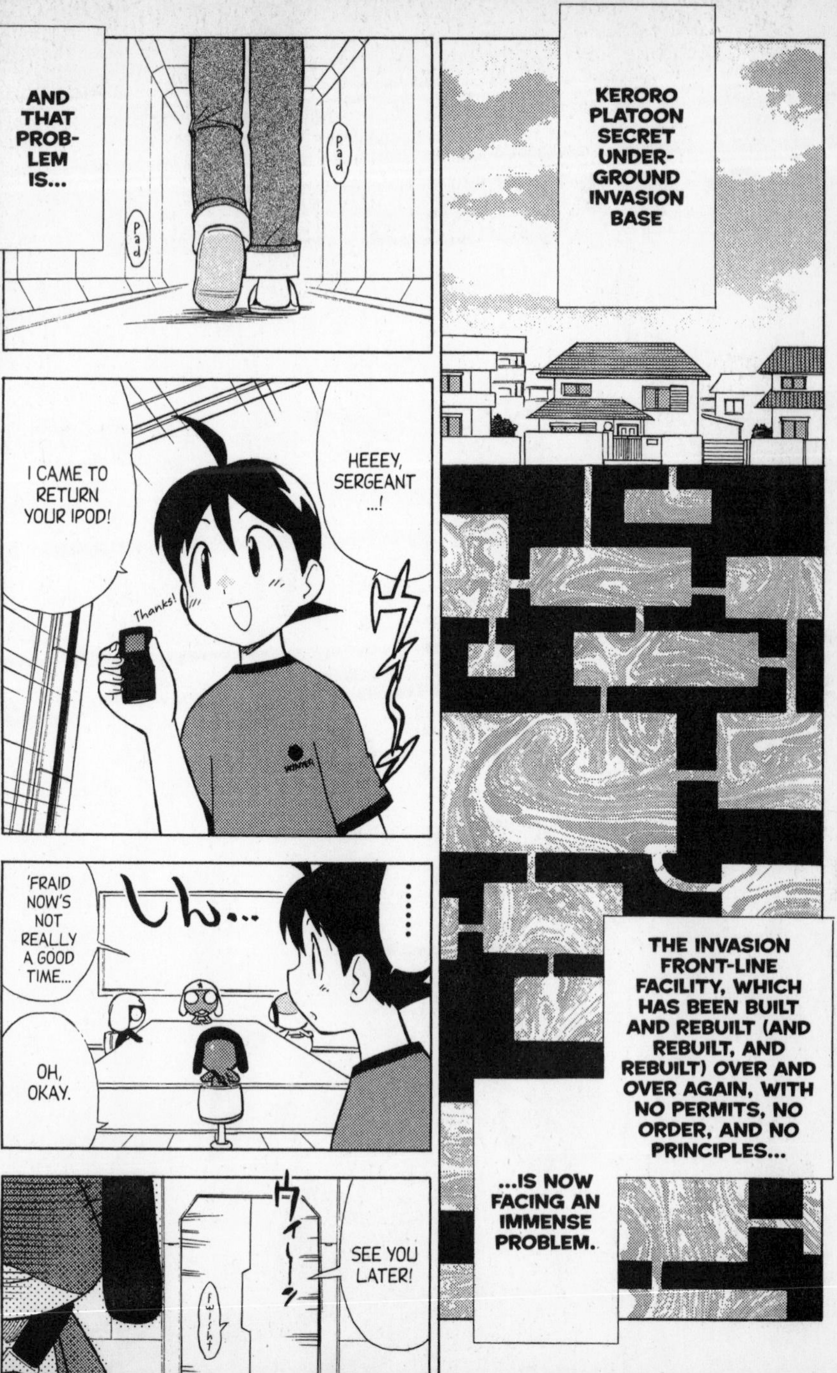
KERORO PLATOON SECRET UNDER-GROUND INVASION BASE
THE INVASION FRONT-LINE FACILITY, WHICH HAS BEEN BUILT AND REBUILT (AND REBUILT, AND REBUILT) OVER AND OVER AGAIN, WITH NO PERMITS, NO ORDER, AND NO PRINCIPLES...
...IS NOW FACING AN IMMENSE PROBLEM.
AND THAT PROB-LEM IS...
Pad
Pad
HEEEY, SERGEANT ...!
I CAME TO RETURN YOUR IPOD!
Thanks!
......
しん...
'FRAID NOW'S NOT REALLY A GOOD TIME...
OH, OKAY.
ウィーッ
SEE YOU LATER!
Fwisht

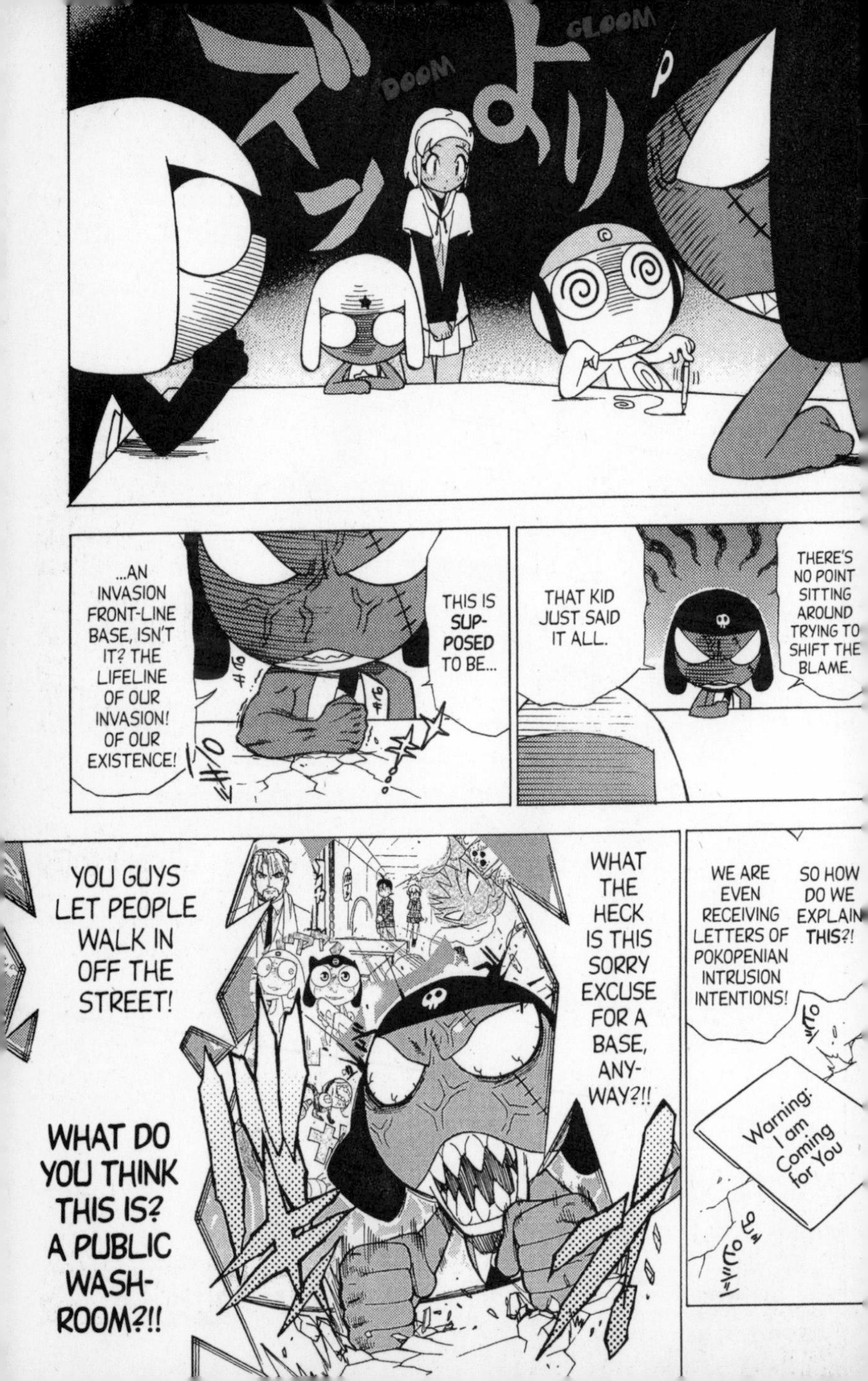
GLOOM
DOOM
THERE'S NO POINT SITTING AROUND TRYING TO SHIFT THE BLAME.
THAT KID JUST SAID IT ALL.
THIS IS SUP-POSED TO BE...
...AN INVASION FRONT-LINE BASE, ISN'T IT? THE LIFELINE OF OUR INVASION! OF OUR EXISTENCE!
SO HOW DO WE EXPLAIN THIS?!
WE ARE EVEN RECEIVING LETTERS OF POKOPENIAN INTRUSION INTENTIONS!
Warning: I am Coming for You
WHAT THE HECK IS THIS SORRY EXCUSE FOR A BASE, ANY-WAY?!!
YOU GUYS LET PEOPLE WALK IN OFF THE STREET!
WHAT DO YOU THINK THIS IS? A PUBLIC WASH-ROOM?!!

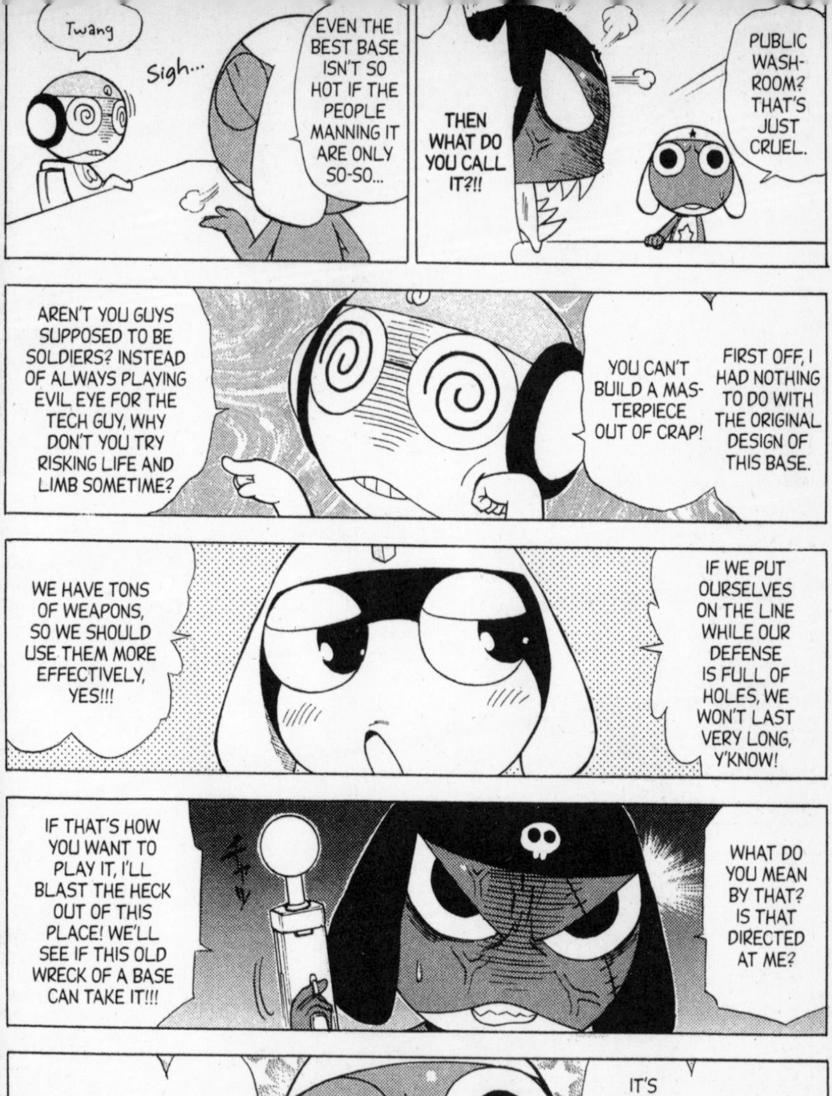
PUBLIC WASH-ROOM? THAT'S JUST CRUEL.
THEN WHAT DO YOU CALL IT?!!
Twang
Sigh...
EVEN THE BEST BASE ISN'T SO HOT IF THE PEOPLE MANNING IT ARE ONLY SO-SO...
FIRST OFF, I HAD NOTHING TO DO WITH THE ORIGINAL DESIGN OF THIS BASE.
YOU CAN'T BUILD A MAS-TERPIECE OUT OF CRAP!
AREN'T YOU GUYS SUPPOSED TO BE SOLDIERS? INSTEAD OF ALWAYS PLAYING EVIL EYE FOR THE TECH GUY, WHY DON'T YOU TRY RISKING LIFE AND LIMB SOMETIME?
IF WE PUT OURSELVES ON THE LINE WHILE OUR DEFENSE IS FULL OF HOLES, WE WON'T LAST VERY LONG, Y'KNOW!
WE HAVE TONS OF WEAPONS, SO WE SHOULD USE THEM MORE EFFECTIVELY, YES!!!
WHAT DO YOU MEAN BY THAT? IS THAT DIRECTED AT ME?
IF THAT'S HOW YOU WANT TO PLAY IT, I'LL BLAST THE HECK OUT OF THIS PLACE! WE'LL SEE IF THIS OLD WRECK OF A BASE CAN TAKE IT!!!
PERHAPS YOU'RE ALL FAILING TO GRASP MY VISION FOR THE BASE.
IT'S INNOVATIVE! CREATIVE! A SOLUTION WAITING FOR A PROBLEM!
TUNE IN TO IT, LADS!
METHINKS THE PROBLEMS LIE IN THE USERS, NOT THE BASE!

(HOW TO GET THE MOST OUT OF THIS PAGE.)

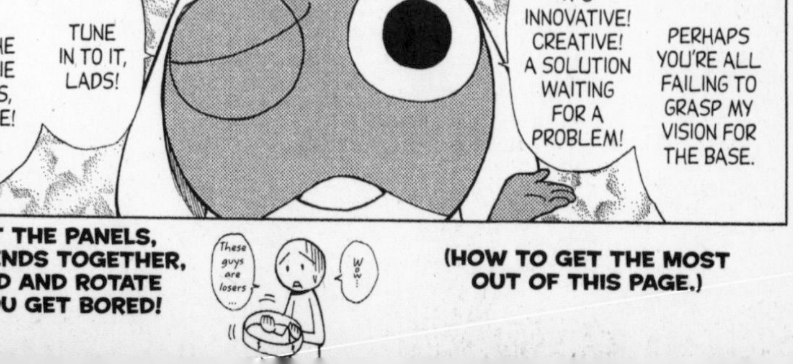
Wow...
These guys are losers...

CUT OUT THE PANELS, TAPE THE ENDS TOGETHER, AND READ AND ROTATE UNTIL YOU GET BORED!

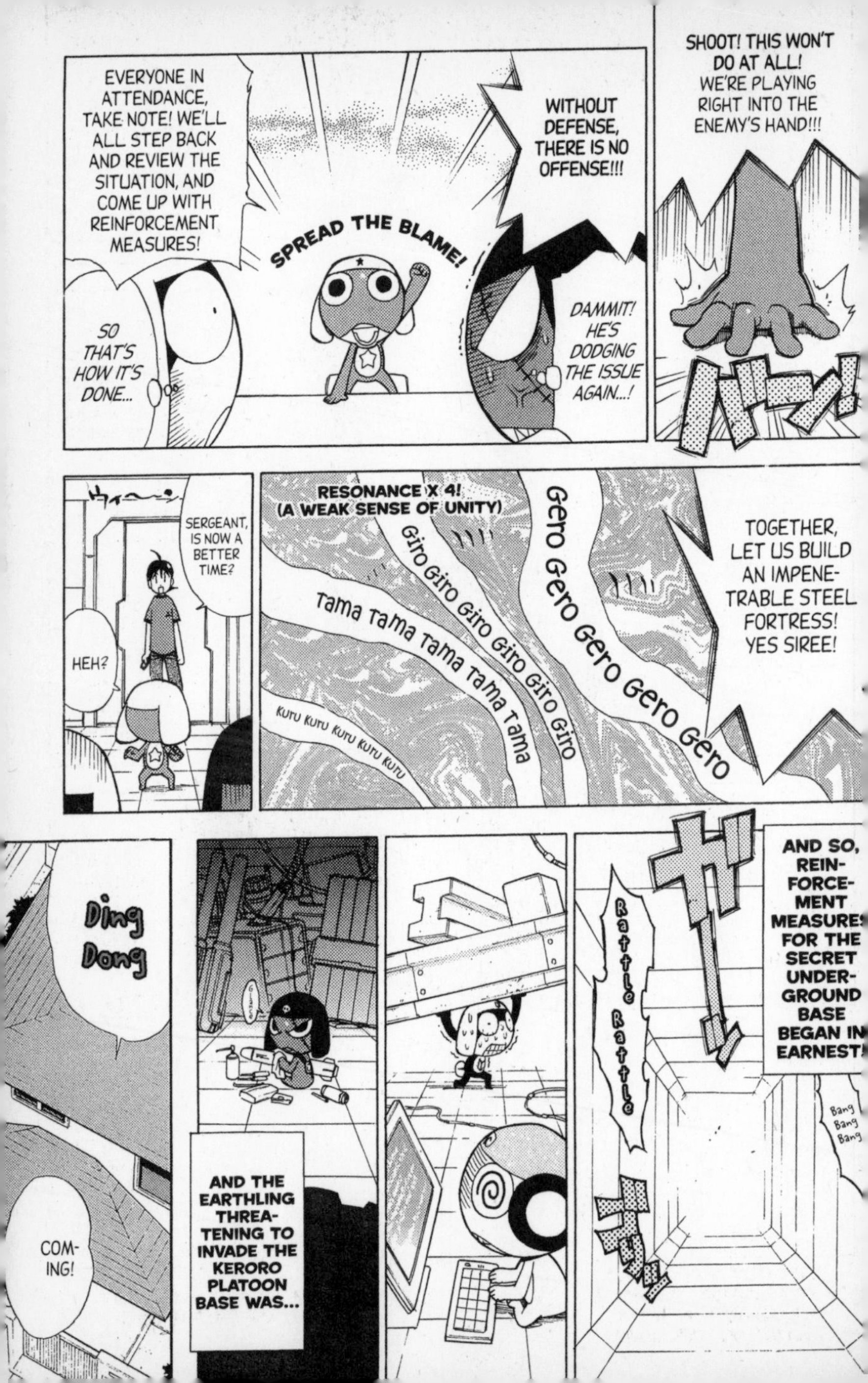
SHOOT! THIS WON'T DO AT ALL! WE'RE PLAYING RIGHT INTO THE ENEMY'S HAND!!!
EVERYONE IN ATTENDANCE, TAKE NOTE! WE'LL ALL STEP BACK AND REVIEW THE SITUATION, AND COME UP WITH REINFORCEMENT MEASURES!
WITHOUT DEFENSE, THERE IS NO OFFENSE!!!
SPREAD THE BLAME!
DAMMIT! HE'S DODGING THE ISSUE AGAIN...!
SO THAT'S HOW IT'S DONE...
TOGETHER, LET US BUILD AN IMPENETRABLE STEEL FORTRESS! YES SIREE!
Gero Gero Gero Gero Gero
RESONANCE X 4! (A WEAK SENSE OF UNITY)
Giro Giro Giro Giro Giro Giro
Tama Tama Tama Tama Tama
Kuru Kuru Kuru Kuru Kuru
SERGEANT, IS NOW A BETTER TIME?
HEH?
AND SO, REINFORCEMENT MEASURES FOR THE SECRET UNDERGROUND BASE BEGAN IN EARNEST!
Bang Bang Bang
Rattle Rattle
AND THE EARTHLING THREATENING TO INVADE THE KERORO PLATOON BASE WAS...
Ding Dong
COMING!

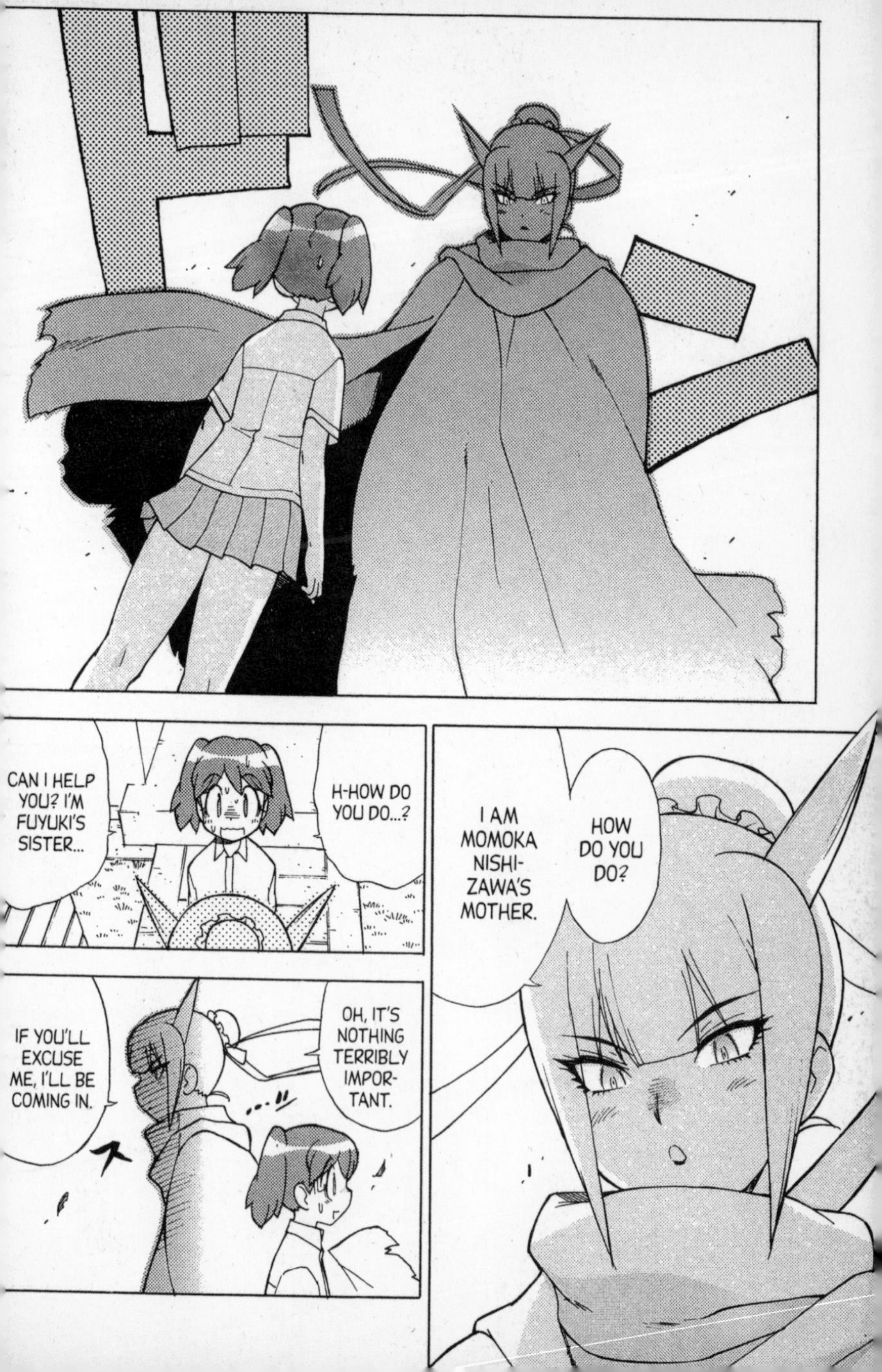
HOW DO YOU DO?
I AM MOMOKA NISHI-ZAWA'S MOTHER.
H-HOW DO YOU DO...?
CAN I HELP YOU? I'M FUYUKI'S SISTER...
OH, IT'S NOTHING TERRIBLY IMPOR-TANT.
IF YOU'LL EXCUSE ME, I'LL BE COMING IN.

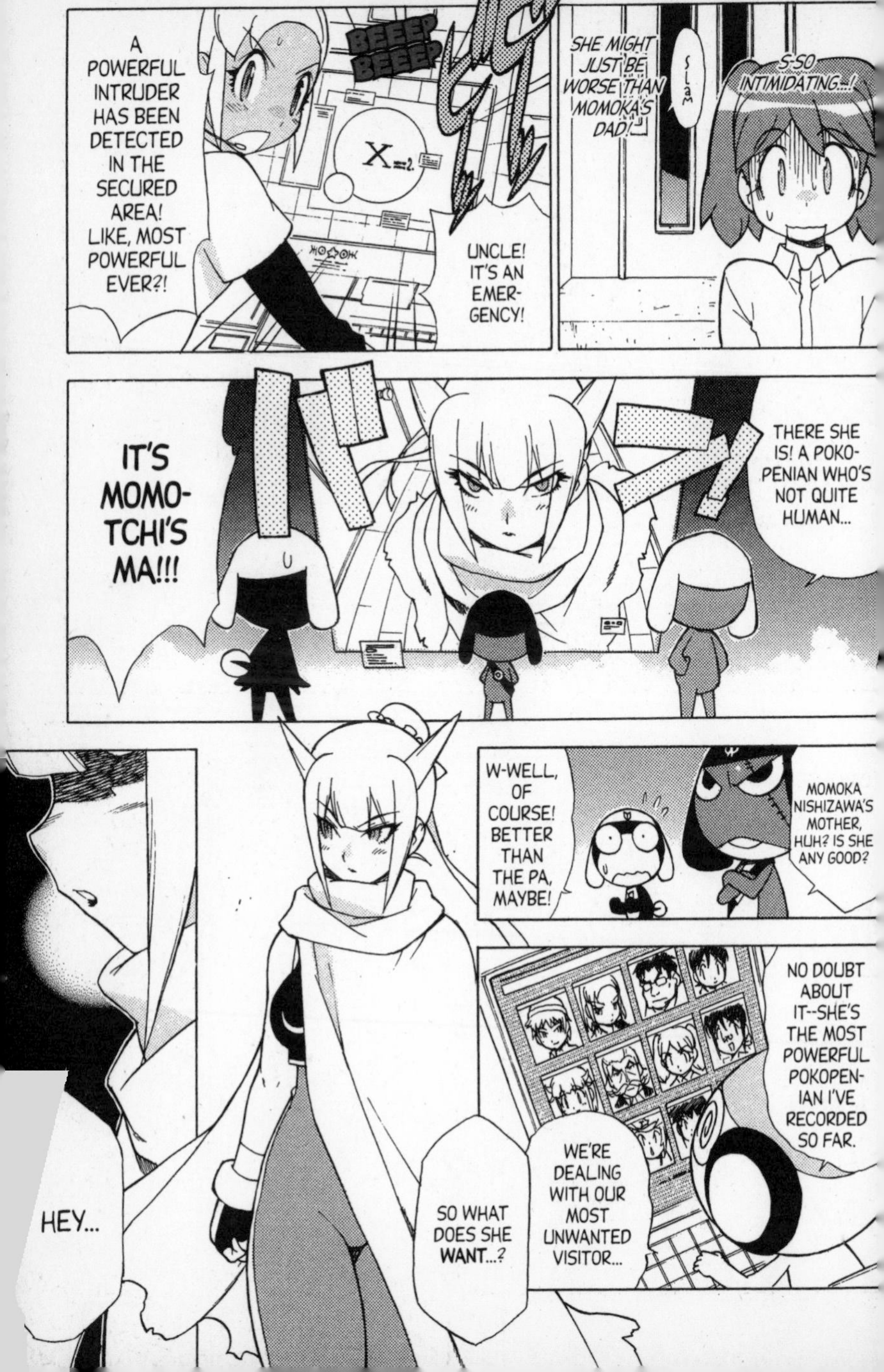
S-SO INTIMIDATING...!
SHE MIGHT JUST BE WORSE THAN MOMOKA'S DAD!
SLAM
BEEEP BEEEP
UNCLE! IT'S AN EMERGENCY!
A POWERFUL INTRUDER HAS BEEN DETECTED IN THE SECURED AREA! LIKE, MOST POWERFUL EVER?!
THERE SHE IS! A POKOPENIAN WHO'S NOT QUITE HUMAN...
IT'S MOMOTCHI'S MA!!!
MOMOKA NISHIZAWA'S MOTHER, HUH? IS SHE ANY GOOD?
W-WELL, OF COURSE! BETTER THAN THE PA, MAYBE!
NO DOUBT ABOUT IT--SHE'S THE MOST POWERFUL POKOPENIAN I'VE RECORDED SO FAR.
WE'RE DEALING WITH OUR MOST UNWANTED VISITOR...
SO WHAT DOES SHE WANT...?
HEY...

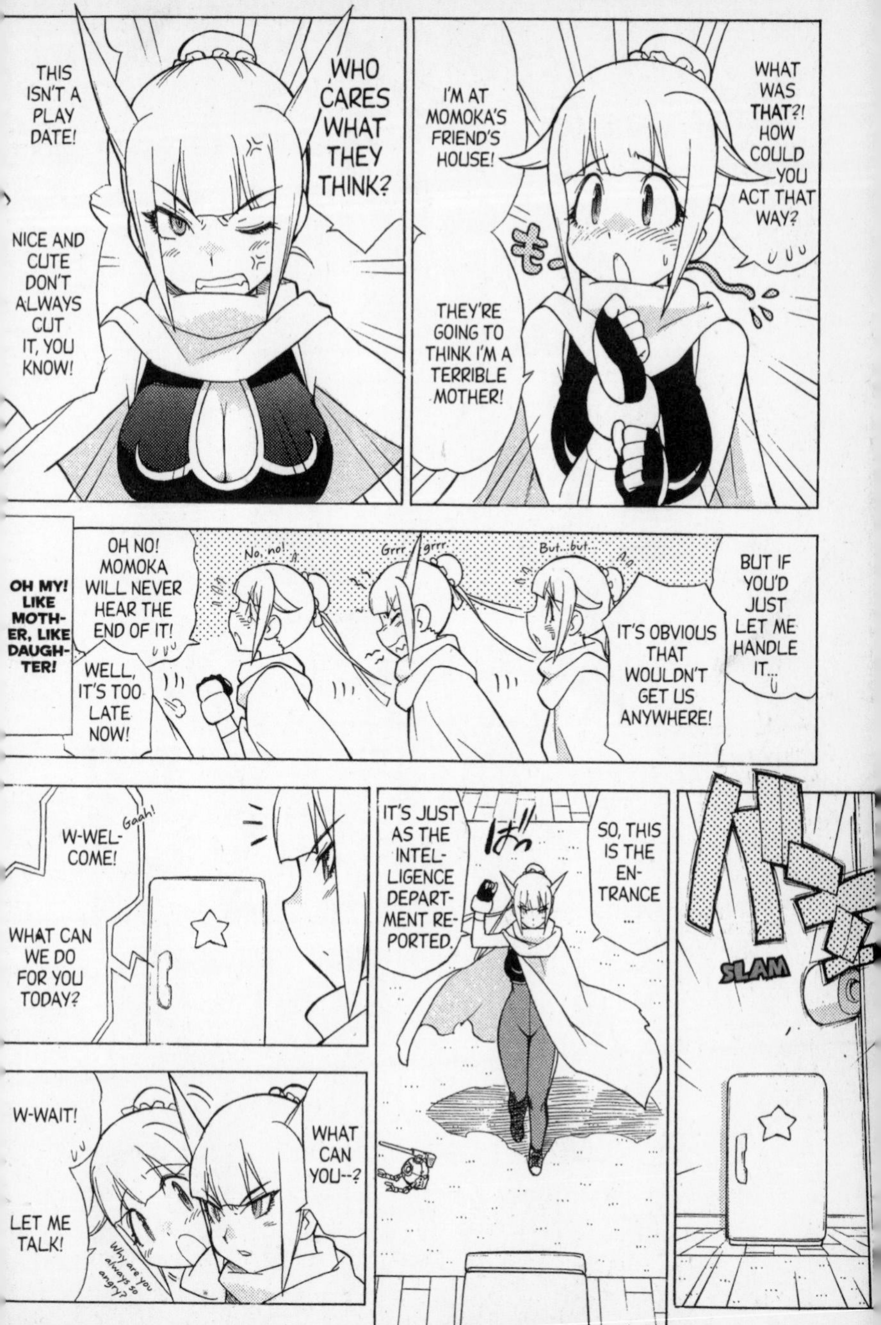
WHAT WAS THAT?! HOW COULD YOU ACT THAT WAY?
I'M AT MOMOKA'S FRIEND'S HOUSE!
THEY'RE GOING TO THINK I'M A TERRIBLE MOTHER!
WHO CARES WHAT THEY THINK?
THIS ISN'T A PLAY DATE!
NICE AND CUTE DON'T ALWAYS CUT IT, YOU KNOW!
BUT IF YOU'D JUST LET ME HANDLE IT...
IT'S OBVIOUS THAT WOULDN'T GET US ANYWHERE!
But...but...
Grrr...grrr...
No, no!
OH NO! MOMOKA WILL NEVER HEAR THE END OF IT!
WELL, IT'S TOO LATE NOW!
OH MY! LIKE MOTHER, LIKE DAUGHTER!
SLAM
SO, THIS IS THE ENTRANCE ...
IT'S JUST AS THE INTELLIGENCE DEPARTMENT REPORTED.
W-WELCOME!
Gaah!
WHAT CAN WE DO FOR YOU TODAY?
W-WAIT!
WHAT CAN YOU--?
LET ME TALK!
Why are you always so angry?

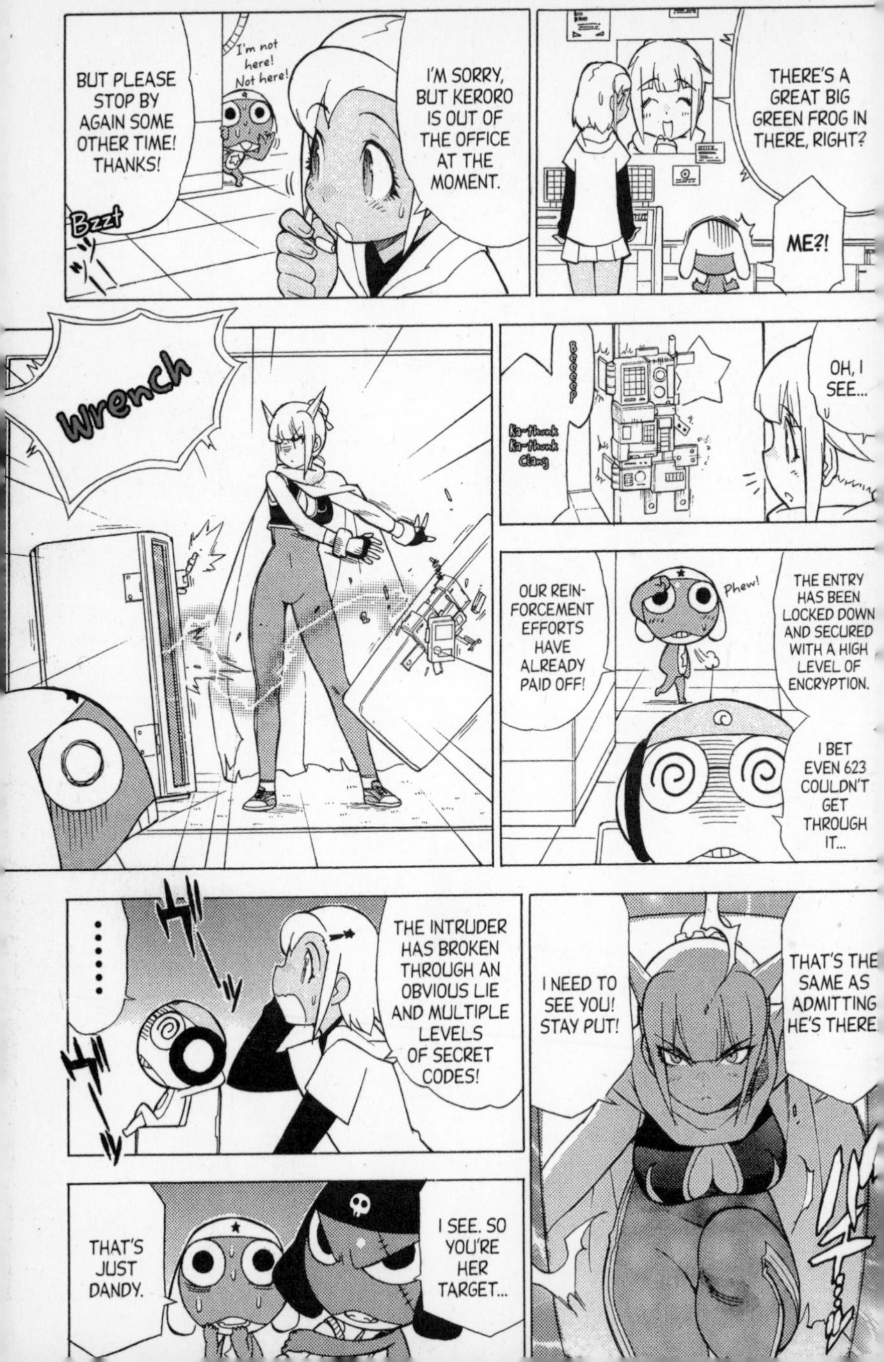
THERE'S A GREAT BIG GREEN FROG IN THERE, RIGHT?
ME?!
I'M SORRY, BUT KERORO IS OUT OF THE OFFICE AT THE MOMENT.
I'm not here! Not here!
BUT PLEASE STOP BY AGAIN SOME OTHER TIME! THANKS!
Bzzt
OH, I SEE...
Beeeep
Ka-thunk Ka-thunk Clang
THE ENTRY HAS BEEN LOCKED DOWN AND SECURED WITH A HIGH LEVEL OF ENCRYPTION.
Phew!
OUR REIN-FORCEMENT EFFORTS HAVE ALREADY PAID OFF!
I BET EVEN 623 COULDN'T GET THROUGH IT...
Wrench
THAT'S THE SAME AS ADMITTING HE'S THERE
I NEED TO SEE YOU! STAY PUT!
THE INTRUDER HAS BROKEN THROUGH AN OBVIOUS LIE AND MULTIPLE LEVELS OF SECRET CODES!
......
I SEE. SO YOU'RE HER TARGET...
THAT'S JUST DANDY.

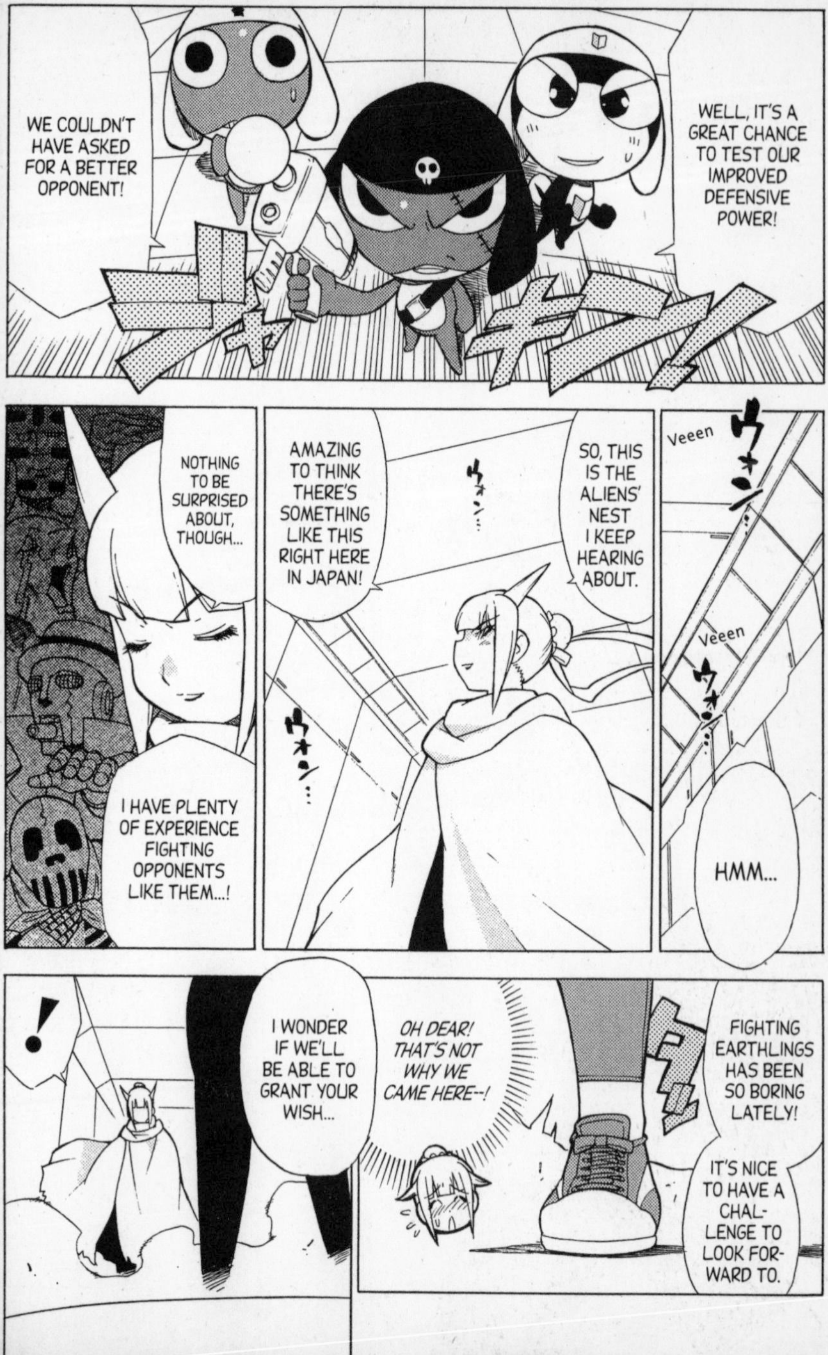
WELL, IT'S A GREAT CHANCE TO TEST OUR IMPROVED DEFENSIVE POWER!
WE COULDN'T HAVE ASKED FOR A BETTER OPPONENT!
Veeen
SO, THIS IS THE ALIENS' NEST I KEEP HEARING ABOUT.
Veeen
HMM...
AMAZING TO THINK THERE'S SOMETHING LIKE THIS RIGHT HERE IN JAPAN!
NOTHING TO BE SURPRISED ABOUT, THOUGH...
I HAVE PLENTY OF EXPERIENCE FIGHTING OPPONENTS LIKE THEM...!
FIGHTING EARTHLINGS HAS BEEN SO BORING LATELY!
IT'S NICE TO HAVE A CHAL-LENGE TO LOOK FOR-WARD TO.
OH DEAR! THAT'S NOT WHY WE CAME HERE--!
I WONDER IF WE'LL BE ABLE TO GRANT YOUR WISH...
!

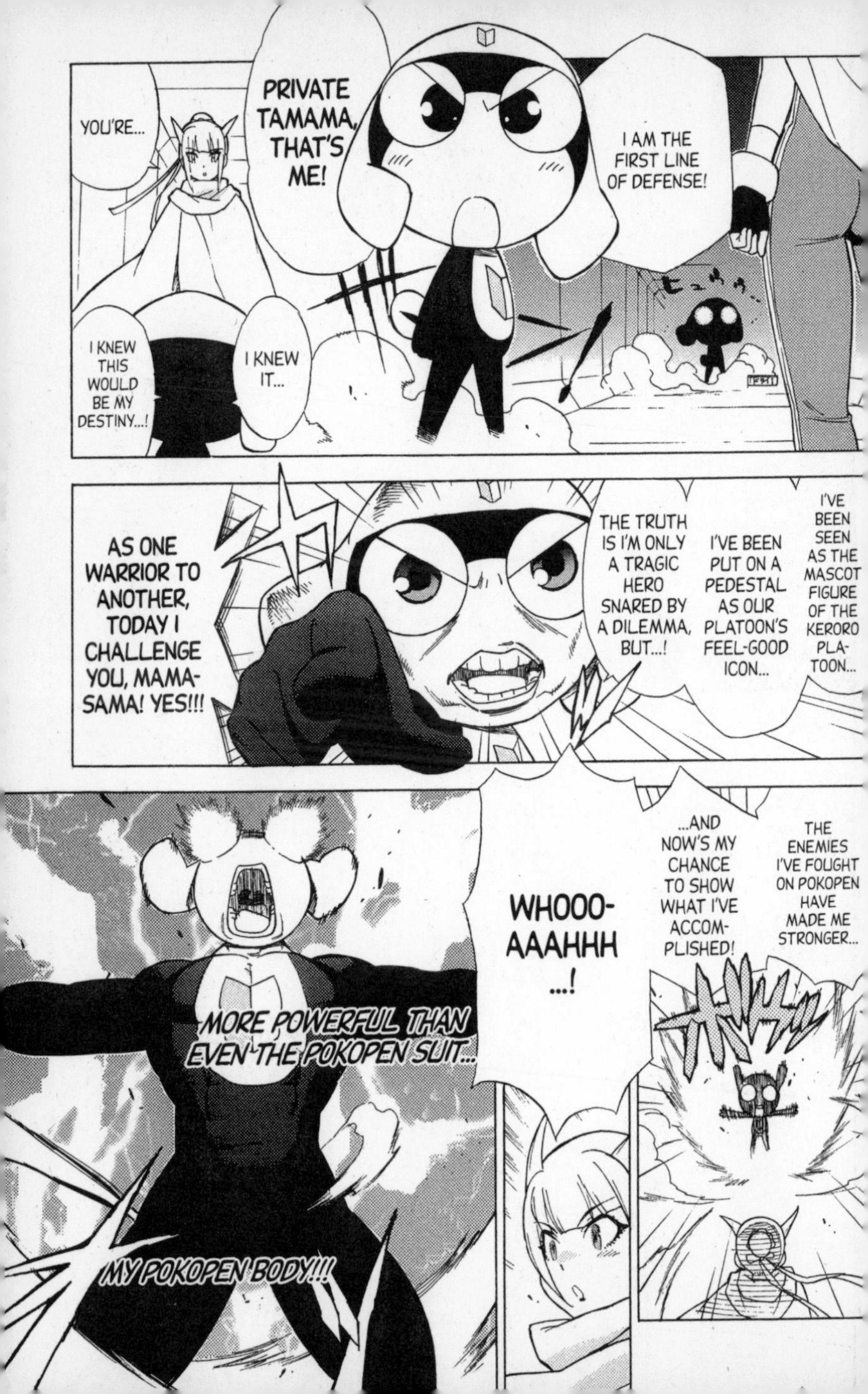
I AM THE FIRST LINE OF DEFENSE!
PRIVATE TAMAMA, THAT'S ME!
YOU'RE...
I KNEW IT...
I KNEW THIS WOULD BE MY DESTINY...!
I'VE BEEN SEEN AS THE MASCOT FIGURE OF THE KERORO PLA-TOON...
I'VE BEEN PUT ON A PEDESTAL AS OUR PLATOON'S FEEL-GOOD ICON...
THE TRUTH IS I'M ONLY A TRAGIC HERO SNARED BY A DILEMMA, BUT...!
AS ONE WARRIOR TO ANOTHER, TODAY I CHALLENGE YOU, MAMA-SAMA! YES!!!
THE ENEMIES I'VE FOUGHT ON POKOPEN HAVE MADE ME STRONGER...
...AND NOW'S MY CHANCE TO SHOW WHAT I'VE ACCOM-PLISHED!
WHOOO-AAAHHH...!
MORE POWERFUL THAN EVEN THE POKOPEN SUIT...
MY POKOPEN BODY!!!

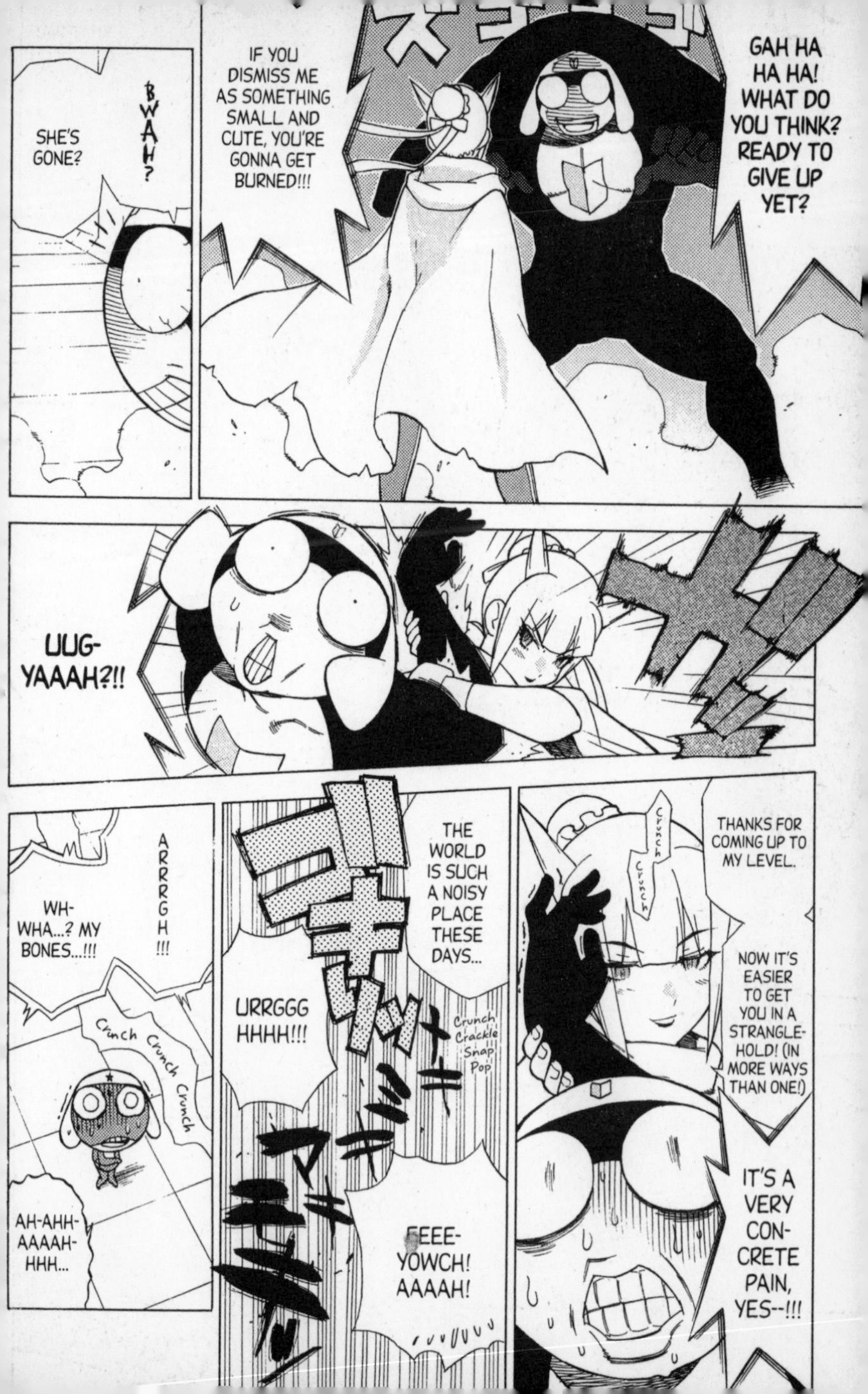
GAH HA HA HA! WHAT DO YOU THINK? READY TO GIVE UP YET?
IF YOU DISMISS ME AS SOMETHING SMALL AND CUTE, YOU'RE GONNA GET BURNED!!!
BWAH?
SHE'S GONE?
UUG-YAAAH?!!
THANKS FOR COMING UP TO MY LEVEL.
Crunch
Crunch
NOW IT'S EASIER TO GET YOU IN A STRANGLE-HOLD! (IN MORE WAYS THAN ONE!)
IT'S A VERY CON-CRETE PAIN, YES--!!!
THE WORLD IS SUCH A NOISY PLACE THESE DAYS...
URRGGG HHHH!!!
Crunch Crackle Snap Pop
EEEE-YOWCH! AAAAH!
ARRRGH!!!
WH-WHA...? MY BONES...!!!
Crunch Crunch Crunch
AH-AHH-AAAAH-HHH...

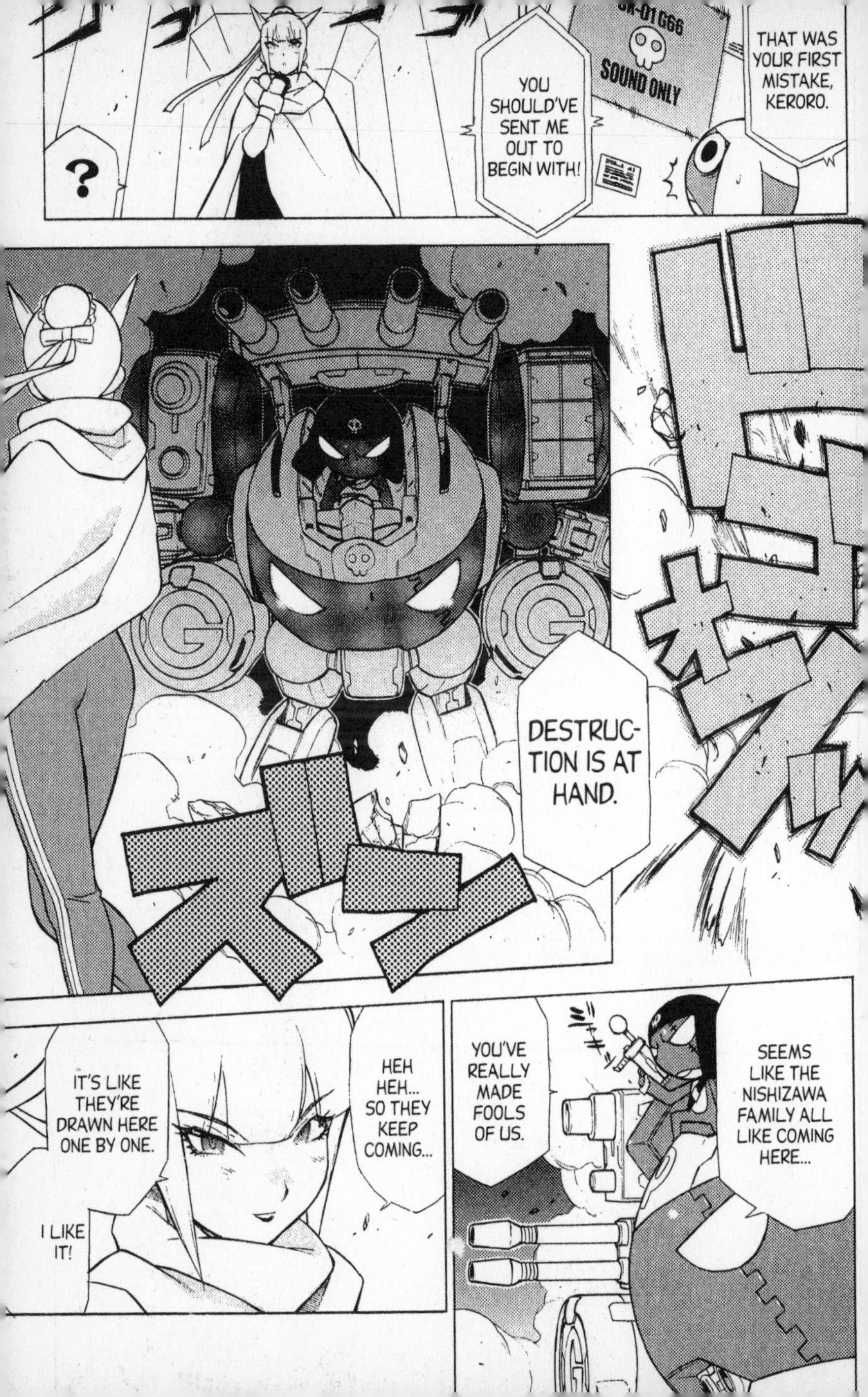
THAT WAS YOUR FIRST MISTAKE, KERORO.
SK-01 G66
SOUND ONLY
YOU SHOULD'VE SENT ME OUT TO BEGIN WITH!
?
DESTRUC-TION IS AT HAND.
SEEMS LIKE THE NISHIZAWA FAMILY ALL LIKE COMING HERE...
YOU'VE REALLY MADE FOOLS OF US.
HEH HEH... SO THEY KEEP COMING...
IT'S LIKE THEY'RE DRAWN HERE ONE BY ONE.
I LIKE IT!

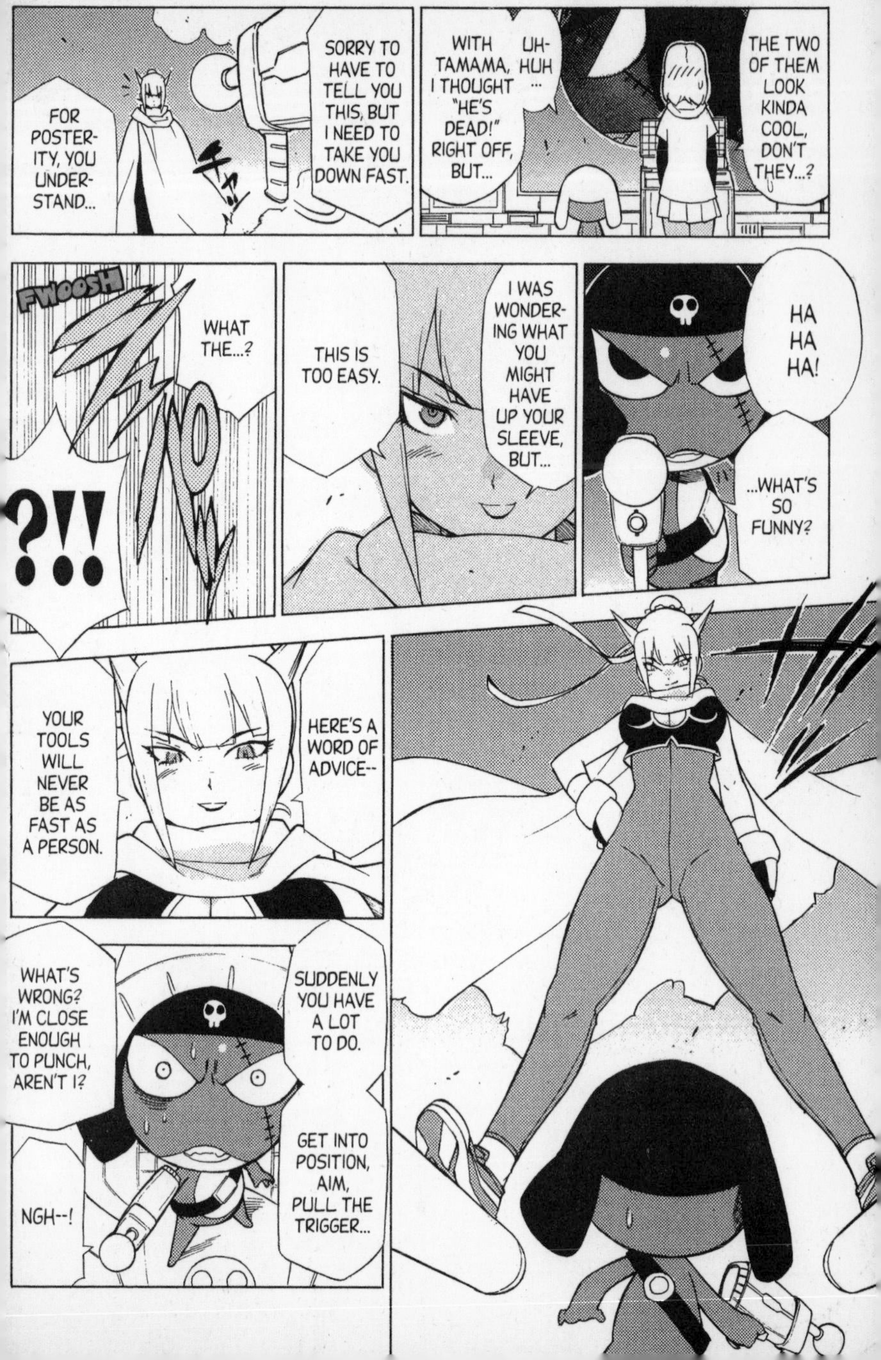
THE TWO OF THEM LOOK KINDA COOL, DON'T THEY...?
UH-HUH ...
WITH TAMAMA, I THOUGHT "HE'S DEAD!" RIGHT OFF, BUT...
SORRY TO HAVE TO TELL YOU THIS, BUT I NEED TO TAKE YOU DOWN FAST.
FOR POSTERITY, YOU UNDERSTAND...
HA HA HA!
...WHAT'S SO FUNNY?
I WAS WONDERING WHAT YOU MIGHT HAVE UP YOUR SLEEVE, BUT...
THIS IS TOO EASY.
FWOOSH
WHAT THE...?
?!!
HERE'S A WORD OF ADVICE--
YOUR TOOLS WILL NEVER BE AS FAST AS A PERSON.
SUDDENLY YOU HAVE A LOT TO DO.
WHAT'S WRONG? I'M CLOSE ENOUGH TO PUNCH, AREN'T I?
GET INTO POSITION, AIM, PULL THE TRIGGER...
NGH--!

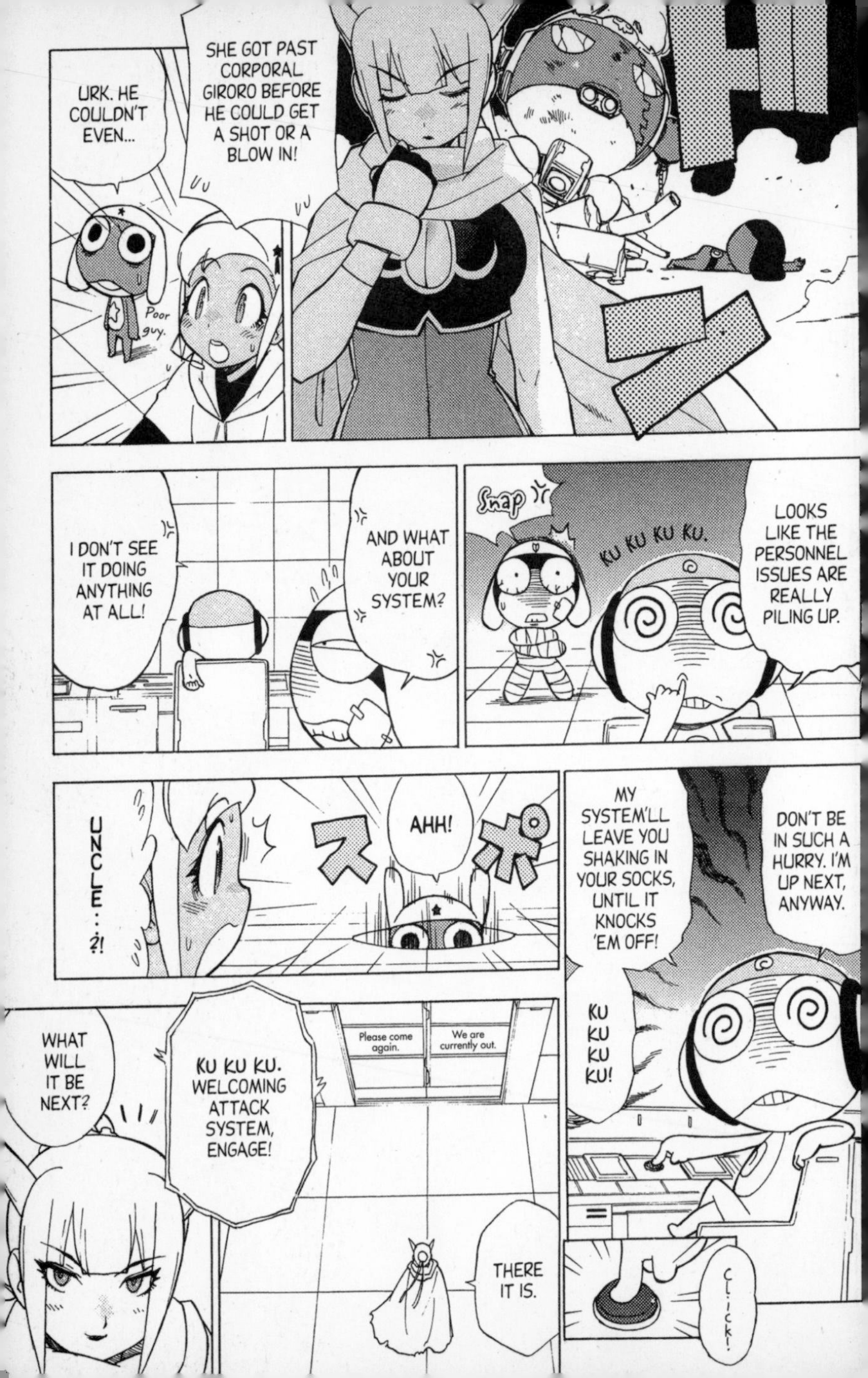
SHE GOT PAST CORPORAL GIRORO BEFORE HE COULD GET A SHOT OR A BLOW IN!
URK. HE COULDN'T EVEN...
Poor guy.
LOOKS LIKE THE PERSONNEL ISSUES ARE REALLY PILING UP.
KU KU KU KU.
Snap
AND WHAT ABOUT YOUR SYSTEM?
I DON'T SEE IT DOING ANYTHING AT ALL!
DON'T BE IN SUCH A HURRY. I'M UP NEXT, ANYWAY.
MY SYSTEM'LL LEAVE YOU SHAKING IN YOUR SOCKS, UNTIL IT KNOCKS 'EM OFF!
KU KU KU KU!
CLICK!
AHH!
UNCLE...?!
KU KU KU. WELCOMING ATTACK SYSTEM, ENGAGE!
WHAT WILL IT BE NEXT?
We are currently out.
Please come again.
THERE IT IS.

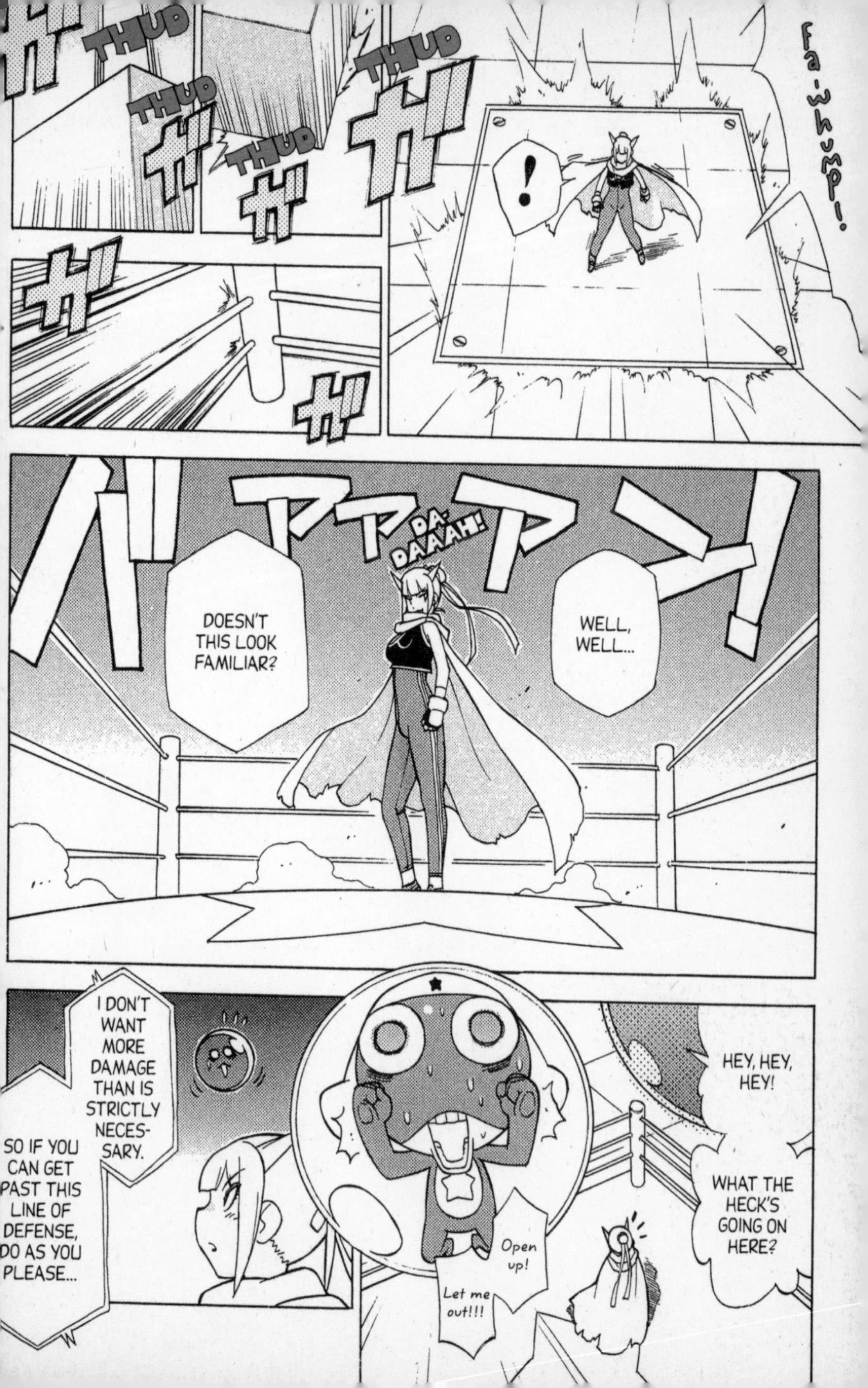
Fa-whump!
!
THUD
THUD
THUD
THUD
WELL, WELL...
DA-DAAAH!
DOESN'T THIS LOOK FAMILIAR?
HEY, HEY, HEY!
WHAT THE HECK'S GOING ON HERE?
Open up!
Let me out!!!
I DON'T WANT MORE DAMAGE THAN IS STRICTLY NECES-SARY.
SO IF YOU CAN GET PAST THIS LINE OF DEFENSE, DO AS YOU PLEASE...

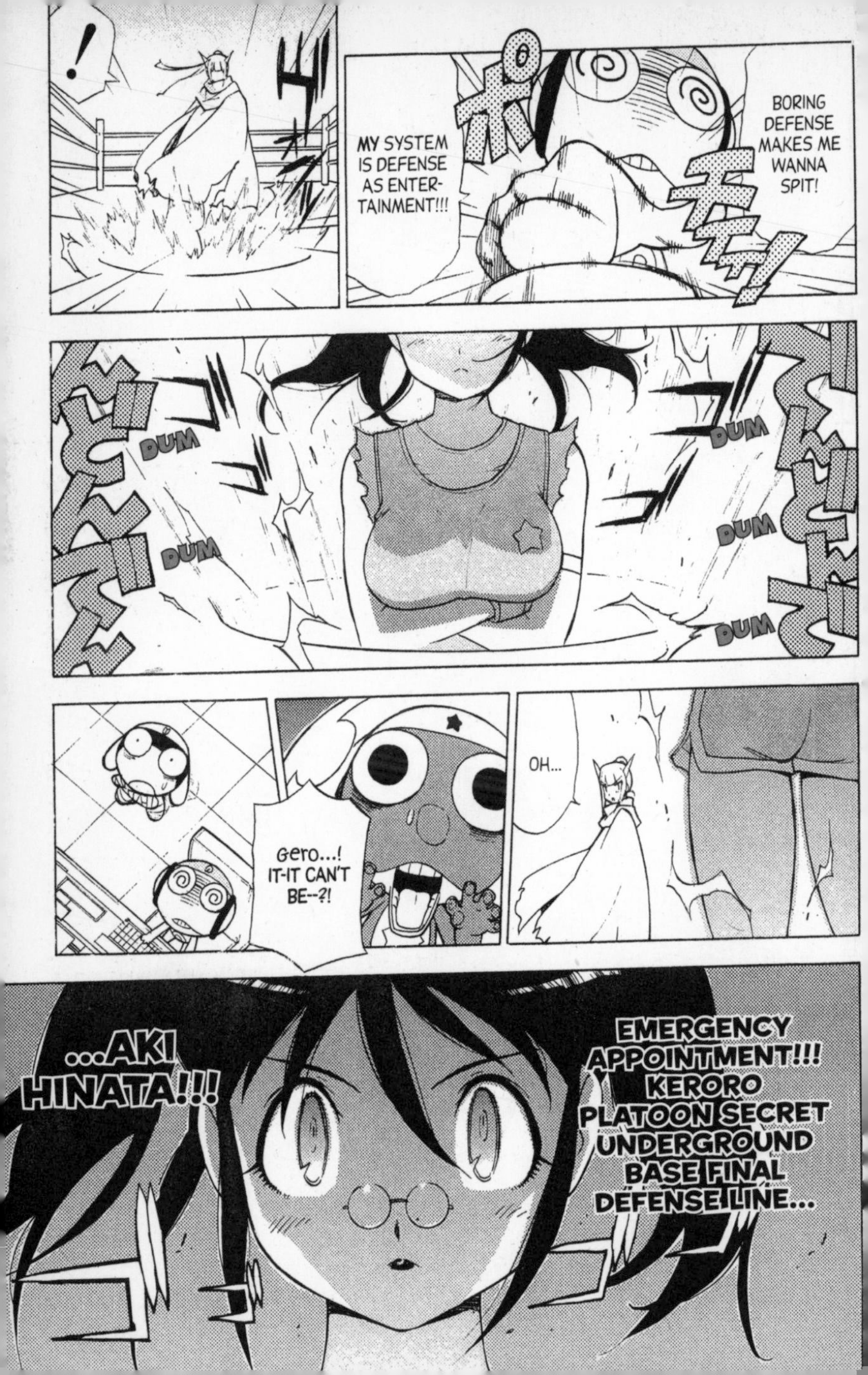
BORING DEFENSE MAKES ME WANNA SPIT!
MY SYSTEM IS DEFENSE AS ENTER-TAINMENT!!!
!
DUM
DUM
DUM
DUM
DUM
OH...
Gero...! IT-IT CAN'T BE--?!
EMERGENCY APPOINTMENT!!! KERORO PLATOON SECRET UNDERGROUND BASE FINAL DEFENSE LINE...
...AKI HINATA!!!

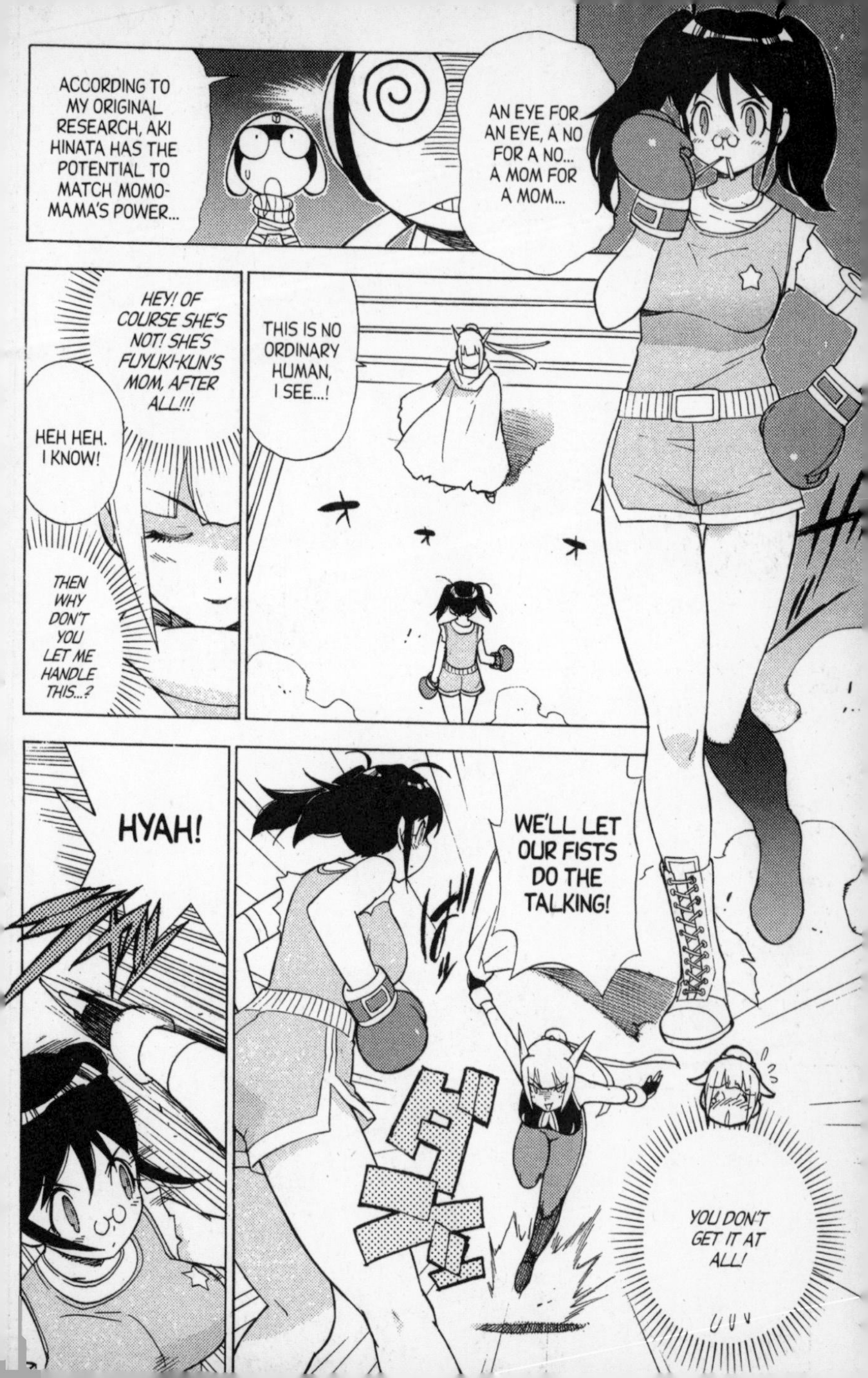
AN EYE FOR AN EYE, A NO FOR A NO... A MOM FOR A MOM...
ACCORDING TO MY ORIGINAL RESEARCH, AKI HINATA HAS THE POTENTIAL TO MATCH MOMO-MAMA'S POWER...
THIS IS NO ORDINARY HUMAN, I SEE...!
HEY! OF COURSE SHE'S NOT! SHE'S FUYUKI-KUN'S MOM, AFTER ALL!!!
HEH HEH. I KNOW!
THEN WHY DON'T YOU LET ME HANDLE THIS...?
WE'LL LET OUR FISTS DO THE TALKING!
YOU DON'T GET IT AT ALL!
HYAH!

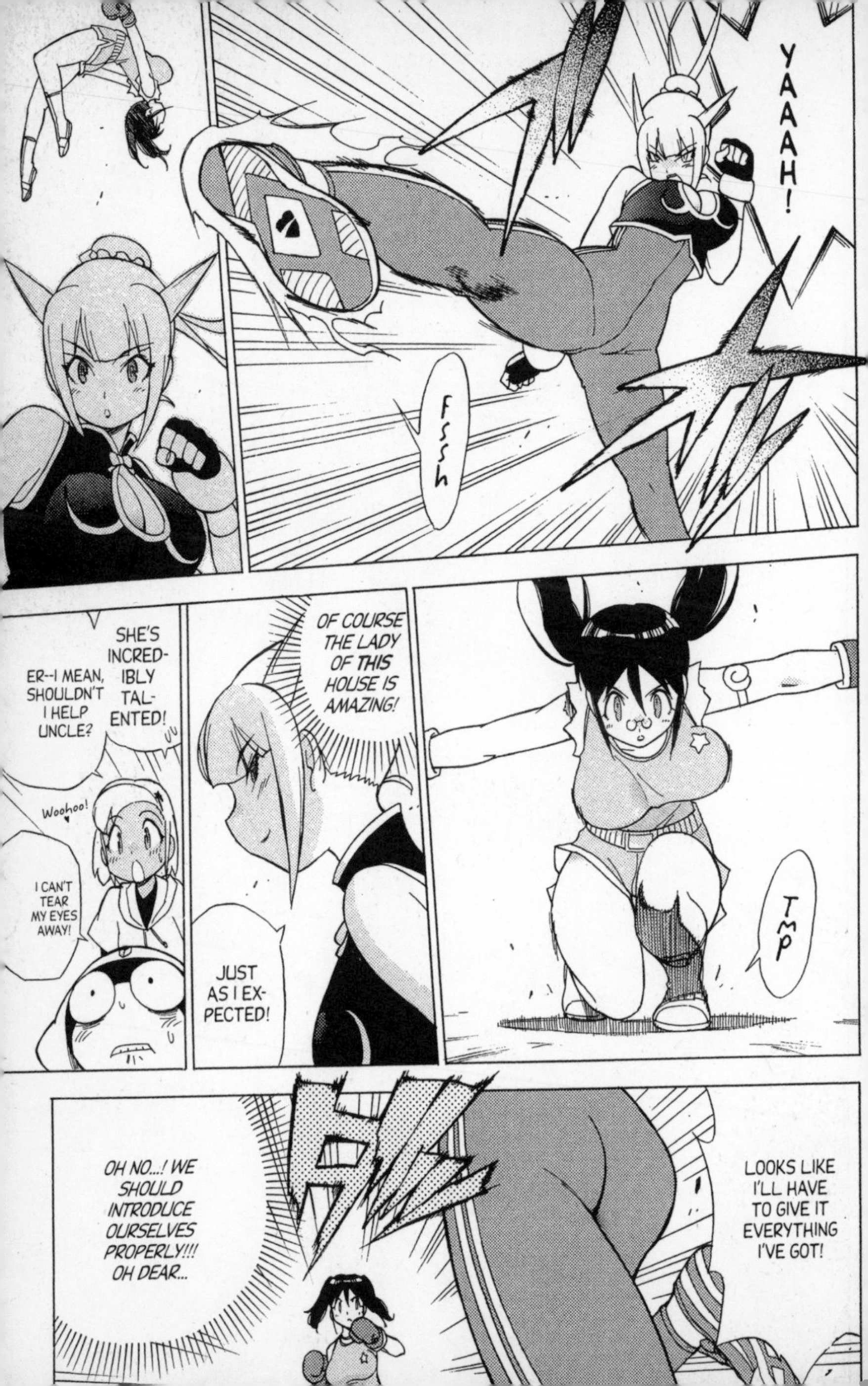
YAAAH!
Fssh
Tmp
OF COURSE THE LADY OF THIS HOUSE IS AMAZING!
JUST AS I EX-PECTED!
SHE'S INCRED-IBLY TAL-ENTED!
ER--I MEAN, SHOULDN'T I HELP UNCLE?
Woohoo!
I CAN'T TEAR MY EYES AWAY!
LOOKS LIKE I'LL HAVE TO GIVE IT EVERYTHING I'VE GOT!
OH NO...! WE SHOULD INTRODUCE OURSELVES PROPERLY!!! OH DEAR...

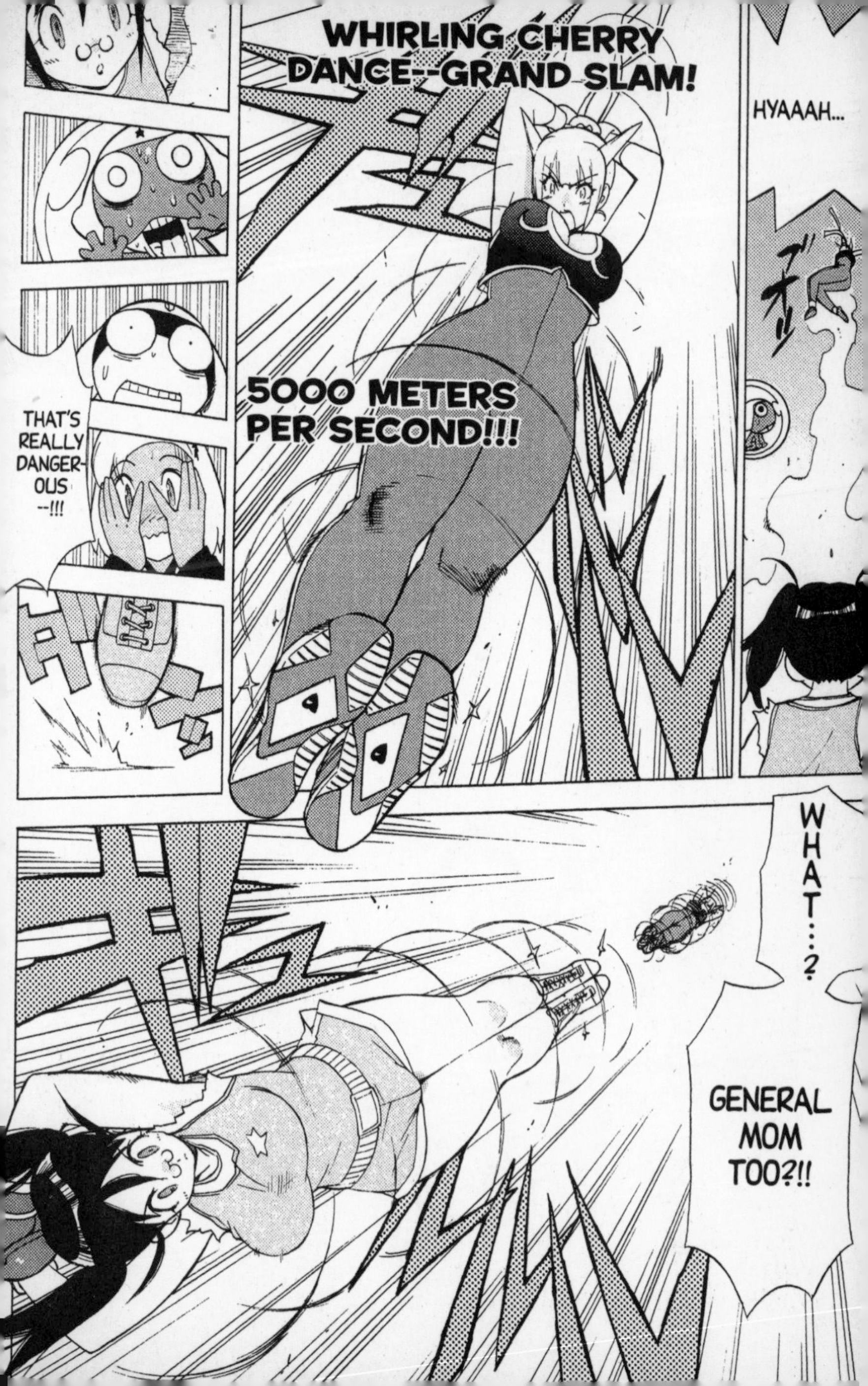
HYAAAH...
WHIRLING CHERRY DANCE--GRAND SLAM!
5000 METERS PER SECOND!!!
THAT'S REALLY DANGER-OUS--!!!
WHAT...?
GENERAL MOM TOO?!!

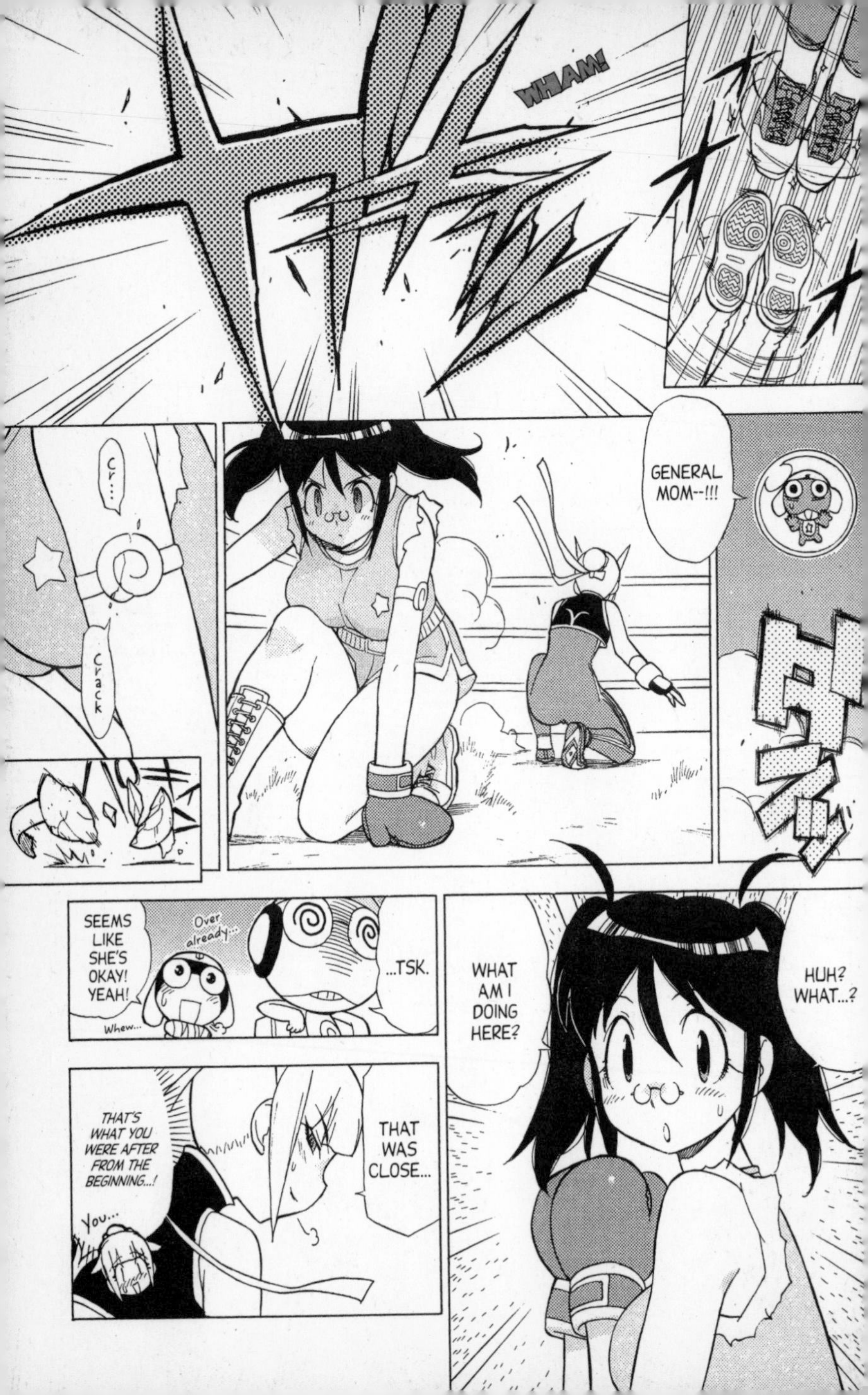
WHAM!
GENERAL MOM--!!!
Cr...
Crack
HUH? WHAT...?
WHAT AM I DOING HERE?
...TSK.
Over already...
SEEMS LIKE SHE'S OKAY! YEAH!
Whew...
THAT WAS CLOSE...
THAT'S WHAT YOU WERE AFTER FROM THE BEGINNING...!
You...

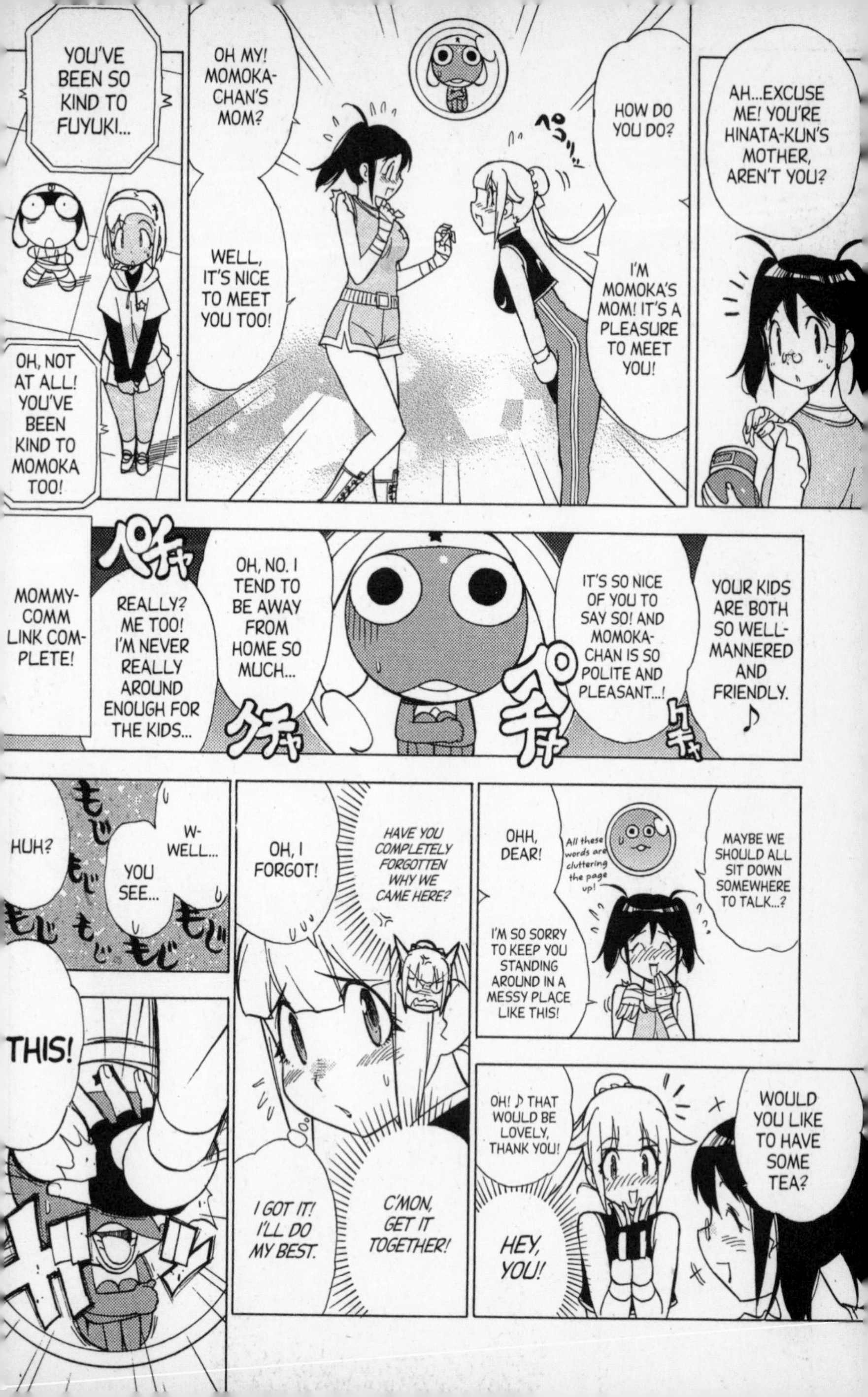
AH...EXCUSE ME! YOU'RE HINATA-KUN'S MOTHER, AREN'T YOU?
HOW DO YOU DO?
I'M MOMOKA'S MOM! IT'S A PLEASURE TO MEET YOU!
OH MY! MOMOKA-CHAN'S MOM?
WELL, IT'S NICE TO MEET YOU TOO!
YOU'VE BEEN SO KIND TO FUYUKI...
OH, NOT AT ALL! YOU'VE BEEN KIND TO MOMOKA TOO!
YOUR KIDS ARE BOTH SO WELL-MANNERED AND FRIENDLY. ♪
IT'S SO NICE OF YOU TO SAY SO! AND MOMOKA-CHAN IS SO POLITE AND PLEASANT...!
OH, NO. I TEND TO BE AWAY FROM HOME SO MUCH...
REALLY? ME TOO! I'M NEVER REALLY AROUND ENOUGH FOR THE KIDS...
MOMMY-COMM LINK COMPLETE!
MAYBE WE SHOULD ALL SIT DOWN SOMEWHERE TO TALK...?
OHH, DEAR!
All these words are cluttering the page up!
I'M SO SORRY TO KEEP YOU STANDING AROUND IN A MESSY PLACE LIKE THIS!
HAVE YOU COMPLETELY FORGOTTEN WHY WE CAME HERE?
OH, I FORGOT!
W-WELL...
YOU SEE...
HUH?
WOULD YOU LIKE TO HAVE SOME TEA?
OH! ♪ THAT WOULD BE LOVELY, THANK YOU!
HEY, YOU!
C'MON, GET IT TOGETHER!
I GOT IT! I'LL DO MY BEST.
THIS!

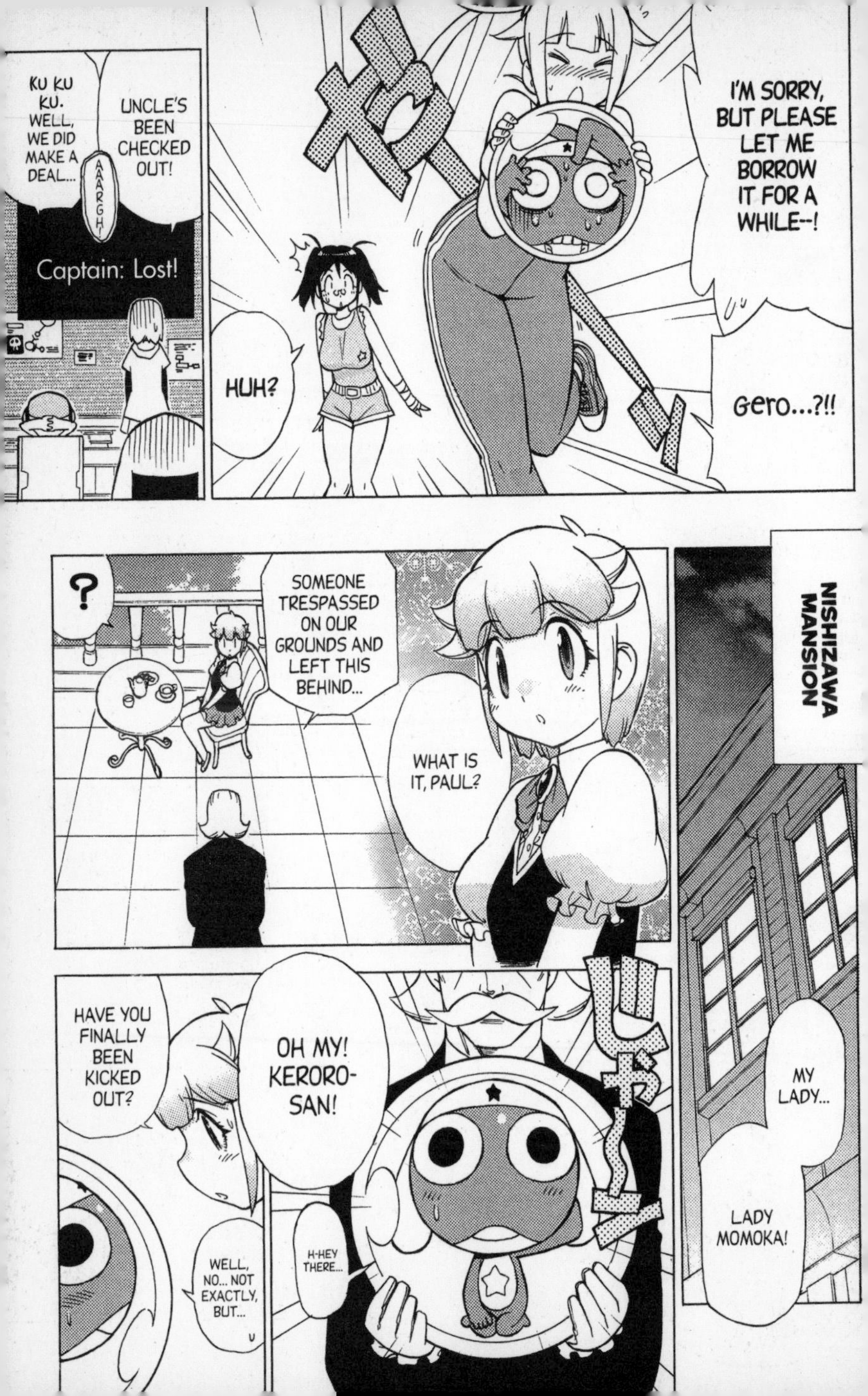
I'M SORRY, BUT PLEASE LET ME BORROW IT FOR A WHILE--!
Gero...?!!
HUH?
UNCLE'S BEEN CHECKED OUT!
AAARGH!
KU KU KU. WELL, WE DID MAKE A DEAL...
Captain: Lost!
NISHIZAWA MANSION
WHAT IS IT, PAUL?
SOMEONE TRESPASSED ON OUR GROUNDS AND LEFT THIS BEHIND...
?
MY LADY...
LADY MOMOKA!
OH MY! KERORO-SAN!
HAVE YOU FINALLY BEEN KICKED OUT?
H-HEY THERE...
WELL, NO... NOT EXACTLY, BUT...

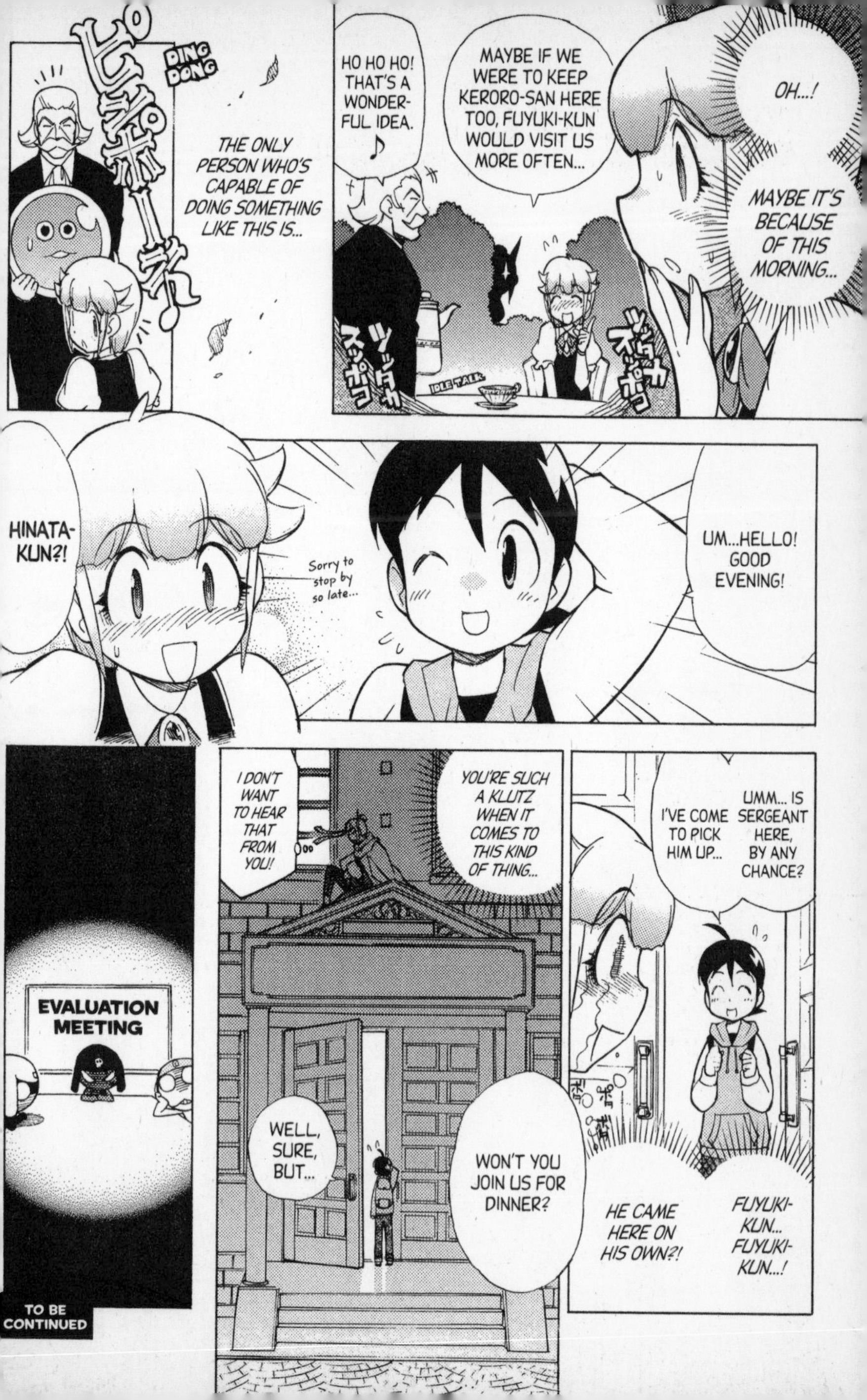
OH...!
MAYBE IT'S BECAUSE OF THIS MORNING...
MAYBE IF WE WERE TO KEEP KERORO-SAN HERE TOO, FUYUKI-KUN WOULD VISIT US MORE OFTEN...
HO HO HO! THAT'S A WONDERFUL IDEA. ♪
IDLE TALK
THE ONLY PERSON WHO'S CAPABLE OF DOING SOMETHING LIKE THIS IS...
DING DONG
UM...HELLO! GOOD EVENING!
Sorry to stop by so late...
HINATA-KUN?!
UMM... IS SERGEANT HERE, BY ANY CHANCE?
I'VE COME TO PICK HIM UP...
FUYUKI-KUN... FUYUKI-KUN...!
HE CAME HERE ON HIS OWN?!
YOU'RE SUCH A KLUTZ WHEN IT COMES TO THIS KIND OF THING...
I DON'T WANT TO HEAR THAT FROM YOU!
WON'T YOU JOIN US FOR DINNER?
WELL, SURE, BUT...
EVALUATION MEETING
TO BE CONTINUED

ENCOUNTER CXXXIII
THE SHOCKING SURVIVALIST SERGEANT!

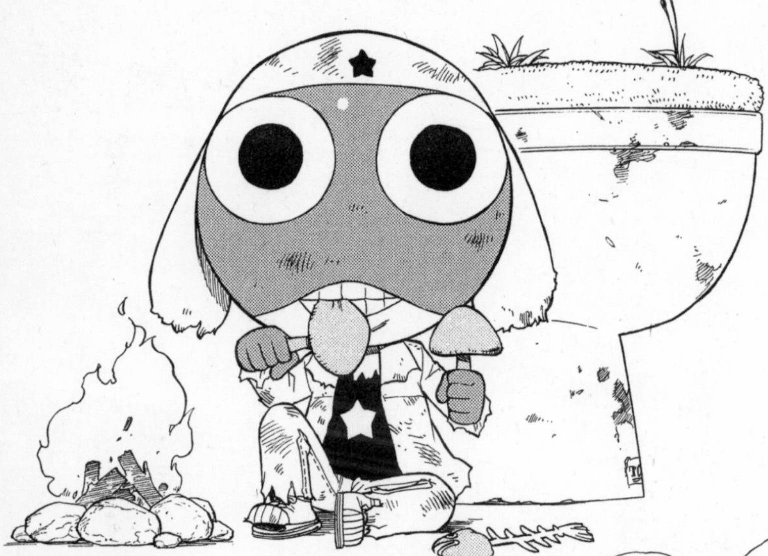

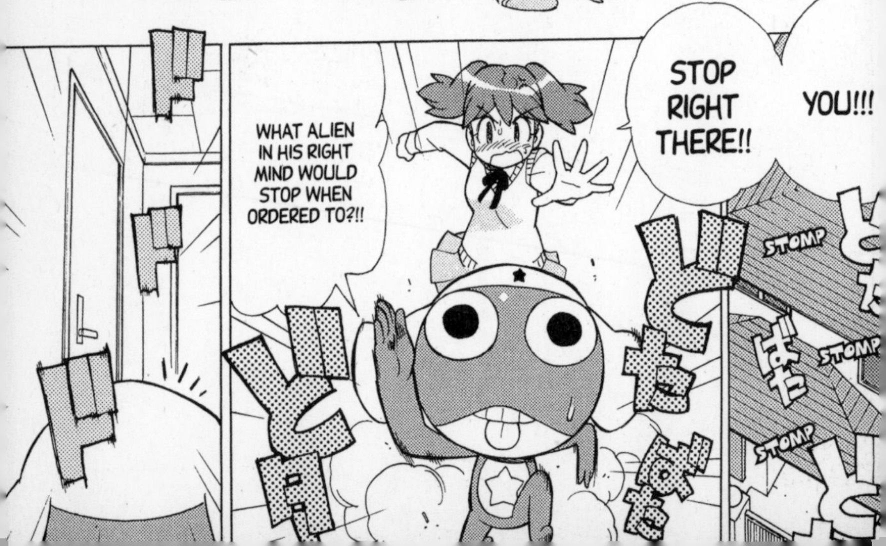
YOU!!!
STOP RIGHT THERE!!
WHAT ALIEN IN HIS RIGHT MIND WOULD STOP WHEN ORDERED TO?!!
STOMP
STOMP
STOMP

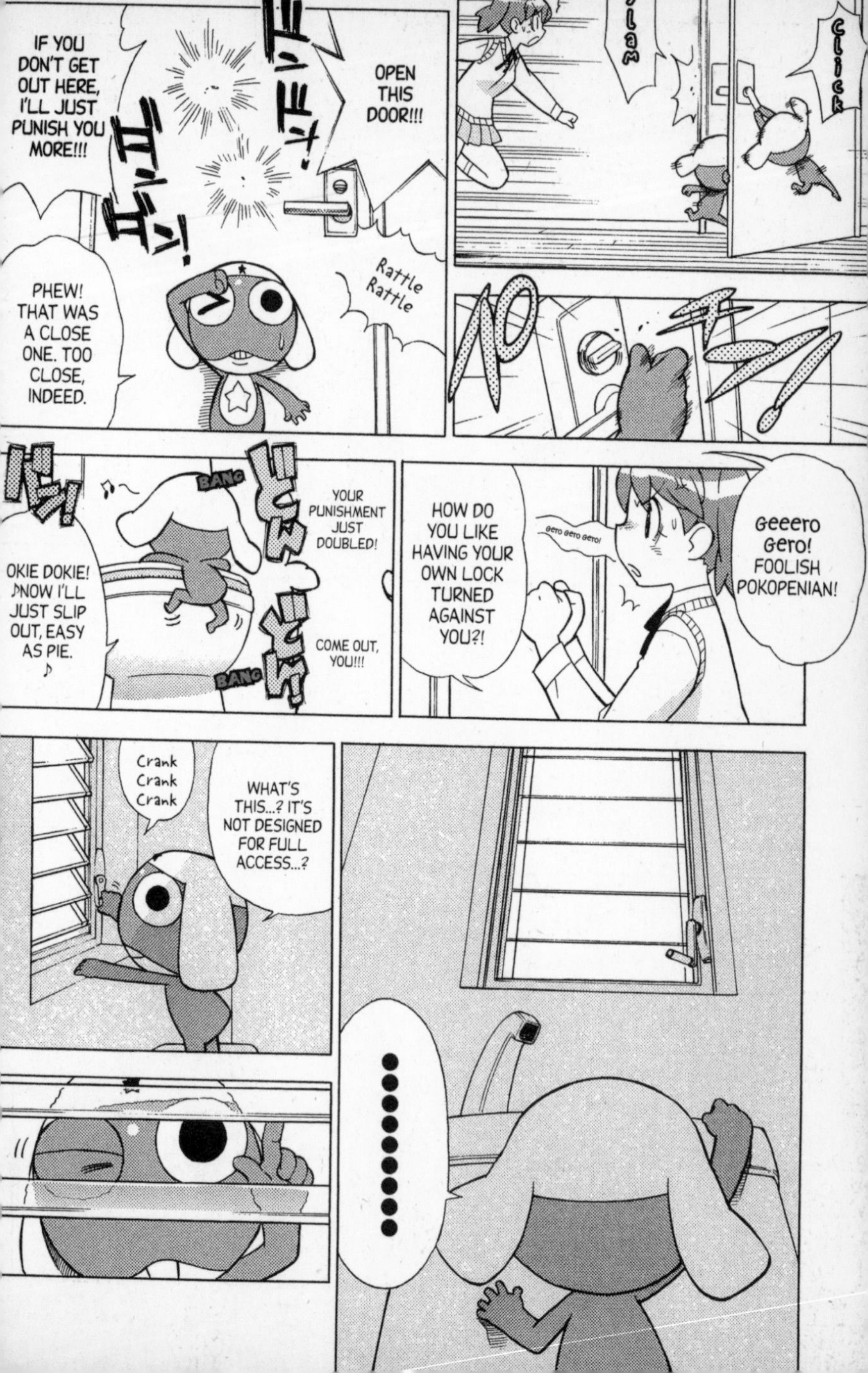
Click
Slam
OPEN THIS DOOR!!!
Rattle Rattle
IF YOU DON'T GET OUT HERE, I'LL JUST PUNISH YOU MORE!!!
PHEW! THAT WAS A CLOSE ONE. TOO CLOSE, INDEED.
Geeero Gero! FOOLISH POKOPENIAN!
Gero Gero Gero!
HOW DO YOU LIKE HAVING YOUR OWN LOCK TURNED AGAINST YOU?!
YOUR PUNISHMENT JUST DOUBLED!
COME OUT, YOU!!!
BANG
BANG
OKIE DOKIE! ♪NOW I'LL JUST SLIP OUT, EASY AS PIE. ♪
....
Crank Crank Crank
WHAT'S THIS...? IT'S NOT DESIGNED FOR FULL ACCESS...?

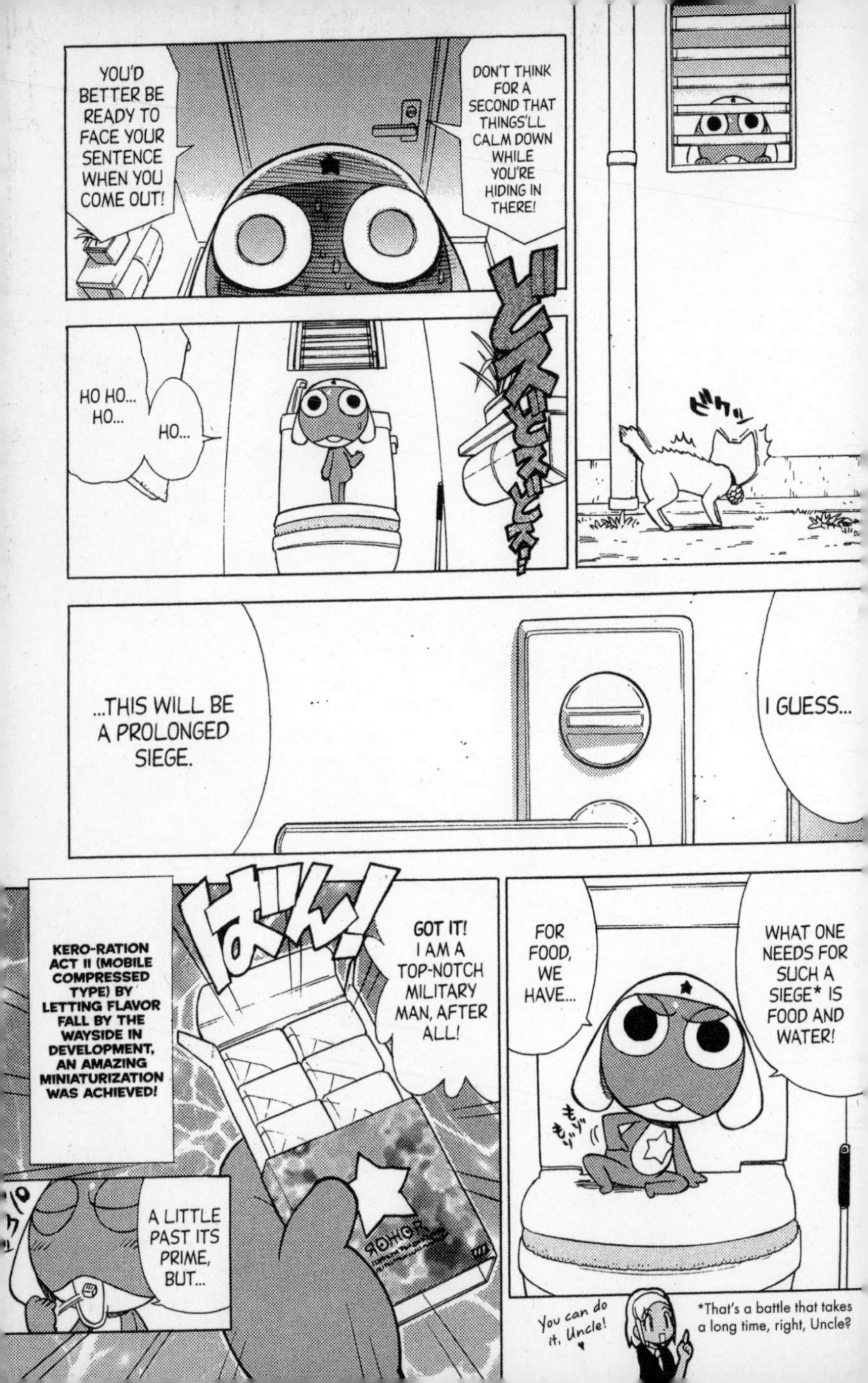
DON'T THINK FOR A SECOND THAT THINGS'LL CALM DOWN WHILE YOU'RE HIDING IN THERE!
YOU'D BETTER BE READY TO FACE YOUR SENTENCE WHEN YOU COME OUT!
HO HO... HO...
HO...
I GUESS...
...THIS WILL BE A PROLONGED SIEGE.
WHAT ONE NEEDS FOR SUCH A SIEGE* IS FOOD AND WATER!
FOR FOOD, WE HAVE...
GOT IT! I AM A TOP-NOTCH MILITARY MAN, AFTER ALL!
KERO-RATION ACT II (MOBILE COMPRESSED TYPE) BY LETTING FLAVOR FALL BY THE WAYSIDE IN DEVELOPMENT, AN AMAZING MINIATURIZATION WAS ACHIEVED!
A LITTLE PAST ITS PRIME, BUT...
*That's a battle that takes a long time, right, Uncle?
You can do it, Uncle!

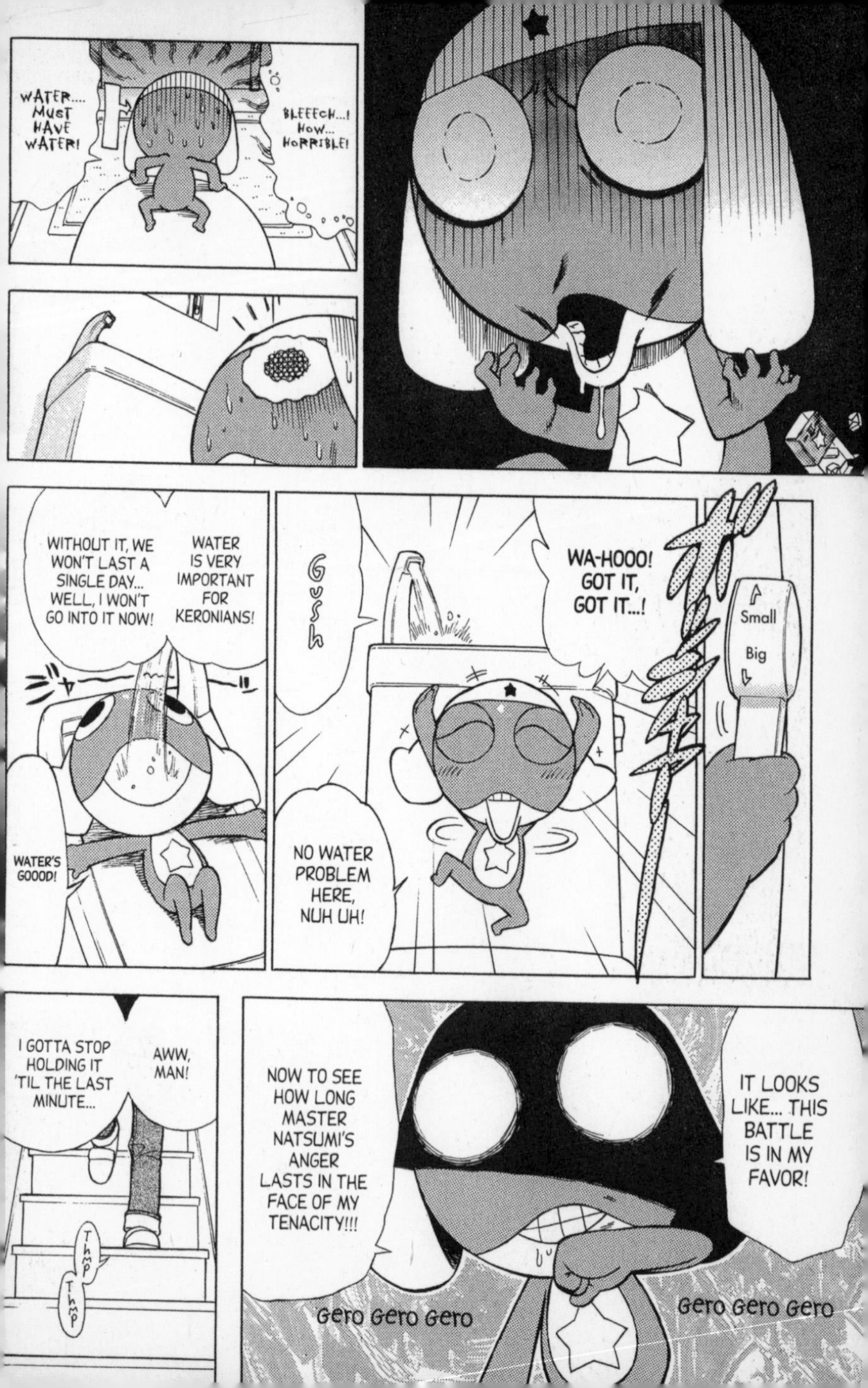
WATER.... MUST HAVE WATER!
BLEEECH...! HOW... HORRIBLE!
Small
Big
WA-HOOO! GOT IT, GOT IT...!
Gush
NO WATER PROBLEM HERE, NUH UH!
WATER IS VERY IMPORTANT FOR KERONIANS!
WITHOUT IT, WE WON'T LAST A SINGLE DAY... WELL, I WON'T GO INTO IT NOW!
WATER'S GOOOD!
IT LOOKS LIKE... THIS BATTLE IS IN MY FAVOR!
NOW TO SEE HOW LONG MASTER NATSUMI'S ANGER LASTS IN THE FACE OF MY TENACITY!!!
Gero Gero Gero
Gero Gero Gero
AWW, MAN!
I GOTTA STOP HOLDING IT 'TIL THE LAST MINUTE...
Thmp
Thmp

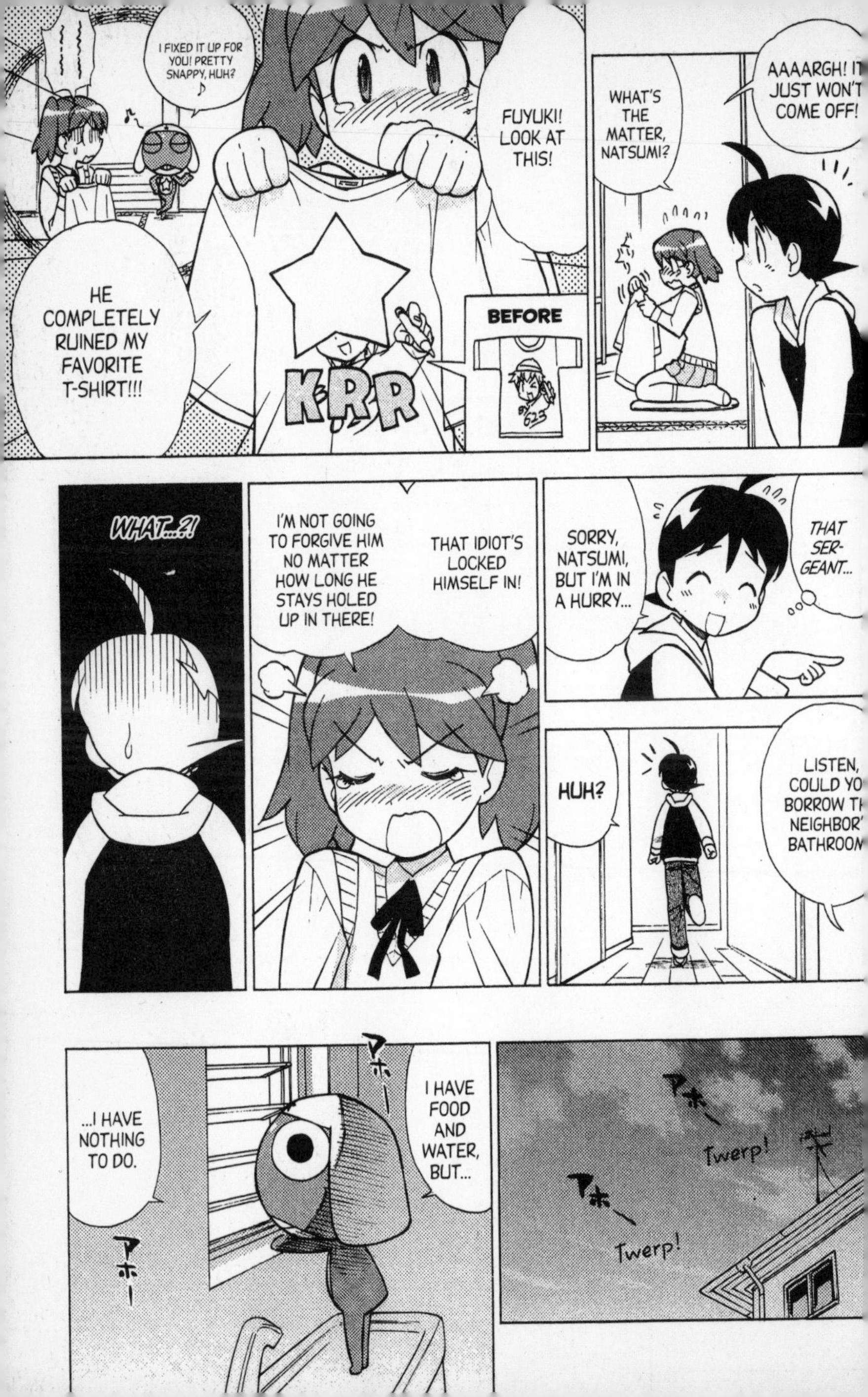
AAAARGH! IT JUST WON'T COME OFF!
WHAT'S THE MATTER, NATSUMI?
FUYUKI! LOOK AT THIS!
I FIXED IT UP FOR YOU! PRETTY SNAPPY, HUH? ♪
HE COMPLETELY RUINED MY FAVORITE T-SHIRT!!!
BEFORE
KRR
THAT SER-GEANT...
SORRY, NATSUMI, BUT I'M IN A HURRY...
LISTEN, COULD YO BORROW TH NEIGHBOR' BATHROOM
HUH?
THAT IDIOT'S LOCKED HIMSELF IN!
I'M NOT GOING TO FORGIVE HIM NO MATTER HOW LONG HE STAYS HOLED UP IN THERE!
WHAT...?!
Twerp!
Twerp!
I HAVE FOOD AND WATER, BUT...
...I HAVE NOTHING TO DO.

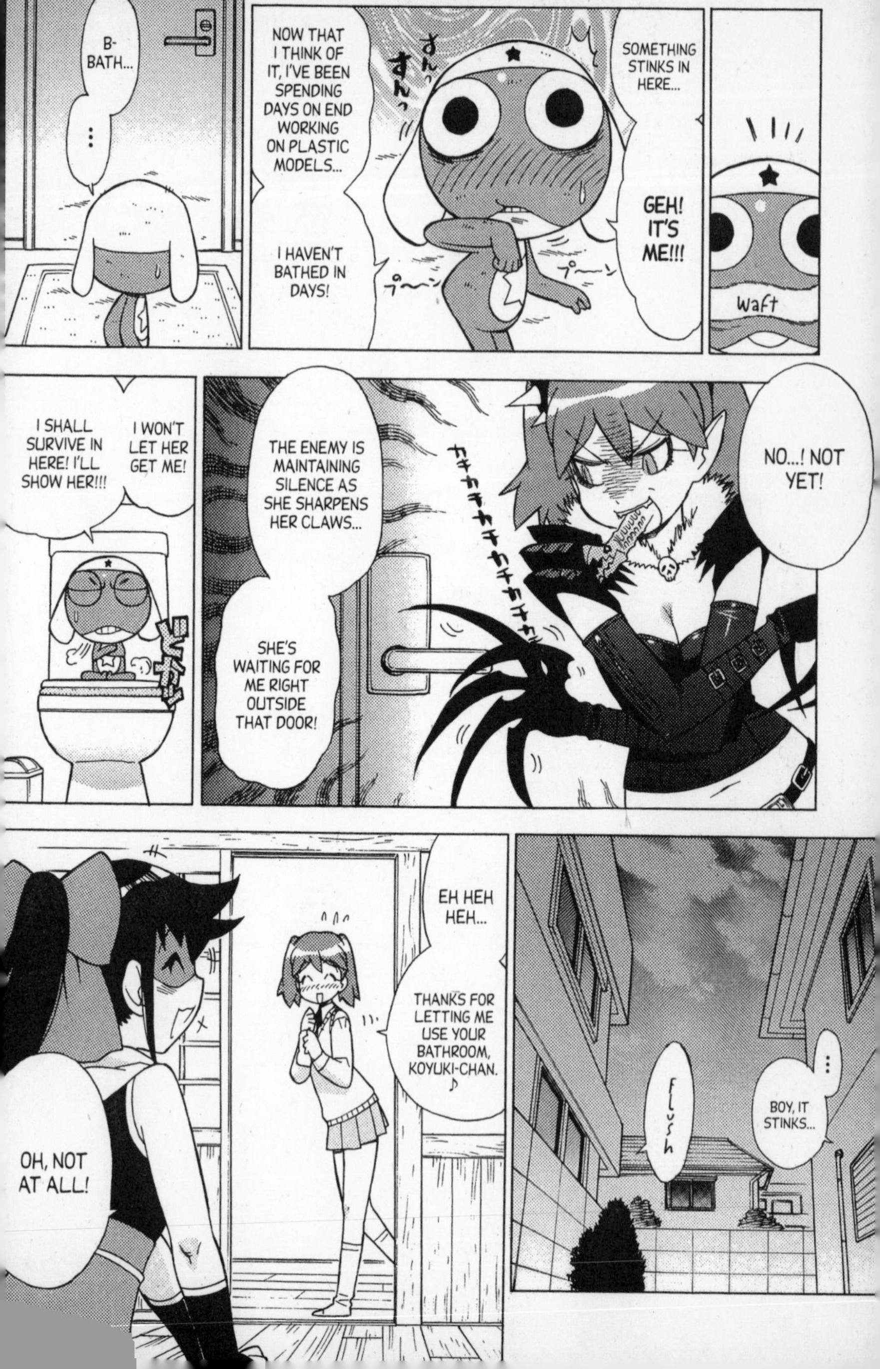
Waft
SOMETHING STINKS IN HERE...
GEH! IT'S ME!!!
NOW THAT I THINK OF IT, I'VE BEEN SPENDING DAYS ON END WORKING ON PLASTIC MODELS...
I HAVEN'T BATHED IN DAYS!
B-BATH...
...
NO...! NOT YET!
THE ENEMY IS MAINTAINING SILENCE AS SHE SHARPENS HER CLAWS...
SHE'S WAITING FOR ME RIGHT OUTSIDE THAT DOOR!
I WON'T LET HER GET ME!
I SHALL SURVIVE IN HERE! I'LL SHOW HER!!!
...
BOY, IT STINKS...
Flush
EH HEH HEH...
THANKS FOR LETTING ME USE YOUR BATHROOM, KOYUKI-CHAN. ♪
OH, NOT AT ALL!

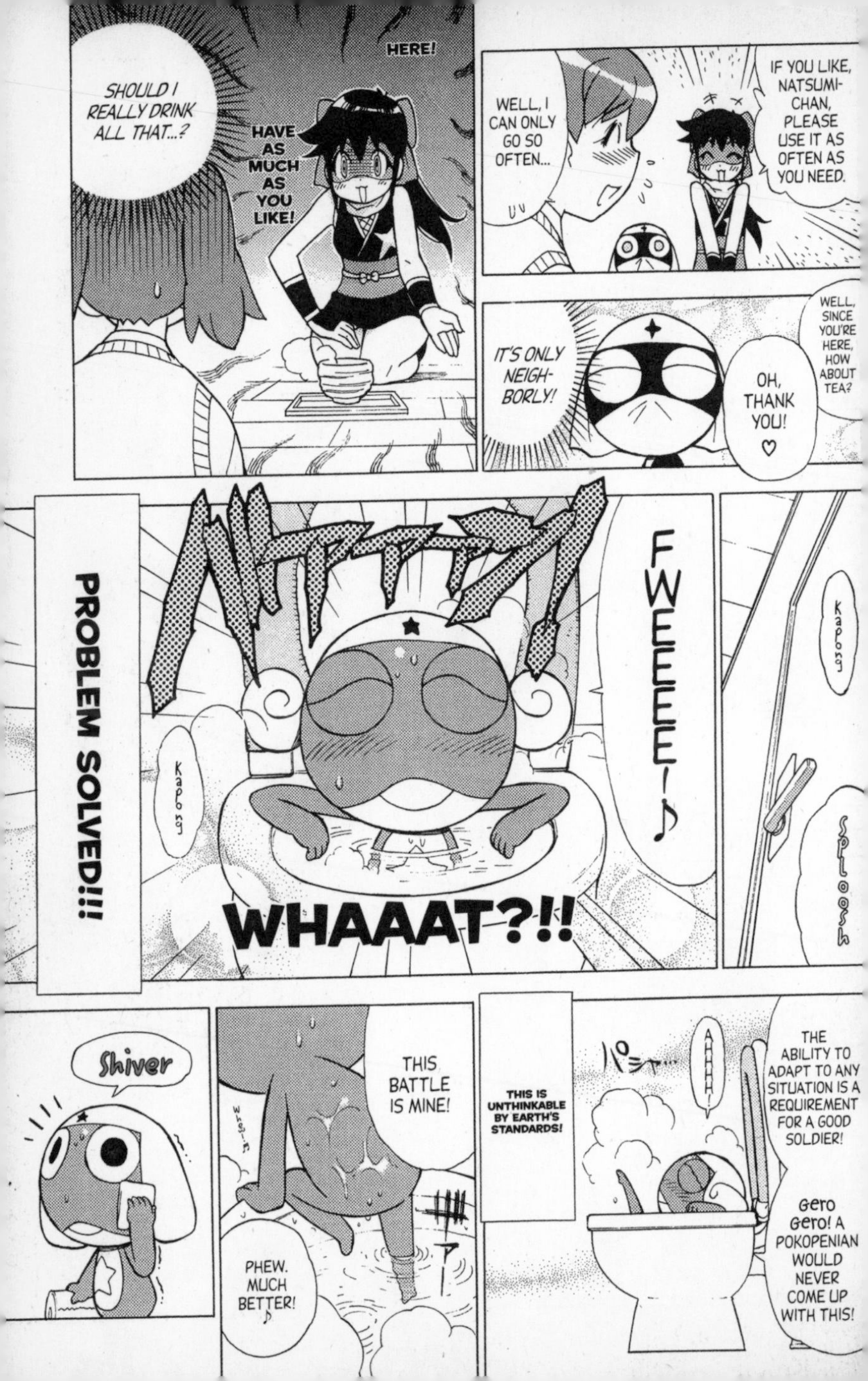

IF YOU LIKE, NATSUMI-CHAN, PLEASE USE IT AS OFTEN AS YOU NEED.
WELL, I CAN ONLY GO SO OFTEN...
WELL, SINCE YOU'RE HERE, HOW ABOUT TEA?
OH, THANK YOU! ♡
IT'S ONLY NEIGHBORLY!
HERE!
HAVE AS MUCH AS YOU LIKE!
SHOULD I REALLY DRINK ALL THAT...?
Kapong
Sploosh
FWEEEEE-!♪
Kapong
WHAAAT?!!
PROBLEM SOLVED!!!
THE ABILITY TO ADAPT TO ANY SITUATION IS A REQUIREMENT FOR A GOOD SOLDIER!
Gero Gero! A POKOPENIAN WOULD NEVER COME UP WITH THIS!
AHHH!
THIS IS UNTHINKABLE BY EARTH'S STANDARDS!
THIS BATTLE IS MINE!
PHEW. MUCH BETTER! ♪
Shiver

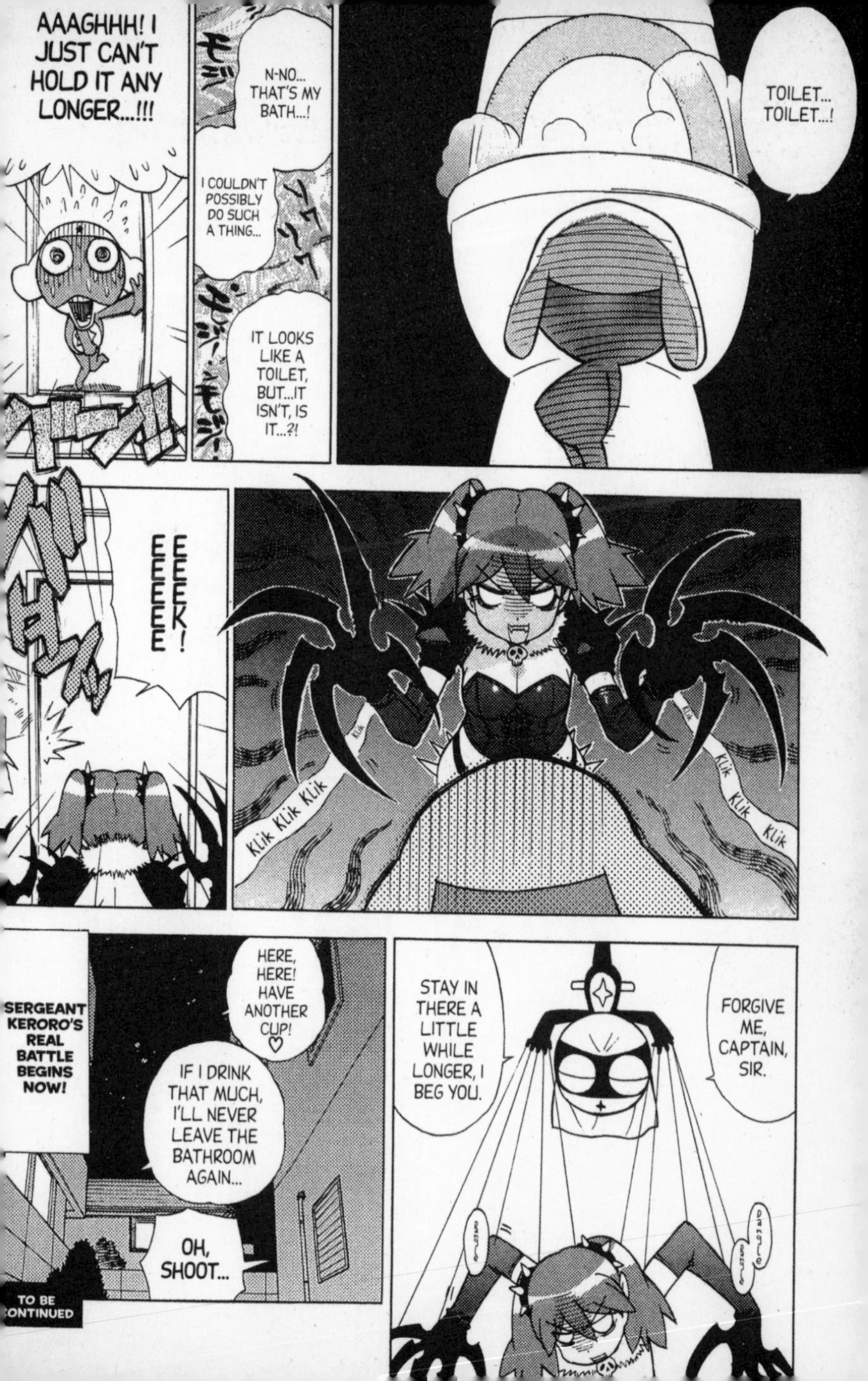
TOILET... TOILET...!
N-NO... THAT'S MY BATH...!
I COULDN'T POSSIBLY DO SUCH A THING...
IT LOOKS LIKE A TOILET, BUT...IT ISN'T, IS IT...?!
AAAGHHH! I JUST CAN'T HOLD IT ANY LONGER...!!!
Klik Klik Klik
Klik
Klik
Klik Klik Klik
EEEEEEEK!
FORGIVE ME, CAPTAIN, SIR.
STAY IN THERE A LITTLE WHILE LONGER, I BEG YOU.
dangle
dangle
dangle
HERE, HERE! HAVE ANOTHER CUP! ♡
IF I DRINK THAT MUCH, I'LL NEVER LEAVE THE BATHROOM AGAIN...
OH, SHOOT...
SERGEANT KERORO'S REAL BATTLE BEGINS NOW!
TO BE CONTINUED

ENCOUNTER CXXXIV
ALL LINE UP!! THE DARK BEFORE THE DAWN

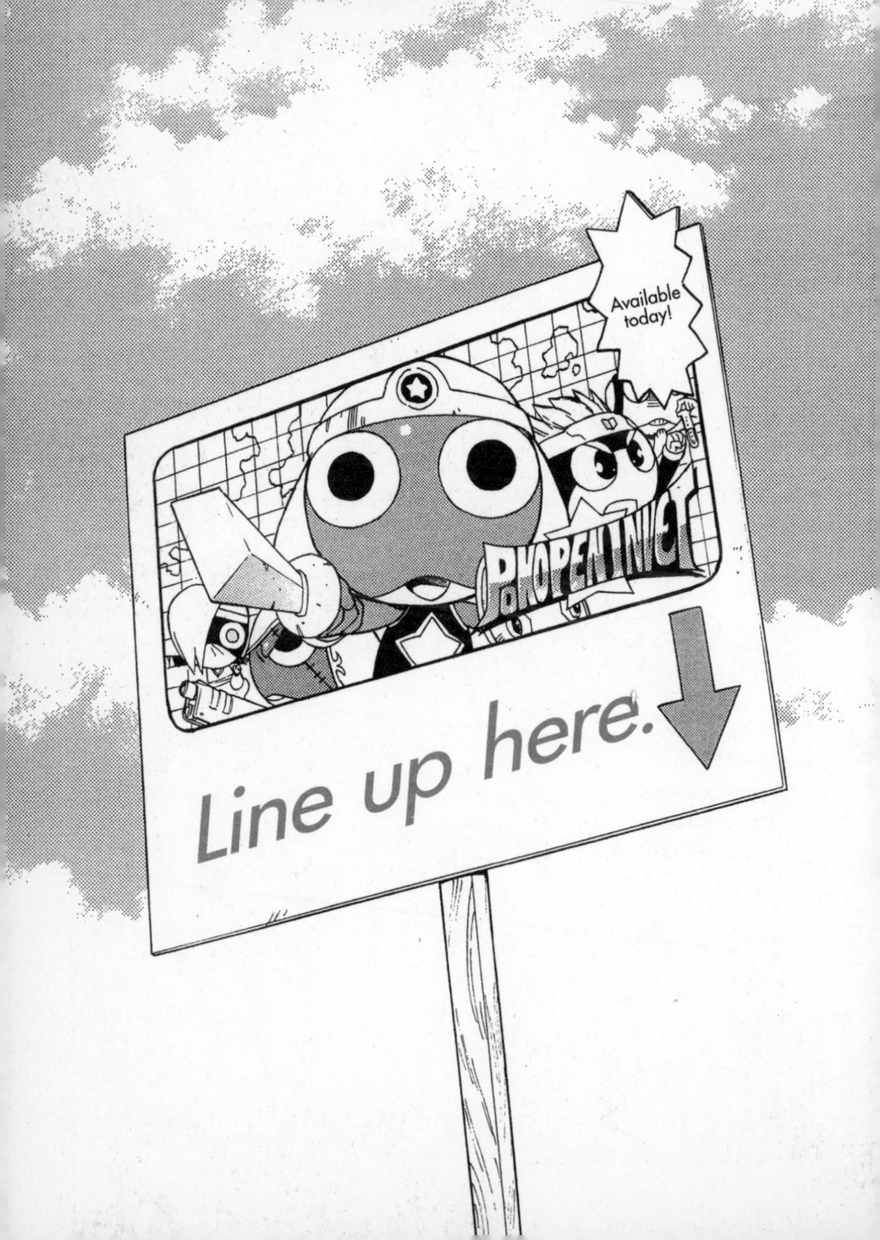
Available today!
Line up here.

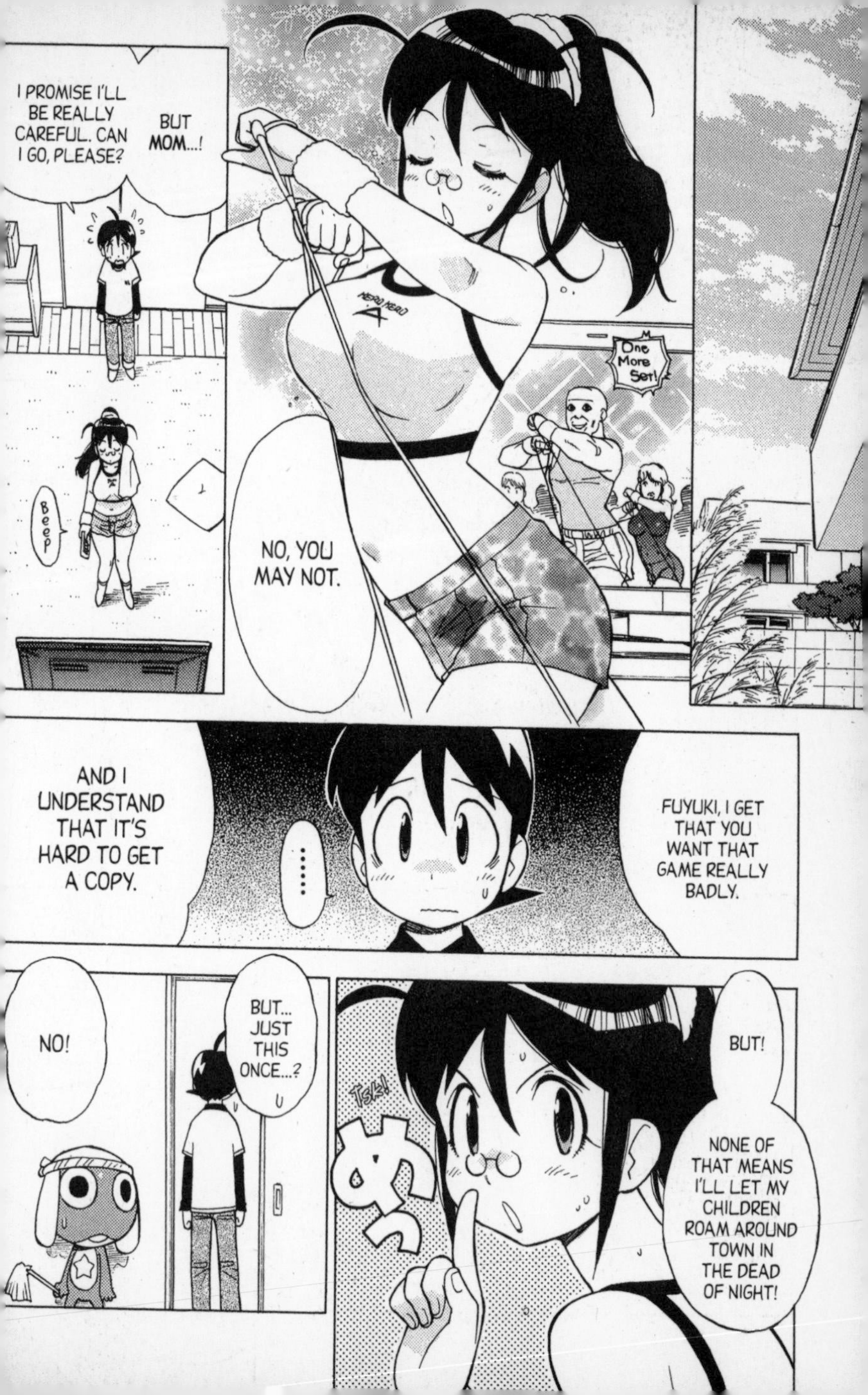
One More Set!
NO, YOU MAY NOT.
Beep
I PROMISE I'LL BE REALLY CAREFUL. CAN I GO, PLEASE?
BUT MOM...!
FUYUKI, I GET THAT YOU WANT THAT GAME REALLY BADLY.
......
AND I UNDERSTAND THAT IT'S HARD TO GET A COPY.
BUT!
NONE OF THAT MEANS I'LL LET MY CHILDREN ROAM AROUND TOWN IN THE DEAD OF NIGHT!
Tsk!
BUT... JUST THIS ONCE...?
NO!

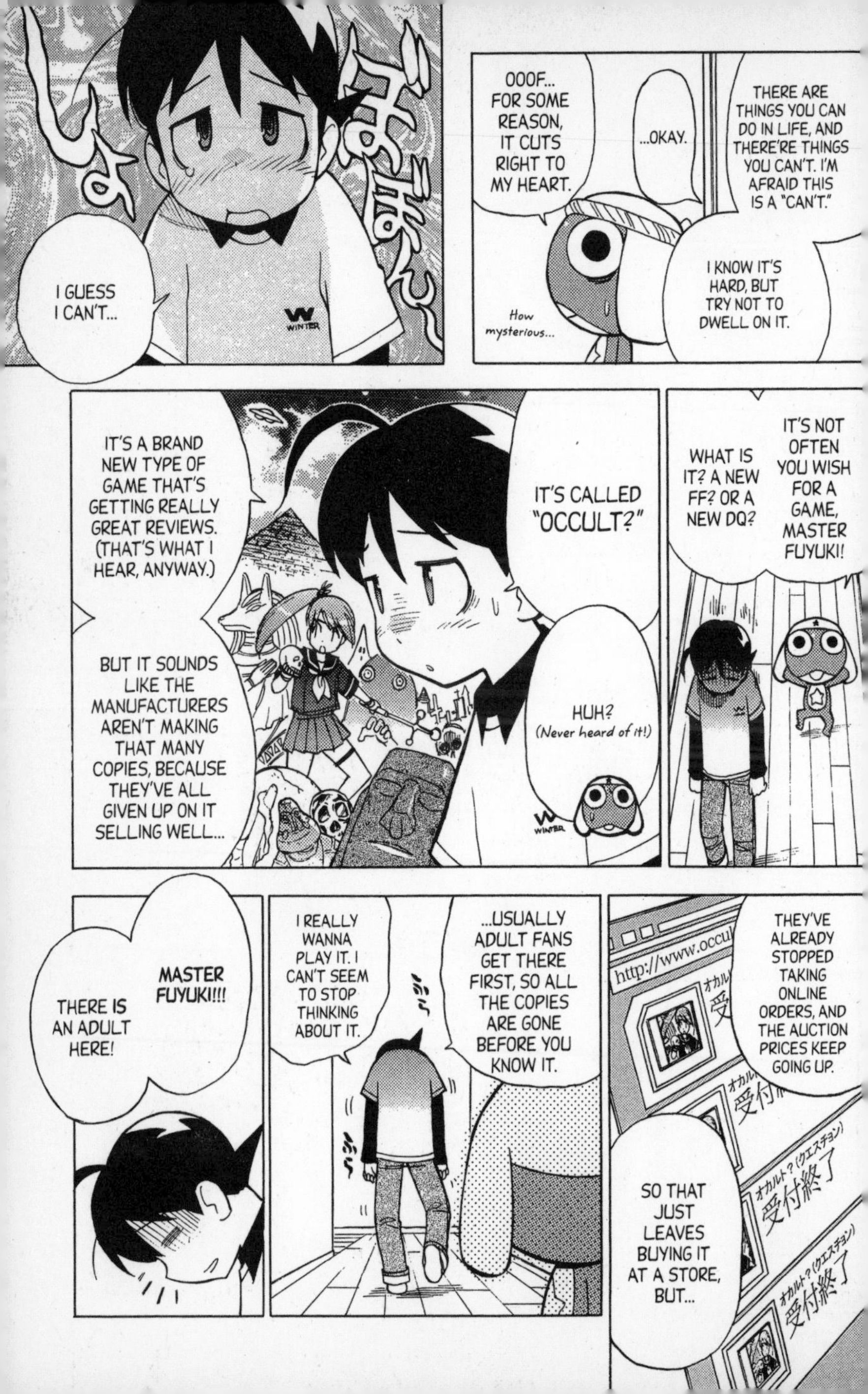
THERE ARE THINGS YOU CAN DO IN LIFE, AND THERE'RE THINGS YOU CAN'T. I'M AFRAID THIS IS A "CAN'T."
I KNOW IT'S HARD, BUT TRY NOT TO DWELL ON IT.
...OKAY.
OOOF... FOR SOME REASON, IT CUTS RIGHT TO MY HEART.
How mysterious...
I GUESS I CAN'T...
IT'S NOT OFTEN YOU WISH FOR A GAME, MASTER FUYUKI!
WHAT IS IT? A NEW FF? OR A NEW DQ?
IT'S CALLED "OCCULT?"
HUH? (Never heard of it!)
IT'S A BRAND NEW TYPE OF GAME THAT'S GETTING REALLY GREAT REVIEWS. (THAT'S WHAT I HEAR, ANYWAY.)
BUT IT SOUNDS LIKE THE MANUFACTURERS AREN'T MAKING THAT MANY COPIES, BECAUSE THEY'VE ALL GIVEN UP ON IT SELLING WELL...
THEY'VE ALREADY STOPPED TAKING ONLINE ORDERS, AND THE AUCTION PRICES KEEP GOING UP.
http://www.occul
オカルト？(クエスチョン) 受付終了
SO THAT JUST LEAVES BUYING IT AT A STORE, BUT...
...USUALLY ADULT FANS GET THERE FIRST, SO ALL THE COPIES ARE GONE BEFORE YOU KNOW IT.
I REALLY WANNA PLAY IT. I CAN'T SEEM TO STOP THINKING ABOUT IT.
MASTER FUYUKI!!!
THERE IS AN ADULT HERE!

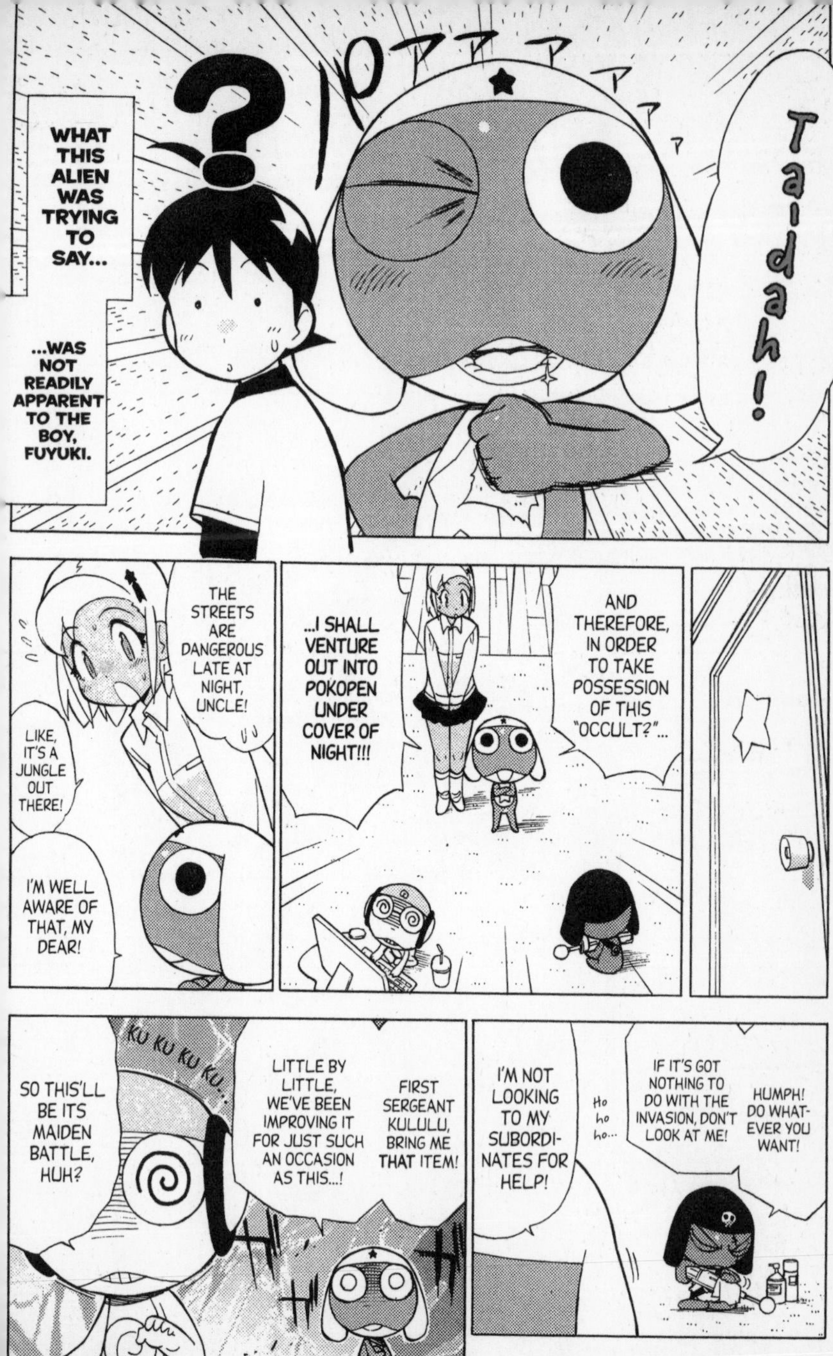
Tadah!
WHAT THIS ALIEN WAS TRYING TO SAY...
...WAS NOT READILY APPARENT TO THE BOY, FUYUKI.
AND THEREFORE, IN ORDER TO TAKE POSSESSION OF THIS "OCCULT?"...
...I SHALL VENTURE OUT INTO POKOPEN UNDER COVER OF NIGHT!!!
THE STREETS ARE DANGEROUS LATE AT NIGHT, UNCLE!
LIKE, IT'S A JUNGLE OUT THERE!
I'M WELL AWARE OF THAT, MY DEAR!
HUMPH! DO WHAT-EVER YOU WANT!
IF IT'S GOT NOTHING TO DO WITH THE INVASION, DON'T LOOK AT ME!
Ho ho ho...
I'M NOT LOOKING TO MY SUBORDI-NATES FOR HELP!
FIRST SERGEANT KULULU, BRING ME THAT ITEM!
LITTLE BY LITTLE, WE'VE BEEN IMPROVING IT FOR JUST SUCH AN OCCASION AS THIS...!
KU KU KU KU...
SO THIS'LL BE ITS MAIDEN BATTLE, HUH?

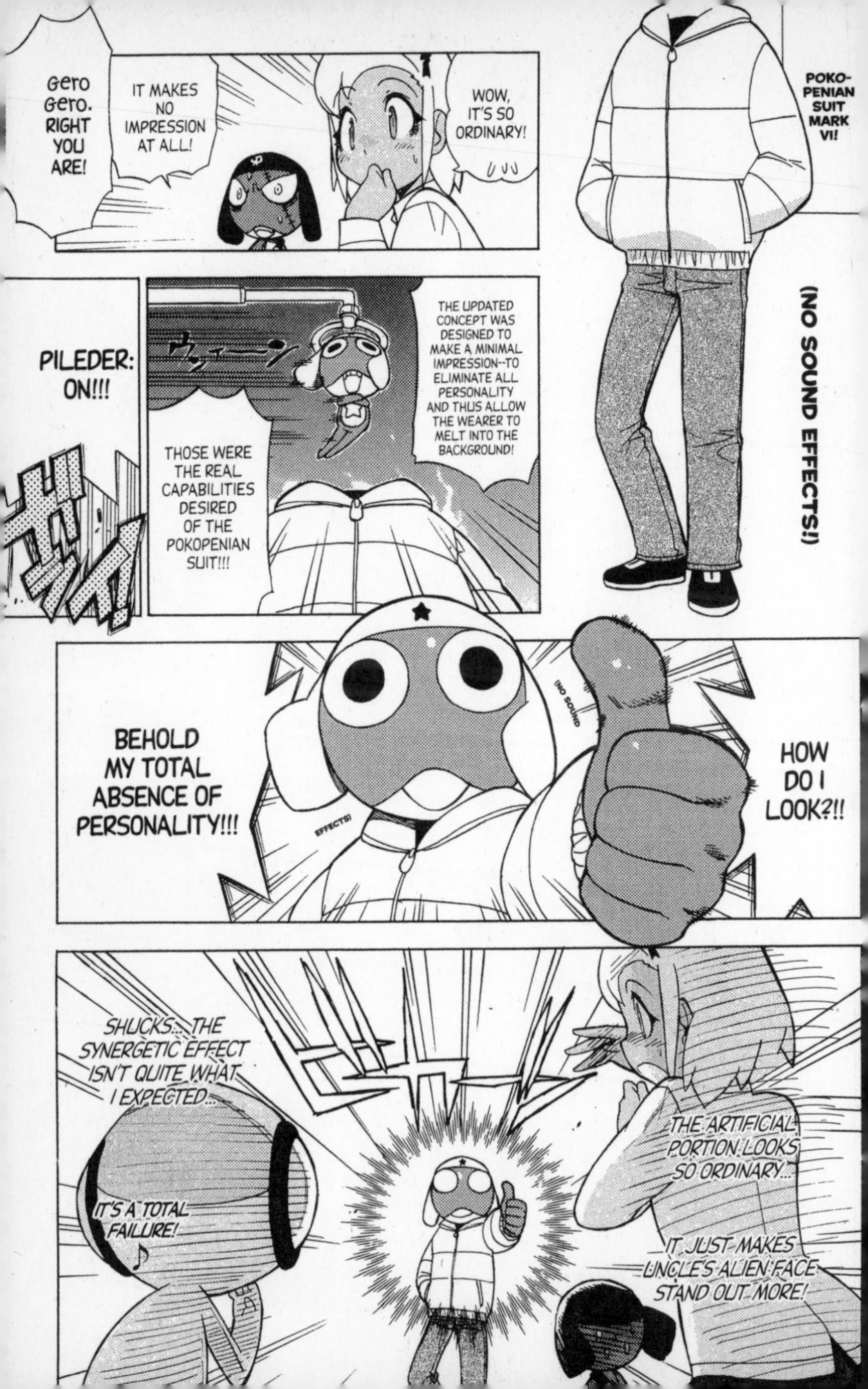
POKO-PENIAN SUIT MARK VI!
(NO SOUND EFFECTS!)
WOW, IT'S SO ORDINARY!
IT MAKES NO IMPRESSION AT ALL!
Gero Gero. RIGHT YOU ARE!
THE UPDATED CONCEPT WAS DESIGNED TO MAKE A MINIMAL IMPRESSION--TO ELIMINATE ALL PERSONALITY AND THUS ALLOW THE WEARER TO MELT INTO THE BACKGROUND!
THOSE WERE THE REAL CAPABILITIES DESIRED OF THE POKOPENIAN SUIT!!!
PILEDER: ON!!!
HOW DO I LOOK?!!
(NO SOUND EFFECTS)
BEHOLD MY TOTAL ABSENCE OF PERSONALITY!!!
THE ARTIFICIAL PORTION LOOKS SO ORDINARY...
IT JUST MAKES UNCLE'S ALIEN FACE STAND OUT MORE!
SHUCKS... THE SYNERGETIC EFFECT ISN'T QUITE WHAT I EXPECTED...
IT'S A TOTAL FAILURE!

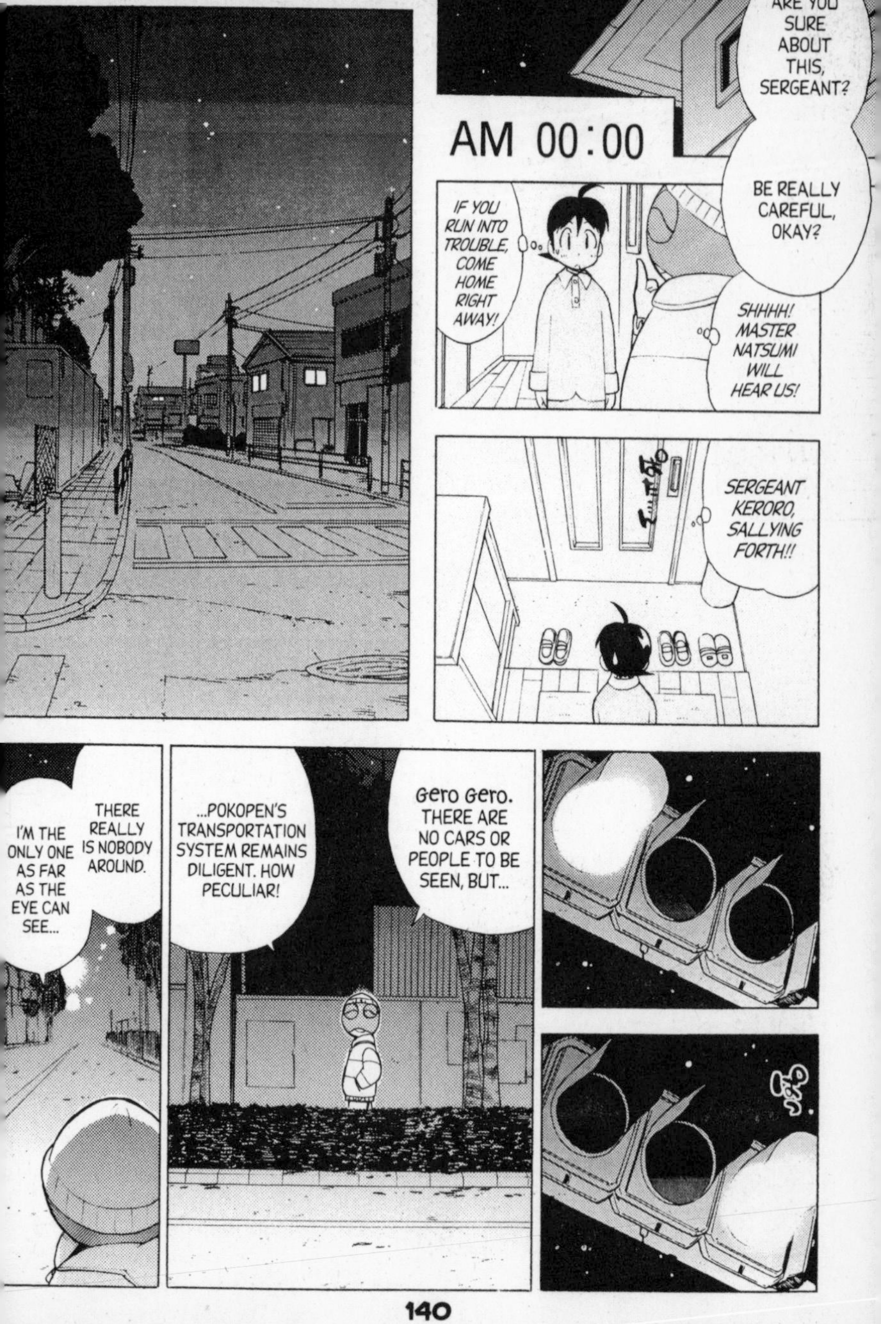
ARE YOU SURE ABOUT THIS, SERGEANT?
AM 00:00
BE REALLY CAREFUL, OKAY?
IF YOU RUN INTO TROUBLE, COME HOME RIGHT AWAY!
SHHHH! MASTER NATSUMI WILL HEAR US!
SERGEANT KERORO, SALLYING FORTH!!
Gero Gero. THERE ARE NO CARS OR PEOPLE TO BE SEEN, BUT...
...POKOPEN'S TRANSPORTATION SYSTEM REMAINS DILIGENT. HOW PECULIAR!
THERE REALLY IS NOBODY AROUND.
I'M THE ONLY ONE AS FAR AS THE EYE CAN SEE...

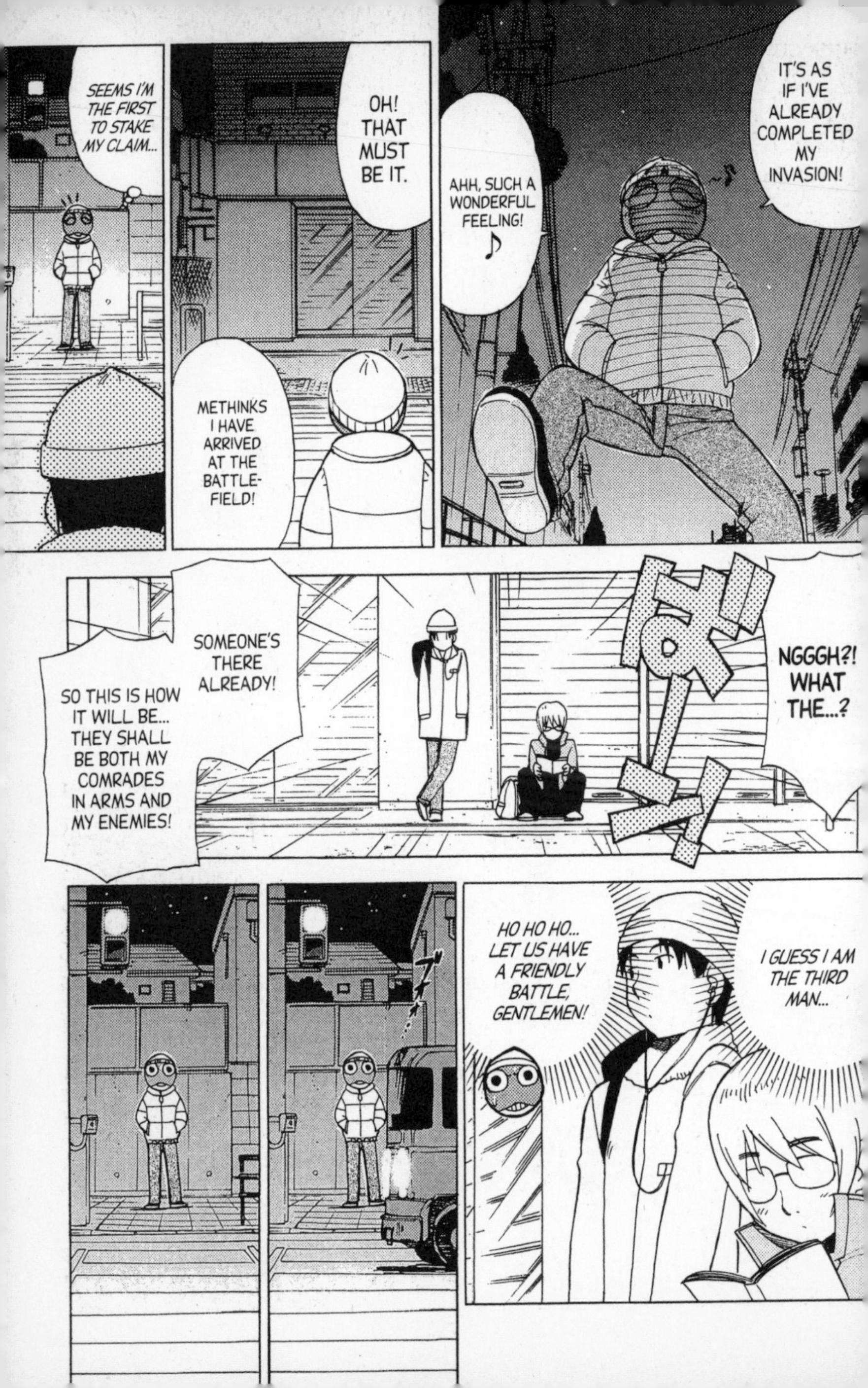
IT'S AS IF I'VE ALREADY COMPLETED MY INVASION!
AHH, SUCH A WONDERFUL FEELING! ♪
OH! THAT MUST BE IT.
METHINKS I HAVE ARRIVED AT THE BATTLE-FIELD!
SEEMS I'M THE FIRST TO STAKE MY CLAIM...
NGGGH?! WHAT THE...?
SOMEONE'S THERE ALREADY!
SO THIS IS HOW IT WILL BE... THEY SHALL BE BOTH MY COMRADES IN ARMS AND MY ENEMIES!
I GUESS I AM THE THIRD MAN...
HO HO HO... LET US HAVE A FRIENDLY BATTLE, GENTLEMEN!

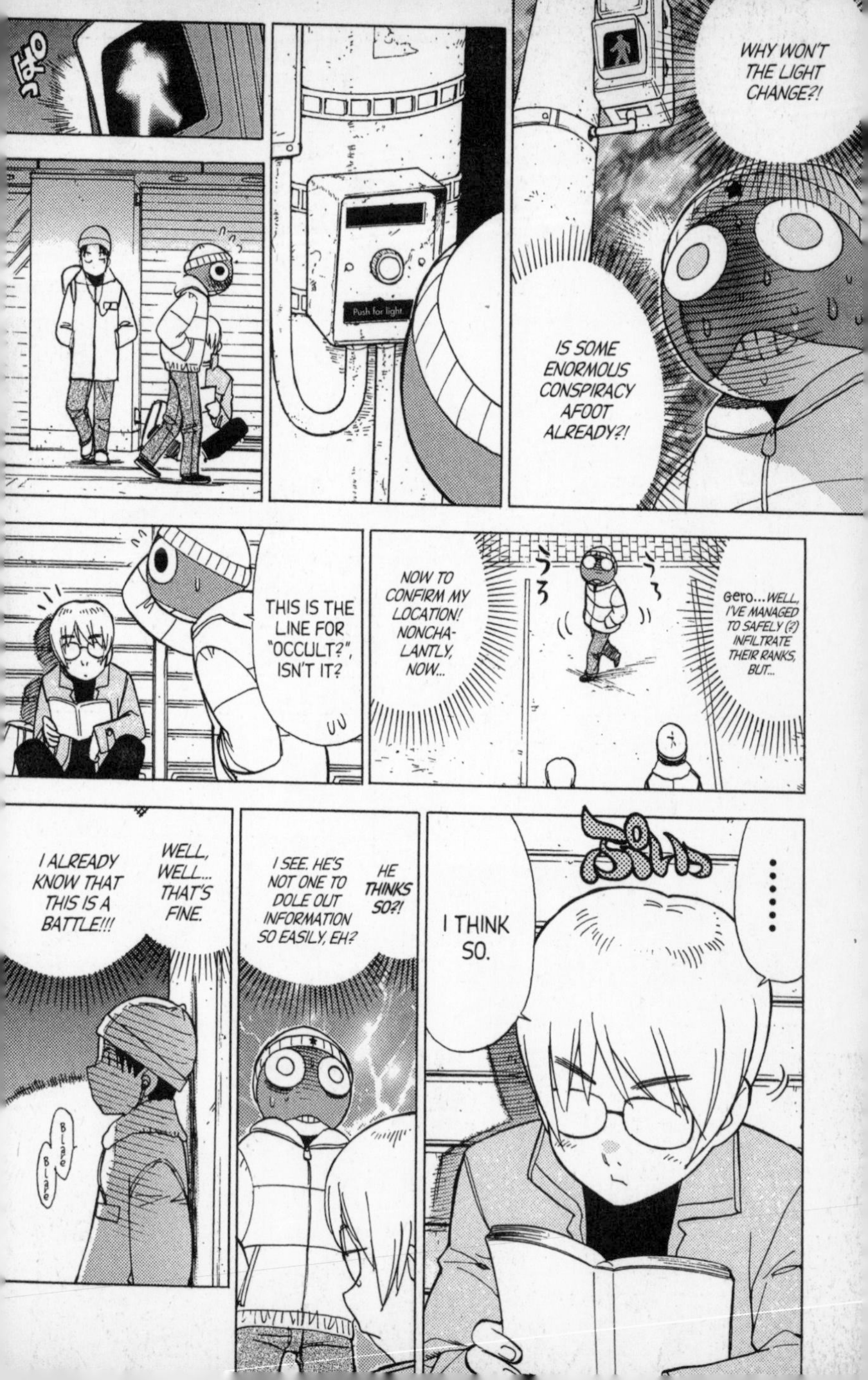
WHY WON'T THE LIGHT CHANGE?!
IS SOME ENORMOUS CONSPIRACY AFOOT ALREADY?!
Push for light.
Gero... WELL, I'VE MANAGED TO SAFELY (?) INFILTRATE THEIR RANKS, BUT...
NOW TO CONFIRM MY LOCATION! NONCHA-LANTLY, NOW...
THIS IS THE LINE FOR "OCCULT?", ISN'T IT?
......
I THINK SO.
HE THINKS SO?!
I SEE. HE'S NOT ONE TO DOLE OUT INFORMATION SO EASILY, EH?
WELL, WELL... THAT'S FINE.
I ALREADY KNOW THAT THIS IS A BATTLE!!!
Blae Blae

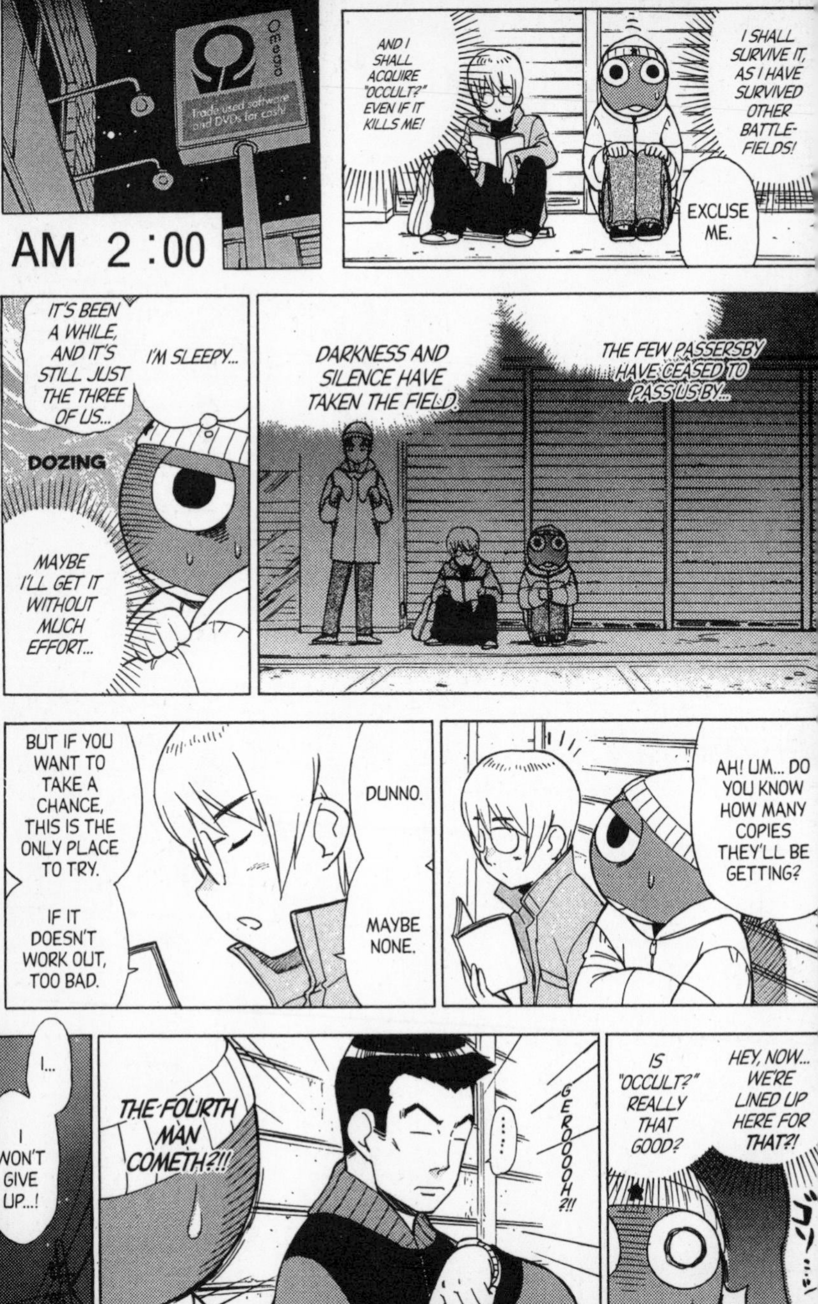
I SHALL SURVIVE IT, AS I HAVE SURVIVED OTHER BATTLE-FIELDS!
AND I SHALL ACQUIRE "OCCULT?" EVEN IF IT KILLS ME!
EXCUSE ME.
Omega
Trade used software and DVDs for cash!
AM 2:00
THE FEW PASSERSBY HAVE CEASED TO PASS US BY...
DARKNESS AND SILENCE HAVE TAKEN THE FIELD.
IT'S BEEN A WHILE, AND IT'S STILL JUST THE THREE OF US...
I'M SLEEPY...
DOZING
MAYBE I'LL GET IT WITHOUT MUCH EFFORT...
AH! UM... DO YOU KNOW HOW MANY COPIES THEY'LL BE GETTING?
DUNNO.
MAYBE NONE.
BUT IF YOU WANT TO TAKE A CHANCE, THIS IS THE ONLY PLACE TO TRY.
IF IT DOESN'T WORK OUT, TOO BAD.
HEY, NOW... WE'RE LINED UP HERE FOR THAT?!
IS "OCCULT?" REALLY THAT GOOD?
Oh!
GEROOOOOH?!!
.....
THE FOURTH MAN COMETH?!!
I...
I WON'T GIVE UP...!

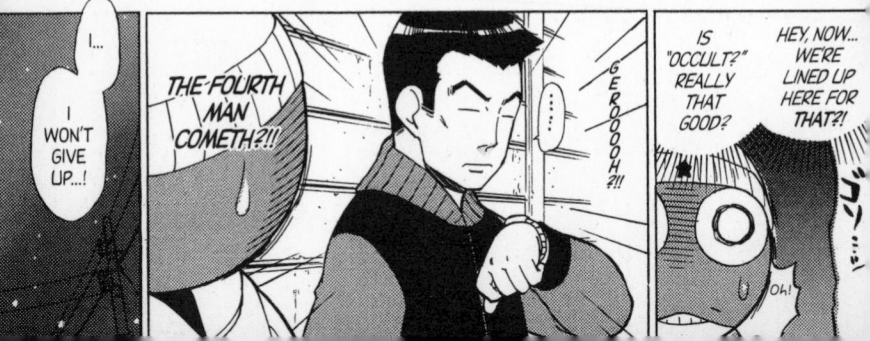

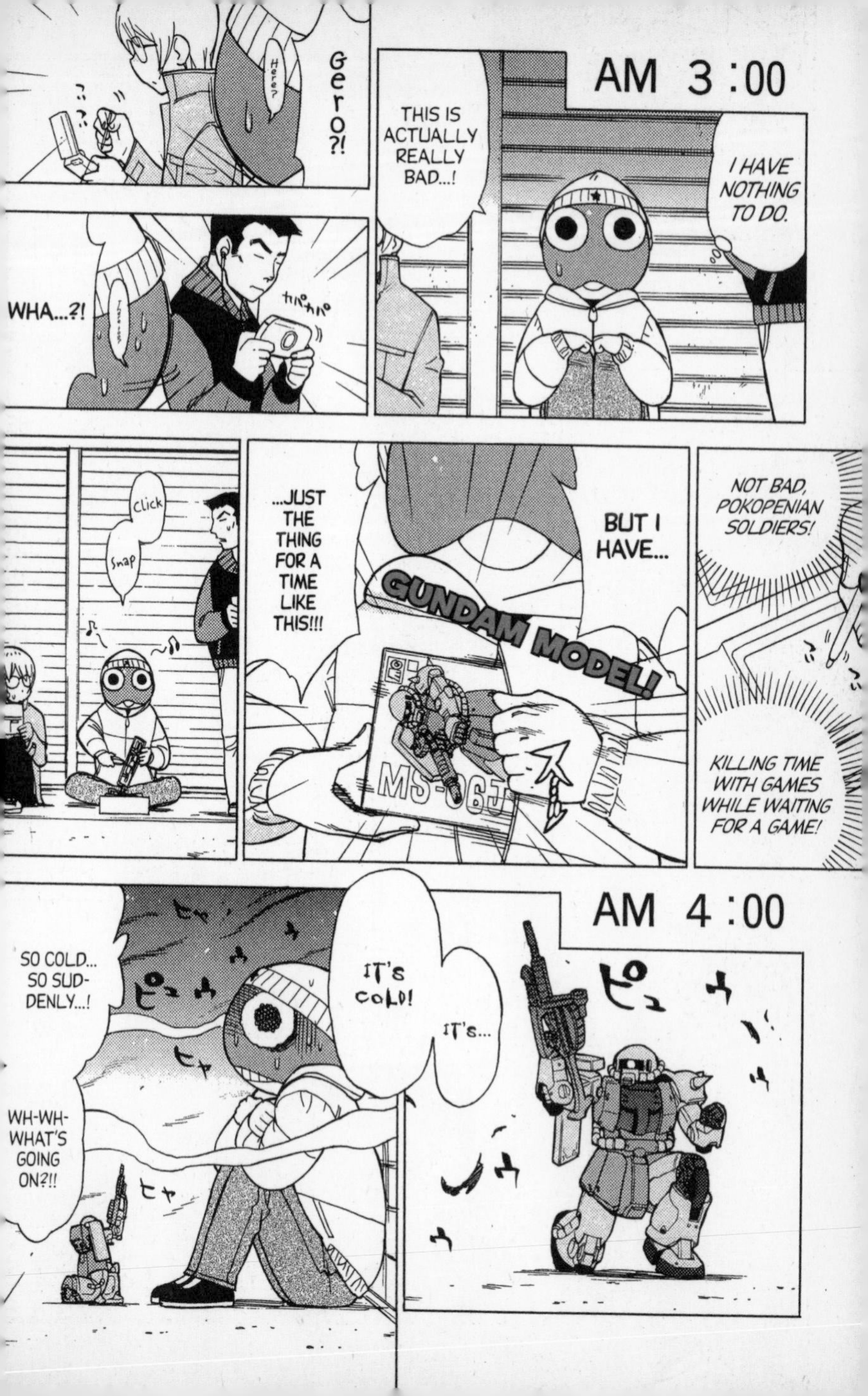
AM 3:00
I HAVE NOTHING TO DO.
THIS IS ACTUALLY REALLY BAD...!
Gero?!
Here?
WHA...?!
NOT BAD, POKOPENIAN SOLDIERS!
KILLING TIME WITH GAMES WHILE WAITING FOR A GAME!
BUT I HAVE...
GUNDAM MODEL!
...JUST THE THING FOR A TIME LIKE THIS!!!
Click
Snap
MS-06J
AM 4:00
IT's...
IT's COLD!
SO COLD... SO SUD-DENLY...!
WH-WH-WHAT'S GOING ON?!!

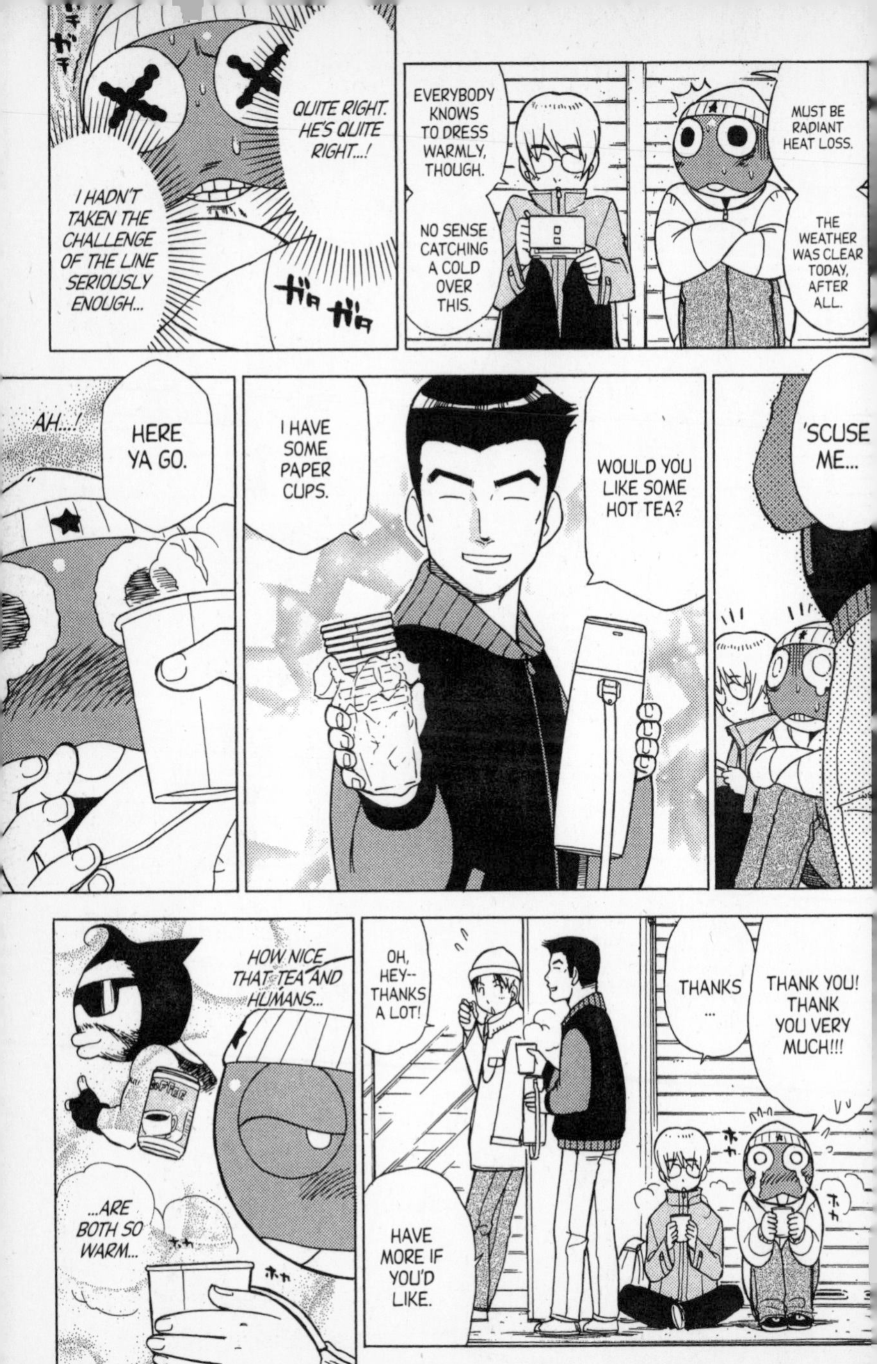
MUST BE RADIANT HEAT LOSS.
THE WEATHER WAS CLEAR TODAY, AFTER ALL.
EVERYBODY KNOWS TO DRESS WARMLY, THOUGH.
NO SENSE CATCHING A COLD OVER THIS.
QUITE RIGHT. HE'S QUITE RIGHT...!
I HADN'T TAKEN THE CHALLENGE OF THE LINE SERIOUSLY ENOUGH...
'SCUSE ME...
WOULD YOU LIKE SOME HOT TEA?
I HAVE SOME PAPER CUPS.
HERE YA GO.
AH...!
THANK YOU! THANK YOU VERY MUCH!!!
THANKS ...
OH, HEY-- THANKS A LOT!
HAVE MORE IF YOU'D LIKE.
HOW NICE THAT TEA AND HUMANS...
...ARE BOTH SO WARM...

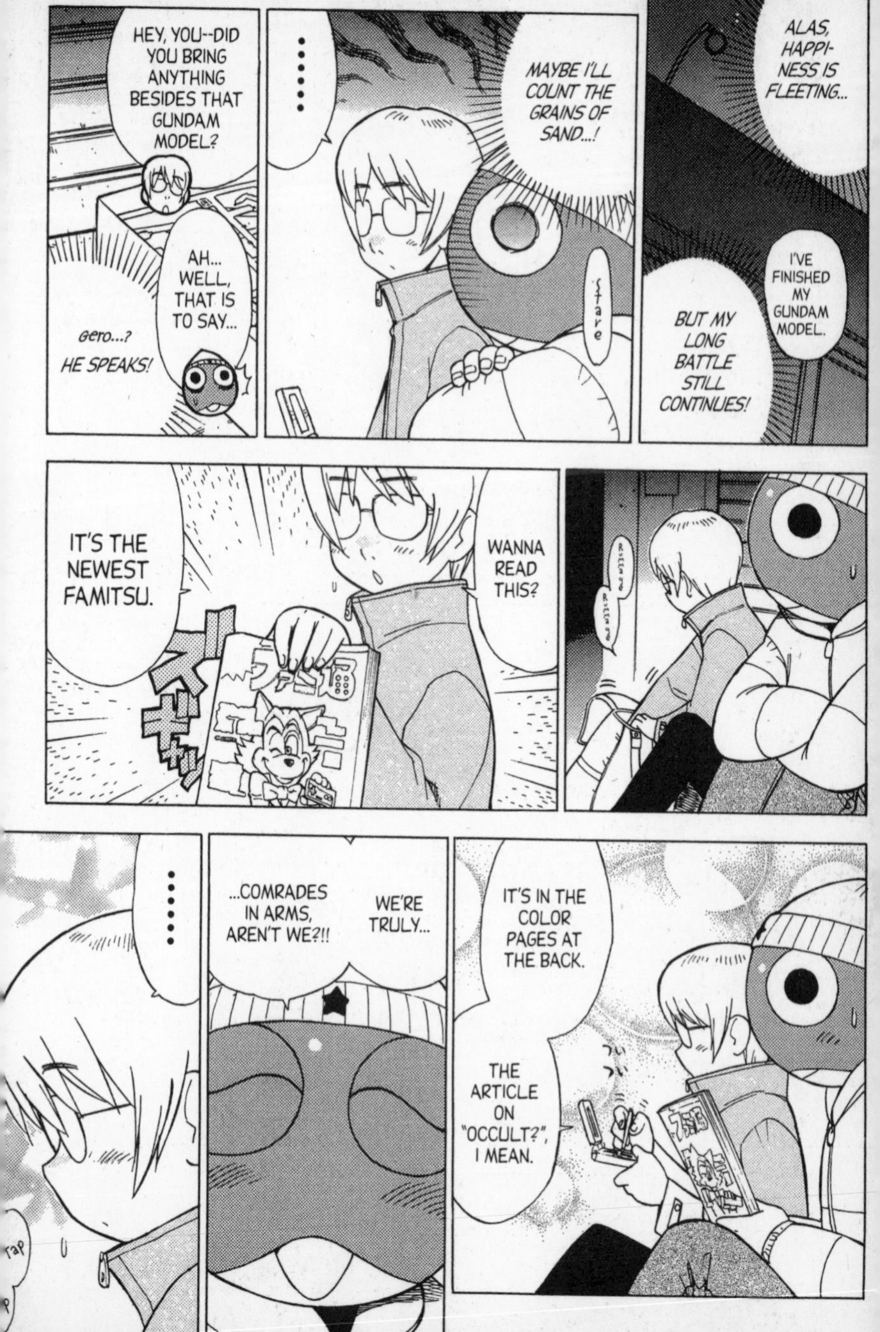

ALAS, HAPPI-NESS IS FLEETING...
I'VE FINISHED MY GUNDAM MODEL.
BUT MY LONG BATTLE STILL CONTINUES!
MAYBE I'LL COUNT THE GRAINS OF SAND...!
......
stare
HEY, YOU--DID YOU BRING ANYTHING BESIDES THAT GUNDAM MODEL?
AH... WELL, THAT IS TO SAY...
Gero...?
HE SPEAKS!
WANNA READ THIS?
IT'S THE NEWEST FAMITSU.
IT'S IN THE COLOR PAGES AT THE BACK.
THE ARTICLE ON "OCCULT?", I MEAN.
WE'RE TRULY...
...COMRADES IN ARMS, AREN'T WE?!!
......

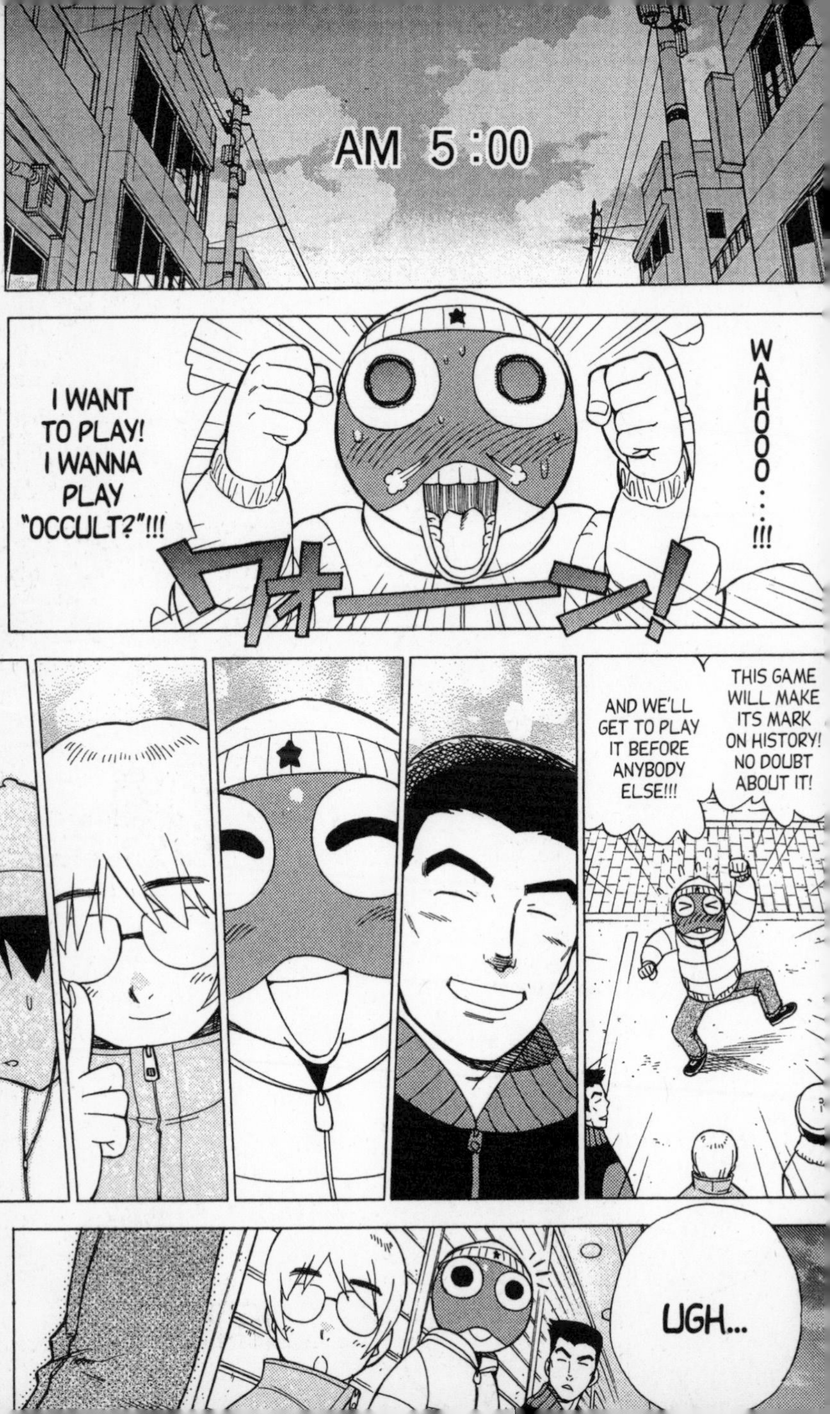
AM 5:00
WAHOOO...!!!
I WANT TO PLAY! I WANNA PLAY "OCCULT?"!!!
ワオーン!
THIS GAME WILL MAKE ITS MARK ON HISTORY! NO DOUBT ABOUT IT!
AND WE'LL GET TO PLAY IT BEFORE ANYBODY ELSE!!!
UGH...

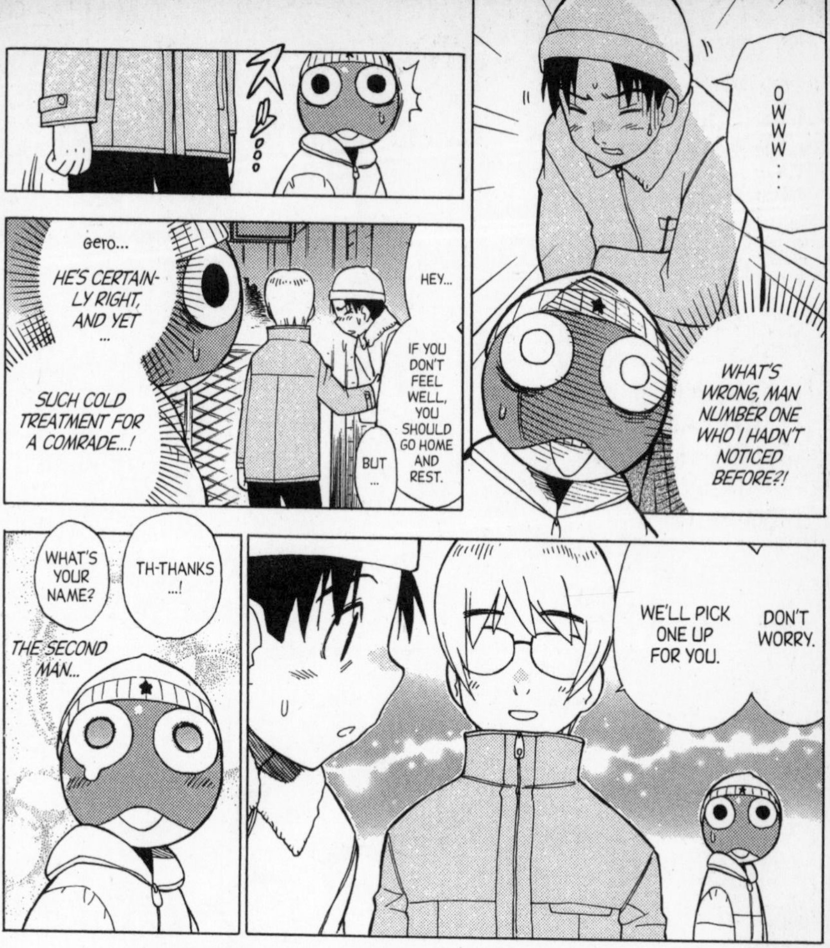
OWWW...
WHAT'S WRONG, MAN NUMBER ONE WHO I HADN'T NOTICED BEFORE?!
HEY...
IF YOU DON'T FEEL WELL, YOU SHOULD GO HOME AND REST.
BUT ...
Gero...
HE'S CERTAIN-LY RIGHT, AND YET ...
SUCH COLD TREATMENT FOR A COMRADE...!
DON'T WORRY.
WE'LL PICK ONE UP FOR YOU.
TH-THANKS ...!
WHAT'S YOUR NAME?
THE SECOND MAN...

FOUR HOURS TO OPENING...

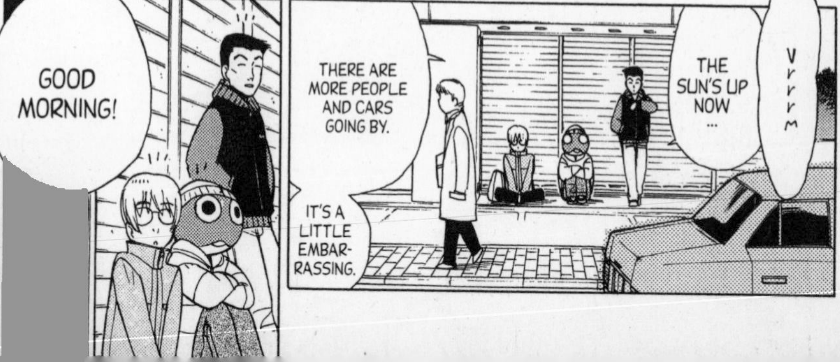
Vrrrm
THE SUN'S UP NOW ...
THERE ARE MORE PEOPLE AND CARS GOING BY.
IT'S A LITTLE EMBAR-RASSING.
GOOD MORNING!

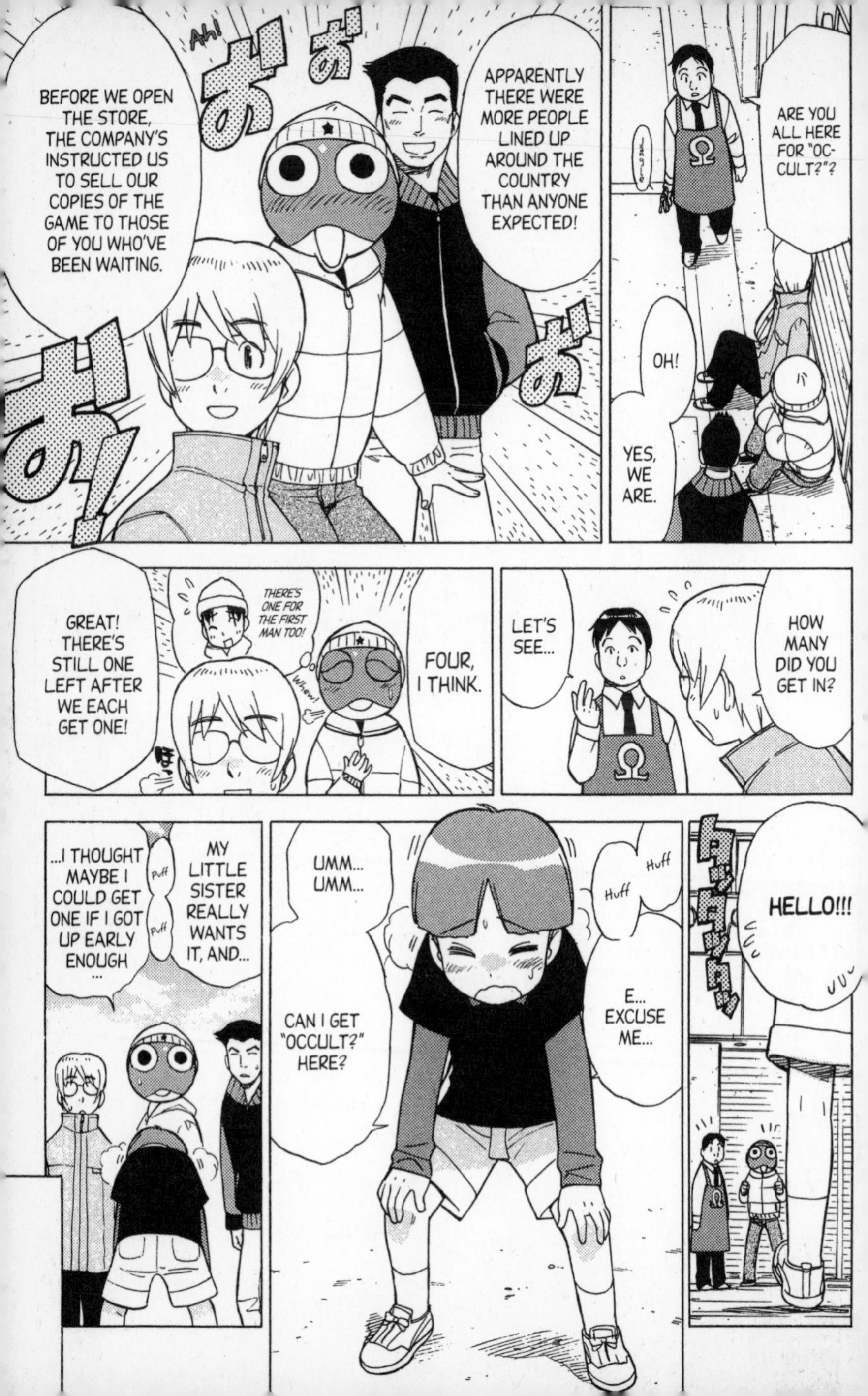
ARE YOU ALL HERE FOR "OC-CULT?"?
OH!
YES, WE ARE.
APPARENTLY THERE WERE MORE PEOPLE LINED UP AROUND THE COUNTRY THAN ANYONE EXPECTED!
Ah!
BEFORE WE OPEN THE STORE, THE COMPANY'S INSTRUCTED US TO SELL OUR COPIES OF THE GAME TO THOSE OF YOU WHO'VE BEEN WAITING.
HOW MANY DID YOU GET IN?
LET'S SEE...
FOUR, I THINK.
THERE'S ONE FOR THE FIRST MAN TOO!
Whew!
GREAT! THERE'S STILL ONE LEFT AFTER WE EACH GET ONE!
HELLO!!!
Huff
Huff
E... EXCUSE ME...
UMM... UMM...
CAN I GET "OCCULT?" HERE?
MY LITTLE SISTER REALLY WANTS IT, AND...
Puff
Puff
...I THOUGHT MAYBE I COULD GET ONE IF I GOT UP EARLY ENOUGH ...

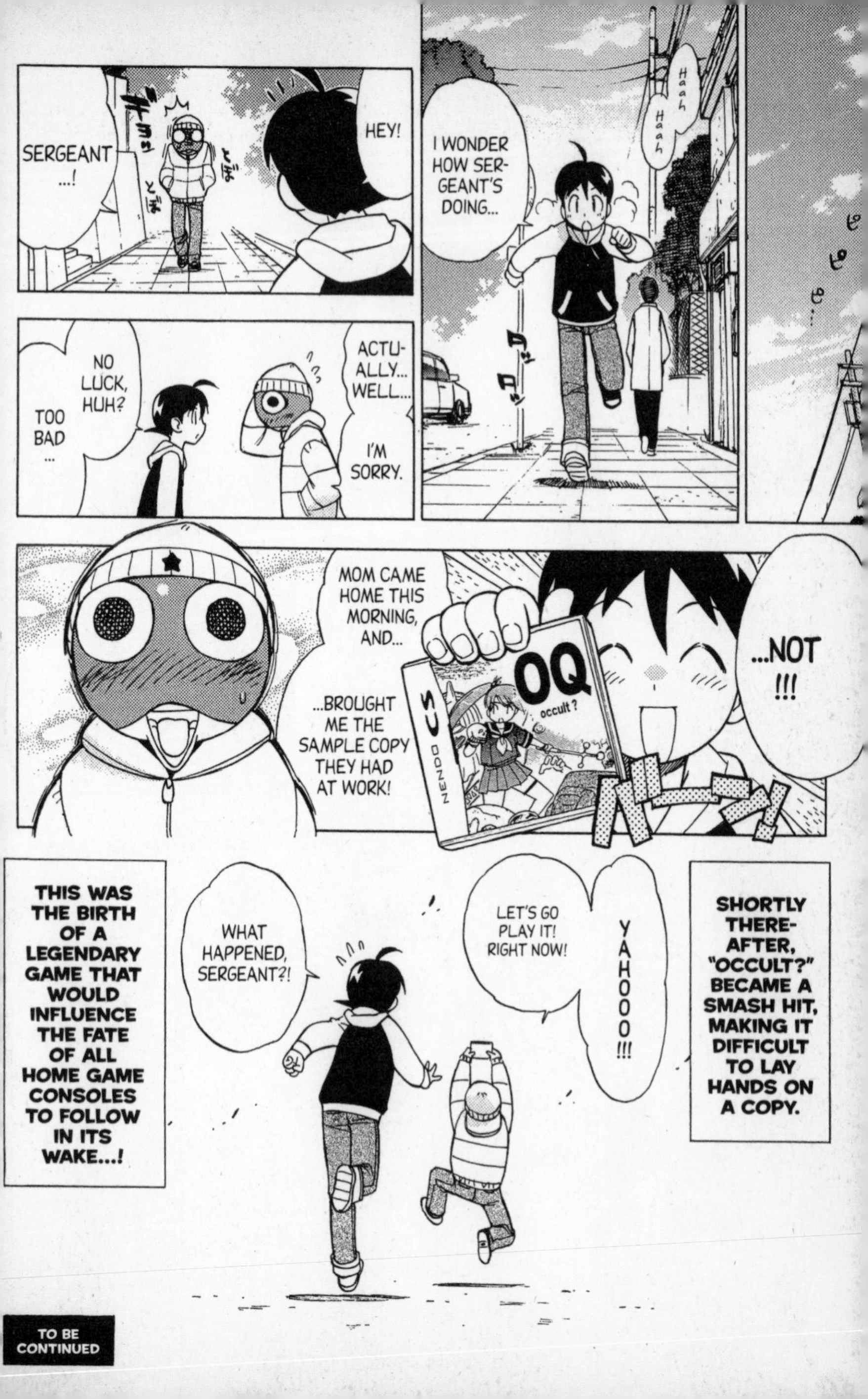
Haah
Haah
I WONDER HOW SER-GEANT'S DOING...
HEY!
SERGEANT ...!
ACTU-ALLY... WELL...
I'M SORRY.
NO LUCK, HUH?
TOO BAD ...
...NOT !!!
OQ occult ?
NENDO CS
MOM CAME HOME THIS MORNING, AND...
...BROUGHT ME THE SAMPLE COPY THEY HAD AT WORK!
SHORTLY THERE-AFTER, "OCCULT?" BECAME A SMASH HIT, MAKING IT DIFFICULT TO LAY HANDS ON A COPY.
YAHOOOO!!!
LET'S GO PLAY IT! RIGHT NOW!
WHAT HAPPENED, SERGEANT?!
THIS WAS THE BIRTH OF A LEGENDARY GAME THAT WOULD INFLUENCE THE FATE OF ALL HOME GAME CONSOLES TO FOLLOW IN ITS WAKE...!
TO BE CONTINUED

ENCOUNTER CXXXV
SLAM! EARTH VS SPACE VIDEO GAME ARMAGEDDON!!

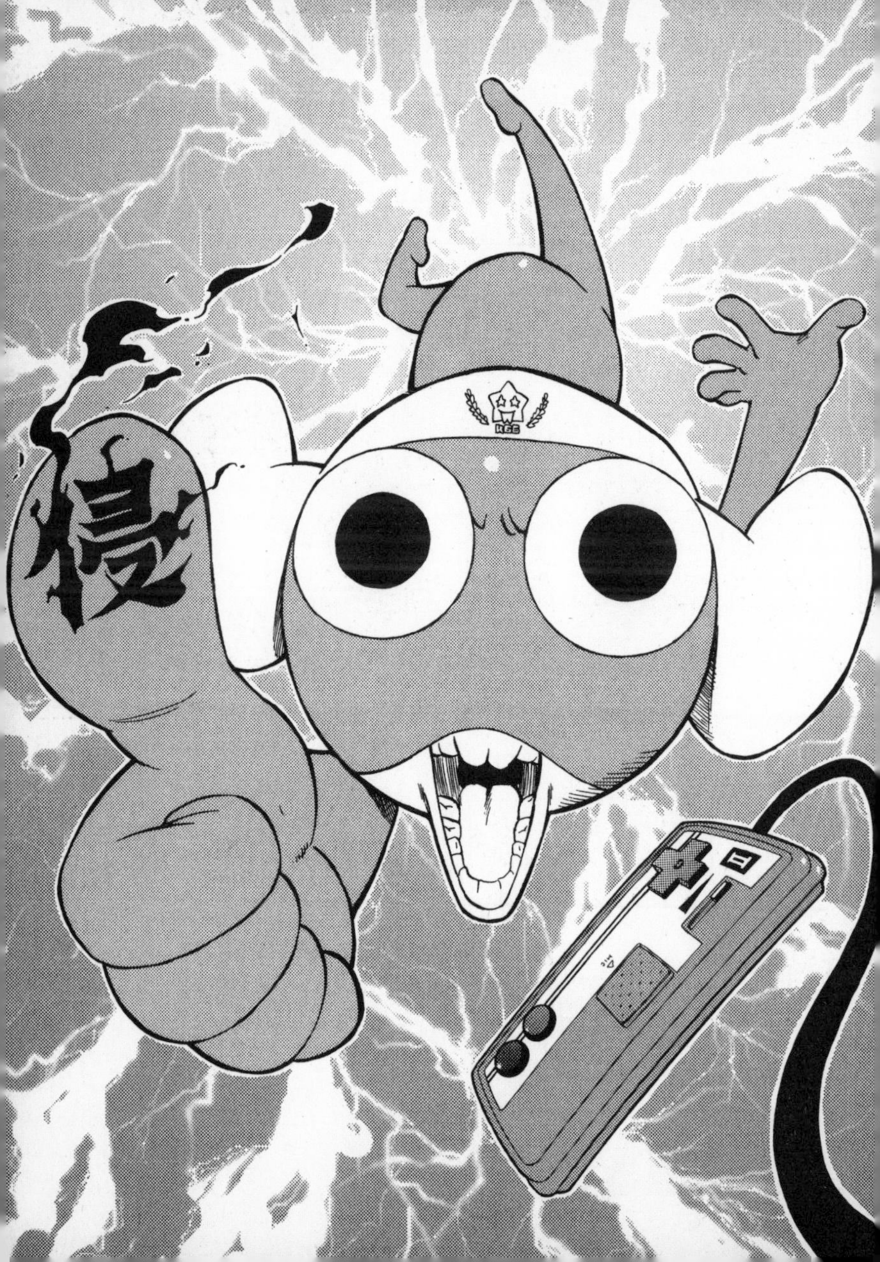
KGE

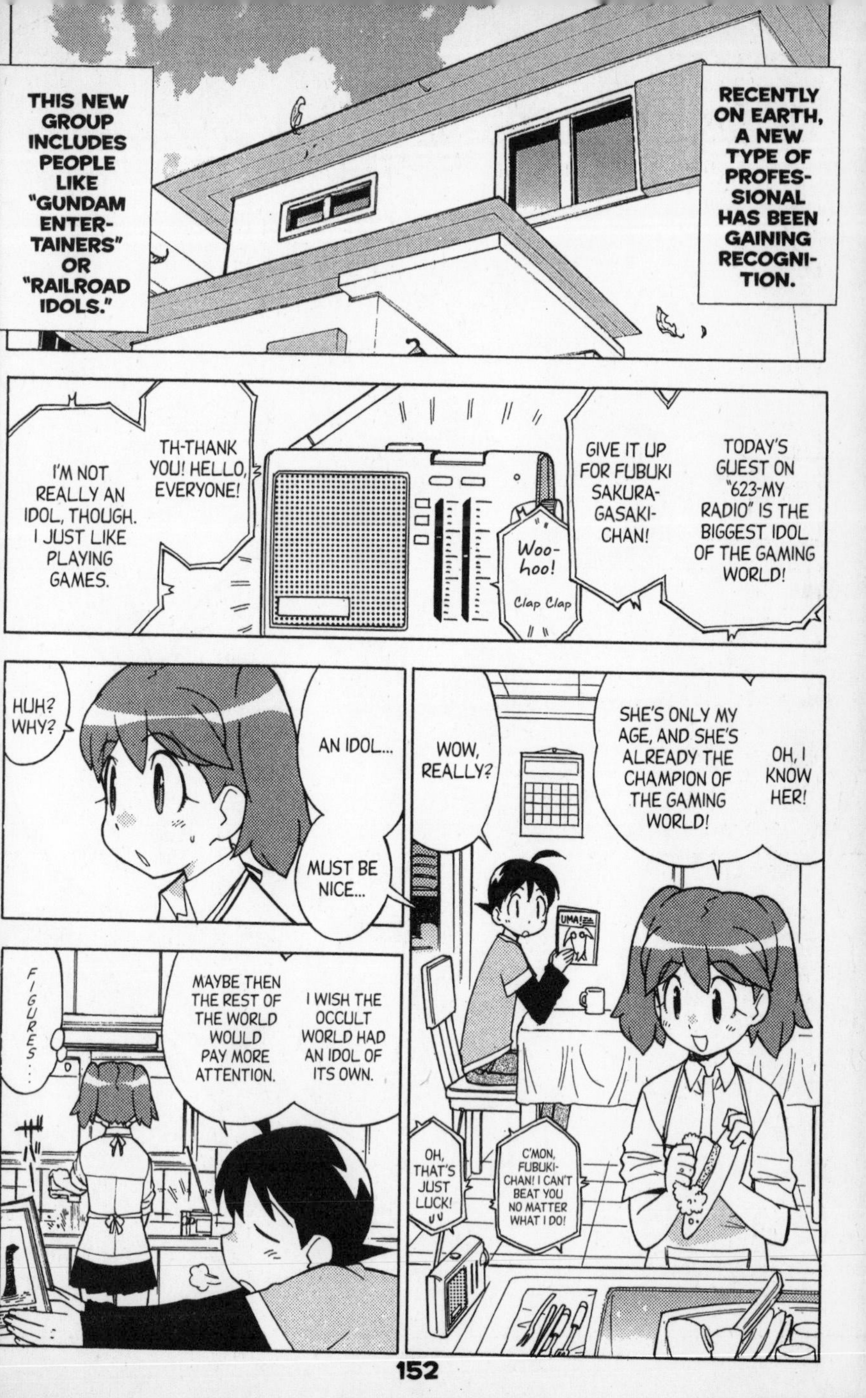
RECENTLY ON EARTH, A NEW TYPE OF PROFESSIONAL HAS BEEN GAINING RECOGNITION.
THIS NEW GROUP INCLUDES PEOPLE LIKE "GUNDAM ENTERTAINERS" OR "RAILROAD IDOLS."
TODAY'S GUEST ON "623-MY RADIO" IS THE BIGGEST IDOL OF THE GAMING WORLD!
GIVE IT UP FOR FUBUKI SAKURA-GASAKI-CHAN!
Woo-hoo!
Clap Clap
TH-THANK YOU! HELLO, EVERYONE!
I'M NOT REALLY AN IDOL, THOUGH. I JUST LIKE PLAYING GAMES.
OH, I KNOW HER!
SHE'S ONLY MY AGE, AND SHE'S ALREADY THE CHAMPION OF THE GAMING WORLD!
WOW, REALLY?
C'MON, FUBUKI-CHAN! I CAN'T BEAT YOU NO MATTER WHAT I DO!
OH, THAT'S JUST LUCK!
AN IDOL...
HUH? WHY?
MUST BE NICE...
I WISH THE OCCULT WORLD HAD AN IDOL OF ITS OWN.
MAYBE THEN THE REST OF THE WORLD WOULD PAY MORE ATTENTION.
FIGURES...

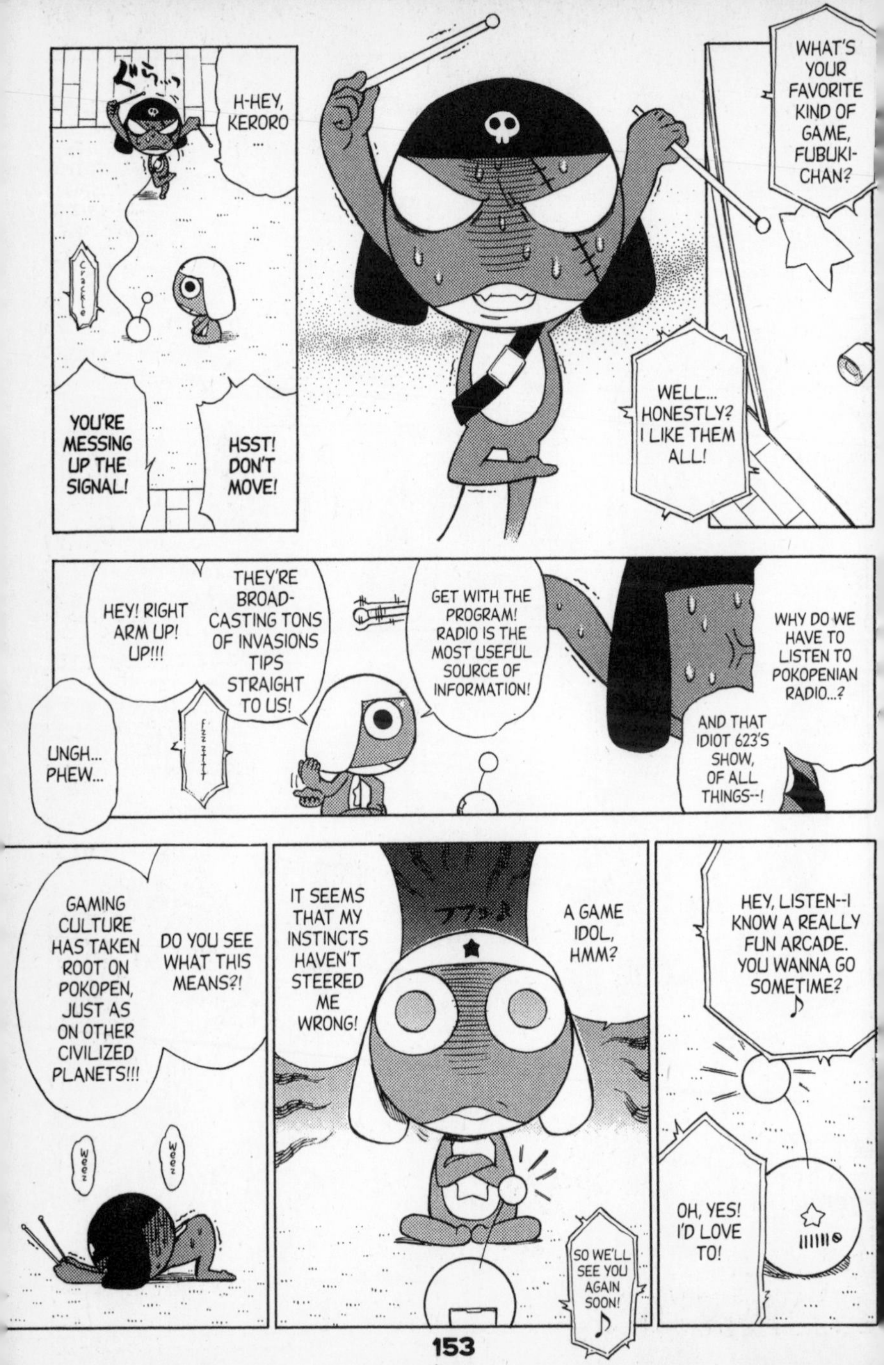
WHAT'S YOUR FAVORITE KIND OF GAME, FUBUKI-CHAN?
WELL... HONESTLY? I LIKE THEM ALL!
H-HEY, KERORO ...
Crackle
HSST! DON'T MOVE!
YOU'RE MESSING UP THE SIGNAL!
WHY DO WE HAVE TO LISTEN TO POKOPENIAN RADIO...?
AND THAT IDIOT 623'S SHOW, OF ALL THINGS--!
GET WITH THE PROGRAM! RADIO IS THE MOST USEFUL SOURCE OF INFORMATION!
THEY'RE BROAD-CASTING TONS OF INVASIONS TIPS STRAIGHT TO US!
HEY! RIGHT ARM UP! UP!!!
FZZ ZZTT
UNGH... PHEW...
HEY, LISTEN--I KNOW A REALLY FUN ARCADE. YOU WANNA GO SOMETIME? ♪
OH, YES! I'D LOVE TO!
A GAME IDOL, HMM?
IT SEEMS THAT MY INSTINCTS HAVEN'T STEERED ME WRONG!
SO WE'LL SEE YOU AGAIN SOON! ♪
GAMING CULTURE HAS TAKEN ROOT ON POKOPEN, JUST AS ON OTHER CIVILIZED PLANETS!!!
DO YOU SEE WHAT THIS MEANS?!
Weez
Weez

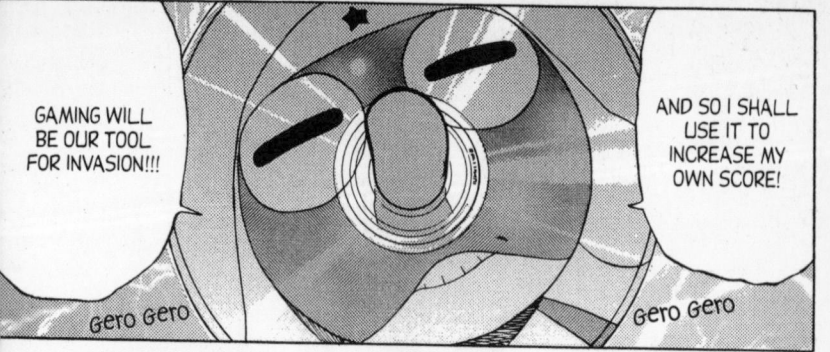

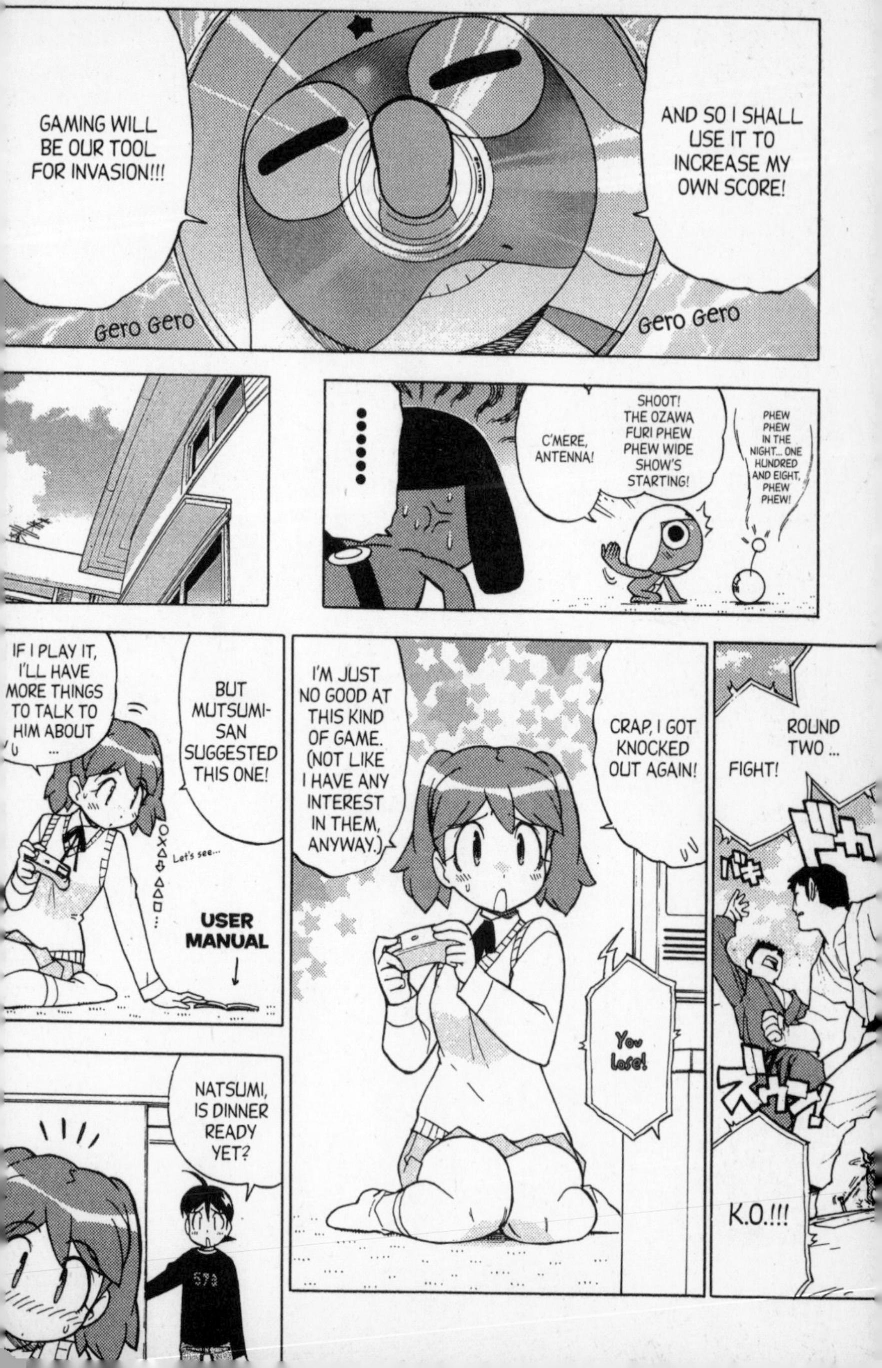

AND SO I SHALL USE IT TO INCREASE MY OWN SCORE!
Gero Gero
GAMING WILL BE OUR TOOL FOR INVASION!!!
Gero Gero
PHEW PHEW IN THE NIGHT... ONE HUNDRED AND EIGHT, PHEW PHEW!
SHOOT! THE OZAWA FURI PHEW PHEW WIDE SHOW'S STARTING!
C'MERE, ANTENNA!
......
ROUND TWO ...
FIGHT!
K.O.!!!
CRAP, I GOT KNOCKED OUT AGAIN!
I'M JUST NO GOOD AT THIS KIND OF GAME. (NOT LIKE I HAVE ANY INTEREST IN THEM, ANYWAY.)
You lose!
BUT MUTSUMI-SAN SUGGESTED THIS ONE!
IF I PLAY IT, I'LL HAVE MORE THINGS TO TALK TO HIM ABOUT ...
Let's see...
USER MANUAL
NATSUMI, IS DINNER READY YET?

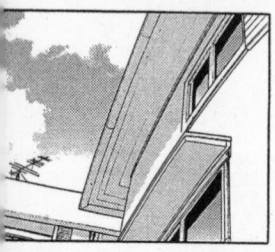

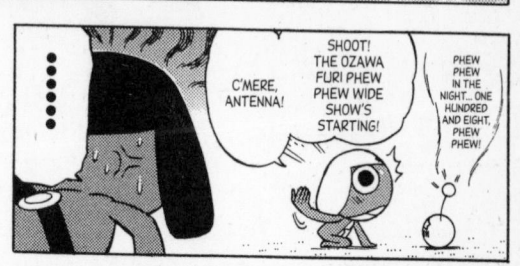

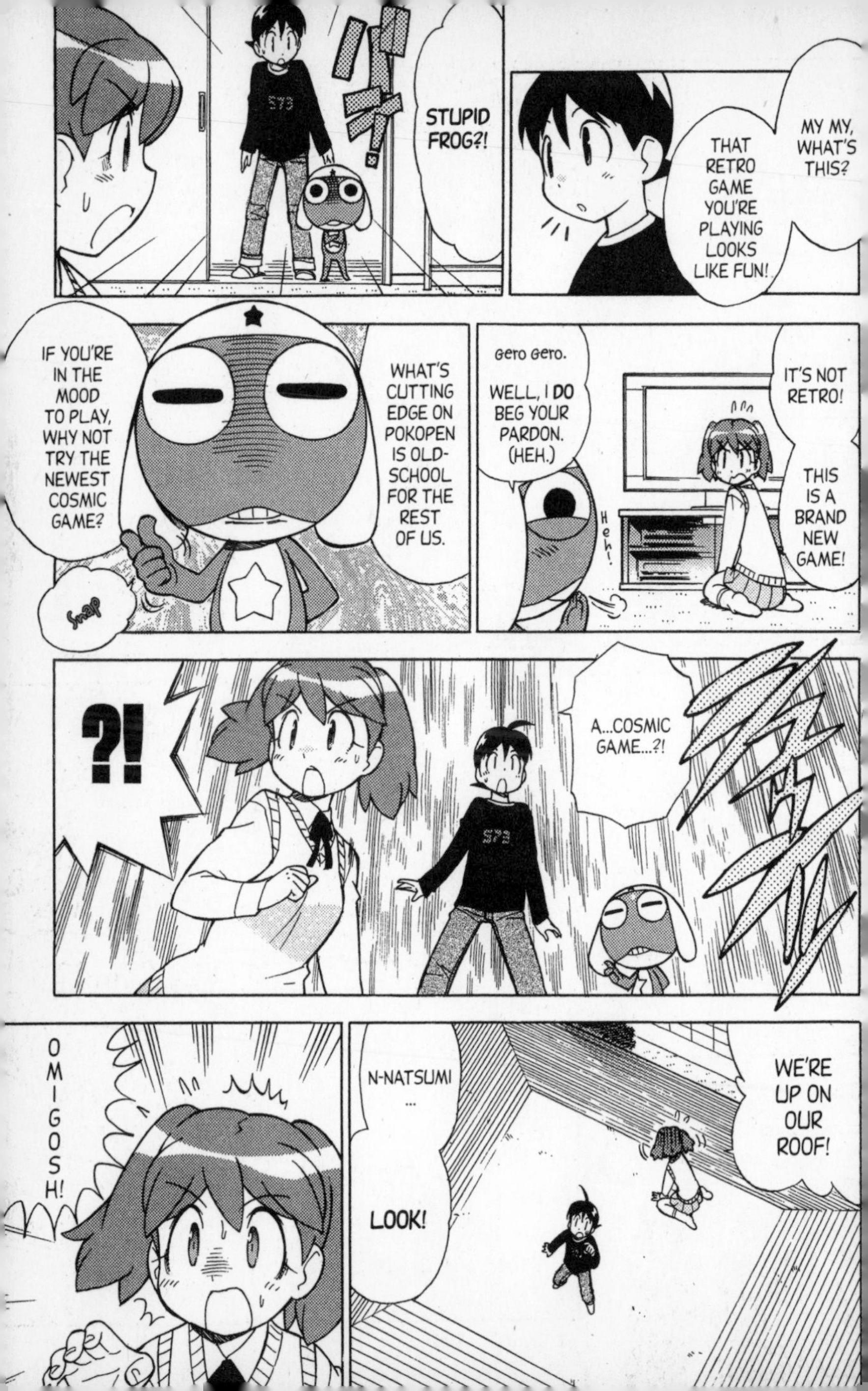
MY MY, WHAT'S THIS?
THAT RETRO GAME YOU'RE PLAYING LOOKS LIKE FUN!
STUPID FROG?!
IT'S NOT RETRO!
THIS IS A BRAND NEW GAME!
Gero Gero.
WELL, I DO BEG YOUR PARDON. (HEH.)
Heh!
WHAT'S CUTTING EDGE ON POKOPEN IS OLD-SCHOOL FOR THE REST OF US.
IF YOU'RE IN THE MOOD TO PLAY, WHY NOT TRY THE NEWEST COSMIC GAME?
Snap
A...COSMIC GAME...?!
?!
WE'RE UP ON OUR ROOF!
N-NATSUMI ...
LOOK!
OMIGOSH!

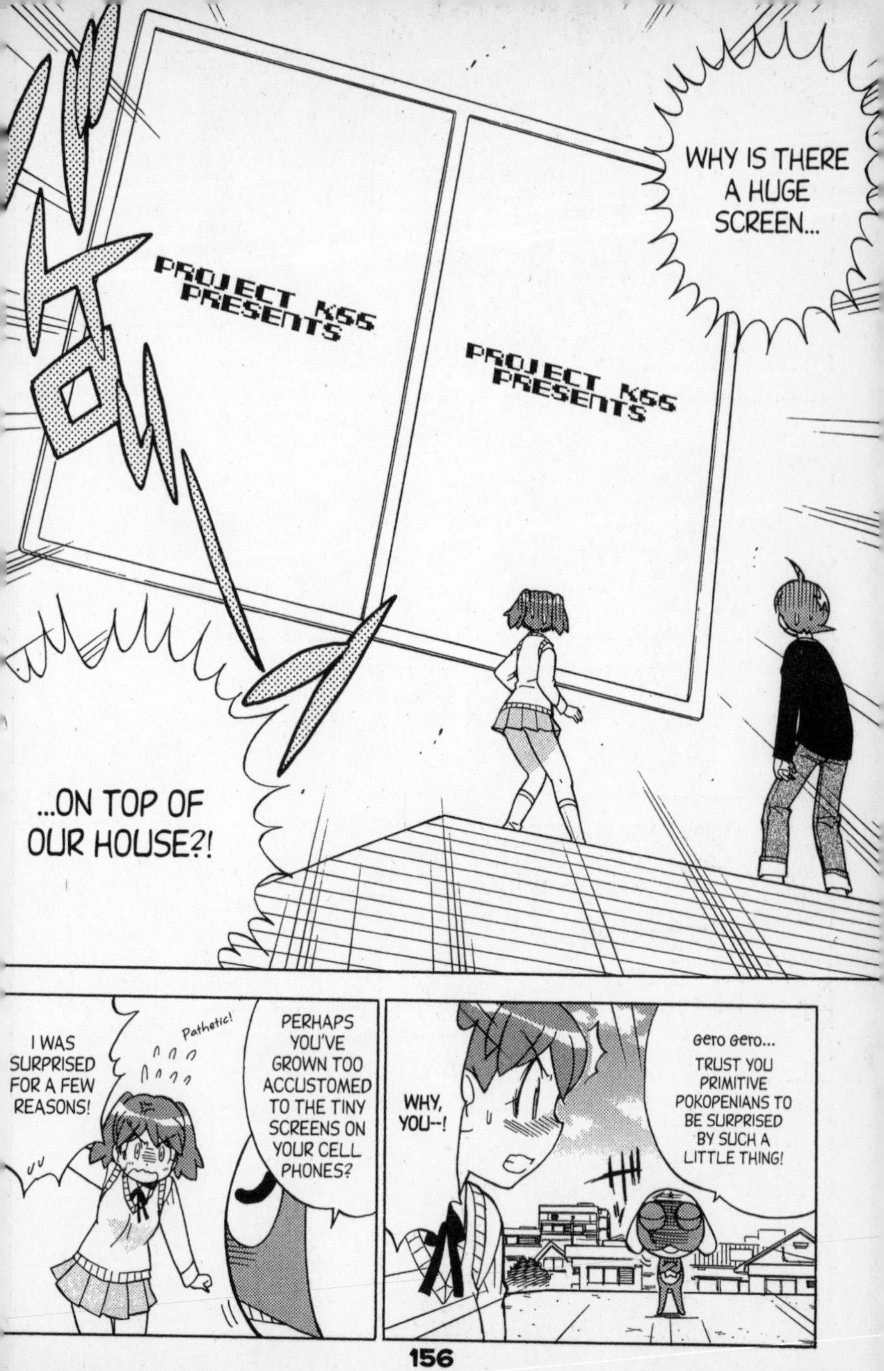
WHY IS THERE A HUGE SCREEN...
PROJECT K66 PRESENTS
PROJECT K66 PRESENTS
...ON TOP OF OUR HOUSE?!
Gero Gero... TRUST YOU PRIMITIVE POKOPENIANS TO BE SURPRISED BY SUCH A LITTLE THING!
WHY, YOU--!
PERHAPS YOU'VE GROWN TOO ACCUSTOMED TO THE TINY SCREENS ON YOUR CELL PHONES?
Pathetic!
I WAS SURPRISED FOR A FEW REASONS!

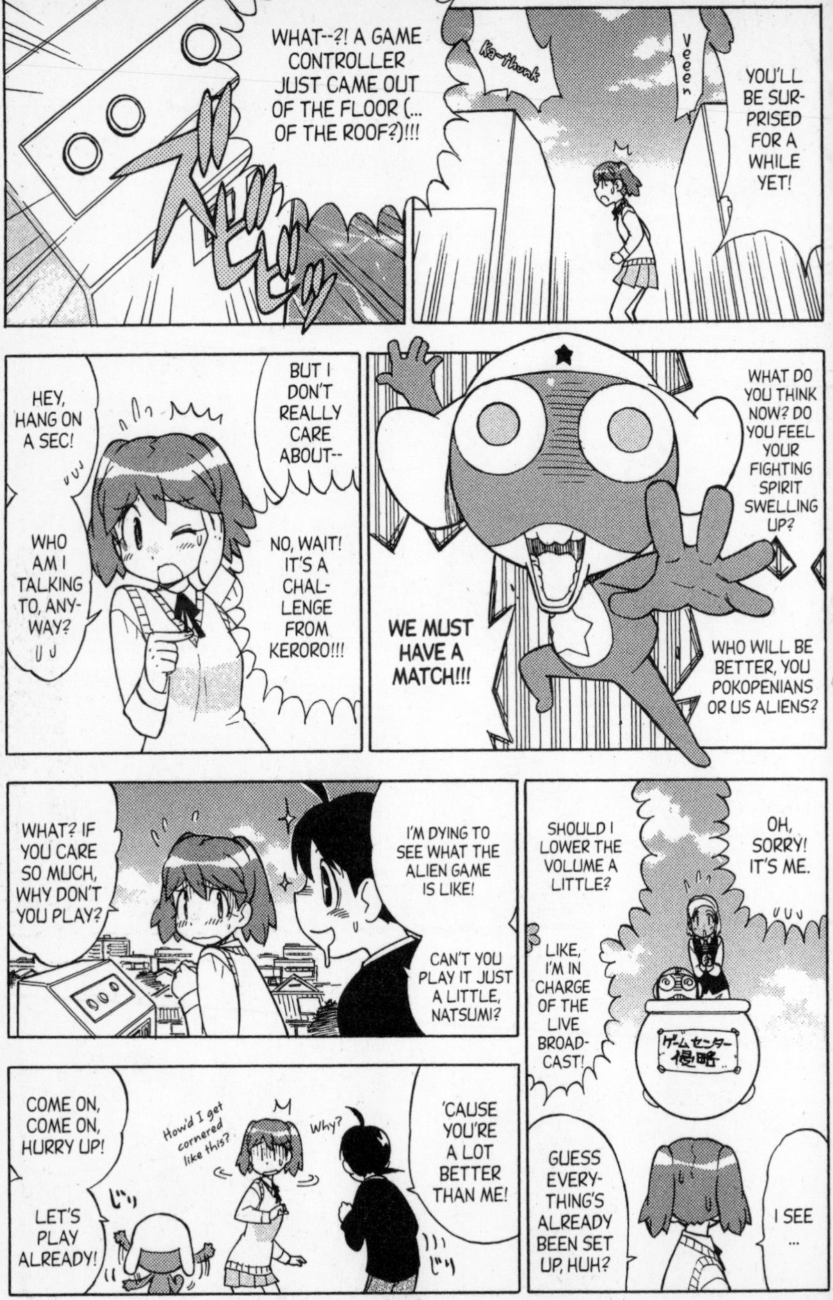
YOU'LL BE SURPRISED FOR A WHILE YET!
Veeen
Ka-thunk
WHAT--?! A GAME CONTROLLER JUST CAME OUT OF THE FLOOR (... OF THE ROOF?)!!!
WHAT DO YOU THINK NOW? DO YOU FEEL YOUR FIGHTING SPIRIT SWELLING UP?
WHO WILL BE BETTER, YOU POKOPENIANS OR US ALIENS?
WE MUST HAVE A MATCH!!!
BUT I DON'T REALLY CARE ABOUT--
NO, WAIT! IT'S A CHALLENGE FROM KERORO!!!
HEY, HANG ON A SEC!
WHO AM I TALKING TO, ANYWAY?
OH, SORRY! IT'S ME.
SHOULD I LOWER THE VOLUME A LITTLE?
LIKE, I'M IN CHARGE OF THE LIVE BROADCAST!
ゲームセンター侵略
I SEE ...
GUESS EVERYTHING'S ALREADY BEEN SET UP, HUH?
I'M DYING TO SEE WHAT THE ALIEN GAME IS LIKE!
CAN'T YOU PLAY IT JUST A LITTLE, NATSUMI?
WHAT? IF YOU CARE SO MUCH, WHY DON'T YOU PLAY?
'CAUSE YOU'RE A LOT BETTER THAN ME!
Why?
How'd I get cornered like this?
COME ON, COME ON, HURRY UP!
LET'S PLAY ALREADY!

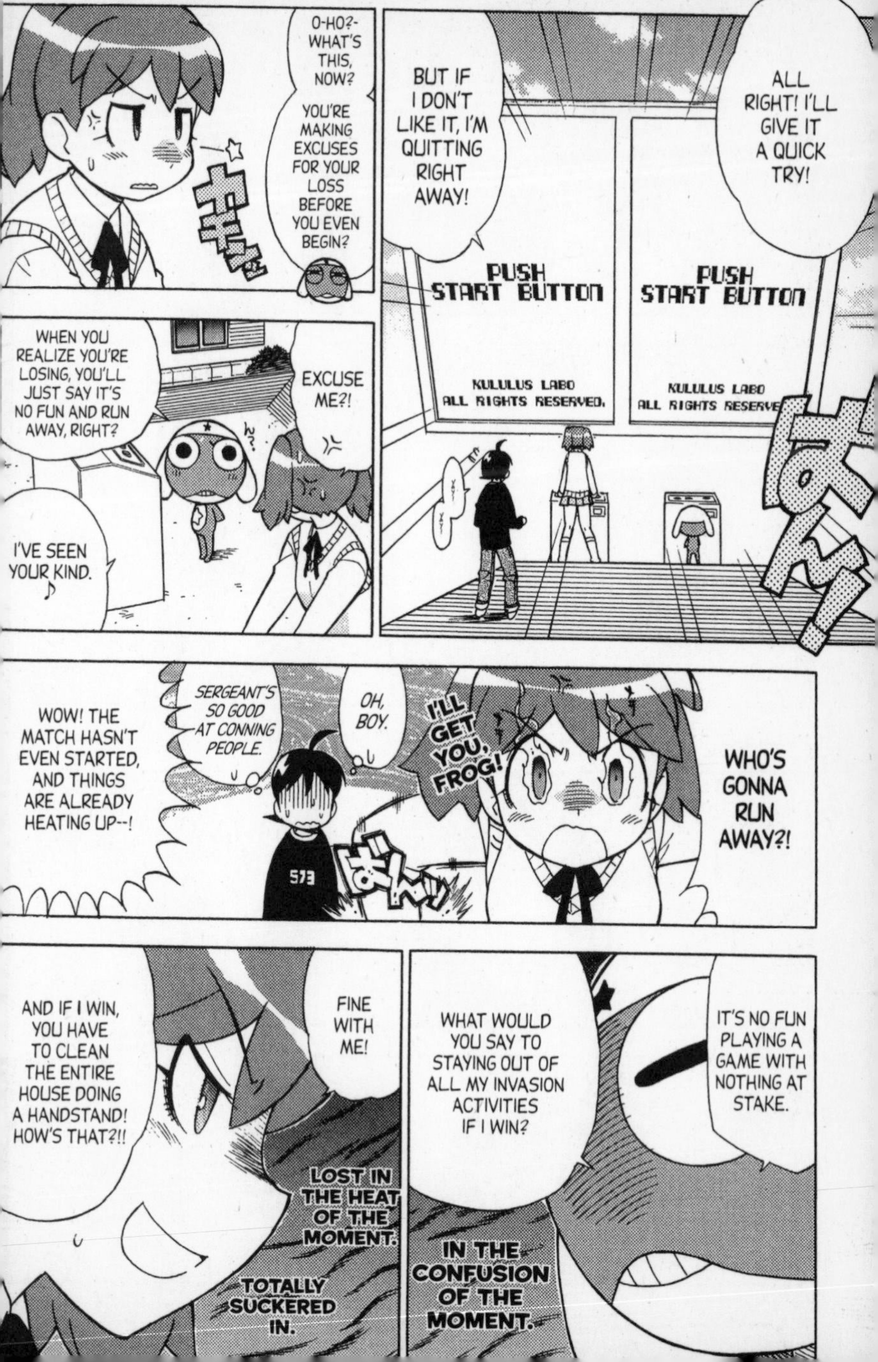
ALL RIGHT! I'LL GIVE IT A QUICK TRY!
BUT IF I DON'T LIKE IT, I'M QUITTING RIGHT AWAY!
PUSH START BUTTON
KULULUS LABO ALL RIGHTS RESERVE
PUSH START BUTTON
KULULUS LABO ALL RIGHTS RESERVED.
O-HO?- WHAT'S THIS, NOW?
YOU'RE MAKING EXCUSES FOR YOUR LOSS BEFORE YOU EVEN BEGIN?
WHEN YOU REALIZE YOU'RE LOSING, YOU'LL JUST SAY IT'S NO FUN AND RUN AWAY, RIGHT?
EXCUSE ME?!
I'VE SEEN YOUR KIND. ♪
WHO'S GONNA RUN AWAY?!
I'LL GET YOU, FROG!
OH, BOY.
SERGEANT'S SO GOOD AT CONNING PEOPLE.
WOW! THE MATCH HASN'T EVEN STARTED, AND THINGS ARE ALREADY HEATING UP--!
IT'S NO FUN PLAYING A GAME WITH NOTHING AT STAKE.
WHAT WOULD YOU SAY TO STAYING OUT OF ALL MY INVASION ACTIVITIES IF I WIN?
IN THE CONFUSION OF THE MOMENT.
FINE WITH ME!
AND IF I WIN, YOU HAVE TO CLEAN THE ENTIRE HOUSE DOING A HANDSTAND! HOW'S THAT?!!
LOST IN THE HEAT OF THE MOMENT.
TOTALLY SUCKERED IN.

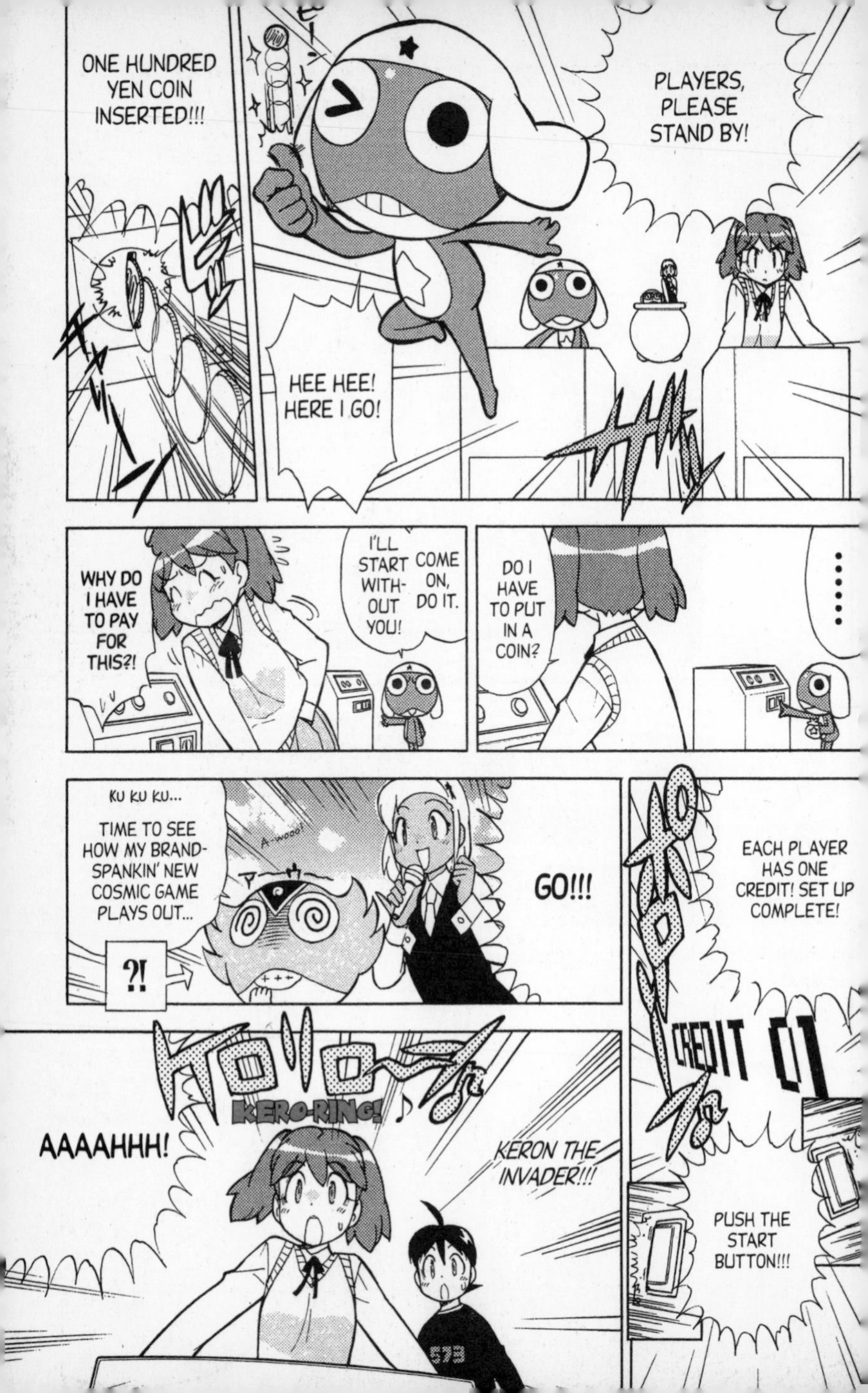
PLAYERS, PLEASE STAND BY!
HEE HEE! HERE I GO!
ONE HUNDRED YEN COIN INSERTED!!!
......
DO I HAVE TO PUT IN A COIN?
COME ON, DO IT.
I'LL START WITH-OUT YOU!
WHY DO I HAVE TO PAY FOR THIS?!
EACH PLAYER HAS ONE CREDIT! SET UP COMPLETE!
CREDIT 01
PUSH THE START BUTTON!!!
GO!!!
KU KU KU...
TIME TO SEE HOW MY BRAND-SPANKIN' NEW COSMIC GAME PLAYS OUT...
A-wooo!
?!
KERO-RING!
KERON THE INVADER!!!
AAAAHHH!

PRESENTING...KERON THE INVADER!

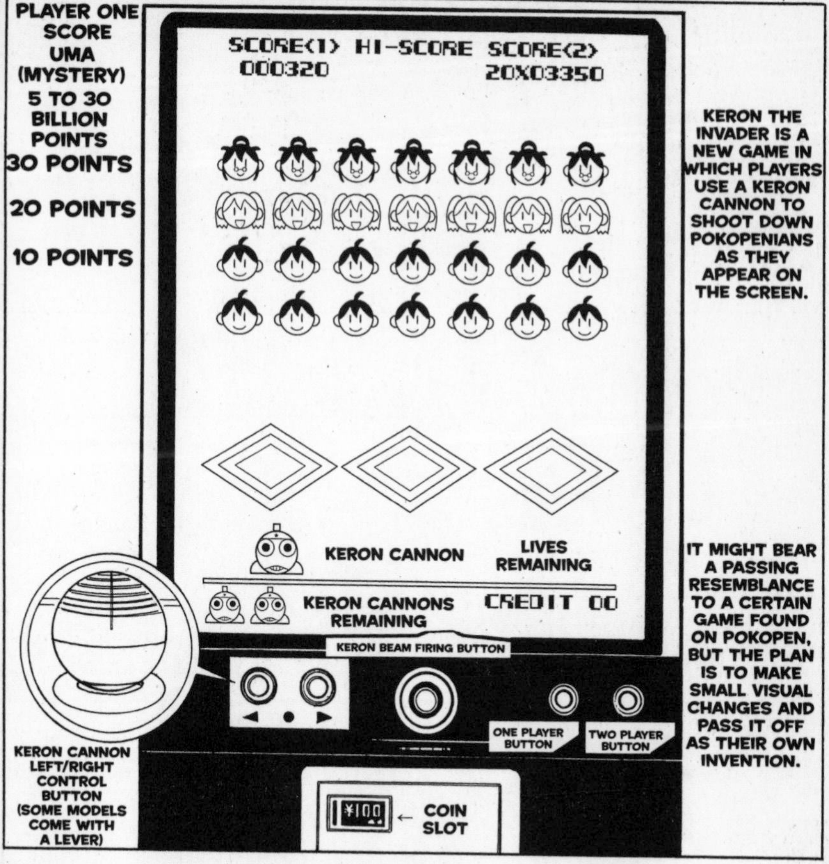

KERON THE INVADER IS A NEW GAME IN WHICH PLAYERS USE A KERON CANNON TO SHOOT DOWN POKOPENIANS AS THEY APPEAR ON THE SCREEN.
PLAYER ONE SCORE
SCORE(1) HI-SCORE SCORE(2)
000320
20X03350
UMA (MYSTERY) 5 TO 30 BILLION POINTS
30 POINTS
20 POINTS
10 POINTS
IT MIGHT BEAR A PASSING RESEMBLANCE TO A CERTAIN GAME FOUND ON POKOPEN, BUT THE PLAN IS TO MAKE SMALL VISUAL CHANGES AND PASS IT OFF AS THEIR OWN INVENTION.
LIVES REMAINING
KERON CANNON
CREDIT 00
KERON CANNONS REMAINING
KERON BEAM FIRING BUTTON
TWO PLAYER BUTTON
ONE PLAYER BUTTON
¥100
COIN SLOT
KERON CANNON LEFT/RIGHT CONTROL BUTTON (SOME MODELS COME WITH A LEVER)

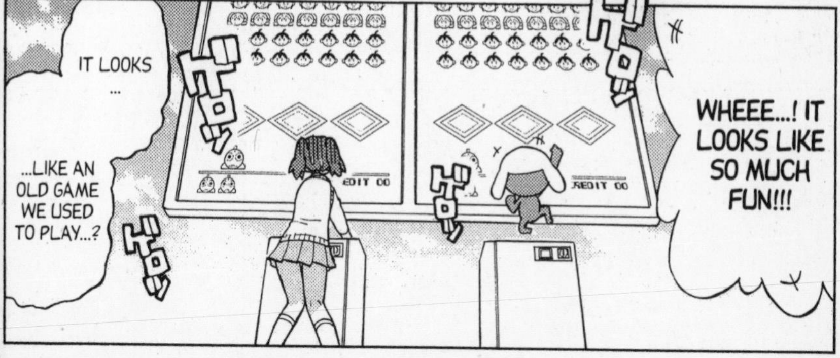

WHEEE...! IT LOOKS LIKE SO MUCH FUN!!!
IT LOOKS ...
...LIKE AN OLD GAME WE USED TO PLAY...?

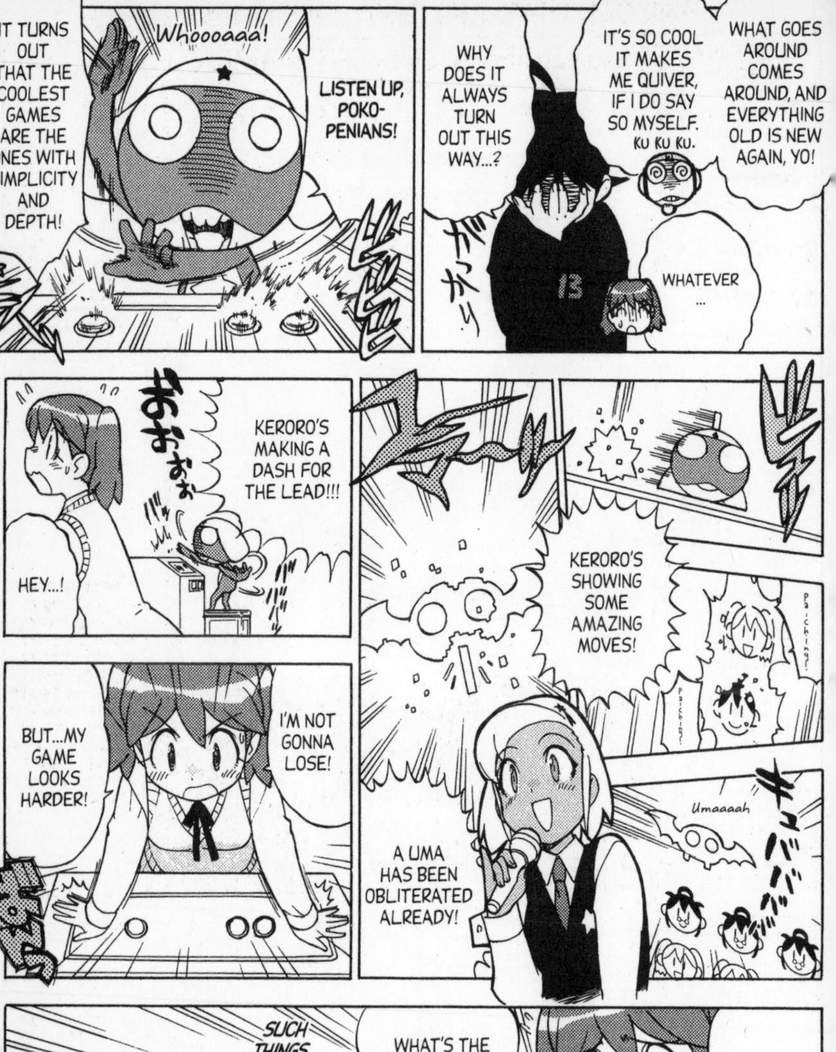
WHAT GOES AROUND COMES AROUND, AND EVERYTHING OLD IS NEW AGAIN, YO!
IT'S SO COOL IT MAKES ME QUIVER, IF I DO SAY SO MYSELF.
KU KU KU.
WHY DOES IT ALWAYS TURN OUT THIS WAY...?
WHATEVER ...
IT TURNS OUT THAT THE COOLEST GAMES ARE THE ONES WITH SIMPLICITY AND DEPTH!
Whooooaa!
LISTEN UP, POKO-PENIANS!
KERORO'S SHOWING SOME AMAZING MOVES!
Umaaaah
A UMA HAS BEEN OBLITERATED ALREADY!
KERORO'S MAKING A DASH FOR THE LEAD!!!
HEY...!
I'M NOT GONNA LOSE!
BUT...MY GAME LOOKS HARDER!
WAIT...! WHERE DO I TYPE IN MY NAME?
WHAT'S THE STORY? WHERE DO I COLLECT ITEMS? WHERE DO I LISTEN TO THE VILLAGERS' STORIES?
SUCH THINGS...
...DO NOT EXIST!!!

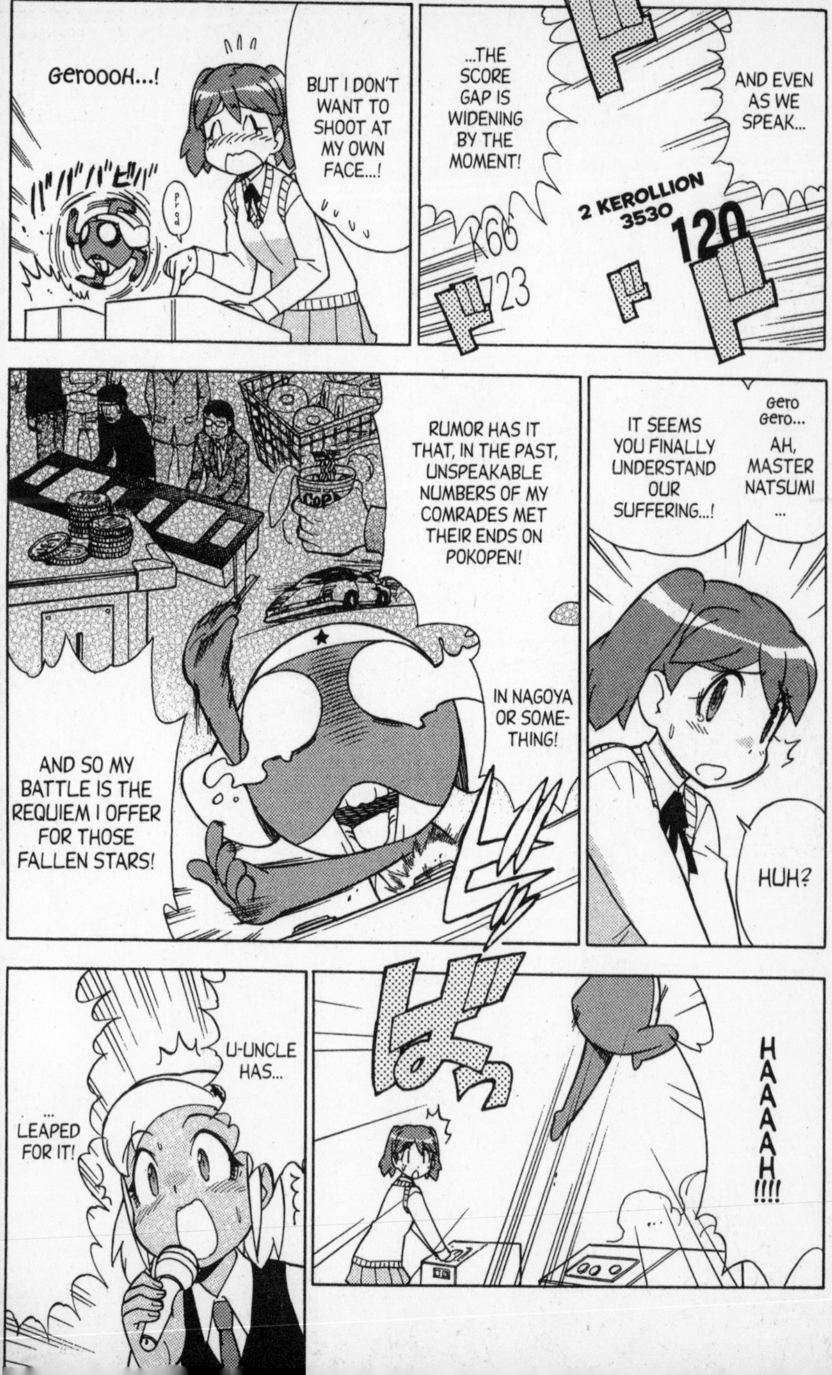
...THE SCORE GAP IS WIDENING BY THE MOMENT!
AND EVEN AS WE SPEAK...
2 KEROLLION 3530
120
K66
723
Geroooh...!
BUT I DON'T WANT TO SHOOT AT MY OWN FACE...!
Gero Gero...
AH, MASTER NATSUMI ...
IT SEEMS YOU FINALLY UNDERSTAND OUR SUFFERING...!
HUH?
RUMOR HAS IT THAT, IN THE PAST, UNSPEAKABLE NUMBERS OF MY COMRADES MET THEIR ENDS ON POKOPEN!
IN NAGOYA OR SOME-THING!
AND SO MY BATTLE IS THE REQUIEM I OFFER FOR THOSE FALLEN STARS!
HAAAAAH!!!!
...
U-UNCLE HAS...
... LEAPED FOR IT!

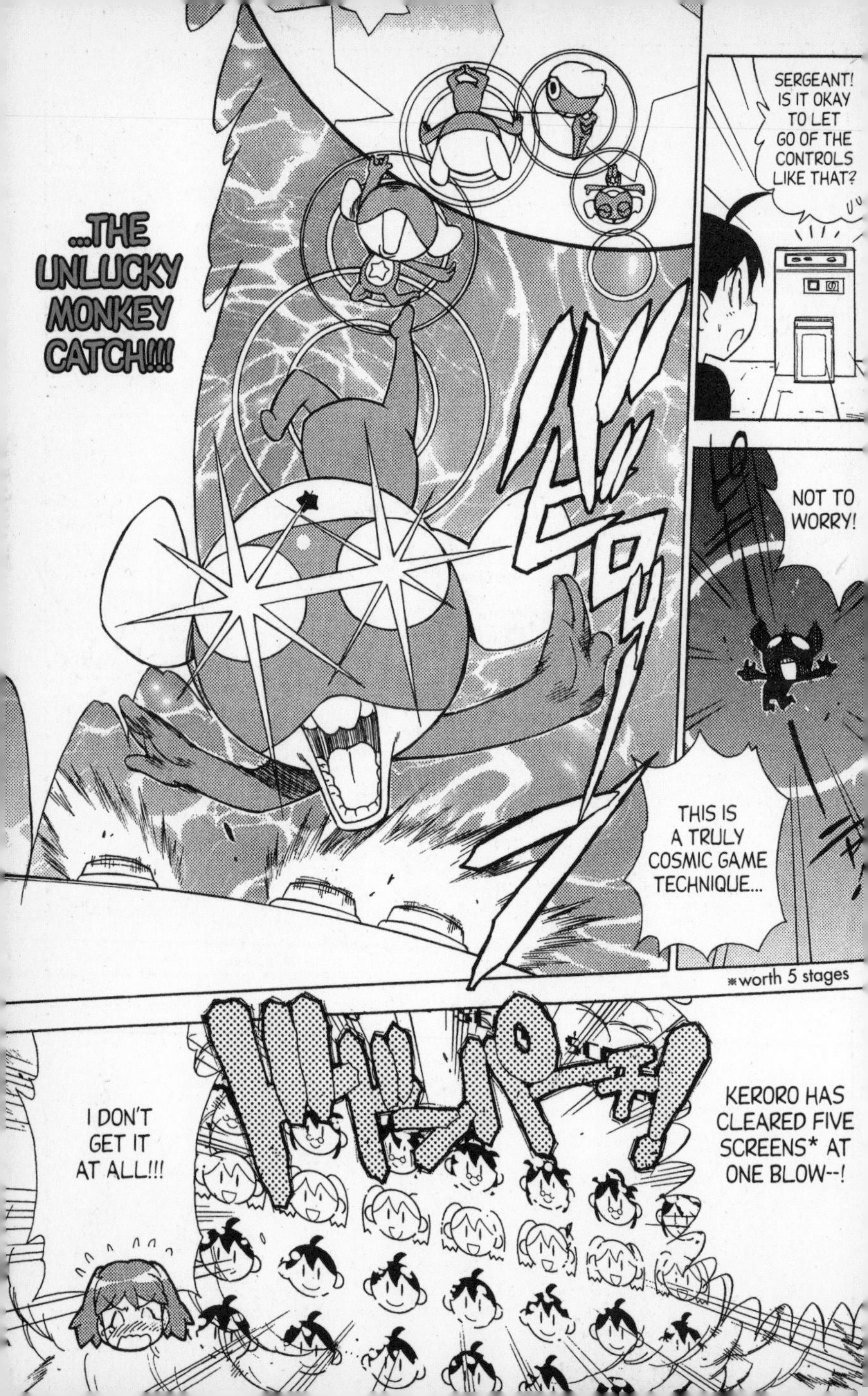
SERGEANT! IS IT OKAY TO LET GO OF THE CONTROLS LIKE THAT?
...THE UNLUCKY MONKEY CATCH!!!
NOT TO WORRY!
THIS IS A TRULY COSMIC GAME TECHNIQUE...
*worth 5 stages
KERORO HAS CLEARED FIVE SCREENS* AT ONE BLOW--!
I DON'T GET IT AT ALL!!!

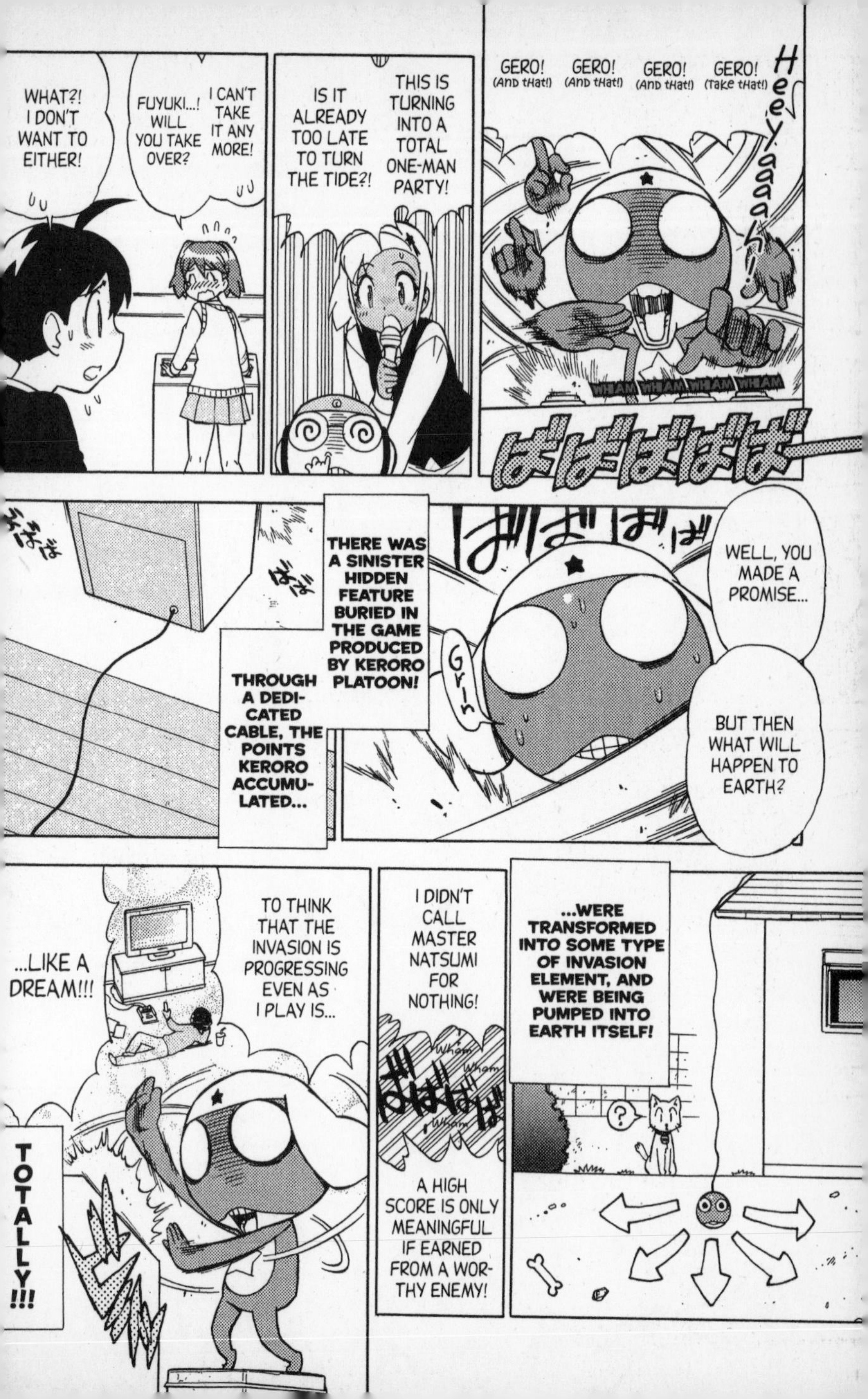
Heeyaaaah!!
GERO! (Take tHat!)
GERO! (And tHat!)
GERO! (And tHat!)
GERO! (And tHat!)
WHAM WHAM WHAM WHAM
THIS IS TURNING INTO A TOTAL ONE-MAN PARTY!
IS IT ALREADY TOO LATE TO TURN THE TIDE?!
I CAN'T TAKE IT ANY MORE!
FUYUKI...! WILL YOU TAKE OVER?
WHAT?! I DON'T WANT TO EITHER!
WELL, YOU MADE A PROMISE...
BUT THEN WHAT WILL HAPPEN TO EARTH?
Grin
THERE WAS A SINISTER HIDDEN FEATURE BURIED IN THE GAME PRODUCED BY KERORO PLATOON!
THROUGH A DEDICATED CABLE, THE POINTS KERORO ACCUMULATED...
...WERE TRANSFORMED INTO SOME TYPE OF INVASION ELEMENT, AND WERE BEING PUMPED INTO EARTH ITSELF!
I DIDN'T CALL MASTER NATSUMI FOR NOTHING!
Wham Wham Wham
A HIGH SCORE IS ONLY MEANINGFUL IF EARNED FROM A WORTHY ENEMY!
TO THINK THAT THE INVASION IS PROGRESSING EVEN AS I PLAY IS...
...LIKE A DREAM!!!
TOTALLY!!!

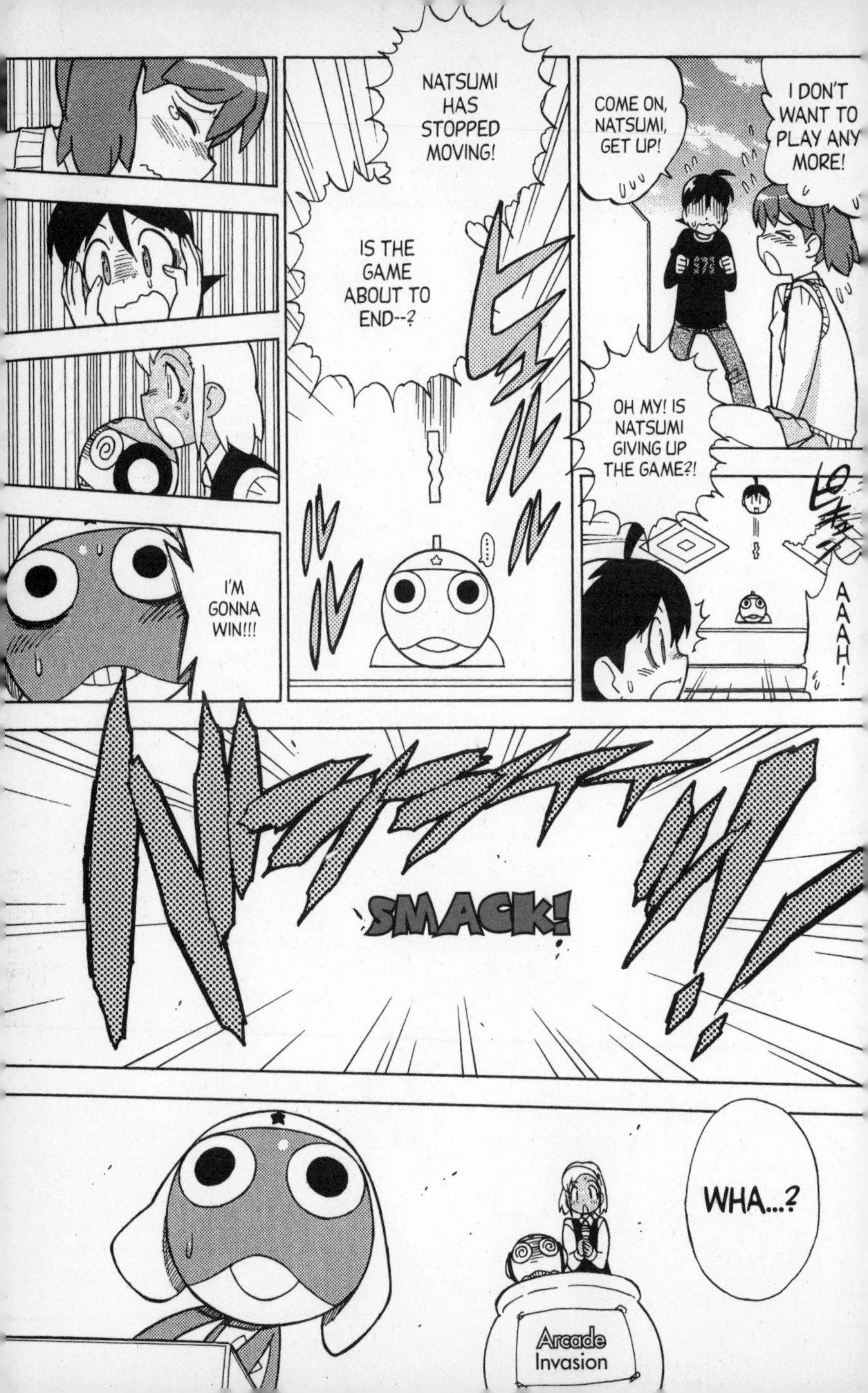
I DON'T WANT TO PLAY ANY MORE!
COME ON, NATSUMI, GET UP!
OH MY! IS NATSUMI GIVING UP THE GAME?!
AAAAH!
NATSUMI HAS STOPPED MOVING!
IS THE GAME ABOUT TO END--?
I'M GONNA WIN!!!
SMACK!
WHA...?
Arcade Invasion

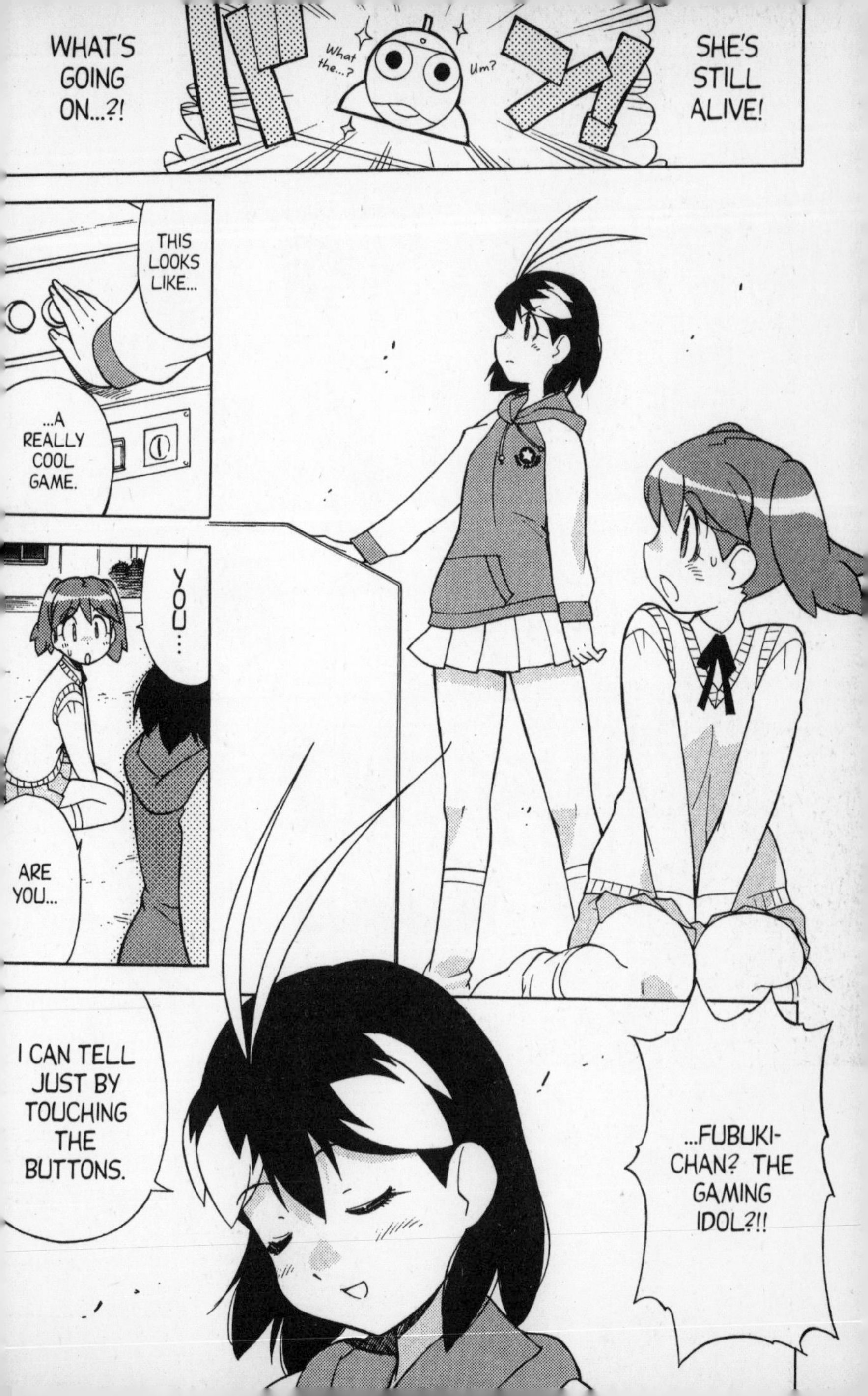
SHE'S STILL ALIVE!
Um?
What the...?
WHAT'S GOING ON...?!
THIS LOOKS LIKE...
...A REALLY COOL GAME.
YOU...
ARE YOU...
...FUBUKI-CHAN? THE GAMING IDOL?!!
I CAN TELL JUST BY TOUCHING THE BUTTONS.

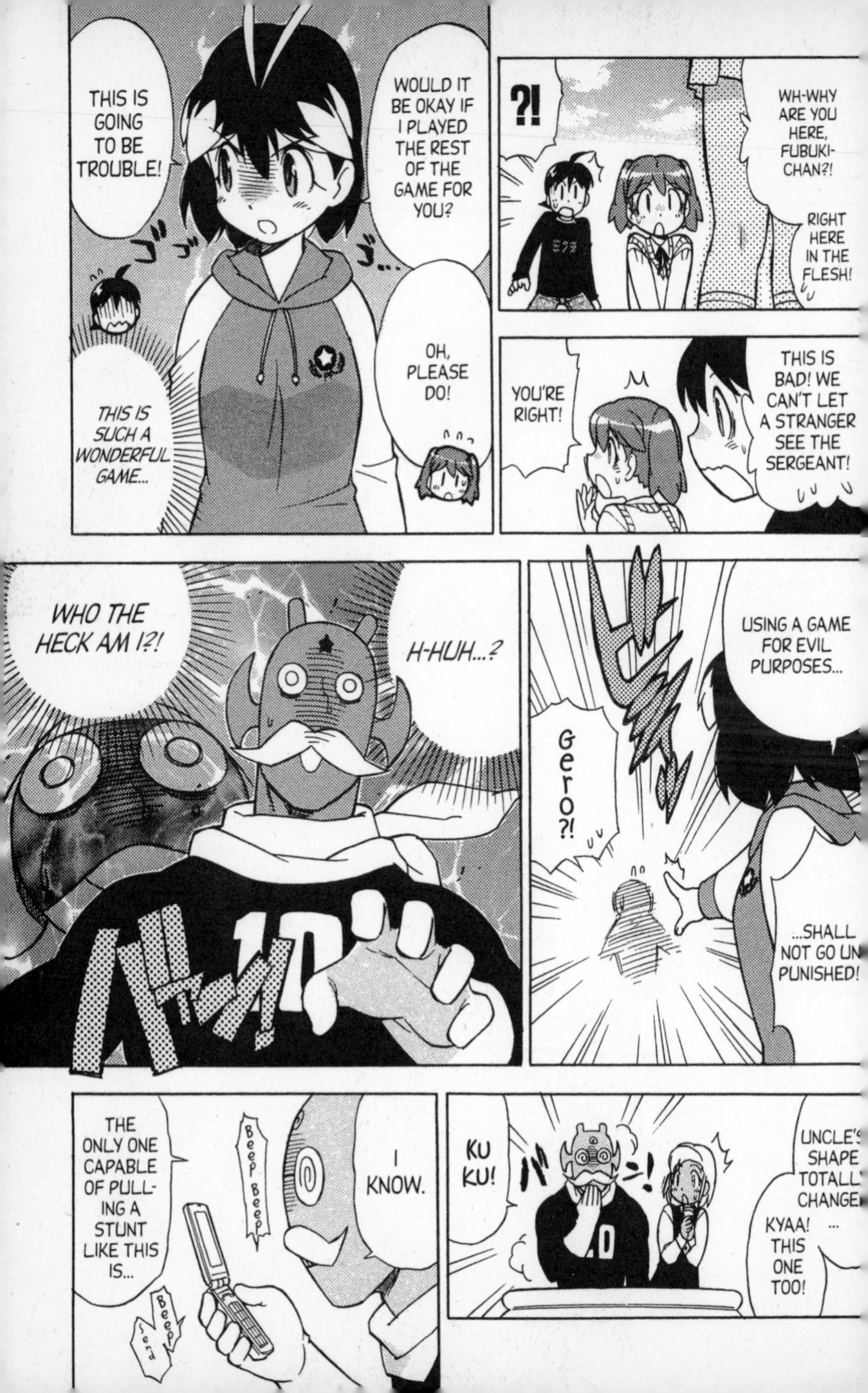
WH-WHY ARE YOU HERE, FUBUKI-CHAN?!
?!
RIGHT HERE IN THE FLESH!
THIS IS BAD! WE CAN'T LET A STRANGER SEE THE SERGEANT!
YOU'RE RIGHT!
WOULD IT BE OKAY IF I PLAYED THE REST OF THE GAME FOR YOU?
THIS IS GOING TO BE TROUBLE!
OH, PLEASE DO!
THIS IS SUCH A WONDERFUL GAME...
USING A GAME FOR EVIL PURPOSES...
Gero?!
...SHALL NOT GO UN
PUNISHED!
H-HUH...?
WHO THE HECK AM I?!
UNCLE'S SHAPE TOTALL CHANGE
...
KYAA! THIS ONE TOO!
KU KU!
I KNOW.
Beep Beep
THE ONLY ONE CAPABLE OF PULL-ING A STUNT LIKE THIS IS...
Beep
Send

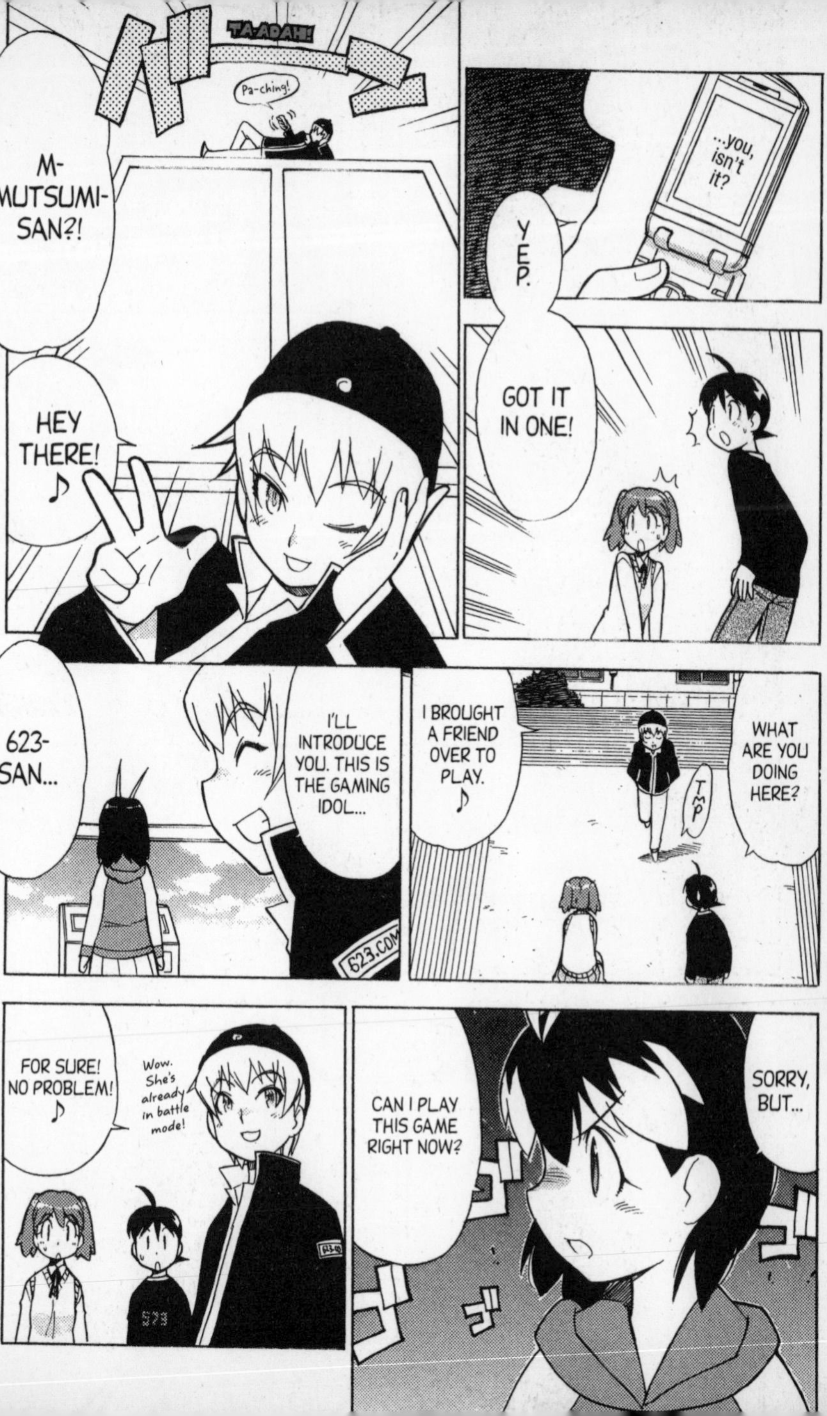
...you, isn't it?
YEP.
GOT IT IN ONE!
TA-ADAH!
Pa-ching!
M-MUTSUMI-SAN?!
HEY THERE! ♪
WHAT ARE YOU DOING HERE?
TMP
I BROUGHT A FRIEND OVER TO PLAY. ♪
I'LL INTRODUCE YOU. THIS IS THE GAMING IDOL...
623-SAN...
SORRY, BUT...
CAN I PLAY THIS GAME RIGHT NOW?
FOR SURE! NO PROBLEM! ♪
Wow. She's already in battle mode!

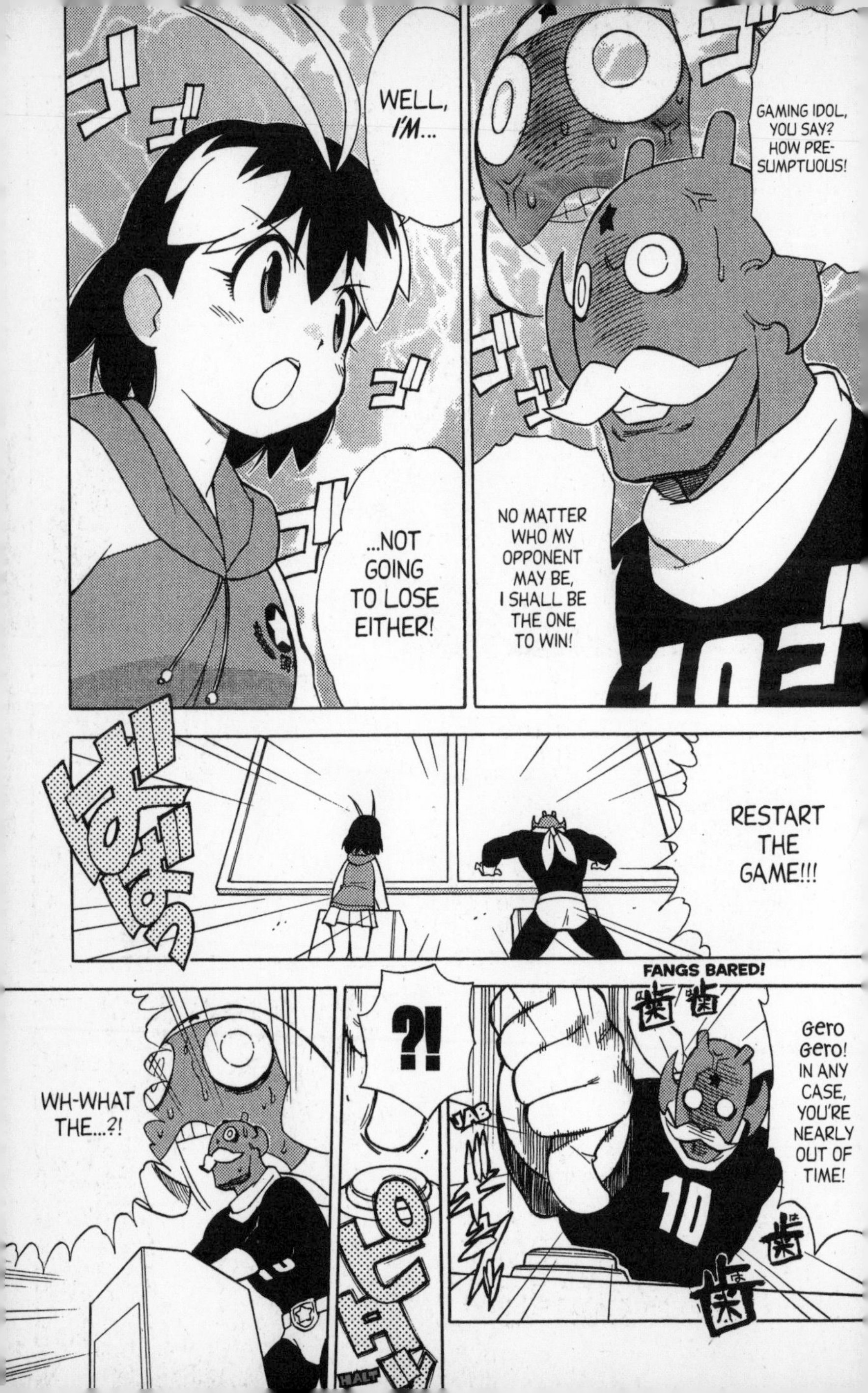
GAMING IDOL, YOU SAY? HOW PRE-SUMPTUOUS!
NO MATTER WHO MY OPPONENT MAY BE, I SHALL BE THE ONE TO WIN!
WELL, I'M...
...NOT GOING TO LOSE EITHER!
RESTART THE GAME!!!
FANGS BARED!
Gero Gero! IN ANY CASE, YOU'RE NEARLY OUT OF TIME!
JAB
?!
HALT
WH-WHAT THE...?!

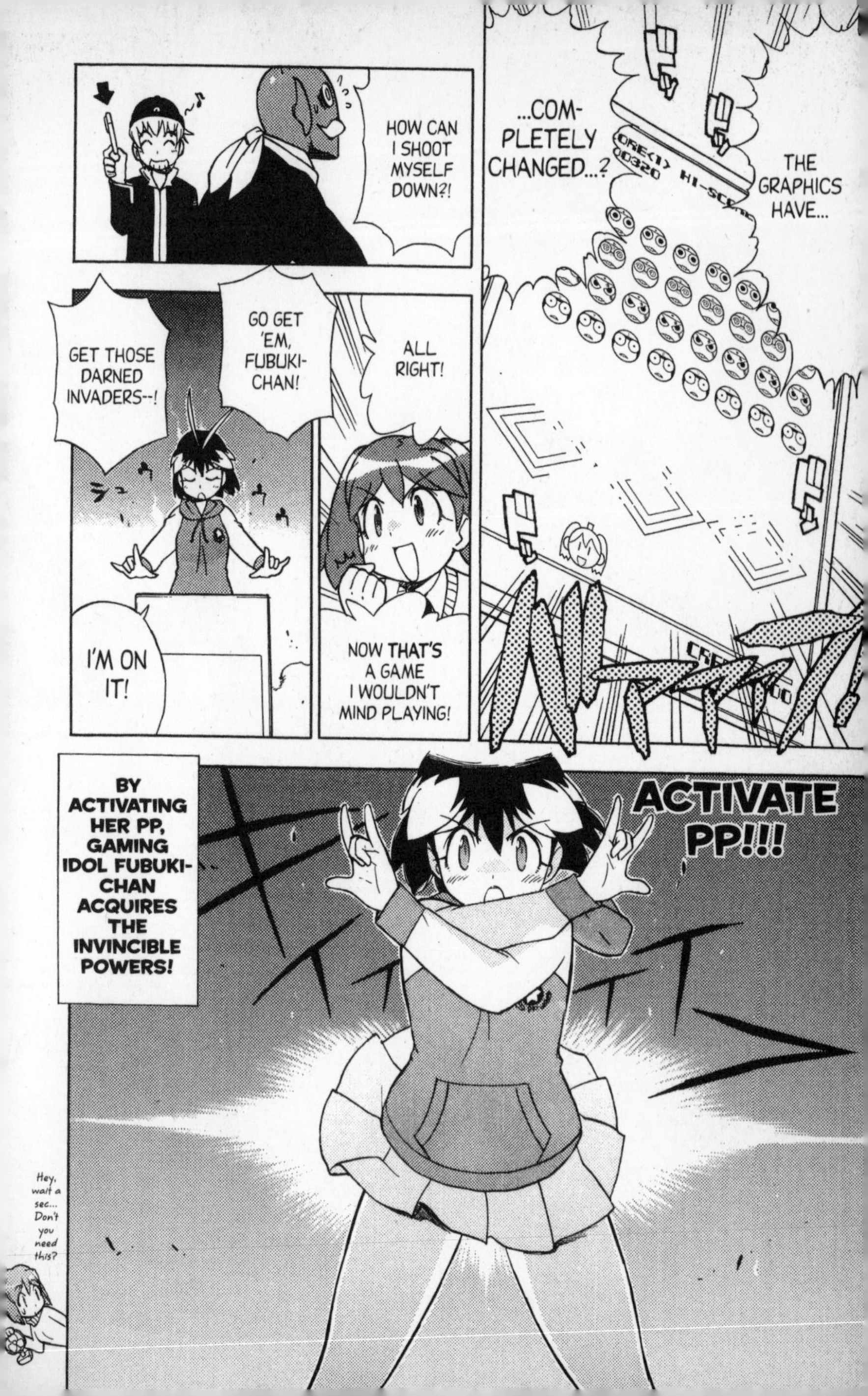
THE GRAPHICS HAVE...
...COM-PLETELY CHANGED...?
HOW CAN I SHOOT MYSELF DOWN?!
ALL RIGHT!
NOW THAT'S A GAME I WOULDN'T MIND PLAYING!
GO GET 'EM, FUBUKI-CHAN!
GET THOSE DARNED INVADERS--!
I'M ON IT!
ACTIVATE PP!!!
BY ACTIVATING HER PP, GAMING IDOL FUBUKI-CHAN ACQUIRES THE INVINCIBLE POWERS!
Hey, wait a sec... Don't you need this?

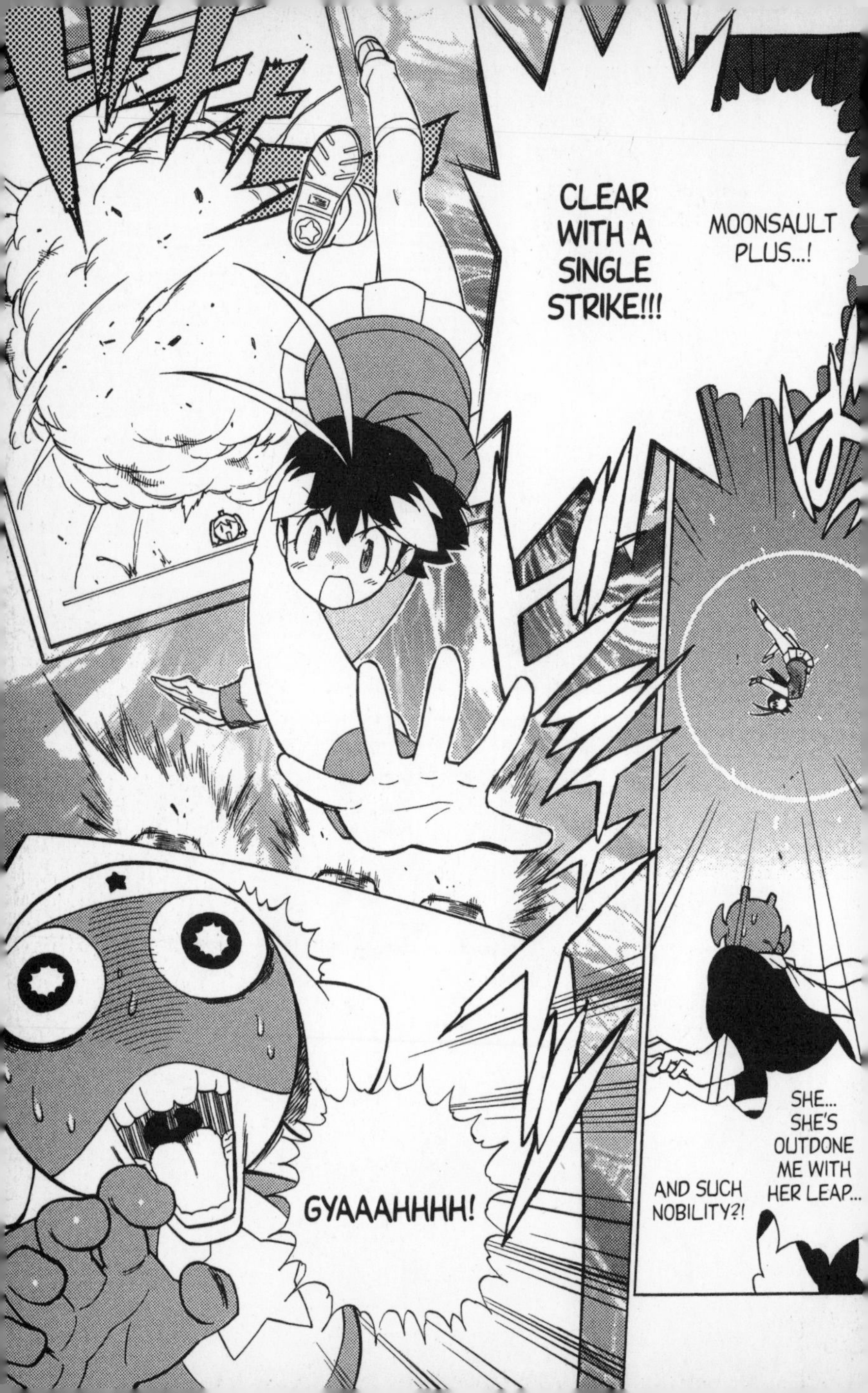
MOONSAULT PLUS...!
CLEAR WITH A SINGLE STRIKE!!!
SHE... SHE'S OUTDONE ME WITH HER LEAP...
AND SUCH NOBILITY?!
GYAAAHHHH!

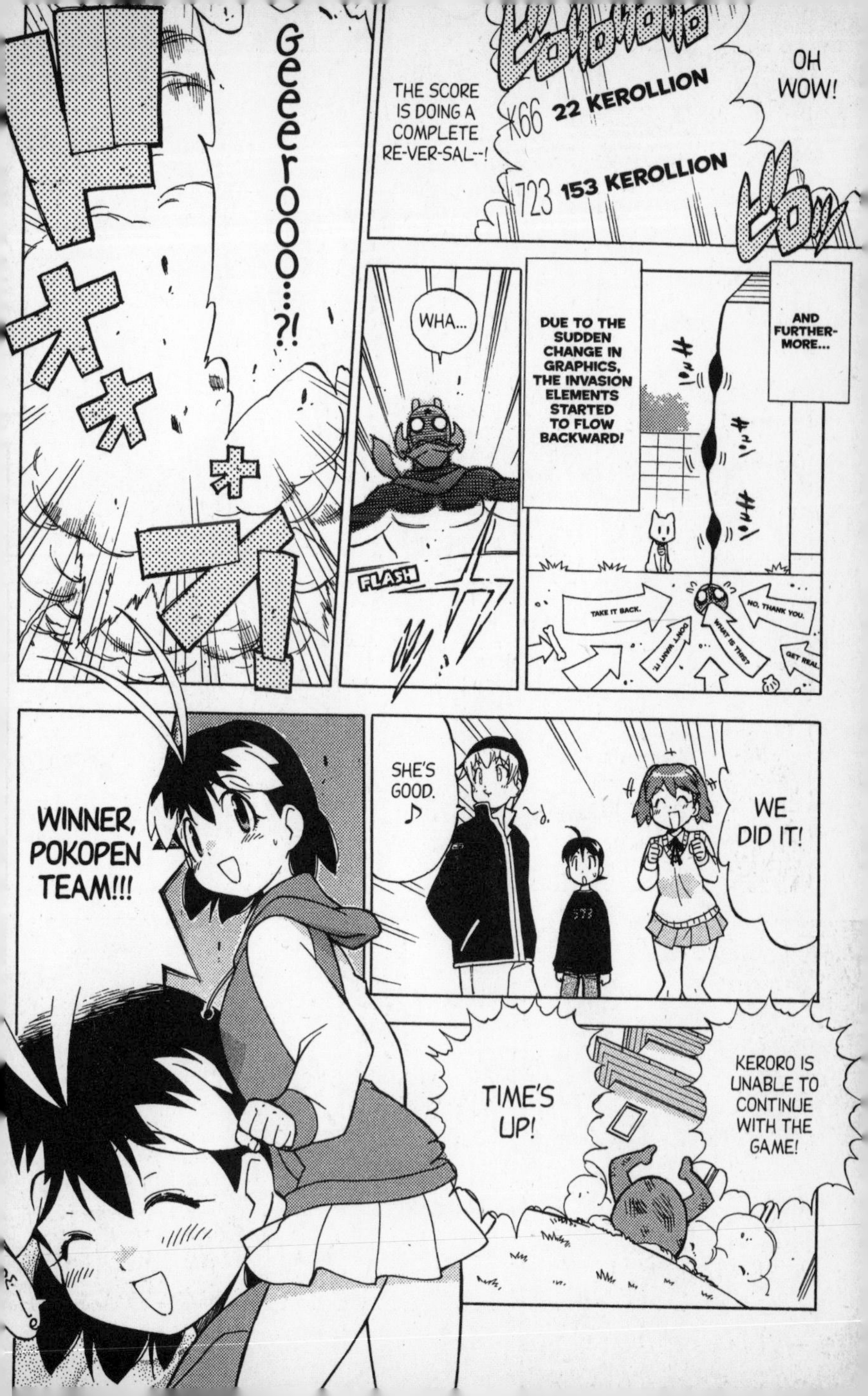
OH WOW!
THE SCORE IS DOING A COMPLETE RE-VER-SAL--!
K66 22 KEROLLION
723 153 KEROLLION
AND FURTHER-MORE...
DUE TO THE SUDDEN CHANGE IN GRAPHICS, THE INVASION ELEMENTS STARTED TO FLOW BACKWARD!
NO, THANK YOU.
TAKE IT BACK.
WHAT IS THIS?
DON'T WANT IT.
GET REAL.
WHA...
FLASH
Geeerooo...?!
WE DID IT!
SHE'S GOOD. ♪
WINNER, POKOPEN TEAM!!!
KERORO IS UNABLE TO CONTINUE WITH THE GAME!
TIME'S UP!

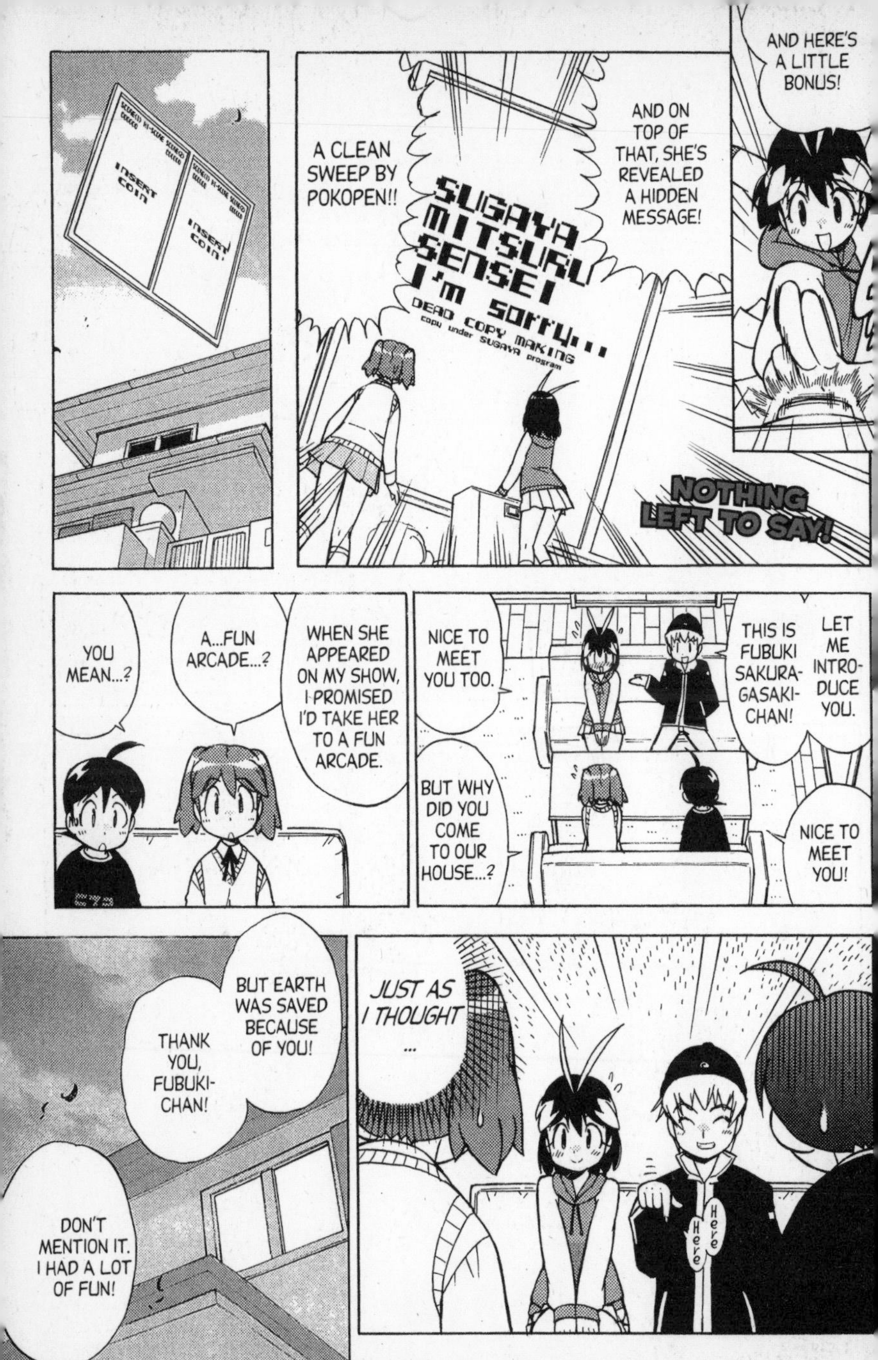
AND HERE'S A LITTLE BONUS!
NOTHING LEFT TO SAY!
AND ON TOP OF THAT, SHE'S REVEALED A HIDDEN MESSAGE!
SUGAYA MITSURU SENSEI I'm sorry...
DEAD COPY MAKING
copy under SUGAYA program
A CLEAN SWEEP BY POKOPEN!!
INSERT COIN
INSERT COIN
LET ME INTRODUCE YOU.
THIS IS FUBUKI SAKURAGASAKI-CHAN!
NICE TO MEET YOU!
NICE TO MEET YOU TOO.
BUT WHY DID YOU COME TO OUR HOUSE...?
WHEN SHE APPEARED ON MY SHOW, I PROMISED I'D TAKE HER TO A FUN ARCADE.
A...FUN ARCADE...?
YOU MEAN...?
JUST AS I THOUGHT...
Here
Here
BUT EARTH WAS SAVED BECAUSE OF YOU!
THANK YOU, FUBUKI-CHAN!
DON'T MENTION IT. I HAD A LOT OF FUN!

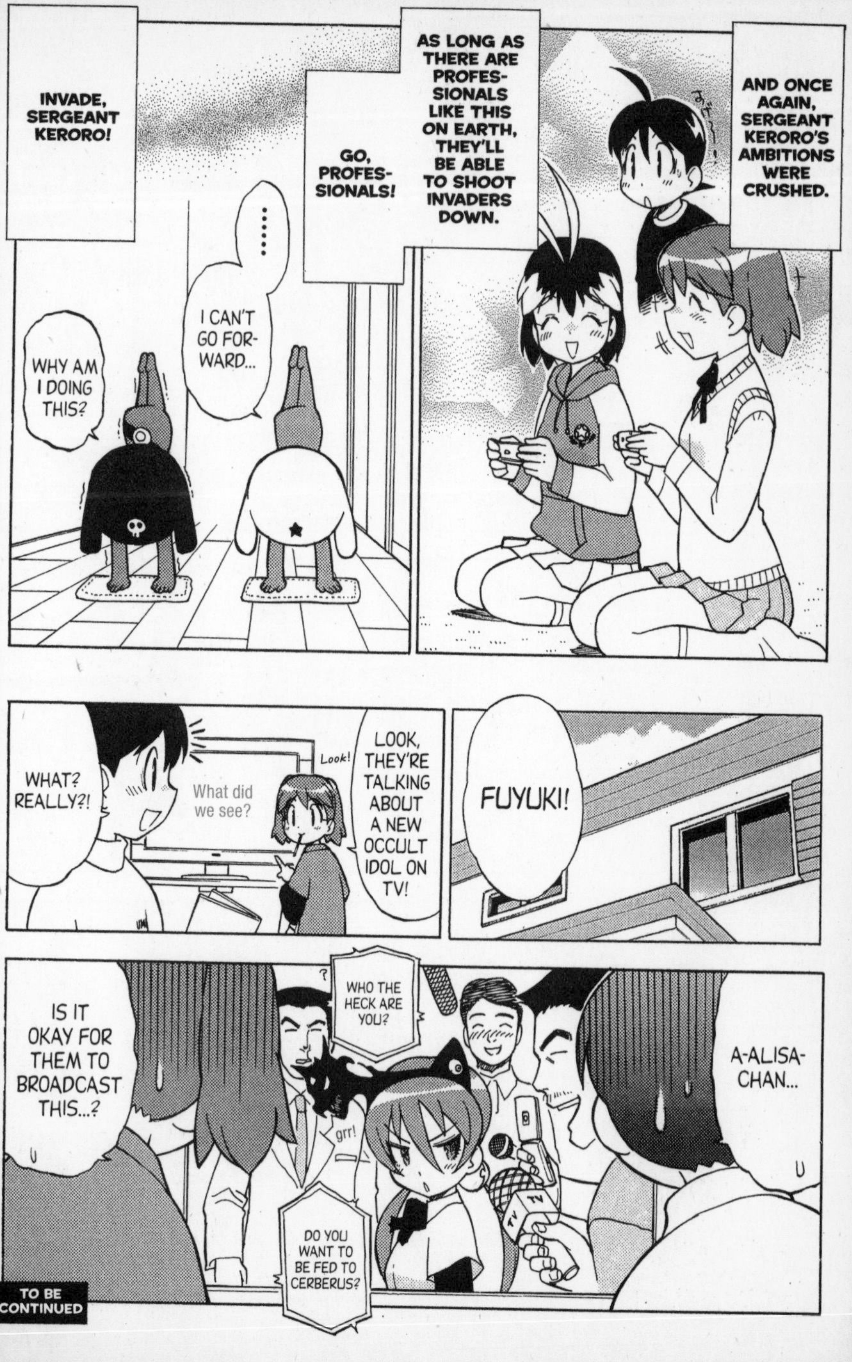
AND ONCE AGAIN, SERGEANT KERORO'S AMBITIONS WERE CRUSHED.
AS LONG AS THERE ARE PROFES-SIONALS LIKE THIS ON EARTH, THEY'LL BE ABLE TO SHOOT INVADERS DOWN.
GO, PROFES-SIONALS!
INVADE, SERGEANT KERORO!
......
I CAN'T GO FOR-WARD...
WHY AM I DOING THIS?
FUYUKI!
LOOK, THEY'RE TALKING ABOUT A NEW OCCULT IDOL ON TV!
Look!
What did we see?
WHAT? REALLY?!
A-ALISA-CHAN...
WHO THE HECK ARE YOU?
grr!
DO YOU WANT TO BE FED TO CERBERUS?
IS IT OKAY FOR THEM TO BROADCAST THIS...?
TO BE CONTINUED

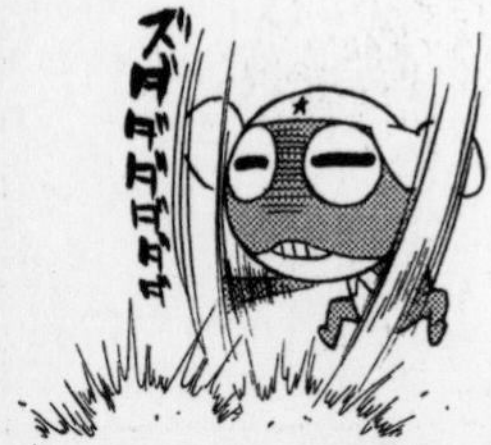
ズダダダダッ

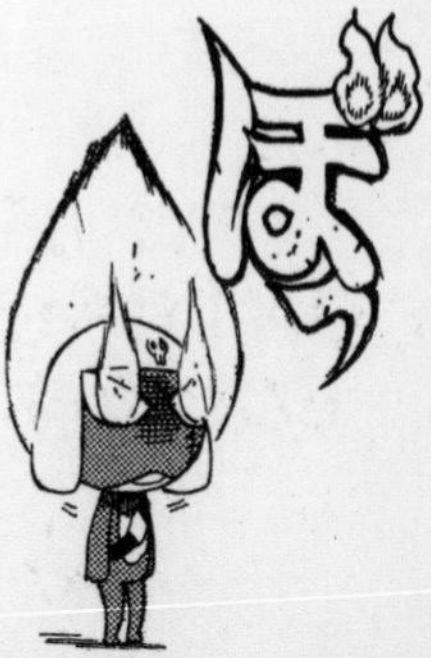
ぼ

JAPAN STAFF

CREATOR
MINE YOSHIZAKI

BACKGROUNDS

OYSTER

FINISHES

AKATSUKI GOMOKU
NARIHARA TOMMI
634
EIJI SHIMOEDA
HAYATO AOKI

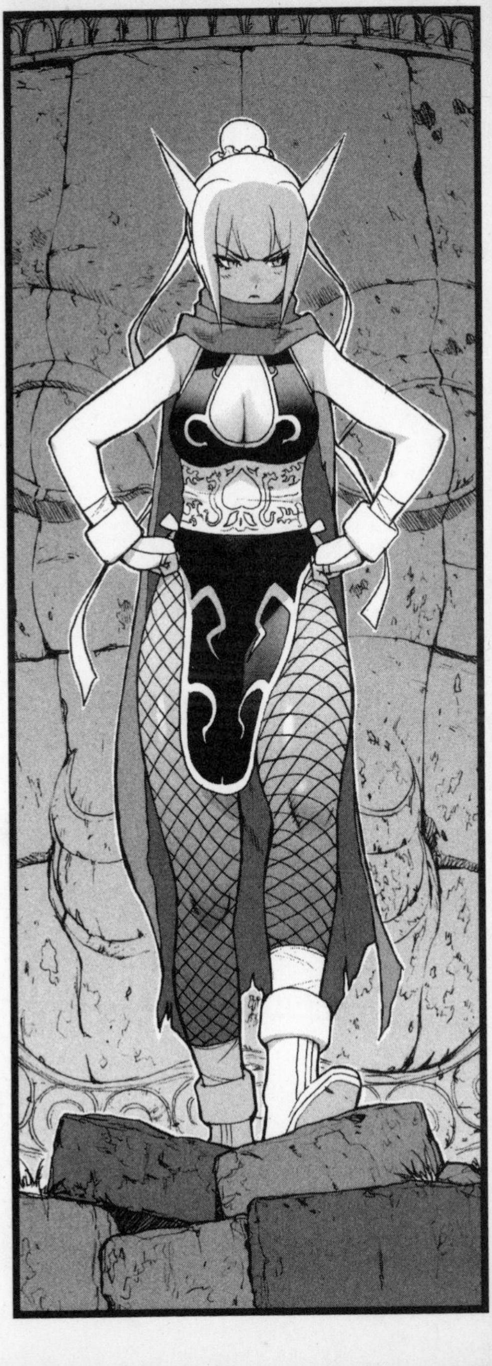

TO BE CONTINUED IN VOLUME 17

OKA-CHAN

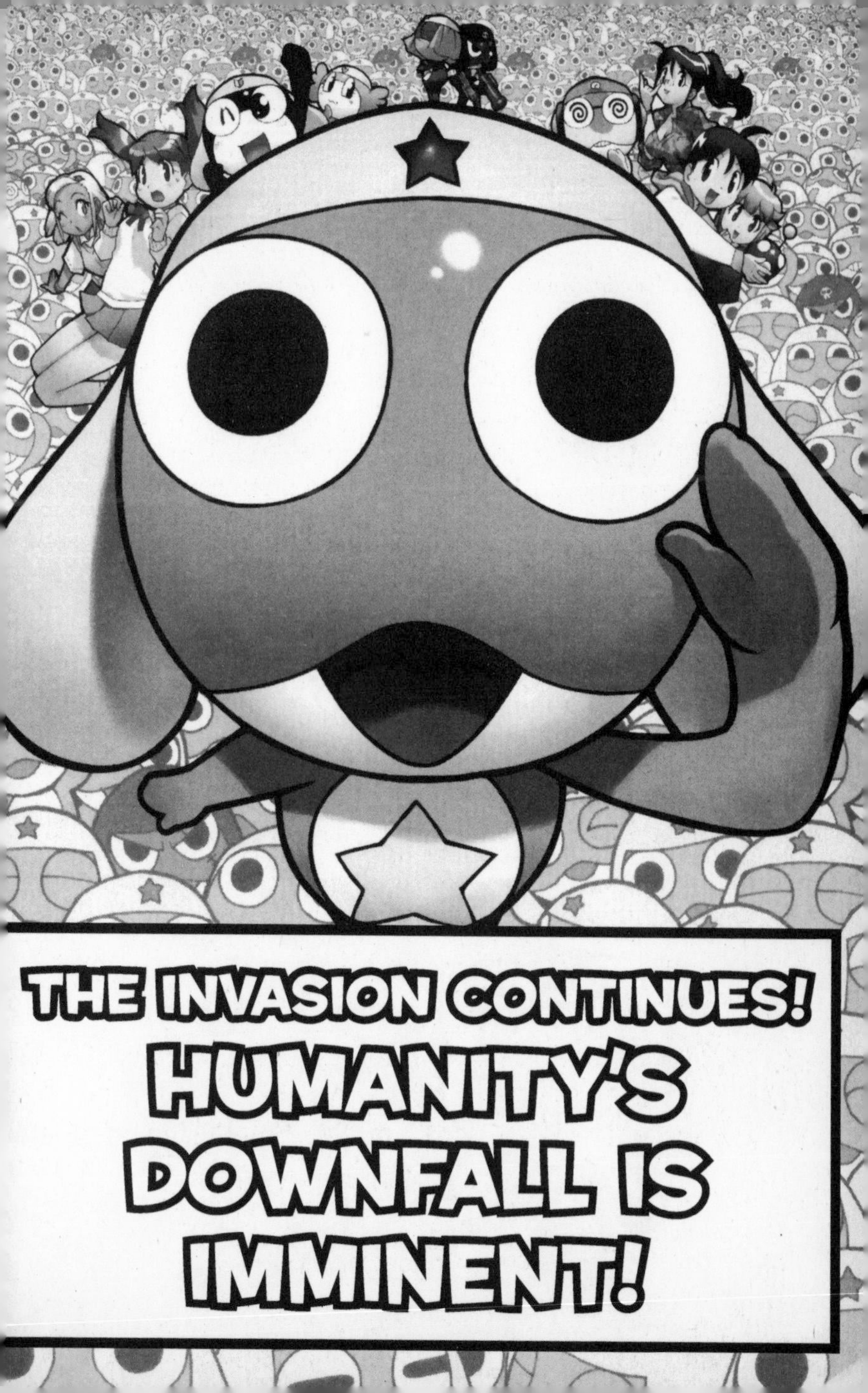
THE INVASION CONTINUES!
HUMANITY'S DOWNFALL IS IMMINENT!

GERO! GERO! GERO!

GREETINGS, POKOPENIANS! HAVE YOU MISSED ANY EXCITING DETAILS SURROUNDING YOUR EVENTUAL SUBJUGATION? FEAR NOT. VOLUMES 1 THROUGH 16 OF *SGT. FROG* WILL BRIEF YOU. AND READING ABOUT ALL OF MY FAILED PLOTS AND SCHEMES WILL ONLY LULL YOU INTO A FALSE SENSE OF SECURITY!

SGT FROG

KERORO GUNSOU

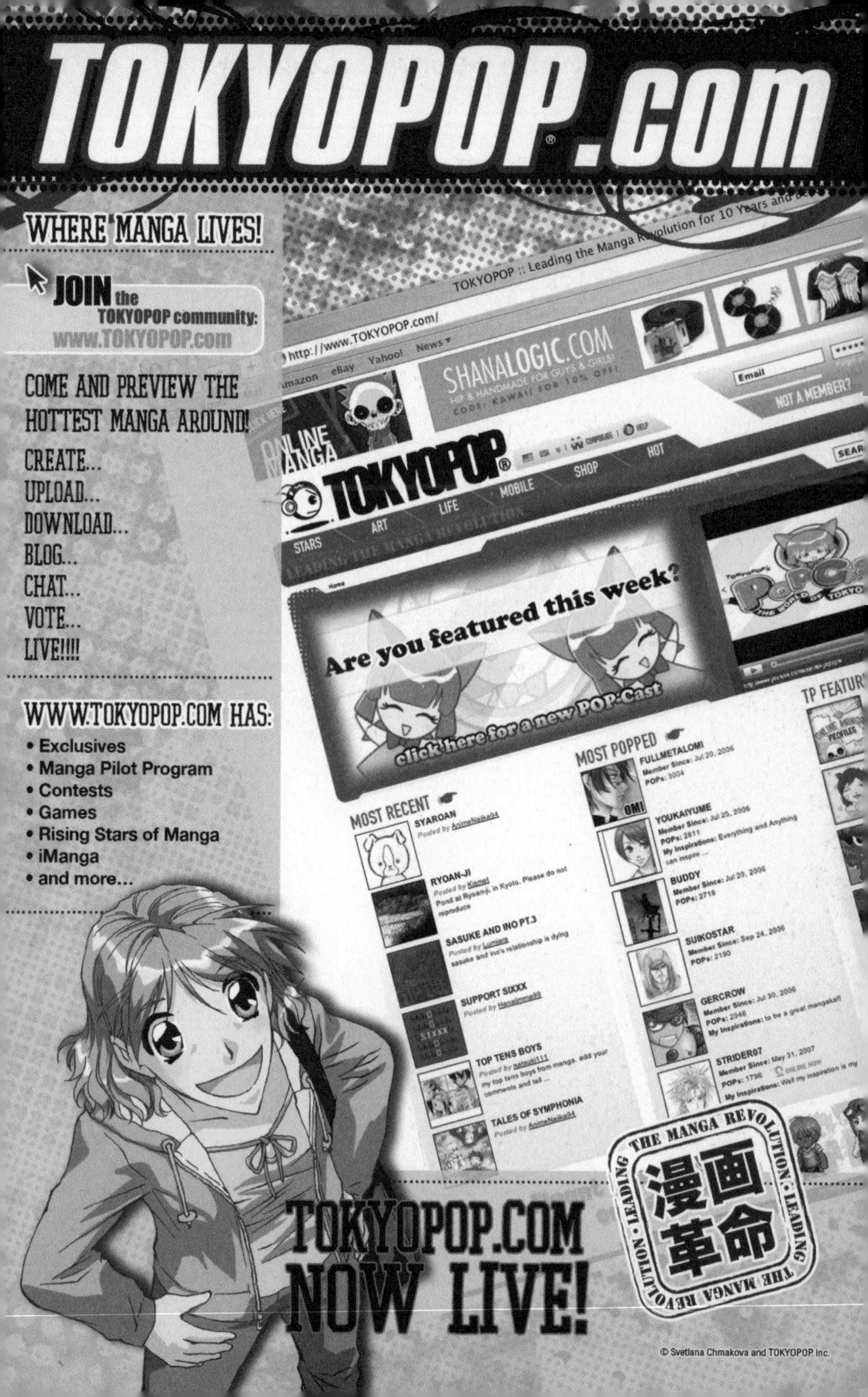
TOKYOPOP®.com
WHERE MANGA LIVES!
JOIN the TOKYOPOP community: www.TOKYOPOP.com
COME AND PREVIEW THE HOTTEST MANGA AROUND!
CREATE...
UPLOAD...
DOWNLOAD...
BLOG...
CHAT...
VOTE...
LIVE!!!!
WWW.TOKYOPOP.COM HAS:
• Exclusives
• Manga Pilot Program
• Contests
• Games
• Rising Stars of Manga
• iManga
• and more...
Are you featured this week?
click here for a new POP-Cast
TOKYOPOP.COM NOW LIVE!
漫画革命
LEADING THE MANGA REVOLUTION
© Svetlana Chmakova and TOKYOPOP Inc.

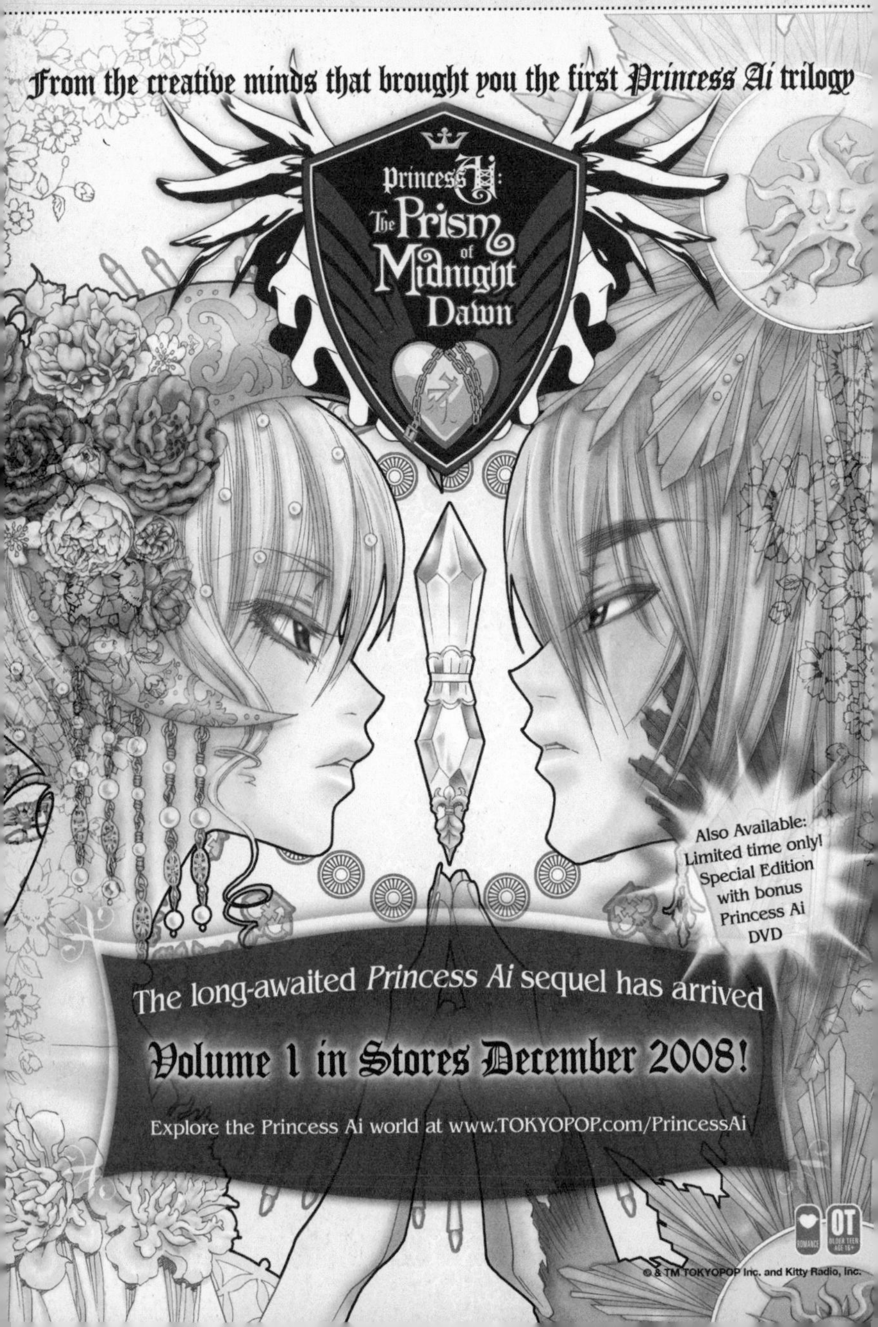
From the creative minds that brought you the first Princess Ai trilogy
Princess Ai: The Prism of Midnight Dawn
Also Available: Limited time only! Special Edition with bonus Princess Ai DVD
The long-awaited Princess Ai sequel has arrived
Volume 1 in Stores December 2008!
Explore the Princess Ai world at www.TOKYOPOP.com/PrincessAi
ROMANCE
OT OLDER TEEN AGE 16+
© & TM TOKYOPOP Inc. and Kitty Radio, Inc.

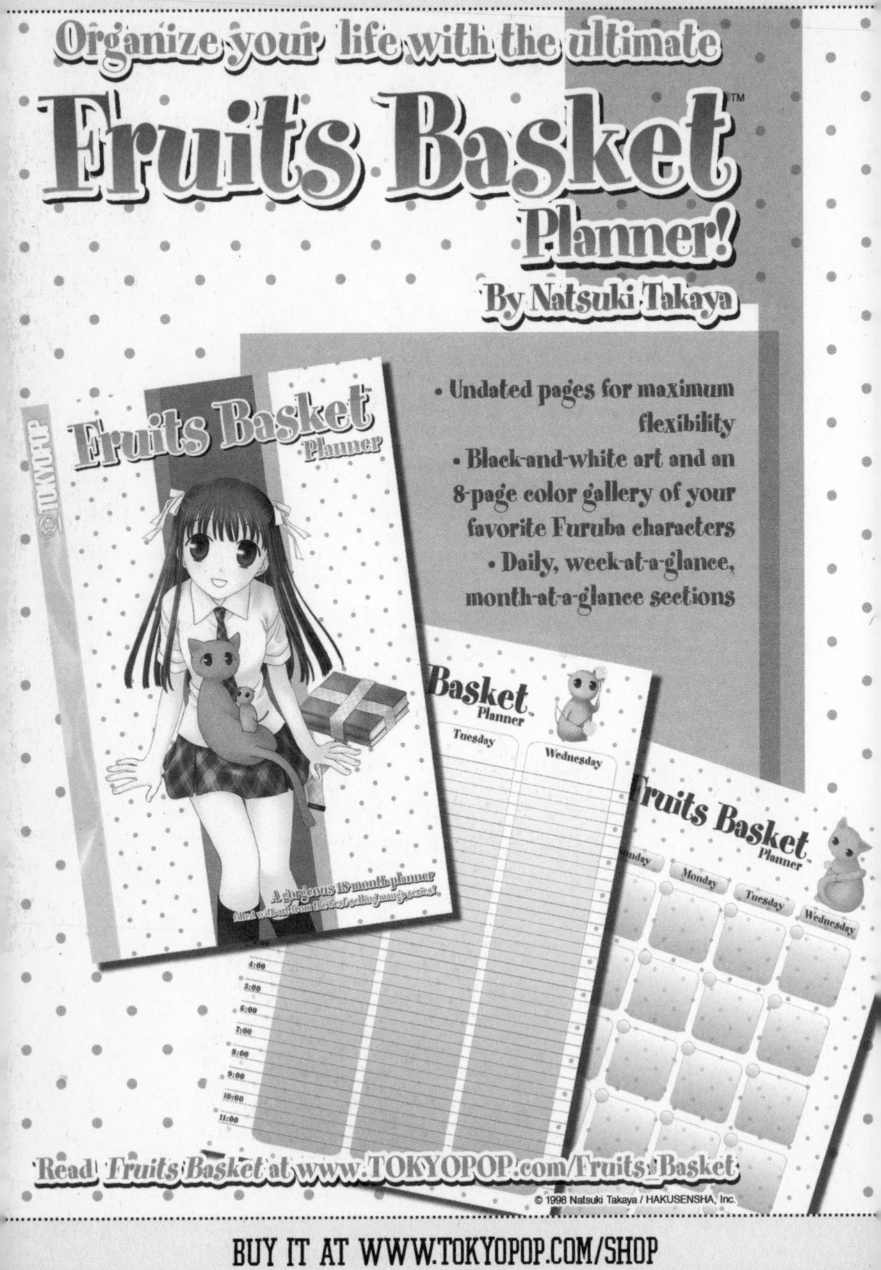
Organize your life with the ultimate
Fruits Basket™
Planner!
By Natsuki Takaya
• Undated pages for maximum flexibility
• Black-and-white art and an 8-page color gallery of your favorite Furuba characters
• Daily, week-at-a-glance, month-at-a-glance sections
Fruits Basket™ Planner
TOKYOPOP
A gorgeous 18-month planner filled with art from the best-selling manga series!
Basket Planner™
Tuesday
Wednesday
4:00
5:00
6:00
7:00
8:00
9:00
10:00
11:00
Fruits Basket Planner™
Monday
Tuesday
Wednesday
Read Fruits Basket at www.TOKYOPOP.com/Fruits_Basket
© 1998 Natsuki Takaya / HAKUSENSHA, Inc.

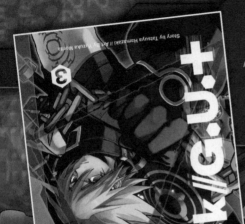

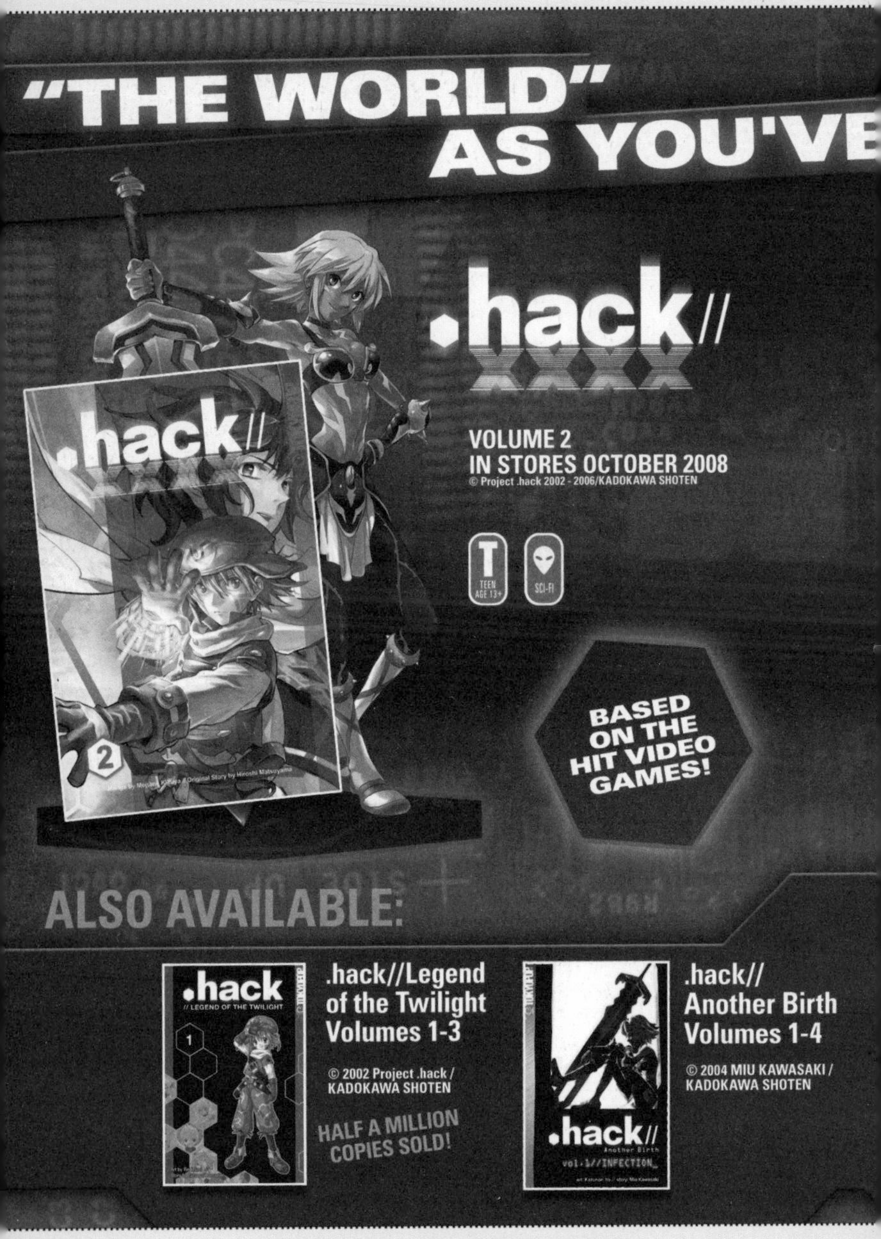

"THE WORLD" AS YOU'VE
.hack//
VOLUME 2
IN STORES OCTOBER 2008
© Project .hack 2002 - 2006/KADOKAWA SHOTEN
TEEN AGE 13+
SCI-FI
BASED ON THE HIT VIDEO GAMES!
ALSO AVAILABLE:
.hack//Legend of the Twilight Volumes 1-3
© 2002 Project .hack / KADOKAWA SHOTEN
HALF A MILLION COPIES SOLD!
.hack// Another Birth Volumes 1-4
© 2004 MIU KAWASAKI / KADOKAWA SHOTEN

FOR MORE INFORMATION VISIT:

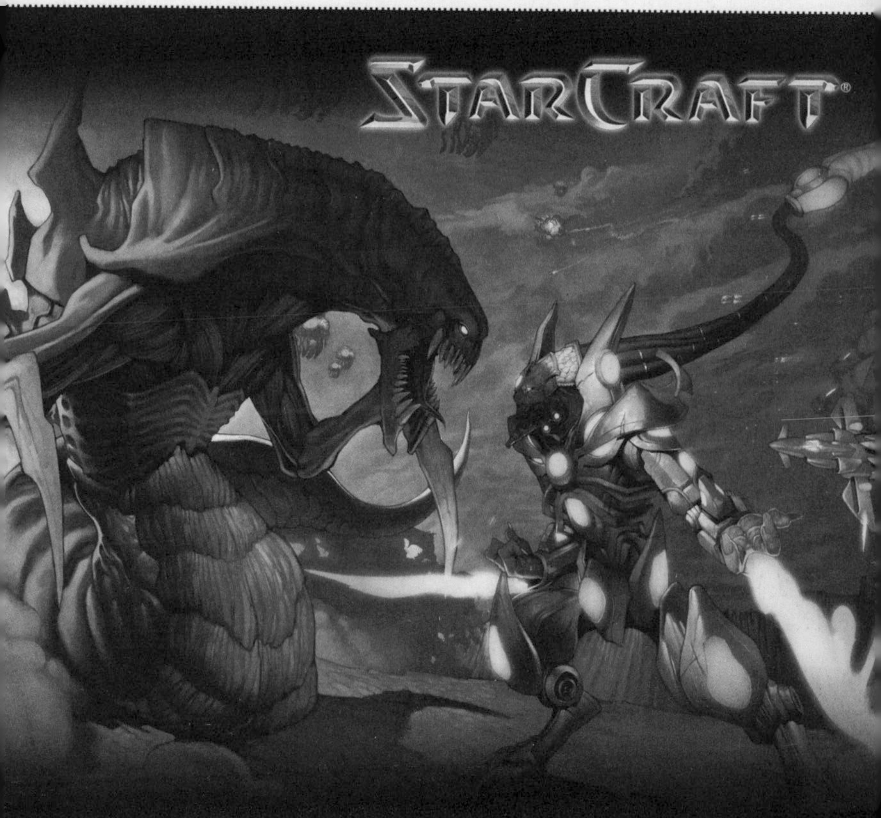
STARCRAFT®

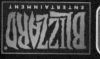

A TALE OF LOYALTY, BLOODLUST AND REVENGE...

In a small village near the Romanian border, young Ted waits for his father, a mercenary in the war against Count Dracula's demon army. Little does he know that he is to become the center of a battle between two of the Count's most powerful generals...

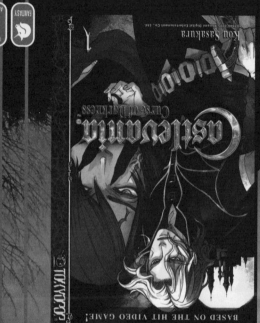

Gothic Manga based on the PS2 and Xbox Video Game!